DEATH
BE NOT
PROUD

CLASS | NEW
200 | STUDIES
| IN
| RELIGION

EDITED BY Kathryn Lofton AND
John Lardas Modern

DEATH BE NOT PROUD

The Art of
Holy Attention

DAVID MARNO

The University of Chicago Press
Chicago and London

The University of Chicago Press, Chicago 60637
The University of Chicago Press, Ltd., London
© 2016 by The University of Chicago
All rights reserved. Published 2016.
Printed in the United States of America

25 24 23 22 21 20 19 18 17 16   1 2 3 4 5

ISBN-13: 978-0-226-41597-0 (cloth)
ISBN-13: 978-0-226-41602-1 (e-book)
DOI: 10.7208/chicago/9780226416021.001.0001

Library of Congress Cataloging-in-Publication Data

Names: Marno, David, author.
Title: Death be not proud : the art of holy attention / David Marno.
Other titles: Class 200, new studies in religion.
Description: Chicago : The University of Chicago Press, 2016. |
    Series: Class 200, new studies in religion
Identifiers: LCCN 2016014272 | ISBN 9780226415970 (cloth : alk. paper) |
    ISBN 9780226416021 (e-book)
Subjects: LCSH: Donne, John, 1572–1631. Holy sonnets. | Donne, John, 1572–1631.
    Holy sonnets. Death be not proud. | Christian poetry, English—Early modern,
    1500–1700—History and criticism. | Death in literature. | Prayer. | Attention—
    Religious aspects—Christianity.
Classification: LCC PR2247.H663 M37 2016 | DDC 821/.3—dc23 LC record available
at https://lccn.loc.gov/2016014272

To the poet, the praying woman, and my mother

———————

"Accept distracted thanks."
Troilus and Cressida, 5.2.189

CONTENTS

ACKNOWLEDGMENTS

THIS BOOK IS ABOUT PRAYER AND poetry, and it is a comedy: it begins with their conflict, and it ends on a note of reconciliation. Like many comedies, it is also about family. I spent a great deal of my childhood observing my mother's negotiations between my father, a fervently skeptical poet, and my maternal grandmother, a devout Catholic with a fondness for liturgy and a distaste for my parents' marriage. I suppose this book might be a belated attempt at peacemaking. It was after completing the manuscript that a conversation with my father reminded me of my mother tongue's familiarity with the idea of a holy attention. We talked about different ways of expressing the act of attending to something, and I was trying to translate the English "pay attention to" but couldn't think of a Hungarian equivalent. He said: "You mean, 'figyelmet szentelni'?" The phrase he used is difficult to translate because it uses the verbal form of the word "szent," meaning "holy." "Devoting attention" comes close, but the literal translation would be "holying attention" to something or somebody. I realized only then that holy attention had been on the tip of my tongue long before I found the term in a little-known seventeenth-century English devotional treatise and became interested in writing about it. I am immensely grateful to my family for their support during the years of articulation.

Thanksgiving is the kind of prayer about which I've been the most curious, and it's a pleasure to now acknowledge all the help I have received over the years. I wish to thank Karl-Heinz Bohrer, Kathryn Crim, Achsah Guibbory, Hans Ulrich Gumbrecht, Amy Hollywood, Victoria Kahn, Jeffrey Knapp, Andrea Nightingale, Maura Nolan, Geoffrey O'Brien, Stephen Orgel, Michael Schoenfeldt, Ethan Shagan, Debora Shuger, Elisa Tamarkin, and James Turner for reading various versions of this book and for offering vital feedback. Roland Greene adopted the project in its infancy, and his always understated but never faltering wisdom made me feel free to learn by making mistakes as I began writing. Steven Justice noticed something worthwhile buried deeply under many flaws in an early draft and helped to dig it out by offering the most erudite and generous advice possible. In tracing the secular afterlives of devotion, Noreen Khawaja was the best accomplice I could have asked for, and every conversation we had about philosophy and religion has left its mark on this book. Joanna Picciotto's readings and comments have put many of my lofty ideas to shame: in scholarship and friendship, she has been my model of attentive thought.

Nourishing conversations with friends and colleagues have shaped this book in crucial ways. For these and more, I thank Hugh Adlington, Lucy Alford, Charles Altieri, Oliver Arnold, Julia Bader, John Bender, Frederick Blumberg, Mitchell Breitweiser, Helen B. Brooks, Teresa DiPasquale, Kathleen Donegan, Diana Dutton, Chiyuma Eliot, Nadia Ellis, Eric Falci, Harris Feinsod, Anne-Lise François, Marisa Galvez, Marissa Gemma, Denise Gigante, Steven Goldsmith, Kevis Goodman, Timothy Hampton, Kristin Hanson, Dayton Haskin, Kathryn Hume, Nicholas Jenkins, Donna Jones, Florian Klinger, David Landreth, Steven Lee, Hanna Marno, Margaret Maurer, Tyrus Miller, Katherine O'Brien O'Keeffe, Samuel Otter, Namwali Serpell, Jonathan Sheehan, George Starr, Richard Strier, Emily Thornbury, Hayden White, and Christopher Wild.

I have benefited from discussions with students and faculty at the Renaissance workshops at Berkeley, Chicago, Harvard, and Stanford, thanks in particular to Ryan Perry, Sarah Kunjummen, Maria Devlin, Elizabeth Weckhurst, Nicole DeBenedictis, and Cécile Tresfels. A memorable Townsend Center seminar at Berkeley on early modern faith and belief was a source of inspiration, and I thank the participants and organizers of the seminar, especially Albert Ascoli and Ethan Shagan. A workshop at Berkeley on the history of prayer has provided exceptionally enjoyable occasions to discuss the paradoxes of devotion, and I owe thanks to my co-organizer Niklaus Largier and to the members of the workshop. The annual meetings of the John Donne Society have been a site of joyful learning, and I thank in particular Theresa DiPasquale, Joshua Eckhardt, Dayton Haskin, Margaret Maurer, Kate Narveson, Robert Reeder, Jeanne Shami, Daniel Starza-Smith, and Kirsten Stirling for their warm welcome and stimulating conversations. Various panels at the Renaissance Society of America and the Modern Language Association conferences have provided a platform to present and revise my argument, and I am grateful to Luke Barnhard, Jessica Beckman, Timothy Harrison, Nigel Smith, David Simon, Ramie Targoff, and Jessica Wolfe for captivating exchanges about literature and devotion. The chapters had already been completed when an opportunity to talk about Donne at Lincoln College, Oxford, gave me the perspective I needed to write the introduction. For the invitation, warm welcome, and exquisite conversations, I thank Peter McCullough and the participants of the conference.

Support from the Hellman Fellows Fund, the Mabelle McLeod Lewis Memorial Fund and the Andrew D. Mellon Foundation has helped me to research and write this book. A fellowship at the Berkeley Townsend Center for the Humanities allowed me to complete it, and I am grateful to Aglaya Glebova, Michael Nylan, and Alan Tansman for their feedback. The publication of this book has been supported by the Arts and Humanities Dean's Office at Berkeley, and I would like to thank Associate Dean Linda Haverty Rugg and Dean Anthony Cascardi for their help.

Parts of chapter 4 have appeared in "Easy Attention: Ignatius of Loyola and Robert Boyle," *Journal of Medieval and Early Modern Studies* 14, no. 1 (2014); "Attention and Indifference in Ignatius's *Spiritual Exercises*," in *A Companion to Ignatius of Loyola*, ed. Aleksander Maryks (Leiden: Brill, 2014); and "Divine Poems," in *John Donne in Context*, ed. Michael Schoenfeldt (Cambridge: Cambridge University Press, forthcoming).

I owe special thanks to my editor, Alan G. Thomas, for his encouragement and insights, to Randolph Petilos, Mark Reschke, and Rose Rittenhouse for taking excellent care of me at the Press, to Jo Ann Kiser for her meticulous and thoughtful copyediting, and to Mark Scott for his scrupulous work on the index. Incisive and generous comments from two anonymous readers for the Press turned the last round of revisions into a series of exciting discoveries. This is a book that reads poetry to make an argument about devotion as a way of thinking, and I am honored that Kathryn Lofton and John Lardas Modern have found in this mix of fields and approaches something worthy of the Class 200 series.

INTRODUCTION

L'attention de l'esprit est la prière naturelle, que nous faisons à
la Verité intérieure, afin qu'elle se découvre à nous. Mais cette
souveraine Verité ne répond pas toûjours à nos désirs, parce
que nous ne sçavons pas trop bien comment il la faut prier.

Nicolas Malebranche[1]

WHAT KIND OF AGENCY DO WE have in thinking? I say, "I think." But
also, "a thought occurs to me." This is not a caprice of language. Between
the passive and active voices, there lurks a familiar experience: in thinking,
I perform an action; but when a thought occurs to me, I become the witness of an event, and suddenly I look back on my thinking as preparation
for an event that was never in my control. Writing at the end of the early
modern era, the philosopher Nicolas Malebranche pondered this experience of limited agency by comparing thinking to prayer. In each, he suggested, the outcome of the action is beyond our control, in the hands of a
sovereign power. Thinking is like prayer because truth is like God: we can
only hope "that it may discover itself unto us; but this Sovereign Truth do-
eth not always answer our expectations, for we do not know how to make
our addresses."[2] But if in this sense both prayer and thinking imply a limited
sense of agency, Malebranche was all the more fascinated with the question
of what the subject could still do within these limitations. In the *Conversations chrétiennes*, he suggests that the answer lies in the act of attention.
Prayer and thinking are analogous activities because "attention is the natural prayer that we make to inward truth." Neither philosophy in the sense
of dialectic nor prayer as conversation with God, acts of attending are in
Malebranche's vision a preparation for both. Attention is the cultivation of
a passive disposition, a solicitous waiting for a conversation to happen. It

is by attending that the subject can fill up the confined but still existing space of agency in thinking and prayer; indeed, it is by attending that he can probe the boundaries of this space. For Malebranche, attention is the foundation of philosophy because it admits the limitations of agency in the production of thought without abandoning the practice of thinking.

In Malebranche's association of prayer with the philosopher's search after truth, there is also an invitation to see religion and philosophy as analogous. To be sure, positing some sort of easy continuity between the two would be both banal and misleading; banal because there is no need for any reminder that seventeenth-century philosophy learned from the theologies and devotions of the time, and misleading because Malebranche's point is that philosophy wasn't a good enough student: it didn't learn how to pray. This might sound like a half-serious admonishment offered by a priest-philosopher (Malebranche was a member of the French Oratory) to modern, secular philosophy, were it not for the additional analogy Malebranche draws between prayer and attention. This is the real core of Malebranche's remarks: what prayer could teach to philosophy isn't a general sense of pious reverence before a sovereign Truth but a specific expertise in attention. The unsaid premise behind Malebranche's characterization of attention as "natural prayer" is that prayer itself is artificial attention, as it were, that prayer includes an art of attending. What Malebranche wants philosophers to emulate is an art of "holy attention."[3]

The purpose of this book is to reconstruct the art of holy attention by following the ways John Donne's devotional poetry enacts it. If in Malebranche's view attention is a hidden connection between religion and philosophy, poetry is the middle realm where this connection may become visible. Most of Donne's devotional poems do not immediately appear to be prayers, and one way of reading them is as poetic meditations in preparation for prayer. Therein lies their promise: for a study about devotional attention, the question is *how* they prepare for prayer, what their preparation involves. Let me evoke Donne's "Death be not proud" as an example. Like many of Donne's devotional poems, the sonnet ends with the speaker's reiteration of a religious commonplace, in this case a phrase from Paul's first letter to the Corinthians that denounces death on the grounds that the resurrection of the body will end its reign (in Donne's paraphrase, "And Death shalbe no more").[4] This raises the question: how does the poem's reiteration of a religious thought differ from the thought as it was given before its integration into the poem? For example, what is the difference between the doctrine of the resurrection of the body, on the one hand, and the poem's use of the doctrine, on the other? A possible answer is that while in the former case the doctrine is a general statement that may or may not apply to any one individual, in the poem's case the speaker reiterates the doctrine as his own, personal belief. But how does a poem allow its speaker to appropriate a doctrine? What can a poem as a linguistic artifact do to help one apply a general doctrine to his singular case?

This question of application isn't unknown to scholarship on post-Reformation devotion and devotional poetry.[5] The conventional wisdom is that in this regard the goal of devotion and devotional poetry is to allow the speaker to "feel" a religious thought, to respond to it emotionally.[6] While this emphasis on emotion bears out in the poetry of George Herbert and other seventeenth-century devotional poets, I think it helps little in making sense of Donne's lyrics.[7] The reason isn't that Donne's poems are worse than, say, Herbert's, but that we haven't been reading them on their own terms: the affect these poems seek to produce has less to do with emotion and more with intellection. My suggestion is that in poems like "Death be not proud," the speaker experiences a given doctrine as his own thought when this thought *occurs* to him. The transition from the general to the personal is still a matter of moving from an abstract idea to a personal experience; but the experience in Donne's case isn't primarily one of emotion but of cognition. To put it bluntly, Donne's poems represent the process of seeking faith by making the reader experience what it feels like to think a thought. This is what makes them valuable for a study of devotion: while the term "affect" is usually associated with desire and emotion, Donne's poems highlight the other, cognitive aspects of affective devotion.[8]

I suggest that the key to this cognitive side of affective devotion is attention. While the occurrence of the thought in the poems must feel like an unexpected event for the speaker, the poem itself is a careful preparation for this occurrence. There is a teleology at work here: the goal of each poem is to generate a state of pure, undistracted attentiveness in which the speaker may feel as if the given idea is occurring to him for the first time, as a cognitive gift given specifically to him. To be sure, a poem may not succeed at producing pure attentiveness, or it may succeed in unexpected ways. We will encounter these complications in the following chapters. What I wish to emphasize for now is how poetry's engagement with attention echoes Malebranche's admonishment. Malebranche's comment is not, as one might assume at first sight, about how philosophers should be more attentive in their thinking. For him, attentiveness is not an accidental feature that may be added to or taken away from the act of prayer but a *mode* of praying and, by extension, also a mode of thinking. Following the ways in which Donne's poems prepare for the occurrence of a thought will help us articulate this devotional mode of thinking.[9] How much one thinks a thought depends, in this model, on how much one becomes capable of attending to it; and perhaps the most interesting question I'll be trying to answer in the chapters is how devotion distinguishes between different quantities and qualities of attention.

This brings me back to a peculiar feature of the argument: the first chapter of this book begins with a reading of "Death be not proud," and the last chapter ends with another reading of the same poem. There are certainly other poems and texts I consider, but insofar as "Death be not proud" guides my argument throughout the chapters and returns at the end to probe my findings, this book is about a single poem. The reasons I have given such priority to one poem are both thematic and methodological, and they follow from what I think is the epistemological status of Donne's devotional exercises. One of my initial claims is that Donne's poems are meant to be devotional *proofs* insofar as their purpose isn't just to allow a speaker to think a Christian doctrine but also to think it with cognitive certainty. This suggests an unusual sense of proof. In the poems, a doctrine appears certain, not when it is logically or empirically proven, but when the speaker experiences it as a thought occurring to him. Since this experience occurs within and because of the poem's attention exercises, the poem turns out to be a type of proof that provides evidence only insofar as it is being attended to. In other words, the poem is a proof that cannot be abstracted from the act of thinking it.

It is therefore important to recall that this is one way of thinking about literature as evidence. Take the Hölderlin and Celan scholar Peter Szondi's formulation: "Philological knowledge possesses a dynamic aspect that is peculiarly its own. This is not simply because, like every other knowledge, it is constantly being altered by new points of view and new findings, but because it can exist, in the first place, only through constantly referring knowledge (*Wissen*) back to its source in cognition (*Erkenntnis*), that is to say, by relating it to the understanding (*Verstehen*) of the poetic word."[10] Donne's poems provide a perspective on Szondi's insight because in the poems the devotional and the literary senses of evidence converge. Before literary criticism (or what Szondi calls "philology") would read the poems as evidence of knowledge, they are designed to be read as proofs of faith.[11] Now, this does not mean that reading Donne's poems must be a devotional act or that we would have to accept the religious beliefs that

Donne's speakers pursue. What it does mean is that studying Donne's poems may offer an insight not only into the history and phenomenology of holy attention, but also into how the protocols of literary close reading are themselves influenced by devotional precedents. In other words, what is at stake in attending to Donne's poems isn't just the knowledge we might gain from them but also how we gain this knowledge. The art of attention is a dispersed phenomenon that affects a wide range of practices both within and beyond religion, and in the course of my argument I consider texts and make claims that belong to fields as diverse as religious studies, history, and philosophy. But it has been my goal to test my claims against the evidence of what Szondi calls "the poetic word." What makes this book a contribution to literary studies is not its subject matter or argument but a consistent prioritization of the literary over other types of evidence. The positioning of "Death be not proud" at the beginning and the end is thus an experiment to stake out the possibilities of literature as proof by testing what we may gain by attending to a single poem.

Of course this raises a question: why this particular poem? I consider other works by Donne, including some of the other poems from the group we know today as the *Holy Sonnets.* As Paul A. Parrish and Gary A. Stringer, the editors of the recent Variorum edition of the *Holy Sonnets* point out, manuscript evidence suggests that Donne never circulated the *Holy Sonnets* individually but always in groups.[12] At the very least, this means that Donne wanted his readers to notice family resemblances between the individual sonnets, and in the second half of the book I compare poems within the group to see how their respective speakers encounter the challenges of holy attention.[13] What makes "Death be not proud" a unique poem in the group, though, is its seemingly unqualified triumph. At the end of the poem, the speaker announces the death of Death and by implication his faith in the resurrection. It is probably the poem's triumphant tone that made it Donne's most popular religious poem for centuries after his death.[14] As late a reader as the Romantic Leigh Hunt, who condemned Donne's other religious poems summarily by stating that "Donne's piety, though sincere, was not healthy," singled out "Death be not proud" as "fortunately the best sonnet he wrote," because "though it is upon a subject on which, generally speaking, he was more than one sense of the word least happy,—Death—is equally unexceptionable and noble."[15] Yet beginning with the second half of the twentieth century, critics began suspecting the speaker's faith in the resurrection and suggested that instead of a triumphant poem about Death's death, the poem is an ironic depiction of one's attempt at self-persuasion.[16]

This was an important discovery that in my view we should see as an opportunity for new approaches to the poem rather than a conclusion to previous queries. If the poem represents a speaker's attempt at self-persuasion, then what would it take for such self-persuasion to *succeed*? After an initial close reading of the poem, the first six chapters of this book articulate the conditions of such a success by examining Christian theological and devotional literature as well as early modern poetry and drama. In the seventh chapter, I return to "Death be not proud" to see how Donne's simultaneously poetic and devotional thought experiment reads in the context of holy attention. It is in this sense that the poem is the "first last end" of my argument.

"THIS FIRST LAST END"

A brief look at the phrase "first last end" in its original context should provide a preliminary sense of why Donne's poetry may be a particularly trustworthy witness to the art of holy attention. The oxymoron appears in *La Corona*, the sonnet crown that introduces Donne's *Holy Sonnets* in a number of manuscripts as well as in the 1633 *Poems by J.D.*, the first printed edition of Donne's poetry.[17] In the first sonnet of *La Corona*, "first last end" is ushered in with a "this" that refers us back to the previous line for a theological meaning.[18] "At our end begins our endless rest," the speaker quips there, preparing an understanding of "this first last end" as simultaneously the end of earthly existence and the beginning of eternal life in what Saint Paul describes as the resurrected, spiritual body. And yet the fact that formally *La Corona* is a crown of sonnets hints at another, poetic meaning. "First last end" is the formula that organizes a sonnet crown: every poem begins with the last line of the previous one, and the crown is completed when the last sonnet ends with the first line of the entire sequence.[19] "First last end" is in this sense a reference to the poem's lines and indeed to the entire poem as stretched out between its self-iterating beginning and end.

A pun that draws a parallel between the lines of the poem and redemption would seem facetious were it not for the fact that "first last end" appears in a sonnet whose task is to think about bridging the gap between poetry and religion. A proem to the entire sequence, the first sonnet of *La Corona* is a meditation on the "ends" or goals of devotional poetry and on the nature of the labor involved in working toward them.[20] In the proem, the speaker offers *La Corona* as a "crown of prayer and praise" whose goal is to earn a "crown of glory," that is, salvation. But what could a poem do to earn this crown of glory? The question emerges only gradually in the first ten lines of the sonnet:

> *Deign at my hands this crown of prayer and praise,*
> Weaved in my low, devout melancholy,
> Thou which of good hast, yea, art treasury,
> All-changing, unchanged Ancient of Days;
> But do not with a vile crown of frail bays
> Reward my Muse's white sincerity,
> But what thy thorny crown gained, that give me,
> A crown of glory, which doth flower always.
> The ends crown our works, but thou crown'st our ends,
> For at our end begins our endless rest.

The meditation follows the unfolding of the different meanings of "crown." In the first line, "this crown of prayer and praise" refers to the sonnet sequence itself. As a virtuosic poetic achievement, a crown of sonnets would seem to merit the traditional headgear of poet laureates from Ovid to Petrarch, a crown of laurel. But Donne's speaker evokes this "vile crown of frail bays" only to reject it in favor of an altogether more ambitious crown, "a crown of glory." This prize, in turn, has been earned by Christ's own "thorny crown," a metonym for the sacrifice that has reinstated the possibility of redemption for mankind. But if salvation is already given, what is the point of the poem? What is the speaker still trying to achieve? This is the question that leads to the recognition in lines 11 and 12, where the speaker offers an answer:

> This first last end, now zealously possessed,
> With a strong, sober thirst, my soul attends.[21]

Commentaries on *La Corona* often argue that the verb "attend" should be understood here in the archaic and now mostly obscure sense of waiting or awaiting.[22] This seems to make sense: the speaker might be saying that he awaits redemption with a "strong, sober thirst," that is, with a patient but confident faith. The adverbial clause of line eleven poses, however, a question: if the point is that the soul awaits the "first last end" in the sense of salvation, why would Donne also suggest that the first last end is zealously possessed *now*? Critics have tried to solve this puzzle by suggesting that the adverbial clause qualifies the "soul," not the "first last end."[23] But the puzzle doesn't need our solution. It belongs to the speaker's train of thought and he himself responds to it. Line eleven articulates the previous lines' conclusion. Redemption is already zealously possessed in the here and the now, in the sense that the speaker believes that Christ has earned it for humankind. In other words, redemption is possessed as a tenet of the speaker's faith. The problem, though, is that while the redemption of mankind is "zealously possessed," what is not present for the speaker in the here and the now is certainty about *his* own redemption. This discrepancy between the general and the particular, the present and the future, is the speaker's existential predicament. But it is also what helps him answer the question about the poem's labor. Since there is a discrepancy between the present but abstract possibility of redemption on the one hand and the concrete but future actuality of the speaker's redemption on the other, the poem's task is to *connect* the present possibility of redemption with its actuality in the future. To put it in other terms, the speaker must translate his faith in the general redemption of mankind that has been earned by Christ's grace into belief in his own, personal salvation.

This is the task of the poem, and this is the labor to which Donne assigns the verb "to attend." If we now rethink what this verb means, two answers emerge. Attending is indeed a kind of waiting, a passive expectation of the speaker's own redemption: although de jure the "first last end" has already been earned by Christ's sacrifice, the speaker has to await its de facto fulfillment. But there is another meaning of "attending" relevant to the poem, one that will allow us to see how Donne redeems the pun implied in "first last end" about the poem's lines. The verb "attend" arrives in English, through Old French, from the Latin *attendere,* meaning stretching toward. Its primary meaning is to direct one's faculties toward something or someone. It is a frequent term in Christian treatises on prayer and handbooks of meditation. For example, early modern discussions of how to pray with the Roman Breviary (one of Donne's likely sources for the first sonnet in *La Corona*) often dedicate sections to the question of how much and what kind of attention one should pay to the words of prayer.[24] The reason this sense of "attending" as "paying attention" isn't immediately obvious in *La Corona* is that in the poem the verb is transitive and takes the direct object "this first last end." This, however, is a matter of historical distance: until the nineteenth century, "attend" in the sense of paying attention was used both transitively and intransitively (and as we shall see, this flexibility between the transitivity and intransitivity of attention has relevance that goes beyond grammar). What we have here is a sense of attending that not only fits in with the sonnet's concern with devotional labor but also completes the pun Donne began with the phrase "first last end." The labor of the poem's speaker, it seems, is both to await his future redemption *and* in the meantime (that is, in the *saeculum*) to attend to the very lines of the poetic prayer that is *La Corona.*

What should we make of this parallel between attending to the poem's lines and awaiting redemption? If *La Corona* is a poetic prayer, what is the significance of paying attention to the prayer's words? Early modern discussions of attention in vocal prayer (*oratio vocalis*) offer little help here. Sermons and devotional handbooks admonish their audiences to fully attend to the words of their prayers; often they acknowledge the difficulty of sustained concentration, and they lament the consequences of inattention or suggest remedies for distraction.[25] But what they don't explain is *why* attention should be necessary for prayer in the first place. Fortunately there is another tradition that provides a clue. Accounts of mental or silent prayer (*oratio mentis*) describe prayer as an act of attention and even suggest that a pure, wordless prayer is nothing but a disposition of undistracted attentiveness (one recalls that the original gesture of prayer in Christianity isn't the familiar folding of the hands—a sign of both obedience and concentration—but the *orans,* a standing position with raised and outstretched arms, a gesture of offering to and opening toward the divine).[26] Now, at first sight these two accounts of attention in prayer appear rather different. Discussions of vocal prayer focus on the difficulty of concentrating on the words of the prayer and reflect skepticism about the possibility of eliminating all distractions. In contrast, the idea of an attentive disposition in silent prayer reminds one of John Ashbery's painter: "just as children imagine a prayer / Is merely silence, he expected his subject / To rush up the sand, and, seizing a brush, / Plaster its own portrait on the canvas."[27] Like the artless painter, the ideal of silent prayer might be accused of a naïve belief in the efficacy of attentiveness in the sense of a passive disposition that will conjure up its subject, and of course this is precisely the error of which both Catholic and Protestant critics accused the most mystical articulations of silent prayer, the so-called pure or perfect prayer.

And yet it is these two different notions of attention in vocal and silent prayer that converge in *La Corona.* The speaker's attending to the words of the poem corresponds to the labor of concentration in vocal prayer, while his awaiting of redemption is reminiscent of silent prayer's passive attentiveness that expects the subject to reveal itself. Indeed, we might go further and assume that much like Ashbery's painter who eventually heeds the advice of his neighbors ("'Try using the brush / As a means to an end'"), the speaker in *La Corona* recognizes that attending to the words of his prayer might help him prepare for the attentiveness that the awaiting of his redemption requires.[28] In other words, when the speaker wants to attend to the first last end, he means attention in two senses. First, he means it as attention to something that is not present and cannot be attended to by an act of transitive attention, *ergo* implying not transitive attention but an intransitive, objectless disposition of attentiveness. Second, however, by "attending" he also means the transitive acts of attending to the words of prayer, which are themselves exercises aiming at creating attentiveness. The ultimate implication of the speaker's pun on attending in *La Corona* is that his poetic prayer is a means toward an end, an exercise in acts of transitive attention in preparation for a disposition of intransitive attentiveness. The pun thus reveals the *interdependence* of vocal prayer's attention and silent prayer's attentiveness: if paying attention to his words helps the speaker toward the attentiveness of mental prayer, the attentiveness that *is* mental prayer provides his vocal prayer with a much-needed foundation. This is circular, of course; but then again *La Corona is* a circle, and perhaps the poem's two iterations of the same prayer (the first line "Deign at my hand this crown of prayer and praise" is repeated as the crown's last line) are connected not only by the words of the poetic prayer that extends between them, but also by the silence that comes after the poem's last line and precedes the first one.

"This first last end . . . my soul attends": reinforcing the semantic relation by the internal rhyme, Donne's double pun is of course still just a hint, a vague indication of the complex role that attention has in prayer. Let me offer a more systematic—though still preliminary—account of this role. I suggest that in the kind of Christian devotion that Donne's *La Corona* emulates, attention isn't a mental faculty or an act of the mind but a *regulative ideal of religious practice.* By this, I mean three things. First, in the context of devotion, attention is a feeling accompanying the disposition of being undistracted. I stress "undistracted" rather than "attentive" to indicate that this understanding of attention as an affect prioritizes intransitive attention over the transitive act of attending to something. Although acts of attending to particular objects may have religious significance, they do so by virtue of entailing an experience of attentiveness or partaking in an exercise toward it. Indeed, the less focused they are on any object, the more religious significance they may have because they thus remain the more open toward the divine.[29] Second, the feeling of being undistracted is associated with

redemption. The roots of this association go back to early Christian asceticism, which suggested that getting rid of *all* distractions would make the
ascetic capable of knowing God and becoming God-like. This ascetic ideal
of pure attention was later criticized on the grounds that it vested too much
confidence in human agency and ignored the need of divine grace in devotion. As a result, the ascetic ideal was marginalized in post-Augustinian
theology, and it was particularly rebuked in the aftermath of the Protestant
Reformation. But it did not disappear. After Augustine the ascetic ideal of
pure, entirely undistracted attention was no longer seen as an actually achievable goal of devotion. Nevertheless, and this is my third point, it was upheld
as a *regulative ideal*. While human actions were no longer perceived to be
capable of realizing perfect attention, approaching this telos as nearly as
possible became their inner logic, sometimes explicitly, though more often
implicitly. Indeed, at stake here isn't mysticism or even heterodoxy but the
degree to which even the most mundane exhortations to pay attention in
prayer carry traces of the ascetic ideal of pure prayer. When I describe attention as a regulative ideal of religious practice, then, I mean to suggest
that in Christian devotion "attention" implies an entire complex of ideas,
actions, and experiences: acts of attention designed to produce the passive
experience of being as undistracted as possible because the experience itself
is associated with redemption. It is this entire complex that I call the art of
holy attention.[30] Let us now see an example of how Donne's work engages
in this art.

POETRY OF ATTENTION

To look for signs of devotional attention in Donne may sound counterintuitive. T. S. Eliot, for instance, accused Donne of habitual distraction and
found Donne's religion for that reason impure.[31] It is true that Donne often
spoke of distraction. When for instance in a sermon he gives a list of possible distractions in prayer, the items include not only sense perceptions
but memories, expectations, and imaginations of any kind: "A memory of
yesterdays pleasure, a feare of to morrows dangers, a straw under my knee,
a noise in mine eare, a light in mine eye, an any thing, a nothing, a fancy,
a Chimera in my braine."[32] What readers from Eliot onward have missed
about this and similar passages is that the interest in distraction here is part
of a broader investment in attention. The point of the list isn't to include

particularly blameworthy sources of distraction but to illustrate how easy it is to get distracted, to demonstrate the mind's inherent proneness to distraction. There is a great deal of theologically inflected epistemology implied in this seemingly personal passage; like his favorite Church Father, Augustine, Donne identified distraction and the resulting scattering of the self with the fallen human condition.[33] But for the same reason he also thought of the experience of being attentive as a minor miracle. Indeed, as I will show in the last chapter, for Donne being attentive in this life was a miracle comparable to the miracle he considered the most important element of the Christian faith, the resurrection. While in the resurrection God miraculously collects the dissolved parts of the human body, in experiences of attention it is the self whose scattered parts are miraculously reunited.[34] Transient and unsustainable, experiences of attentiveness nevertheless have one advantage over resurrection: they belong to this life.

The thirst for the experience of being attentive appears often in Donne's letters and provides some of the most memorable passages in the sermons, moments when Donne abandons the role of the preacher and talks to the audience in a far more intimate voice, appealing to their shared experience of distraction and desire for attentiveness. The gesture is of course ingenious because it capitalizes on the audience's experience of distraction and turns it into attention. But at stake in such passages is more than a rhetorical strategy to keep the audience attentive: Donne is intrigued by how much attention one could possibly have. The love poems of the *Songs and Sonets* are also attempts to imagine moments of wholly absorbing, undistracted attentiveness. Indeed, one of the ways in which he casts love as a religious experience is by drawing a parallel between the exclusive attention that lovers pay to each other and the holy attention that Christian prayer pursues.[35] But while in the *Songs and Sonets* Donne plays with the idea of holy attention, in the devotional poems and particularly in the *Holy Sonnets* the game becomes altogether more serious. In these poems, Donne seeks to bring about the undistracted attention that the *Songs and Sonets* only imagine.

The first four lines of the Holy Sonnet "This is my Playes last Scene" offer an example:

> This is my Playes last Scene, here heavens appoint
> My Pilgrimages last Mile, and my race,
> Idely, yet quickly run, hath this last pace
> My Spanns last inche; my Minutes last pointe.[36]

More than half a century ago, Louis Martz cited these lines as a paradigmatic example of the influence he thought early modern spiritual exercises
had on seventeenth-century English devotional poetry.[37] At first, the poem
seems to bear out Martz's thesis by performing a systematic meditation
guided by images. The first couplet appears to rely on the technique known
as *compositio loci,* a concerted effort to imagine a soteriologically significant scene to stir up one's religious feelings. Such a scene might come from
the Scriptures, an image of the crucifixion, for instance; or it might be, as
in this poem, one's last moment before death. And yet there is something
amiss with describing the poem's first four lines as an attempt to *imagine*
the moment of death. There are images, sure, but they come very quickly
and disappear even faster. Play, pilgrimage, race replace each other too
easily, and their rapid succession suggests that precisely as images, they
are transient and disposable. Indeed, there is in the first four lines an entropic movement away from images: while at first the speaker imagines
the last moment in grand theatrical images of climax, by the end of the
quatrain these images give room to the mere "last inch" and the last instant
of the speaker's bare self. The entropic move from imagining death toward
focusing on an imageless and bare last instant of the self also appears in
the poem's self-consuming prosody. From the beheaded *pies* rhymes ("ap-
point" and "point") to the enjambment that gradually shortens its overflow to disappear entirely by the last line, and to the caesuras that undergo
an entropic process and find their most neutral, central position by the
last line, all the formal poetic institutions participate in the performative
movement whereby the poem internalizes and produces its initial deixis.
It is as if the initial images constituted the flesh of the poem that is now
gradually falling off its body; and by the end, the skeleton is revealed in
the only two words that have remained constant throughout: "my" and
"last." Small and insignificant as they appear, together these two words
offer a complete expression of the poem's subject, the last of the self.

The way the poem's first four lines deconstruct the very images they
initially build could be seen as an iconoclastic Protestant response to the
emphasis on images in Jesuit meditations. And yet the iconoclastic motive
is here also in the service of a seemingly rather un-Protestant search for pure
attention. The images are left behind as mere distractions, and the poem
proceeds in the opposite direction, toward limiting the possibility of distraction to a minimum by confining the speaker's attention. The fourth line
feels almost claustrophobic, and that is its point: it is as though the poem

tried to create, out of its own material of words and images, a trap for attention, a *locus* where attention cannot look anywhere beyond the limits of this "my last." By the end of the fourth line where the speaker identifies the reference of the first "this" as a mere "last pointe," it seems that what the stanza has achieved is not an act of imagining the "this," but an act of forcing attention to hold onto the "last pointe" as an infinitesimal, incomparable, and therefore unimaginable entity. Death isn't imagined here; rather, it is thought in the specific sense of being attended to by a stripped-down, pure act of attention.

So far, the poem's first four lines may be seen to be performing the labor of attending that the speaker of *La Corona* assigned to devotional poetry. But after the first quatrain, the poem offers a new surprise. We could expect the speaker to now pause and reflect on this moment of attending to death. But for some reason, as though carried away by its own performance, the poem does not stop but, with a gesture that is characteristic of the *Holy Sonnets,* goes on to work itself into a frenzy of imagination and speculation.[38] The attention exercise of the first quatrain seems to fall apart in the next eight lines:

> And gluttonous death will instantly unioynt
> My body and Soule, and I shall sleepe a space,
> Or presently, I know not, see that face
> Whose feare allredy shakes my every ioynt.
> Then as my Soule, to' heaven her first Seate takes flight,
> And earthborne body in the earth shall dwell,
> So fall my Sins, that all may have their right,
> To where they'are bred, and would presse me, to hell.

An allegorical Death has entered the stage to perform the surgical work of separating body and soul; the speaker briefly notes the theological conundrum of whether or not after death the soul immediately faces judgment or rests with the body until the resurrection; and in the third quatrain, he delves into a rather fantastic vision of what might happen after the judgment.[39] In contrast to the first four lines that seemed to work methodically toward a moment of pure concentration, these lines undo the first quatrain's work by indulging in unrestrained imagination. The speaker's distractedness now parallels the scattering of the self after death. Yet after these agitated images of death and its aftermath, the final couplet is an altogether different, somber petition for grace:

Impute me righteous, thus purg'd of evill,
For thus I leave the world, the fleshe, and devill.

"Impute me righteous" turns the Protestant doctrine of salvation *sola gratia* into an act of asking for divine grace. This is the moment where the poem becomes a prayer in the proper sense of addressing God. But how did we get here?[40] Where does the prayer for grace come from? What allows the speaker to utter its words? And what is its relation to the poem's initial exercise of attention? In order to answer these questions, we have to temporarily turn away from Donne's poem and consider the ideal of *grace*.

PRACTICES OF GRACE

When Malebranche wryly notes that "truth doesn't always respond to our desires because we don't know how to pray to it," he makes a demand: in order to think better, first we have to learn how to pray better. Seeing the outlines of holy attention brings us a step closer to understanding this demand. In the art of holy attention, one becomes better at prayer by learning how to exercise attention toward an ever more undistracted disposition of attentiveness, which in turn is also a condition of a thought occurring to the thinker.

One benefit of this emphasis on prayer as an exercise of attention is that it helps us move away from the still predominant model of prayer as an *expression* of religious feeling.[41] Malebranche's concept of prayer doesn't express a preconceived content but instead summons a new recognition; similarly, prayer in a general sense that includes vocal and mental exercises is a *technē*, a set of acts and techniques aiming to achieve a desired effect. And yet characterizing prayer as *technē* is slightly misleading. A modern, science-inflected understanding of technology associates *technē* with control, predictability, and consistency. One of the things setting technology apart from other realms of life is its reliability in producing the goods we expect from it. Although prayer may be *technē* in the sense of involving a set of practices and techniques, it is precisely *not* technology in the modern sense because it not only admits the limits of its own agency but cultivates this limitation in order to create space for transcendence.

One of the Latin tradition's terms for prayer will help to clarify this. *Gratiarum actio* is a phrase that survives today in the context of Christianity, where it is a translation of the Greek *eucharistia*. Its primary reference is not just the rite of the Eucharist, however, but a wide range of devotional actions from thanksgiving prayers to confession and repentance.[42] For the purposes of this book, it will be important to remember that just like its Greek predecessor, the Latin phrase contains the word *grace*; indeed, the French translation is *action de grâce*, and a hyperliteral English rendering would be "action of graces." This translation might offend the ear, and with good reason: we are used to thinking of "action" and "grace" as antithetical categories. Grace is "beyond the reach of art," and by extension, beyond the reach of human action.[43] But the point of actions of grace is to invite that which is always and by definition beyond their control and yet what is nevertheless required for their efficacy. Because of the Protestant emphasis on grace, and because of Donne's conversion to Protestantism, discussions of grace in Donne's poetry often restrict the relevance of this ideal to its post-Reformation religious contexts. As a result, readers of Donne often get lost in the intricate details of Catholic and Protestant debates about the theological definitions of grace. But the ideal of grace is neither something exclusive to post-Reformation theological debates nor a solely religious ideal. For this reason, and precisely in order to understand its relevance for early modern devotion, it is best if for a moment we take grace out of the post-Reformation context and place it in a longer, transhistorical, and interdisciplinary one.

When we look up the word "grace" in a dictionary today, we encounter a number of meanings that are not obviously related to each other. Grace is an aesthetic quality in a somewhat vague sense; it is like beauty but unlike beauty, it cannot be held onto (hence the oft-repeated statement that "grace is beauty of movement," as we read it for instance in G. E. Lessing's *Laokoon*).[44] It is also a social quality, the elegance or attractiveness of one's manners, again in a rather elusive sense. (William Hazlitt describes the duke of Marlborough as having been "eminently illiterate" but nevertheless capable of winning over anyone he met seemingly effortlessly because "his engaging, graceful manner" was "irresistible by either man or woman.")[45] Most strikingly, it is a theological term that Western languages inherit from the Latin *gratia*, itself a translation of the Greek *charis*, both of which refer in early Christian writings to the mercy of God that saves mankind from the consequences of sin.

What the dictionary does not say is that for the larger part of Western history, these meanings of grace are intimately bound together by the sense of *charis* as gift or favor. Whether aesthetic, social, or theological, the qualities of grace belong to a human subject only by virtue of being given to him as a gift.[46] It is in this broad sense that grace is connected to a notion of transcendence: it transcends the agency of the subject, it is outside the scope of the subject's intentional actions. When Alexander Pope writes about "a grace beyond the reach of art," he summarizes this tradition of grace's transcendence of human agency. Early modern treatises on painting and sculpture, while highly concerned with technique and praxis, praise grace as the ultimate aesthetic quality that cannot be achieved by mere human action. Michelangelo, whose style was considered in many ways distinct from the "graceful" style of Raphael, is the painter of *una grazia più interamente graziosa* insofar as his skills are so extraordinary that they seem to be a divine gift.[47] In the context of courtly manners, grace too appears as something that one may or may not have, depending on one's social position, physical beauty, and other "given" factors. Thus grace is the courtier's ultimate virtue: in order to ask for the *grazia* (grace as favor) of the prince, the courtier must already possess a kind of behavioral *grazia* (grace as effortless elegance) that enables him to win the prince's attention and benevolence. Finally, the Pauline tradition of Christian divine *charis* or grace is based on the notion that humankind cannot earn its salvation by following the Judaic law; it also needs God's forgiveness, the free divine gift of mercy that makes up for the original sin of the first couple. Whether in the context of religion, aesthetics, or manners, grace is an ideal that is defined by its very inaccessibility to human action.

This tradition is evoked in what is perhaps the most radical post-Enlightenment confrontation of the category, the German dramatist Heinrich von Kleist's parable "Über das Marionettentheater."[48] I evoke Kleist's parable here because it sheds light on the fundamentally different attitudes that pre- and post-Enlightenment accounts have toward the ideal of grace. First published in the *Berliner Abendblätter* in 1810, the *Marionettentheater* reports of a conversation that the author purportedly had with Herr C., the first dancer of the local opera of an unnamed city. At the beginning of the conversation, Herr C. suggests that the puppets of the *Marionettentheater* set up in the local marketplace are more graceful dancers than their human counterparts. As a connoisseur of high arts, the narrator first assumes that Herr C. is jesting; but the dancer turns out to be so serious he even has a soteriological theory to explain the puppets' advantage. The *Marionetten*, he argues, are better dancers because they have more aesthetic grace than humans do; and they have more aesthetic grace because unlike humankind, they have never fallen from *divine* grace.[49] In fact, Herr C. insists, grace is something only puppets can have; humans are irreparably fallen, and they may only receive their lost grace back when history comes to an end. The myth of the fall here becomes the general framework in which grace both as an aesthetic quality and as a divine gift is defined by its inaccessibility to human action. As a consequence, in the *Marionettentheater* grace is something that one may or may not *have*—and not something that one may or may not *seek*.

What is missing from the *Marionettentheater* is what is so prevalent in pre-Enlightenment contexts and particularly in the Renaissance: the act of asking for grace. One of the most influential early modern books of courtesy, Baldassare Castiglione's *Book of the Courtier,* contrasts strikingly with Kleist's *Marionettentheater* in its attempt to make grace available to human action. The famous word *sprezzatura* is coined in the *Book of the Courtier* to cover up what might seem to be a logical contradiction between the impossibility of achieving grace and the interest in actions that seek to achieve it nevertheless.[50] At first, the characters in *Il cortegiano* discuss grace as a quality beyond the reach of human action: grace as the highest and most useful quality of the courtier, they insist, is exclusively a matter of noble birth and natural talent.[51] Soon, however, they turn to the question of what a courtier who has no such natural grace could still do, and it is here that they introduce *sprezzatura*. A courtier who lacks natural grace should acquire and perfect every skill a courtier needs. But this is not enough to have grace; what is also needed is the semblance that these skills are not acquired through practice but are merely the result of birth and talent. *Sprezzatura* is the air of nonchalance that erases the traces of the actions leading to technical perfection and thereby creates a simulacrum of grace. It is, we might say, a mimesis of grace—and of course once the courtier has won the *grazia,* the favor of the sovereign, this virtual grace turns into real grace. Castiglione's contemporaries were fascinated with actions that imitated, invoked, or requested grace, that is, with *prayers* in the broadest sense of the term. *Sprezzatura* itself is a kind of prayer: in making use of aesthetic and social grace, Castiglione's courtier is in fact asking for the prince's favor. Actions of grace are prayers in the sense of petitions for the grace of a sovereign, of God, or anyone and anything that is seen as capable of granting a favor. In the early modern period, such actions are part of what we might call the *practice of grace;* that is, they are not isolated individual actions but elements of a framework of rules, or *technē*: they constitute various practices of praying for grace.

Focusing on theological debates about grace is always in danger of missing the point that practices of grace reveal: the limited sense of human agency that actions associated with grace always cultivate.[52] When we use the term "agency" in the sense of capacity to act, we think of it as a self-evident value: the more agency I have, the better off I am. The Renaissance interest in grace reveals a fundamentally different attitude: as much as Castiglione's contemporaries were obsessed with the sheer political and military power that we associate with Machiavelli's *Prince,* they were also deeply invested in an altogether different, limited kind of agency, which they valued because of its liminality. Actions of grace are marked by an absence, a hollow spot; they not only acknowledge but cultivate and indeed create this hollow spot. This emphatic cultivation of what in theory appears as the impossible is what sets actions of grace apart from other cultural practices. The reason, for example, that Renaissance poetry calls the gift of sleep "heavy grace" is that the process of falling asleep is neither entirely active nor merely passive.[53] Falling asleep is not, properly speaking, an action, because a person is only "asleep" when sleep itself comes. Yet there is in fact a range of actions that the seeker of sleep can choose from, to prepare for and invite sleep. These actions are often mimetic: in trying to fall asleep, we imitate our sleeping selves by closing our eyes, assuming the position of the body asleep, breathing the way a sleeping person does.[54] The preparatory actions to fall asleep are "secular prayers," to use Kenneth Burke's term, prayers that try to "invite" sleep by imitating it.[55] In this sense, sleep's "heavy grace" is a partial result of the sleeper's actions; as Malebranche would say, our actions constitute an "occasion" for the event of sleep to occur. Actions associated with grace, from prayer to Malebranche's notion of thinking are all similar to the "act" of falling asleep: they are actions, often highly developed and ritualized actions, but they are also actions that admit a space in which agency is truncated in order to allow the event that completes them to occur. In fact, actions that seek grace do not only admit this space but cultivate it and ascribe to it centrality and privilege; the impossibility of action becomes a norm of action.

THANKSGIVING

Donne's life was a series of prayers for grace. The story is well known, and I revisit it here only to show how Donne's devotional poems belong to the poet's lifelong concern with asking and thanking in a sense that goes beyond the realm of religion.[56] Born into a Catholic family, Donne began his career as an aspiring courtier whose poetic talent was immediately recognized, giving him promising prospects in the late Elizabethan coterie world. His conversion to Protestantism in the Church of England probably helped him secure a position as secretary to Sir Thomas Egerton, the lord keeper of the Great Seal.[57] Instead of patiently working on his fortunes, however, he clandestinely married the niece of his employer. The letter to Anne More's father in which Donne, though ostensibly apologizing for the marriage, in fact rather arrogantly demands Sir George More's support, proved to be a fatally misconceived petition. The spectacular fall from social grace that Donne subsequently experienced left a mark on his mind.[58] For decades to come, he cultivated a personal mode of melancholy, the melancholy of the fallen courtier, an outcast waiting for readmission into society, crafting in solicitation some of the most original poetry and letters of the era. Indeed, if Donne circulated his poetry as (mostly) implicit requests for patronage, the verse and prose letters not only perform similar requests but also reflect on how to ask and thank for favors. Still, social grace evaded him for a long time, and when it finally came, it was tied to divine grace. James I was willing to consider the employment of Donne, who by this time had proven his usefulness by authoring several pamphlets supporting the king's position in religious matters.[59] But, according to Donne's first biographer, Izaak Walton, the king insisted that he would only employ the now middle-aged Donne if he took holy orders and became a preacher in the Church of England.[60] Walton claims that Donne first rejected the offer, and only after a period of hesitation did he finally accept the king's repeated requests and take holy orders in 1615. Once he did, he rapidly became one of the most successful and famous preachers of the time, eventually as the dean of St. Paul's.

A number of the nineteen extant poems that we know today as the *Holy Sonnets* might have been written during the period when Donne was hesitating over the decision of taking holy orders.[61] Whether this is the case, the poems are witnesses to the ways in which Donne works through his fears and doubts and desires about Christianity in general and Protestantism in particular; they are simultaneously attempts at thinking about religion and attempts at being religious.[62] As Martz argued half a century ago, some of the poems might be influenced by early modern systematic spiritual exercises in the Ignatian tradition—perhaps in the very sense Ignatius intended, as meditations to help the exercitant make a decision, including a decision about a vocation in religion.[63] But as Barbara Lewalski and others have shown, the poems also display a consistent concern with the Protestant doctrine of salvation *sola gratia*.[64] At times it feels tempting to characterize Donne's speakers as Catholic actors but Protestant think-ers, constantly wavering between the different modalities of early modern Christianity.[65] Yet to reduce the poems to either of these influences or even to their combination would be a mistake. The *Holy Sonnets* enact a vari-ety of devotional actions, from confession and repentance to petition and thanksgiving. They are actions of grace in every sense of the word: aesthetic artifacts carefully crafted to ask for divine grace that meanwhile also solicit the favors of an ostensibly accidental human audience. They belong to the realm I described above as the realm of Renaissance practices of grace. They also go beyond it: in the *Holy Sonnets,* Donne not only performs actions of graces but also seeks to understand what it means to do so by contemplat-ing the very conditions of *gratiarum actio.*

Let's return to "This is my Playes last Scene" to see how Donne's mani-fold investment in grace inflects the poem's search for attention; indeed, how it is both the challenge and the solution in the quest for attentiveness. As I argued above, the poem's initial exercises of attention give room, by the second and third quatrains, to a frenzy of images that scatter the speaker's hard-won initial attention and indulge in distractedness:

> This is my Playes last Scene, here heavens appoint
> > My Pilgrimages last Mile, and my race,
> > Idely, yet quickly run, hath this last pace
> My Spanns last inche; my Minutes last pointe.
> And gluttonous death will instantly unioynt
> > My body and Soule, and I shall sleepe a space,
> > Or presently, I know not, see that face
> Whose feare allredy shakes my every ioynt.
> Then as my Soule, to' heaven her first Seate takes flight,
> > And earthborne body in the earth shall dwell,
> So fall my Sins, that all may have their right,
> > To where they'are bred, and would presse me, to hell.

Yet by the final couplet the distraction disappears:

> Impute me righteous, thus purg'd of evill,
> For thus I leave the world, the fleshe, and devill.

The tone of the final couplet suggests that something must have happened in between the first twelve lines of the poem and the final rhyming couplet.

Why and how such a turn might have happened would remain hidden were it not for the poem's prosodic structure, which offers a few initial hints. The final rhyming couplet is prefigured by the first two quatrains, both of which work with *pies* rhymes: in the embrace of the first and last lines of each quatrain, the two middle lines constitute an enclosed rhyming couplet. If we turn to these middle lines, we notice that their rhyming ends speak of an absence. "Race," "space," "pace," and "face" are all words early modern poets were fond of rhyming with the ever-present word "grace." As if silenced by the imprisonment of the sonnet, however, the language does not arrive at "grace" itself: amidst all the soteriological fantasies, the very condition of salvation remains absent, and by the third, most distracted quatrain even its echoes die out. That is, until the final couplet where, escaped from the embrace of the first two quatrains' rhymes, it is finally evoked in the form of the couplet's prayer. As if it has just occurred to the speaker that during all his thinking about salvation he has forgotten the one thing necessary for it, he now asks for grace: "Impute me righteous." It seems as though the final prayer for grace emerges not out of the poem's initial exercise of attention but out of the poem's forgettings, absences, distractions. What's left, by the end of "This is my Playes last Scene," of the art of holy attention?

It will be helpful here to remember the significance of Donne's choice of the sonnet form for his devotional poems. By the early seventeenth century, the sonnet shows signs of age, and Donne carefully avoids it in his love poetry. Every poem of the *Songs and Sonets* is written in a different stanzaic form; forty of them are Donne's own innovations. The sonnet's absence is striking amidst this proud display of poetic invention: Donne seeks to refashion love poetry by cutting it loose from its centuries-old association with the sonnet and the sonnet sequence. Donne's turn to the sonnet in his devotional form is sometimes seen as a provocative gesture of originality; but equally relevant is the degree to which by choosing the old form, Donne imposed a highly artificial restraint on his devotional experiments—as one reader noted, the sonnet form in the *Holy Sonnets* feels a bit like a monastic habit, a deliberate attempt to discipline the body of the poem and the imagination of the poet.[66] The *Holy Sonnets'* reinterpretation of the sonnet's signature *volta* is a case in point. Traditionally, the *volta* brings about a sudden, new and surprising perspective on the sonnet's subject. In the *Holy Sonnets,* this kind of *volta* is upstaged by the more emphatic turn that comes at the very end of the poems. The final rhyming couple often turns toward a basic element of Christian faith—a Scriptural quotation, a liturgical phrase, always something that is already *given* outside and prior to the poem, in religion. Take again the prayer at the end of "This is my Playes last Scene":

> Impute me righteous, thus purg'd of evill,
> For thus I leave the world, the fleshe, and devill.

What is remarkable about this *volta* is that when the missing grace finally comes forth in the poem, it does so not as a rhyme, not even as a word (the word "grace" remains missing from the poem), but as something already given: grace is invoked by reiterating the given words of doctrine and liturgy. The last line is a near-verbatim quotation of the prebaptismal renunciation in the Book of Common Prayer; the penultimate line is of course a reference to the Protestant doctrine of justification by grace.[67] The dominance of the Christian given is even more conspicuous if we compare the couplet with the rest of the poem, which, as we noted above, parodies the Ignatian *compositio loci* and uses poetry to imagine not only the moment of death but its aftermath:

> Then as my Soule, to' heaven her first Seate takes flight,
>   And earthborne body in the earth shall dwell,
> So fall my Sins, that all may have their right,
>   To where they'are bred, and would presse me, to hell.

The logical dilation of the end that we saw earlier in the second quatrain is followed in this quatrain by yet another lastness, an extended, partly scatological, partly eschatological fantasy.[68] The scattering of the postmortem self reflects the speaker's distractedness in the here and the now of the poem. But the technique of *compositio loci* is taken so far that it is in danger of turning into a farce: parts of the self—soul, body, sins—move according to their soteriological vectors in this fantastical space of salvation history, and by the end of the quatrain one wonders: what could the "me" possibly still consist of when all its parts are taken away? And yet it is this "me" that, in the final couplet, pronounces the concluding prayer of the poem:

> Impute *me* righteous, thus purg'd of evill,
> For thus *I* leave the world, the fleshe, and devill.[69]

The final prayer responds to the speaker's recognition that he has lacked the grace he would have needed for salvation by quoting the given words of

Christianity. The final couplets at the end of the *Holy Sonnets* regularly perform this kind of turn to a religious given after the first twelve lines of poetic abundance. The gesture has confounded readers. Although the *Holy Sonnets* are well-respected poems with a firm place in the canon, readers have not always shown the kind of fondness for them that the *Songs and Sonets* usually evoke. One speculates that the reason is the seemingly formulaic, at times even mechanistic, turn to religion at the end of these poems.[70] It is as if in these last couplets Donne turns away from poetry itself. For the modern reader, who reads poems for their reinvention and resuscitation of language, such a turn-away may even feel like a betrayal.[71]

Yet when at the end of "This is my Playes last Scene" the speaker prays, "Impute me righteous," this prayer poses a question dictated by the logic of grace. Stripped of all its constitutive parts, the "me" of the poem after the end of the third quatrain recognizes that grace has remained absent throughout the poem and responds to this recognition by voicing a petition. But in order for this prayer to be efficacious, the "me" would already have to possess grace. Donne articulates this paradox in another Holy Sonnet as a problem of repentance: "grace, if thou repent thou canst not lacke. / But who shall give thee that grace to begin?"[72] In order to be able to ask for grace, one has to repent; but in order to repent, one has to have grace. The problem is not exclusive to repentance; it is a problem of any prayer. Grace is both the desired ideal of devotional action and at the same time its very prerequisite. If "This is my Playes last Scene" ends with the given, the question is whether this given is *given to the speaker*—or whether it is merely *a given* that exists prior to and independent from the speaker.

The difference between a given and something that is given to the speaker is the difference between a given and a *gift*. If the given is what already exists, temporally preceding "me," and existentially independent of "me," a gift by contrast is what is being given to "me" right now in this very moment as a present (to give a gift is *mettre une chose en present à quelqu'un*, to place something in a person's presence), and what is addressed to "me" personally, calling for "my" action. Putting the matter this way helps to articulate the problem of grace in phenomenological terms: grace is not a miraculous gift that appears *ex nihilo*, but an already existing X that is now perceived as Y; a given that appears to the perceiver as gift.[73] The term "given" might sound vague here, but its generality is the point: from the perspective of Christian devotion, the given can be any particular detail of the natural world (in which case the datum of nature becomes the gift of creation), or something as complicated as the incarnation and the crucifixion of Christ (in which case a historical and doctrinal given is rediscovered as a living truth). Let's recall again that the Greek phrase usually rendered as *gratiarum actio* is *eucharistia:* the Eucharistic transformation of the bread into the body of Christ is certainly the most spectacular (and in the early modern period most controversial) instance of this recognition of an X as Y, a given piece of bread as *charis anti charitos,* Christ's body as God's gift to mankind. But while transubstantiation is a Roman Catholic tenet of faith, the aspiration to see the divine gift in the given is shared in both Protestant and Catholic devotion. In his commentary on Psalm 139, Calvin puts the matter in these terms:

> Then is there not set downe here, suche a knowledge as may subdue that thyng to our senses, which David hath under the name of wonderfull, confessed too unable to comprehend (lyke as the overweening of the Philosophers so puffeth them up, that they leave nothing for God to be privie unto:) but only here is betokened such a godly attentivenesse [*pia attentio*] as may waken us to render glorye unto God.[74]

The condition of perceiving the given as a divine gift, in Calvin's polemic against philosophy, is not comprehension but what he calls "pia attentio." Something similar happens in the *Holy Sonnets:* Donne's speakers pursue the ideal of holy attention as a disposition of receptivity, a cognitive foundation for discovering the given as grace. In ascetic discussions of attentiveness and distraction in devotion, holy attention is the implicit but prevalent promise that an entirely undistracted attention would make God's truth directly available to the believer. This promise arises from the conviction that the only reason one would not find divine grace already given in any perceptual experience is due to the distractions of the flesh. If one could attend not *kata sarka,* according to the flesh, but *kata pneuma,* according to the spirit, with a holy attention, the given would immediately reappear as a divine gift, created and given to the person in the moment of its apperception. But of course the human condition *is* the condition of being in the flesh, which means that even if one managed to approximate the ideal of pure attentiveness by laborious acts of transitive attention, distraction would inevitably return and scatter the self again amidst the world and his own thoughts and fantasies. This is why in the second and third quatrains of "This is my Playes last Scene" Donne's speaker leaves behind the first quatrain's hard-won attentiveness and sinks into distraction. And yet without this distraction, the given couldn't appear as a gift at the end of the poem. It is the poem's distractions that in "This is my Playes last scene" spew out the missing grace so that the speaker's attention might find it as an unexpected gift: the final couplet is a surprise that the poem has carefully solicited by its volatile dialectic between attention and distraction. The sonnet becomes a site for making the two sides of grace, its transcendence and its liminality as action, work together.

It is here, between the work of attention and the event of grace that we can catch a glimpse of how the poems perform the kind of thinking that prayer implies.[75] Let's return for a moment to the question of prayer. Malebranche's demand that philosophy should learn from prayer might at first appear rather counterintuitive: after all, unlike philosophy, prayers do not seem to be *about* anything. Aristotle notes that prayers escape the requirements of propositional statements; they are neither true nor false because they do not make any propositional claim (in this they are similar to poetic fictions, and Aristotle asserts that their study belongs to rhetoric or poetics).[76] But Malebranche's comments begin to make more sense if we remember that Christian authors from Clement of Alexandria to Saint Augustine considered prayer and theology as aspects of the same practice. They saw in prayer not only a petition to God but an attempt to *think* God; prayer was for them also *theologia,* logos coming from and returning to God.[77]

Holy attention is the condition of this practical, devotional sense of *theologia.* When prayer is a movement toward *theologia,* its aim isn't to know God in terms of propositional, universal statements that describe verifiable truths, but by experiencing him. The condition of this experience is the speaker's openness toward it; it is, in other words, the ideal of an entirely undistracted attentiveness. Like lyric address, in this sense prayer might seem like an atavistic act, insofar as it appears to believe that the object *will* actually reveal itself to prayer's attention.[78] But the point is that the quest for a holy attention aims at the elimination of all preexisting assumptions as distractions; this is why in perfect prayer even the thought of God's existence is an obstacle to devotion. To be sure, prayer may never reach the goal of an entirely undistracted attention; perhaps the goal itself is impossible. Still, insofar as prayer is striving toward this goal, it includes the possibility of a mode of thinking in the specific sense of preparation for a thought to occur without obstructing its occurrence by presuming anything about it.

In a post-Hegelian perspective, philosophical thinking has become an ideal of thinking as such, in the specific sense of a process of creating one opening after another, as a movement whose strength and appeal lie in its capability to overcome its own limitations by reflecting on them. From this perspective, religion might seem a primitive precedent at best, and at worst, the very opposite of thinking or at least of *good* thinking. As an institution it may appear to impose artificial limits on thinking, and as a set of doctrines it may seem to inhibit autonomous thought. Prayer as an art of holy attention contradicts this dichotomy between philosophy and religion by offering a model of cognitive receptivity rivaling the philosophical ideal. In the conception of holy attention, a "thought" isn't just a mental proposition but an event occurring to the attentive mind, and thinking isn't merely an attempt to formulate mental propositions but a set of techniques whose goal is, paradoxically, to allow the unpredictable to happen.

Donne's devotional poems depict the ways in which individual speakers may arrive at the experience of this sort of thought. The reason these poems cannot and shouldn't be read for their propositional statements about doctrines is that they are not expressions of any specific belief but preparations for the very faith that such beliefs require. In this sense, the poems are the speakers' attempts to see whether an individual doctrine may be turned into practice, whether the poem itself can become the proof of a doctrine's possibility by translating the abstract thought of the doctrine into living experience. We have seen this in *La Corona*, where the speaker aims at translating his faith in Christ's redeeming sacrifice into certainty in his own salvation; and we have seen it in "This is my Playes last Scene," where it is the Protestant doctrine of salvation only by grace that has to occur to the speaker as his own faithful request for grace. In "Death be not proud," the poem that plays a central role in this book, Donne's speaker seeks to think another Christian tenet, this time the Pauline doctrine of the resurrection of the body. But here too, what is at stake in the poem's specific movements is whether the speaker becomes able to transition from the given Pauline doctrine to experiencing the thought of the resurrection as his own. In all of these poems, the art of holy attention becomes part of the speaker's attempt to appropriate specific Christian doctrines as his own thoughts. This is why the poems often waver between commonplaces and strikingly original thoughts, between doctrines and heterodox or near-blasphemous ideas, between certainty and disbelief. Donne's devotional poems are experiments in prayer and poetry, but above all they are thought experiments. They seek to transition from the given to the gift so that they can appropriate doctrines: it is by thanking that they think.

CLOSE READING AND ATTENTION EXERCISES

In a sense, the intuition that Donne's poems include exercises of attention has influenced modern literary criticism since at least I. A. Richards and the New Critics, and it has contributed to the centrality of close reading in the academic study of literature. Recall that the story of modern, professionalized literary criticism begins with the rediscovery of Donne.[79] In his poetry, the New Critics found a blueprint for all good poetry:

> Certainly Shakespeare's LXXXVII, "Farewell! thou art too dear for my possessing," already quoted as an instance of good structure is in the style [of metaphysical poetry]. Three times, in as many quatrains, the lover makes an exploration within the field of the figure. The occasions are fairly distinct, though I should think their specifications are hardly representative enough to have satisfied Donne. But the thing which surprises us is to find no evidence anywhere that Shakespeare's imagination is equal to the peculiar and systematic exercises which Donne imposed habitually upon his.[80]

It is not simply that, for John Crowe Ransom, Donne was a better poet than Shakespeare. Reading Donne is seen here as a systematic and rigorous exercise preparing the critic for the reading and judging of *any* poetry. This could be a remarkable insight into the devotional purposes of Donne's poetry and a beginning of thinking about devotion's relevance for aesthetics and literary criticism. Yet when the New Critics considered Donne's poetry a model of poetry as such, what they had in mind was more often Donne's secular poetry, particularly the *Songs and Sonets:*

> Since . . . the *Songs and Sonets* of Donne . . . requires . . . "a perpetual activity of attention . . . on the part of the reader from the rapid flow, the quick change, and the playful nature of thoughts and images," the discipline gained from reading Donne may allow us to see more clearly the survival of such qualities in the later style of Shakespeare.[81]

When the New Critics noticed the significance of attention in Donne's poetry, they thought that it was a sign of Aristotelian invention, of rigorous but free poetic creation. That their author also wrote devotional poems,

INTRODUCTION 29

which, however much they displayed the same artistic virtues, ultimately gave the last word (literally) to religion, posed a challenge to the New Critics and their predecessors in Cambridge.

I. A. Richards's *Practical Criticism* offers an example. In Richards's book, a Holy Sonnet appears not only as one of the thirteen "practice" poems, but as the paradigmatic example of the difficulty of "doctrine in poetry," an issue to which he later dedicates an entire chapter. The responses sum up the difficulty: readers disapprove of Donne's "At the round earth's imagined corners" either because they are religious (and they find Donne's treatment of Christianity frivolous) or because they are agnostic or hold different religious views (and find Donne's Christianity off-putting). Thus when Richards returns to the question in his chapter 7, his concern is how to overcome doctrinal differences altogether in reading poetry. His formulation of the problem is striking: "In the end, with Donne's Sonnet (*Poem III*), for example, it becomes very difficult not to think that *actual belief* in the doctrine that appears in the poem is required for its full and perfect imaginative realisation."[82] To overcome this difficulty, Richards suggests that even if we "intellectually" disagree with the poem's beliefs, we can still offer our emotional belief. When he goes on to ponder how we might be able to separate our intellectual beliefs from our emotional beliefs and still be *sincere* readers, he finds a solution for the problem by proposing meditative exercises for "heightening sincerity." Indeed, he concludes that "the value of poetry lies in the difficult *exercises in sincerity* it imposes upon its readers."[83] Except for mistaking attentiveness for sincerity (a mistake that has to do with the significant overlap between attention and intention), Richards here rediscovers the purpose of Donne's poetry as spiritual exercise. But instead of recognizing that this was the original purpose of these poems, he assumes that the necessity of these "exercises in sincerity" emerges because of the historical and religious distance between the author and the reader. Despite the Christian overtones of the exercises that Richards then describes in detail, he concludes by evoking Confucianism as a model that should help us with the difficulties of Donne's poem.[84]

It was not until Louis Martz's *Poetry of Meditation* appeared in 1954 that the New Critical interest in Donne's poems as exercises was put in a historical perspective. Martz was sympathetic to many New Critical claims and even to Eliot's thesis about the "association" of sensibility in early modern lyric poetry. But for him, what these views referred to were not aesthetic standards of poetry as such, but historically specific poetic strategies grounded in the devotional concerns of the post-Reformation era. The reason Donne and his contemporaries wrote poetry that appeared to offer systematic exercises was that these poems *were* systematic exercises. *Poetry of Meditation* is a historical case study: it suggests that the early modern fascination with meditation and spiritual exercises in the Ignatian tradition was the main influence behind the poetry that the New Critics called "metaphysical." From Robert Southwell to Donne and Herbert, poets of the seventeenth century appear in Martz's work as Christians enacting the Ignatian exercises and their Catholic and Protestant variations. Explaining the modernist affinity for their poetry, Martz quotes D. H. Lawrence to suggest that meditation, and by extension the seventeenth-century poetry of meditation, "was a discipline directed toward creating an 'act of pure attention.'"[85]

Martz's *The Poetry of Meditation* could have been a turning point in the scholarship on early modern devotional poetry; it could have led to further thinking about the nature of religious actions and their relationship to doctrine; it could have led to a recovery of the art of attention in poetry. Unfortunately, in making an extraordinary effort to show the *historical* connection between meditation and poetry, Martz often failed to acknowledge those aspects of the poems that resisted assimilation into his argument. Most strikingly, even though Martz did emphasize that meditation was not an exclusively Catholic concern in the period, he all but ignored the recurrent and rather obvious insistence on Protestant doctrines and especially on the tenet of salvation only by grace in the poetry of Donne and others. In terms of the scholarship on Donne and early modern devotional poetry, this oversight proved to be a fatal mistake because it distracted from the conceptual insights of Martz's argument and focused the debate almost entirely on questions of confessional identity.[86] Provoked by what they saw as Martz's privileging of Catholic contexts for Protestant poetry, critics rushed to prove Martz wrong on this account. The most eminent instance of this backlash is Barbara Lewalski's *Protestant Poetics and the Seventeenth-Century Religious Lyric* (1979). This work, which its author characterizes as "revisionist," is a monumental effort to show that instead of a continental, Catholic, and specifically Ignatian tradition, the main context in which most of seventeenth-century devotional poetry ought to be read is English and Protestant. Lewalski suggests that Protestant devotional poetry is a poetry of the Bible: it follows biblical models of poetry (the Psalms, in particular) and biblical materials (from stories and figures to particular doctrines).

Lewalski's book proved immensely influential, particularly in demanding closer attention to seventeenth-century poetry's immediate religious contexts. It helped to revive interest in the poetry of George Herbert, whose *Temple* has since become the subject of some of the best work on early modern devotional poetry.[87] But Lewalski's emphasis on confessional identity had some unfortunate consequences as well. If in Martz's *Poetry of Meditation* Donne and his contemporaries appear as exercitants of Catholic spiritual meditations, in Lewalski's *Protestant Poetics* they are often reduced to spokespeople for Protestant doctrine.[88] Take the book's chapter on Donne. Lewalski begins by admitting that Donne's religious poetry does not always appear to be as Protestant and biblical as one might expect. Nevertheless, she suggests that there is a chronological development in Donne's poetry toward an ever greater emphasis on the Bible. After tracing this development, Lewalski sums up her view: "the pillars of Donne's biblical, Protestant poetics are: that the scriptures are the most eloquent books in the world, that God is a witty and also 'a figurative, a metaphoricall God,' and that the religious lyric poet should endeavor to 'write after . . . [his] Copie.' "[89] In other words, Lewalski's final word on the subject is that the more poetic and "witty" Donne is in his poetry, the more Protestant he becomes. It's a conclusion that makes it hard to see how any (good) poetry could ever escape being an instance of Protestant poetics.

If we look at the scholarship since Lewalski's work, it is striking to see that in contrast to Herbert's *The Temple,* Donne's devotional verse has still not seen a book-length study. It is as if Donne's devotional poems yield less easily to historicist and new historicist methods than Herbert's, and certainly less than Shakespeare's or Milton's work. Arthur Marotti's *John Donne, Coterie Poet* is perhaps the most successful attempt to integrate Donne's devotional poems into their social context.[90] Marotti's general claims that "Donne's religious poems, particularly those pieces he composed in the decade preceding his ordination, were fundamentally coterie literature" and that Donne "expected this poetry to help him win patronage" are entirely convincing, and as Marotti himself acknowledges, the emphasis on social performance doesn't exclude the possibility that the poems also represent genuine devotional quests.[91] But then how much insight does the characterization of the poems as "witty performances" yield into the specific details of the poems? Like Lewalski's Donne who is Protestant by virtue of his wit, Marotti's Donne is a coterie author because his poetry is complex. The price of integrating Donne's poetry into a specific historical context seems to be the specificity of the poems.

The flip side of this problem appears in Ramie Targoff's *Common Prayer,* a book that elegantly challenges the notion that seventeenth-century devotional poetry was modeled on private devotional practices. Donne remains a curious exception in Targoff's argument: at first, Targoff cites Donne's sermons and dedicatory poem to the Sidney psalms as documents of the early seventeenth-century English interest in public forms of devotion, but then she sets aside the *Holy Sonnets* as idiosyncratic poems that aren't representative of early modern devotional poetry's concern with public devotion.[92] When Targoff does return to the *Holy Sonnets* in *John Donne: Body and Soul,* her exquisite close readings of the poems provide evidence for an argument that is about Donne the person and his lifelong interest in both the body and the soul.[93] Donne appears here as a *sui generis* poet who must be considered on his own terms, and the *Holy Sonnets* as unique poems that must be interpreted in the context of their author's life. Indeed, a similar resistance to assimilating Donne's devotional poems into any larger interpretative scheme characterizes some of the best work on Donne today.[94] While between the New Critics and Marotti, scholars proposed broad historical or conceptual frameworks for reading Donne's poetry, today many critics acknowledge Donne's sources and contexts but insist that the poems cannot and shouldn't be reduced to any one of their influences. We continue to close-read the poems, we delight in their formal complexity and internal integrity, and we appreciate the ways they appear to resist religious or other forms of certainty. In this sense, our practices of reading Donne's poems resemble those of the New Critics. But of course what we no longer possess is the confidence that the New Critics had about the inherent value of close reading as a critical and educational practice.

My point here isn't to debate the uniqueness of Donne's poetry, much less to argue against close reading, which is something I do extensively in this book. But the ways in which Donne's poetry seems to continually demand close reading does raise the question: why should we give in to their demand? Franco Moretti's critique comes to mind: "At bottom, [close reading] is a theological exercise—very solemn treatment of very few texts taken very seriously—whereas what we really need is a little pact with the devil: we know how to read texts, now let's learn how *not* to read them. Distant reading: where the distance, let me repeat it, *is a condition of knowledge.*"[95] Moretti is mainly thinking about novels here, and one immediately suspects that his advice may not apply in the case of Donne's poems, but the interesting question is *why* not. If my argument about Donne's poems being representations of attention exercises has any merit, we may articulate an answer. I have suggested that Donne's speakers train and test their attentiveness by attending to the very words they utter in their prayers and meditations. It is only natural, then, that their words invite a similar kind of close attending from us. Of course, while this explains why Donne's poems would appear to resist distant reading, it only amplifies Moretti's claim that close reading is a "theological exercise" that doesn't provide knowledge. But then we must ask: what kind of knowledge? Presumably, what Moretti means by knowledge is a set of general propositional statements that convey information on the ground of inductively collected, quantitative evidence. Donne's poems, however, are invested in a very different kind of knowledge. As attention exercises, they are aimed at allowing the speaker to think a religious doctrine with a certainty that is subjective and existential. In other words, they are meant to create a very specific kind of knowledge: faith.

If we close-read Donne's poems without realizing that their search for faith and our own close reading of the poems share the same origins, we will simply engage in the same theological exercises Donne's speakers do (indeed, as I showed above this is what Richards did in *Practical Criticism,* without recognizing it). But if we close-read the poems *and* keep in mind their relationship to theology, what we gain is an opportunity to think about "theological exercises" and their relationship to literary criticism. Then, and only then, can we start debating the question of whether the knowledge we expect from reading literature is closer to the objective and propositional knowledge of Moretti's scheme, or whether it has more in common with the subjective and existential experience of thought that Donne's poems pursue.

Methodologically, this means that my readings of Donne's poems are *formal* in the sense that I read the poems to uncover how their language may thwart or help their speakers' attention, how it may be seen as a means of preparing attentiveness.[96] To be sure, attention is at work in any text. A major character in the novel is major because it demands more attention than a minor character. The reason this statement is not entirely banal is that attention is a limited resource: every text's economy determines the distribution of the reader's attention.[97] What makes the poetics of the *Holy Sonnets* singular in the early modern period yet paradigmatic of the art of holy attention and formative for later poetry is that in these poems, the issue is not only *what* attention is drawn to—that is to say, the objects of attention from a rhyme to an idea—but how these objects affect attention itself, how they may or may not contribute to the clearing of attention of any distractions.

This focus on forms of attention renders the question of *whose* attention the poems cultivate methodologically irrelevant. The "I" who speaks in the *Holy Sonnets* is a locus of experimentation that Donne or any reader may inhabit by following its movements of attention. In other words, the speaker of the poems is a self insofar as it is a stretching-toward in the original sense of *ad-tendere*. In order to understand what the poems do, we as readers must follow the motions of this attending self. But whether we want to identify with this self is a separate question that is left for each individual reader to decide. The same applies to the poems' first reader, Donne himself. Given the facts of Donne's life and the impression one gets about his personality from his writings, it is likely that Donne more often than not personally identified with the speakers of his poems. But this must remain a matter for speculation, and in the following chapters my goal is to focus not on Donne's personal motives but on how the collaboration of formal and semantic elements in the poems guide, distract, and often surprise the speakers' attention.

While my readings are formal, however, they are not formalist; rather, I follow a literary-critical version of the approach that phenomenologists call *epochē*. I seek to let the poems raise their own questions about their historical and conceptual contexts, and instead of making assumptions about the ontological status of any entity the texts refer to (the ego, God, the resurrected body), I try to rely on the poems' language to recover how these entities are construed in and by the poems. This means that even when poems gesture toward a theological concept or a devotional practice whose understanding necessitates going beyond the poem itself, I always return to the poetry to see how it might confirm or problematize the conceptual or historical information that I gathered from external sources. As exercises of attention and as lyric addresses that do not posit propositionally anything about their references, the *Holy Sonnets* not only allow but invite this phenomenological approach.[98] Indeed, as representations of their speakers' thought experiments, the poems are *already* phenomenologies.

ARGUMENT

The book's argument works on four levels, two pertaining to literature, and two to religion. First, the book is an extended close reading of Donne's "Death be not proud," which I analyze in its entirety in the first and the last chapters. The sonnet functions as a kind of envelope, as if all the historical and conceptual issues about attention that occupy the intervening chapters were folded into the single poem that begins and ends the book. Second, I argue that reading Donne's poem in the context of Christian devotional practices reveals how early modern poetry and prayer share an investment in using language to cultivate attentiveness. In order to understand where this investment comes from and what kind of attentiveness it seeks, I ask why Christian prayer requires attention in the first place. This leads to the third aspect of the argument: I uncover a mostly latent tradition of holy or devotional attention within Christian devotion and theology, which I suggest originates in the ascetic ideal of attentiveness as a way of knowing God.[99] Finally, the book as a whole is an argument about how the previous three levels are connected: I suggest that Christian ideals and practices of holy attention are a significant influence not only for early modern devotional poetry but for the modern protocol of close reading. In other words, the book's form as an extended close reading of Donne's poem is also its final argument, an invitation for the reader to consider the devotional precedents of literary criticism and to compare the kinds of knowledge devotion and literary criticism are supposed to yield.

Accordingly, the first two chapters do not yet discuss attention itself but seek to find out what model of devotion Donne's "Death be not proud" follows. In chapter 1, I argue that the poem's purpose is to *prove* the Pauline doctrine of the resurrection. A survey of Aristotelian and Pauline notions of proofs shows, however, that in the case of the resurrection the proof that is sought isn't a matter of logical or theological demonstration. Much like the Corinthians in Paul's letters, Donne's speaker already accepts Christ's resurrection as a fact. The goal of the poem is to make the speaker certain of his own resurrection, to generate personal faith in the doctrine. In this sense, its purpose is to provide a radically subjective proof, a proof that is certain because it pertains only to the subject.

In chapter 2, I suggest that insofar as its goal is the transition from doctrine to faith, the devotion that "Death be not proud" implies is oriented toward *thanksgiving*. A consideration of classical and Christian accounts of thanksgiving shows why this is the case. While a doctrine is given prior to and independent of the subject's thinking, it becomes the gift of faith when it is available for the speaker as his own thought. I suggest that in Donne's poem, the doctrine is placed at the end of the poem because the poem itself is an invention of the given as a gift, a preparation for seeing the given doctrine as the speaker's own thought. This leads to yet another hypothesis: if devotion's telos is thanksgiving in the sense of acknowledging the divine gift, the preparation for thanksgiving is *prayer* in the specific sense of asking for the gift.

Chapter 3 turns from poetry to theater in order to see what we might learn about the conditions of prayer's success from the ways in which prayer is dramatized for early modern audiences. My central text in this chapter is the most famous theatrical representation of prayer in the seventeenth-century, Claudius's failed devotion in Shakespeare's *Hamlet*. Older accounts of this scene assumed that Claudius's attempt to pray for mercy failed because the king didn't sincerely repent his murder of Hamlet's father. More recent and particularly new historicist interpretations suggest that in fact Claudius's prayer might be seen as a proper attempt to pray by performing the words and gestures associated with prayer. In my reading, the point of the scene is to allow these two perceptions of the scene clash. Claudius's prayer is both an appropriate attempt to pray *and* a failure at praying. By emphasizing the tension between these two aspects of Claudius's prayer, Shakespeare poses the question of why a prayer might fail despite the subject's sincere intention to pray and despite his adequate attempt to perform prayer. The scene offers an answer: Claudius's prayer fails because the king remains unable to pay full attention to the words of his own prayer.

Does this mean that attention is requisite for prayer's success? Chapters 3 and 4 seek to answer this question by surveying late antique, medieval, and early modern discussions of attention in devotion. The first answer, emerging especially from scholastic theology, is that attention isn't necessary in vocal prayer, but it is essential for mental prayer. This raises the further question of how vocal prayer is related to mental prayer. In this context, the idea of pure prayer emerges as an ideal of an attentiveness stripped not only of vocalized words but of all words, images, even thoughts. Pure prayer and the ideal of a holy attention that it entails were marginalized in post-Augustinian theology. Yet in Western monasticism and its early modern revivals, holy attention was turned into a regulative ideal structurally influencing rather more mundane devotional acts, including vocal prayer. The conclusion of this survey is that vocal prayer may paradoxically be seen as preparation for the holy attention of pure prayer, despite the widespread early modern view that the entirely undistracted attentiveness of pure prayer is outside the reach of human devotion.

This understanding of vocal prayer's relation to holy attention leads to a reformulation of the book's inquiry: if Donne's poems are preparations for faith, thanksgiving, and prayer in the specific sense of exercises that use poetic language to overcome distraction, how could they defeat the very distraction that their poetic language provides? In order to answer this question, in chapter 5 I turn to Saint Augustine, whose works offer the most complete account of attention's role in vocalized devotion. Augustine's central thesis is that a perfectly pure, holy attention is impossible for created beings because of their flesh. By embedding it in space and time, the flesh is attention's permanent blind spot, constantly producing distraction as a by-product of every act of attention. For this reason, Augustine sees distraction and the resulting scattering of the self as the defining qualities of the human condition. Poets in the Petrarchist tradition follow him: works from the *Canzoniere* to the Sidney psalm translations present lyric poems as illustrations of the scattered, distracted self of Augustine's *Confessions*. Donne's devotional poems are a response to this tradition. In the *Holy Sonnets*, Donne uses the signature sonnet form of Petrarchism not to associate poetry with distraction but to overcome distraction by poetic means, by turning distraction against itself.

The last two chapters describe how the *Holy Sonnets* perform this task by turning to Donne's profound interest in both distraction and the body. In chapter 6, I argue that Donne uses the early modern trope of *sarcasmos* to figure the poem's own distracting language as flesh. While early modern rhetoricians defined *sarcasmos* as a mockery of the flesh (*sarx*), in Donne's hands *sarcasmos* becomes a peculiar *imitatio Christi*: the sonnets mock their own language as a distraction much like the crucifixion mocked the flesh and its mortality. While in this sense chapter 6 focuses on Donne's negative technique of mocking the poem itself, in the last chapter I return to "Death be not proud" to show how the poem might be seen as a victory over distraction. This chapter is called "The Spiritual Body" because in the letter to the Corinthians that Donne emulates in the poem, Paul's final "proof" for the resurrection of the body is the idea of a spiritual body, the purpose of which is to show that the resurrection of the body is possible. The argument of the final chapter is that "Death be not proud" is an attempt to prove the spiritual body by allowing the speaker to experience its figure in the poem itself. For Donne, the crucial difference between the body of the flesh and the spiritual body is in their capability to attend. While the body of the flesh can never overcome its distraction because it always attends *kata sarka*, according to the flesh, the spiritual body attends *kata pneuma*, according to the spirit and thus without any distraction. What is at stake in "Death be not proud," therefore, is whether the poem succeeds at making its speaker experience the idea of the spiritual body as his own thought. After the last chapter's answer to this question, the Coda concludes the argument

by considering the role of doubt in Donne's devotional poems, and by offering some remarks about the aftermath of holy attention in the early modern
philosophies of René Descartes and Nicolas Malebranche.

In the past century, Simone Weil argued that devotional models of attending should serve as models for modern thought in education, ethics, and
philosophy.[100] On the other hand, Walter Benjamin suggested that religious
ideals of attention were obsolete and the modern world required a different, distracted sensibility.[101] But neither they nor any more recent authors
have actually offered a full account of attention's role in Christian devotion;
instead, it is too often assumed that religion posits an unproblematic distinction between the virtue of attentiveness and the vice of distraction. As
I will try to show in this study, the extended attention that Donne's poems
pursue has in fact a lot in common with Benjamin's "reception in a state of
distraction."[102] How the poems search for this extended, holy attention, and
how in this search they make devotion and thinking converge in poetry, is
the subject of this book. I follow the ways in which the *Holy Sonnets* attempt
to pray by gathering attention; the ways they often fail to do so; the ways
they think about their distractions; and ultimately the ways in which they
sometimes succeed in accepting them. In sum, this is a book about poems
that pray, prayers that think, and thinking that attends, a book that tries to
extend Donne's poetic invitation to rethink each of these three categories.

1

THE *PISTIS* OF THE POEM

THE PROBLEM THAT I AM GOING to address in this chapter is that poems sometimes end by reiterating a religious doctrine. It may not be immediately obvious why this is a problem at all, and much of what follows is an articulation of the problem itself. For now, let me offer this preliminary formulation: a poem ending with a religious doctrine constitutes a problem because the domain of poetry is *invention,* while the domain of religion is the *given.*[1] The problem emerges from the intuition that these two domains may not be compatible with each other. The final rhyming couplet of "Death be not proud" offers the example I focus on in the chapter:

> One short sleepe past, we live eternally
> And Death shalbe no more, Death thou shallt dy.[2]

What makes the speaker of the poem certain that what he is saying is true? The last line's "Death thou shallt dy" proclaims a coming final victory over death. It announces a future event, an event that is expected to happen. To expect, *ex-spectare,* is to look beyond the spectacle of the present, beyond what merely *is.* Yet if it is to be uttered with any measure of confidence, expectation must also rely on something that is already present, either by virtue of having happened in the past and continuing into the present or by happening right now, in this instant. It needs *proof* in the rhetorical sense of the term: ground for believing in the truth of what it states. It needs a proof to rely on in order to be able to both look at the spectacle of the present and yet not be distracted by it but look also beyond it, into the future. But what is the proof for the proclamation that "Death thou shallt dy"? On what grounds would, and indeed on what grounds could, anyone believe in the coming death of Death?

This question might appear naïve because there are two answers readily available to it, answers that have been repeated time and again over the last two millennia of Western literature. The first is the answer formalist poetics offers, and it is dismissive: it suggests that any question concerning proofs in poetry is mistaken and based on a fundamentally flawed view of what poetry is and does. This answer, which can be traced back to Aristotle's *Poetics* but which has flourished particularly since the Renaissance rediscovery of Aristotle's text, claims that poetic works cannot be held responsible for their statements in the way everyday language can, because poems refer to invented worlds, and not to the world as we know it.[3] The realm of poetry is imagination, and the mode proper to poetic statements is the hypothetical. As one of Aristotle's early modern readers, Philip Sidney, asserts, the poet "nothing affirms, and therefore never lieth," because he invents his own world, instead of relying on what is already given.[4]

But any reader familiar with the history and literature of Christianity will offer a different answer. Not only does Donne's speaker rely on a proof in proclaiming the death of Death—the proclamation is a reiteration of this very proof. The poem's penultimate line, "One short sleepe past, we live eternally," is a paraphrase of the Christian doctrine of the resurrection of the dead. "Death shalbe no more" is a concise expression of the same doctrine; and when the speaker turns to a personalized Death to say, face to face, "Death, thou shallt dy," he can do so because he relies on the authority of Christian doctrine. In fact, if we take into account that Donne thought the doctrine of resurrection encapsulated all other doctrines of Christianity, it may be more accurate to say that at the end of the poem the speaker doesn't simply invoke a particular Christian doctrine, but rather Christianity as such.[5] What it means to invoke Christianity in this undefined but essential sense is a question I will return to later in this chapter; what matters for now is that a Christian reading of the poem would recognize the grounds for the poem's last taunting of Death in the doctrine of the resurrection as a doctrine central to Christianity.

No proof on the one hand, and Christianity itself as a proof on the other: on purely a priori grounds these two approaches seem mutually exclusive. The Aristotelian tradition of poetics suggests that the only proof on which a poetic speaker can rely is a proof located within the poem's invented world; ultimately, the poem is the only "proof" of itself. And if the poem is a self-referential invention that requires no proof other than the poem itself, the last proclamation of the end of death appears to be a mere fiction. A Christian perspective suggests, in contrast, that the poem relies on the evidence of Christianity. Poetic invention may contribute to the form of the speaker's final proclamation; it may change the words, shape their prosody, form them into figures, but the substance of "Death thou shallt dy" remains the doctrine that is already given in Christianity independent of any poetic invention on Donne's part. A Christian reading departs radically from the Aristotelian approach and reclaims truth value for the poem: it suggests that the speaker's final utterance, far from being a mere fiction, is a truth supported by the testimony of Christianity. We might be inclined to prioritize either of these two approaches, according to our own literary or religious preferences. But doing so would mean ignoring the very poem we want to decipher: it is Donne's "Death be not proud" that demands to be read as *both* poetic and religious. It is the poem that invites us to see it as an invention of the given.[6]

In the first section of this chapter, I briefly discuss how literary history has dealt with the problem of devotional poetry and explain why I am interested in a different, conceptual approach. In the second section, I compare two antique conceptions of proofs, Aristotle's in the *Rhetoric* and Paul's in the letter to the Corinthians (which is Donne's main source in "Death be not proud"). The third section concludes the chapter's argument by returning to "Death be not proud" and by showing how the poem may be seen as an attempt to invent the doctrine not as proof but as faith.

THE ONE VERSUS THE MANY: THE QUESTION OF HISTORICISM

The promise of reading Donne's poem in the double bind of the religious given and poetic invention is that it allows us to reopen the conceptual question of devotional poetry. In the first half of the twentieth century the standard solution for the problems I stressed above would have been that Donne's poem is poetic fiction and therefore shouldn't be held responsible for its content the way propositional statements are. In contrast, the past half-century has been dominated by historicist approaches that suggest that we read early modern devotional poems from the perspective of their own authors and readers and therefore from the perspective of the ostensible beliefs that they may have had. Conceptual problems such as the apparent incompatibility between invention and givenness tend to disappear when they are placed in a historical perspective; after all, the poem exists, so speaking of its conceptual impossibility seems moot. So why return to questions that seem to belong to a previous era?

Since Herbert Grierson in 1921 defined the field's central explanandum by insisting that "in no poetry more than the religious did the English genius in the seventeenth century declare its strong individuality," the most influential attempt to offer a historical account for the flourishing of religious lyric in early seventeenth-century England has been Barbara Lewalski's *Protestant Poetics*.[7] In the Introduction I showed how Lewalski's book ignited a debate about early modern devotional poets' confessional identity. The relevance of Lewalski's book for my purposes here is that in characterizing seventeenth-century English devotional poetry as "biblical poetry," Lewalski's argument offered a clear and unanimous answer to the questions I posed above about the role of religion and invention in the devotional poem. In Lewalski's view, the majority of seventeenth-century religious lyrics in England fall into the specific category "Protestant poetics," meaning that these poems do not seek to conform to the Aristotelian principle of invention as the essence of *poesis* but deliberately release their claims to poetic autonomy and submit themselves to the authority of the Christian Bible and its Protestant interpretations. Lewalski quotes Herbert's "Jordan" to this effect: "Who sayes that fictions onely and false hair / Become a verse? Is there in truth no beauty?" Truth is of course biblical truth here; Lewalski reads "Jordan" as a manifesto of what she calls biblical poetics. "The poetics of much seventeenth-century religious lyrics," she asserts, "derives primarily from Protestant assumptions about the poetry of the Bible."[8]

The enormous achievement of Lewalski's account is that it casts light on the aspirations of Protestant devotional poetry. The downside of her argument is that it overshadows the difficulties that these aspirations face. Herbert may ask rhetorically "Who says that fictions only and false hair / Become a verse," but the answer is not only that Aristotle does, but that Herbert's intimation is hardly satisfying because the original question isn't whether truth and beauty are incompatible, but whether religious doctrine and poetic fiction are. While early modern statements about religious poetry often support Lewalski's account of biblical poetry, instead of taking these statements at their face value we need to ask whether they talk about the aspirations of Protestant poets or about actual poetic practice. A look at Philip Sidney's *Defence of Poesy* will be helpful here. Although Sidney develops a category of "religious poetry" that would seem to support Lewalski's notion of Protestant poetics, when we trace the ways he manipulates this concept to make it fit to the local needs of his argument, we recognize how acutely aware Sidney remains of the concept's inherent logical difficulties.

The first time Sidney makes a reference to Christian religious poetry in *Defence of Poesy* is in the introductory narration. Rather than making any particular argument, Sidney here simply lists instances of poetry whose authority cannot be called into question, and which therefore provide him with a springboard to get to the more difficult problems that arise from the definition of poetry, which he offers only *after* these introductory comments. This is what Sidney has to say about Christian poetry in this preliminary context:

> And may not I presume a little farther, to show the reasonableness of this word *Vates*, and say that the holy David's Psalms are a divine poem? If I do, I shall not do it without the testimony of great learned men, both ancient and modern. But even the name of Psalms will speak for me, which, being interpreted, is nothing but Songs; then, that it is fully written in meter, as all learned Hebricians agree, although the rules be not yet fully found; lastly and principally, his handling his prophecy, which is merely poetical. For what else is the awakening of his musical instruments, the often and free changing of persons, his notable *prosopopeias*, when he maketh you, as it were, to see God coming in his majesty, his telling of the beasts' joyfulness and hills' leaping, but a heavenly poesy, wherein almost he showeth himself a passionate lover of that unspeakable and everlasting beauty to be seen by the eyes of the mind, only cleared by faith?[9]

Note the degree of specificity with which Sidney operates in this passage: "poetical" refers not to a text's ontological status but to its use of particular poetic devices, from prosody to personae and *prosopopeias*. Since biblical texts, first and foremost the Psalms, seem to use such devices, they qualify, for now at least, as poetry, and thus help Sidney make a preliminary defense of poetry on the basis of the Bible's authority. The Psalms are "divine poems" and thus offer a first proof in poetry's defense.[10]

But shortly after this passage, Sidney introduces his ontological definition of poetry: poetry is invention ("the poet . . . lifted up with the vigor of his own invention, doth grow in effect another Nature"), and more specifically it is mimesis, that is, it is invention that imitates ("Poesy, therefore, is an art of imitation, for so Aristotle termeth it in the word μίμησις; that is to say, a representing, counterfeiting, or figuring forth").[11] Once his subject is defined, Sidney returns to the Psalms and to the matter of divine poetry one more time: "The chief [poems], both in antiquity and excellency, were they that did imitate the unconceivable excellencies of God. Such were David in his Psalms; Solomon in his Songs of Songs, in his Ecclesiastes, and Proverbs; Moses and Deborah in their Hymns; and the writer of Job; which, beside other, the learned Emanuel Tremellius and F[ranciscus] Junius do entitle the poetical part of the Scripture. Against these none will speak that hath the Holy Ghost in due holy reverence."[12] The last sentence is telling. If it is indeed the case that Sidney's argument is a response to Puritan accusations that there is no difference between poetic invention and mere lies, it makes sense that Sidney repeatedly uses the Psalms and other biblical texts to show that poetry has biblical authority. It also makes sense that he should not delve into the details of just how these biblical poems might be seen as inventive. Rather, he goes on to define two further types of mimetic poetry: the generic category of all poetry that imitates facts of history or knowledge (that is, historical and philosophical poetry) and the poetry that departs from the historical-philosophical poet in taking "the free course" of its "own invention."[13] Sidney's preference for this third kind of poetry is evident throughout: those who write this third type of poetry are the "right poets," so much so that he wryly notes about the philosophical and historical poets, "whether they properly be poets or no let grammarians dispute."[14] What distinguishes the third kind of poetry from both religious and historical-philosophical poems is that in its essence it is not concerned with the given but invents its own subject. It imitates "nothing of what is, hath been, or shall be"; instead, it may only "range . . . into the divine consideration of what may be, and should be."[15] Sidney leaves the relationship between the divine poetry of the scriptures and this third, "right" kind of poetry unspecified, though if we follow the line of his argumentation, we must conclude that the Psalms are poetry only in the sense historical or philosophical poems are "poems": their status is a debate for the grammarians.

It seems fair to conclude that within this essay Sidney's interest is in an Aristotelian, *secular* concept of poetry as pure invention.[16] His purpose is to defend this secular poetry from religious-cultural criticism by establishing it as an ethically committed mode.[17] Within this argument, the category of "divine poetry" is a sleight of hand, a trick that is useful insofar as it serves Sidney's purpose of defending "poetry" and that proves useless and problematic as soon as he defines poetry as invention.[18] For the rest of the *Defence of Poesy,* divine poetry becomes something of a specter of the "right" kind of poetry. Even though "poems" like David's Psalms use certain poetic devices like *prosopopeia* or meter, they can no longer be seen as poetry in the full sense of the term. Since they do not freely invent their subjects but instead imitate "divine excellencies," they are poetry only in a limited sense of the term, however sublime they might be as another kind of discourse. Sidney's *Defence of Poesy* thus bears witness to how "religious poetry," far from a clear explanatory category, is in fact merely another name for what remains a problem, the problem of how poetic invention and the religious given could possibly coexist. And while it is understandable why Sidney would rely on this argument in defending poetry, it remains surprising that a significant trend in modern literary criticism after Lewalski's *Protestant Poetics* would essentially accept Sidney's or Herbert's accounts as objective descriptions of religious poetry's stakes and challenges in the period.

Kimberly Coles has argued against Lewalski's thesis on the grounds that it prevents us from seeing how difficult it was for Protestant poets to begin writing *authorial* religious poetry, that is, poetry that reclaims poetic invention and acknowledges poetic authority.[19] When placed in the longer context of post-Reformation English literary history, early seventeenth-century devotional poetry appears as a novelty because it follows in the footsteps of sixteenth-century Protestant poets from Wyatt to Sidney who tended to shy away from writing authorial religious lyrics and concentrated their efforts on translating and paraphrasing biblical texts instead.[20] It took English Protestant poets almost a century to begin to write religious verse that went beyond mere translation of divine revelation—and even then, as the poetry of Herbert in particular demonstrates, the problem of how to negotiate the competing claims of divine and human authorship remains central to the actual poems. In other words, the fundamental problem with Lewalski's account is that it considers Protestantism as the primary enabler of seventeenth-century religious lyric, when the evidence suggests that on the contrary, Protestantism was one of the reasons it was so challenging for these poets to write religious verse.

While Coles I think offers a very persuasive historical account of how Protestant poetry became possible, my rather more modest interest here is in how individual poems negotiate the apparent logical incompatibility between religious givenness and poetic invention. Every text that brings together poetry and religion faces this challenge of incompatibility between the two modes, and every single poem must offer its own answer to the challenge. Some poems may do this by abandoning poetry as invention; they are poetic expressions of religion, which means they use poetry in a limited sense as a set of formal techniques to convey a specific content (in chapter 4 we will see how Anne Lock's sonnet sequence exemplifies Lewalski's Protestant poetics). Some poems may follow the opposite path and absorb the religious into their own invented world (arguably some of Donne's love poems do exactly this when they appropriate religious ideas for their own poetic and rhetorical purposes—think of the moment of resurrection turning into an opportunity for one final tryst in "The Relique"). But the really fascinating question is whether poems could achieve what seems impossible and become religious poems in the full sense of the term, that is, as inventions of the given. This is not a question of genres and movements but of individual poems, a question of whether *this* particular poem has succeeded in achieving the goal its authors set out to do in it. This is why I want to insist on the conflict between poetic invention and the religious given: my concern is how "Death be not proud" articulates and resolves this conflict, and what we might learn from the ways in which it does so.[21]

PROOFS IN ARISTOTLE AND PAUL

The view that poetry is a mode of invention begins with an explicit exclusion of the given from its domain. Aristotle's text inaugurates the tradition with the famous assertion that "it is not the poet's function to relate actual events, but the kinds of things that might occur and are possible in terms of probability or necessity."[22] Since the first Renaissance Italian treatises on the *Poetics,* the second part of this definition has been widely discussed: the domain of poetry is the possible, the probable, and the necessary.[23] The first part of Aristotle's definition deserves equal or even more attention, however, because it is here that the beginning of Western poetics is marked by exclusion. The poet's work (*ergon*), Aristotle declares, is *not* to say (*legein*) what is already given, what has already come about (Aristotle uses the plural, *ta genomena*) before the poem itself.

What Aristotle expels here from the realm of poetry, the *genomena,* the things and events that have already come about, cannot be properly rendered by words like "actuality" or the "past." Just a few lines later Aristotle in fact admits that poems can and do on occasion integrate the given (he specifically refers to tragedy's use of the *genomenon onomaton,* the already existing, historical or mythical name).[24] Rather, what is excluded, what the poet is *not* supposed to say is the given in its givenness, as opposed to the given in its potentiality.[25] Aristotle explains that since "the possible seems credible," the poet may include events that have actually taken place because "it is evident that actual events [*ta genomena*] are possible—they could not have otherwise occurred" (60).[26] What the poet cannot do, however, is to make use, in the poetic work, of the given as proof, as something that is relevant for the poem's internal world insofar as it is being given to it from the outside. The poet's work in the case of the given consists in stripping the given from its givenness so that it can become part of the purely possible world of the poetic saying.[27]

When approached from this Aristotelian perspective, the proclamation at the end of "Death be not proud" should belong to the fictional world of the poem and require no proof other than the poem itself. Indeed, when we return to Donne's poem, we notice that the poem ends with a proclamation of a future event, that is, an event that by definition cannot be given, cannot be already in existence. It would seem, then, that the announcement that "Death shalbe no more" should belong to the poetic realm of the possible already by virtue of being in the future tense.[28]

But it is here that Christianity introduces a different perspective. When read against the background of Christian history and doctrine, Donne's poem does appear to recall the future as already given. Donne's speaker does not simply pronounce a future event; he does so by reiterating the given words of the Bible. The poem recollects and reiterates St. Paul's mockery of Death as a defeated enemy: "Death is swallowed up in victory. O death, where is thy victory? O death, where is thy sting?"[29] Although written in the future tense, the last couplet of the poem is not spoken in the voice of the *vates*-poet; no one here claims to have received any sort of immediate divine revelation. The poem does not prophesy the future, nor does it simply express an opinion about it; instead, it proclaims a future event by remembering the past, by reiterating the given.

What is invention's role in this reiteration of the given? Perhaps rhetoric offers an answer. Until this point I have used "invention" to refer to the Aristotelian notion of poetry as the making of fictions. But in the more influential tradition of classical rhetoric, a tradition that, unlike Aristotle's *Poetics*, was continuous from antiquity to the Middle Ages and the Renaissance, invention appears as a broader and far more fluid category. In Aristotle's *Rhetoric*, *heuresis* refers to the first part of rhetoric defined as the discussion of all the possible means of "coming upon" the proofs (*pisteis*) that the orator may employ in his argument.[30] In accordance with the pragmatic approach that is at the heart of the rhetorical tradition, *heuresis* may include the finding of proofs that already exist as given (a witness, or a piece of physical evidence), as well as the creation of new proofs (the logos, the very argument that the orator crafts belongs to the category of the created, artificial proofs). When the authors of the first Roman rhetorical treatises translate *heuresis* as *inventio,* they preserve this ambiguity of the category: up until the seventeenth century, *inventio* may refer to both the discovery of a given proof and the creation of a new one.[31] The story of how authors exploited this duality of the rhetorical category of invention, and how the meaning of the term changed in Christian contexts, has been widely discussed in the scholarship.[32] The relevance of this story for the case of religious poetry is that it might answer our question: perhaps "religious poems" ought to be understood not on the grounds of Aristotelian poetic invention, but as rhetorical constructs in which invention might mean the discovery of already existing proofs. What would it mean to think about Donne's poem as a deliberate attempt to find proofs to support the speaker's mockery of death?

The text that Donne's speaker ultimately "finds" at the end of "Death be not proud," St. Paul's first letter to the Corinthians, will show that a rhetorical approach is illuminating but ultimately insufficient. The mockery of death that Donne's speaker echoes at the end of the poem comes at the end of Paul's argument as well. In fact, the original of Donne's mockery is itself a repetition: in referring to Isaiah 25:8 and Hosea 13:14, Paul introduces his final mockery of death by characterizing it as the fulfillment of an ancient prophecy:[33] "Then shall be brought to pass the saying that is written, Death is swallowed up in victory. O death, where *is* thy sting? O grave, where *is* thy victory?" (1 Cor., 15:54–56). The last line of Donne's poem, "And Death shalbe no more, Death thou shallt dy," is not just a close variation on Paul's proclamation. Donne also follows Paul's apostrophe, the turn from talking about death in the third person to a direct address of a personified death (one recalls how impressed Sidney was with the prosopopeias of the Bible). The difference between Donne's poem and Paul's letter, of course, is that Paul's letter is explicitly framed as an argument. While in the case of Donne's poem the question of proof may have sounded unusual, the same question could not be more appropriate in the context of 1 Corinthians. What is the proof that the Pauline speaker relies on in announcing the coming victory over death? How does this speaker know, how could he know that death will die?[34]

At the beginning of 1 Corinthians 15, it seems Paul wants to invoke the testimony of material witnesses: the resurrected Christ was seen, he reminds the Corinthians, by Cephas, by James, and by many other witnesses, including Paul himself. The testimony of these witnesses, some dead but some alive and one speaking these very lines, offers a proof that Christ was indeed resurrected. But this is misleading. The testimony of these witnesses may prove that Christ was resurrected, but Paul's goal in the chapter is not to prove Christ's resurrection. From the letter it soon becomes clear that the Corinthians do not need to be convinced of this; they share Paul's conviction that Christ was resurrected, and Paul's invocation of the witnesses is just a reminder, an admonishment that they should keep Christ's resurrection in mind. The problem that Paul faces is rather more difficult. The Corinthians seem to accept the fact of Christ's resurrection, but they do not incorporate this knowledge into their lives. According to Paul they do not do so because while they believe in Christ's resurrection, they deny the general resurrection of the dead.

This leads to a second possibility: it now seems that Paul's goal is to remind the Corinthians of Christ's resurrection because he thinks that Christ's resurrection is proof of the general resurrection of the dead. How would this notion of Christ's resurrection as a proof fit in with the principles of classical rhetoric? From an Aristotelian point of view, Christ's resurrection seems to fall in the category that Aristotle calls *atechnoi,* nontechnological or inartificial proofs.[35] The *pisteis atechnoi,* inartificial proofs, are proofs that the orator can find as given, and in the *Rhetoric* Aristotle contrasts them with the technological or artificial proofs (the *pisteis entechnoi*), which are the orator's own work to produce.[36] The three main categories of artificial proofs, the orator's manifest character (*ēthos*), the emotional response that he induces in the audience (*pathos*), and the oration's logical or pseudo-logical arguments (*logos*), include proofs that the orator is expected to produce in and through the oration. In contrast, Aristotle identifies torture, material witnesses, and laws as inartificial proofs that exist before the oration and can thus simply be pointed out by the orator.[37] The resurrection of Christ seems to be an inartificial proof, or rather, it seems to be *the* given of Paul's proclamation, the absolute and entirely external foundation of everything Paul has to say in this letter, his eschatological message about the Parousia and the resurrection of the dead.

But here a difficulty emerges in reading Paul through ancient rhetoric: the use of an inartificial proof for announcing a future event. This does not seem to be compatible with the way in which Aristotle thinks about inartificial proofs, or, for that matter, with the Aristotelian notion of proof in general. In the *Rhetoric* inartificial proofs belong to only one of the three branches of rhetoric: while deliberative and epideictic rhetoric relies only on artificial proofs, forensic rhetoric is set apart from them by its exclusive right to rely *both* on artificial and inartificial proofs. The reason for this is not just in the particularities of the Greek juridical system.[38] Aristotle distinguishes the three branches of rhetoric in terms of their temporal relevance, and in this distinction it is forensic rhetoric that emerges as responsible for that which has already happened, the *genomenon*. Forensic rhetoric uses given, inartificial proofs, proofs that are rooted in the past, because its subject is the given past.

The stake of Paul's argument is not to prove the fact that Christ was resurrected. Since the Corinthians already accept this as a fact, Paul's concern is that they do not understand how Christ's resurrection is not a mere fact but a proof of the general resurrection. Therefore Paul's task is *not* to prove a fact—that is, the fact of Christ's resurrection—but to present the fact *as proof*: the notion that Christ's resurrection was not simply an individual case, but a sign, a proof of God's will to fulfill the ancient promise of defeating death. Nor can we make this way of thinking about proof compatible with Aristotelian rhetoric by suggesting that Paul uses an inartificial proof to make an artificial *logos*—the argument of the letter itself. The incompatibility between classical rhetoric and Paul's use of proofs concerns the very foundations of rhetoric.[39] In Paul's letters, an inartificial, given proof is to prove a future event, the resurrection of the dead.

There is no such possibility in the *Rhetoric*. Aristotle designates deliberative rhetoric to concern itself with the future, and deliberative rhetoric can rely only on artificial proofs, proofs that the orator produces through the rhetorical performance. The reason deliberative rhetoric can rely only on such artificial proofs is that the future that this particular branch of rhetoric is concerned with is itself "artificial," that is, brought about by those human actions that deliberative rhetoric is supposed to urge or admonish. To use an inartificial, given proof to foretell the future is therefore entirely outside the scope of what Aristotle considers to be the core of rhetoric, invention.[40]

Christ's resurrection in Paul's letter defies this logic. It is a given proof, belonging to an already existing reality (both past and present), and at the same time it is the proof of a future reality. Behind it, there is a notion of time entirely different from the threefold temporality that serves as the basis of Aristotle's theory of invention. Christ's resurrection is not a proof of human actions or intentions, but of the divine will (that is, of divine grace) that transcends and indeed creates the threefold temporality of past, present, and future, in which human actions takes place. The resurrection as a given proof can in Paul's letter become the ground of a given future because from the perspective of eternity the future is given exactly the same way the past is. What biblical scholars call the Christ event is a proof of God's grace, of the mercy manifest in his willingness to sacrifice his son for the sins of mankind, which makes Christ's resurrection the proof of the future resurrection of the dead. In short, it is the proof of God's will to save humankind from his own wrath; and every particular detail and consequence of the process of salvation follow from this one proof. Insofar as the subject of Paul's proclamation (*kērygma*) is Christ, his resurrection is proof of every particular detail and consequence of Paul's good message (*euangelion*), including the final victory, the victory over death by the resurrection of the dead.

All this sheds light on what at first appears as a spectacularly circular argument at the heart of Paul's message:

> But if there be no resurrection of the dead, then is Christ not risen: And if Christ be not risen, then *is* our preaching vain, and your faith [*pistis*] *is* also vain. . . . But now is Christ risen from the dead, *and* become the firstfruits of them that slept. (1 Cor. 15:13–14, 20)

If Christ's resurrection were a logical proof of the general resurrection, this would be a circular argument. But in fact there is no circularity here; the reason the argument appears circular is that it destabilizes the very status of proofs.[41] The argument here is not "A (Christ is risen) therefore B (general resurrection is going to happen)." Instead it is: if you do not believe the resurrection of the dead, then you don't *really* believe Christ's resurrection either, then your faith in Christ's resurrection is in vain—it is uncertain, purposeless, empty, hasty.[42] Ergo: You *have* to believe that Christ is resurrected *and* that this means he's firstfruits, a proof of the resurrection of the dead.[43]

This explains a curious fact that to my knowledge New Testament scholarship has never really clarified, despite the increasing consensus concerning Paul's reliance on the rhetorical foundations of the first-century Hellenistic culture, namely the question of why Paul doesn't use the word "pistis" in the sense of proof but only in the sense of faith (with one, rather fascinating, exception).[44] The term that Greek rhetoric uses to refer to "proof" is *pistis,* the very same word that Paul in the letter to the Corinthians that ends with the mockery of death uses for "faith."[45] This is no coincidence; in Greek rhetoric, proof (*pistis*) is what the orator uses to induce a particular belief (*pistis*) in his audience: the task of *heuresis* is to find the means (the proofs, or *pisteis*) by which the orator can convince the audience to have belief (*pistis*) in his assertion.[46] In Paul's passage, the two rhetorical senses of *pistis,* proof and faith, are collapsed into each other: the proof of the resurrection of the dead is not Christ's resurrection as a given fact, but the belief that the Christ event as such is a divine gift to mankind, that it is an act of grace. In other words, the proof for the final victory over death is faith in the *euangelion* that suggests that Christ's resurrection is proof of God's will to resurrect the dead.[47]

In 1 Corinthians 15, the act of faith replaces the rhetoric of proofs by reflecting a transition from the given to grace: since Christ's resurrection is a proof of the resurrection only if it's not a mere given but an act of grace, the question of *inventio* in Paul's argument is not one of finding available proofs, but of inventing one's own faith as proof. The Pauline proclamation is "foolishness" for the Greeks because faith does not follow from the proof, but on the contrary, constitutes the proof: it is only through faith that the crucifixion is no longer seen as a mere given but as a proof of grace, only through faith that the death of the Messiah becomes the life of Christians. This unity of proof and faith is behind the argument of 1 Corinthians 15. In the *euangelion,* everything follows from the crucifixion, not only as from a proof, on the basis of probability, and thus inductively, but also as from faith, deductively, and therefore with apodictic necessity.

With this, we are in the position to assess Paul's mockery of death as the last, concluding gesture at the end of the "argument" of 1 Corinthians 15. This argument appears circular if we analyze it in logical terms: Paul argues that the resurrection of the dead must be true, because otherwise the *euangelion,* that is, the proclamation that Christ is God's grace, would not be true. And if that is the case, Paul says, then "is our preaching vain, and your faith is also vain" (1 Cor. 15:14). The foundation of the resurrection of the dead is not Christ as given, but Christ as grace, and therefore to not believe in the resurrection of the dead means that one does not believe in Christ either. To believe in the resurrection of the dead, however means that one has an active, "working" faith. To mock death the way Paul does at the end of the letter, to be able to utter the words "O death, where is thy victory? O death, where is thy sting?" is in turn to demonstrate one's faith in practice: it is only from the position of faith that one can challenge death. The final personification and mockery of death at the end of 1 Corinthians

15 is Paul's own, personal demonstration of his faith, an exemplary *devotional* act that he sets forth in order to show the Corinthians in action that which he has argued for throughout the letter in theory, the faith that relies on itself as its own proof. Far from being a mere figurative play with words, the mockery of death signals the completion of one's faith because it means that one has become able to stand in faith-as-proof, which Paul expresses by the phrase "in Christ." The question of *inventio* in Paul's argument is not one of finding available proofs. It is of seeking and finding one's own faith in the sense of a capacity of seeing the given as gift. It is, therefore, a question of inventing the given as grace.

POETIC PROOF IN "DEATH BE NOT PROUD"

In the more than fifteen centuries that separated Paul's message to the Corinthians from Donne's *Holy Sonnets,* Christian theologians produced innumerable logical and theological arguments and proofs to add to Paul's original announcement, and Paul's faith-as-proof has become one of the central doctrines of Christianity, an article of faith. And yet one must not think of this history as one beginning with an original, faith-as-inartificial-proof, which then leads to a series of artificial proofs, resulting in the set of doctrines that we call Christian theology. The reason the distinction between artificial and inartificial proofs in Aristotle's rhetoric is not absolute is that the question of whether a proof is *entechnos* or *atechnos* cannot be decided on the basis of whether the proof in question is constructed.[48] Rather, the categorization of the proof is determined by its relation to the artifact that the orator produces. The inartificial proofs, the *pisteis atechnoi,* are inartificial or "nontechnological" only because they are given before the oration itself, because they precede the technology of the oration, as it were, because their production does not belong to the *technē* of rhetoric. If we were to imagine a Pauline rhetoric, we might think of Paul's letters as attempts to turn their given, the *euangelion* of Christ, into proofs of grace through the work of *pistis* as faith.

But from the perspective of Donne's poem, it is the Pauline letter itself, and specifically the Pauline mockery of death, that is given. Therefore the question becomes: what does Donne's poem do with *this* given?[49] Until now, I have avoided quoting the poem in full so that we could focus on its doctrinal end. It is now time to listen to the poetic beginning:

> Death be not proud, thou some have called thee
>> Mighty and dreadfull, for thou art not so.[50]

The voice, both petulant and affected, is loudly and almost gleefully poetic
here, as if its goal were not just to launch an attack on death but to announce
that the attack belongs to the realm of poetry. The poem is of course a sonnet, the paradigmatic form of Western lyricism since Petrarch's *Canzoniere.*
In just four monosyllables ("Death be not proud"), the beginning displays
some of the essential features of the Western poetic tradition. The first line
constitutes a poetic address in the form of an apostrophe, a turning-away
from the reader toward an absent addressee, a figure that Jonathan Culler
once described as the embarrassingly ubiquitous figure of the lyric itself. In
naming this addressee, the poem uses the classical figure of *prosopopeia,*
the figure of putting face on an abstraction or absence.[51] Indeed, the words
"Death be not proud" are a paradigmatic *prosopopeia* in that they summon
not the dead but Death itself, thus bringing together the abstract and the
absent in a single call. We could paraphrase these two lines as a challenge
posed to death by the hubris of poetry.

Facing such an early and conspicuous display, we might rightly expect
the poem to go on in this poetic manner; we might rightly expect it to unfold its invention, its "work," in the Aristotelian sense of the word. Indeed, it
does continue in the same poetic manner for ten lines, teasing death:

> For those whom thou thinkst thou dost overthrow
> Dy not poore death, nor yet canst thou kill mee.
> From rest and sleepe which but thy pictures bee
>> Much pleasure; then from thee much more must flow,
>> And soonest our best men with thee do go,
> Rest of ther bones, and Soules deliveree.
> Thou art Slave to Fate, Chance, kings, and desperat men,
>> And dost with poyson, warr, and sicknesse dwell;
>> And Poppy or Charmes can make us sleepe as well,
> And easier then thy stroke, why swellst thou then?[52]

But as we reach the end of the poem, searching to see its work, its invention,
we find that it is here, in the final couplet, that the poem sheds this poetic
tone and most directly closes in on its given, the Pauline mockery of death.
We might note that the poem's initial provocation of death used the imperative mood, and indeed, what could be more appropriate for such a display of

poeticity than the grammar of the imperative, the very index of the potential power of words to create, *poiein*? But this imperative recedes, and in the final line, we are faced with the two plain, declarative phrases:

And Death shalbe no more, Death thou shallt dy.[53]

If the poem followed the Aristotelian model of poetic *ergon*, it would move from the facticity of the given to the fictionality of the invented. But Donne's poem does the opposite: it goes from the fictional to the given. In other words, if the end of the poem is the given Pauline doctrine, it seems that the poem's movement is directed toward this preexisting given from its first line onward, doing nothing to the doctrine except for reiterating it at the end. Admittedly, the Christian doctrine of the final victory over death is expressed in a poetic form, that is, at the end of a sonnet, using metrical structure, poetic address, and so forth. But if this is all, we have to conclude that poetry here is merely an ornate cornice, an aesthetic framework around the religious content that is lifted into this framework from the outside. And then we have to ask: if this framework is just an addition to the already existing content, if the poem's circle merely repeats something that is already given before the poem's coming to being, doesn't poetry run the risk of doing nothing? Doesn't it risk being nothing but a pretty way of saying what religion already knows (and what those who don't believe it will not accept anyway)?

There is another possibility, one that allows us to see the poem's ending with the given as the point of the poem. In Paul's letter, the transition from searching for proofs for the resurrection of the dead toward faith in Christ was based on the recognition that the Christ event was not a given (and thus a potential proof) but a gift (that is, an act of grace, and thus requiring faith). What if we see Donne's poem as an attempt to follow this model? If this were the case, the poem's ending with the Pauline mockery of death wouldn't be a simple reiteration of an already existing proof of authority but the speaker's demonstration of his faith in the resurrection of the dead. We would have to see Donne's poem not so much as an attempt to invent the given but as an attempt to reinvent the given as a gift.

This difference between the given and the gift is crucial for understanding the poem as a proof. As I explained in the Introduction, if the given is what already exists, temporally preceding the subject and existentially independent of it, a gift by contrast is what is being given to the subject *in* the present and *as* a present, addressed to this particular subject and calling for its action. When the given is seen as a gift, it becomes a practical, experiential, radically subjective proof: no longer a mere datum, the gift belongs to its recipient. What this means for Donne's poem is that the poem might be seen as an attempt to prove the Pauline doctrine for the speaker of the poem by preparing him to see it not just as a given but as a gift, not just as an abstract doctrine but as his own thought, a thought given specifically to him in the course of speaking the poem's words. And this offers an explanation for the fact that the doctrine comes at the end of the poem: it does so because it can appear only after the poem's labor of preparing for seeing the given as a gift has already been completed. In the next chapter, I show that Donne articulated exactly this conception of devotion and devotional poetry when he envisioned the goal of devotion in the act of *thanksgiving*.

THE THANKSGIVING MACHINE

"Étant donné."

Jean-Luc Marion

IN THE PREVIOUS CHAPTER, I ARGUED that "Death be not proud" was an attempt to prove the Pauline doctrine of the resurrection of the dead by translating it from a mere given into a gift. In this sense, the poem may be seen as a practical proof: rather than proving the doctrine by providing universal logical or external empirical evidence for its validity, it seeks to give the doctrine to the speaker of the poem as his own thought, as a gift that he can experience as his own. The consequence of this argument is that the doctrine is placed at the end of Donne's poem for the sole reason that the end of the poem is where the acknowledgment of the gift must have become possible. In other words, the end of the poem is the locus of *thanksgiving*, and the poem itself is preparation for this act of thanksgiving. In this chapter, I suggest that in one of his sermons Donne articulates exactly this theory of devotional poetry as thanksgiving. The first section shows that Donne's concern in the sermon is with the process of *becoming* thankful. The second section places Donne's sermon in the larger context of Christian thanksgiving. The third section explains how Donne's discussion of thanksgiving in the sermon suggests a theory of devotional poetry.

The sermon I focus on in this chapter belongs to Donne's middle period at St. Paul's, and it has acquired some fame among Donne scholars on account of a passage about poetry and specifically about the end of the poem. Donne suggests that the end is the poem's most important part: "The force of the whole piece, is for the most part left to the shutting up." What has been overlooked in the scholarship is that Donne makes this comment about poetic ending in the context of a larger argument about thanksgiving. The end of the devotional poem and the act of giving thanks are, as we will see, intimately connected. Indeed, Donne makes his point about poetry in response to a question that echoes our questions about the end of "Death be not proud." Thinking about Psalm 6, Donne wonders why David defers the act of thanksgiving to the very end of the psalm's verses. What is at stake in Donne's sermon, then, isn't just thanksgiving. By discussing thanksgiving and poetry side by side, Donne develops a robust poetics of devotion that also elucidates his poetic practice.

BECOMING THANKFUL

Let's listen to Donne's words from the proemium of the sermon, as he detects the theme of thanksgiving in his chosen text, the last three verses of the sixth psalm:

> A man perchance may be safe in a Retrait, but the honour, the victory, the triumph lies in enforcing the enemy to fly. *To that is David come here, to such a thankfull sense of a victory;* in which we shall first consider Davids thankfulnesse, that is, his manner of declaring Gods mercy, and his security in that mercy. (Emphasis mine)[1]

Donne's sermon is *not* what has come to be known as a thanksgiving sermon. In the sixteenth and seventeenth centuries, thanksgiving sermons were an established subgenre. Protestant preachers relied on them to respond to particular events, usually political in nature, such as the defeat of the Spanish Armada or the succession of a new sovereign.[2] In such thanksgiving sermons, the event in question served as evidence of God's generosity in general, a reminder of divine grace. By contrast, Donne's sermon neither focuses upon any particular external occurrence nor performs an act of giving thanks. It is rather a sermon *about* thanksgiving, about the act of thanksgiving that Donne finds in the sixth psalm. Yet Donne's sermon is about a text that isn't usually seen as an example of thanksgiving. A number of the psalms are identified as thanksgiving psalms, either explicitly, for instance in the Book of Common Prayer, or in a more indirect manner within the broader devotional tradition.[3] Psalm 6 is not one of them. Known after its initial Latin words as *Domine, ne in furore,* it is one of the traditional penitential psalms.[4]

It is precisely Donne's unorthodox decision to think about thanksgiving in the context of a psalm that isn't usually associated with it that makes his discussion pertinent to my concerns. As Donne points out in the premium, Psalm 6 does not begin with thanksgiving; rather, David comes "to such a thankfull sense of victory" by the end of the psalm. This allows Donne to consider thanksgiving not as a static formula but as the end of a dynamic process. The speaker of the psalm *becomes* thankful in front of our eyes, within the text recorded for us. In other words, Donne's sermon is not simply about thanksgiving, but about coming to thanksgiving. The end of this becoming thankful, not simply in itself but together with the process that has led to it, is what interests Donne when he poses the question: why does thanksgiving come only at the very end of the psalm?

> First then we consider David's thankfulnesse: But why is it so long before David leads us to that consideration? Why hath he deferred so primary a duty, to so late a place, to so low a roome, to the end of the Psalme? (6:40)

What makes Donne's question intriguing is not just the range of potential answers to it, but the very fact that he finds it noteworthy. It is not an obvious question. In the *divisio* of this sermon, and in his other sermons on the previous verses of Psalm 6, Donne explains that before it comes to the final act of thanksgiving, Psalm 6 includes prayers of penitence and petition. If thanksgiving is an expression of gratitude for a gift, it stands to reason that the act of thanking should come after the act of asking for the gift.[5] But Donne is less interested in this temporal logic than in a different, devotional and teleological relationship between prayer and thanksgiving:

> Not that the duty of thanksgiving is lesse then that of prayer; for if we could compare them; it is rather greater; because it contributes more to Gods glory, to acknowledge by thanks, that God hath given, then to acknowledge by prayer, that God can give. (6:40)

The deferral is all the more curious, Donne suggests, because in devotional import, thanksgiving equals or even surpasses prayer. Prayer and thanksgiving are not, in this account, fundamentally different actions insofar as their goal is concerned.[6] Even when we talk about prayer in the specific sense of petition, this petitionary prayer shares the purpose of thanksgiving insofar as it acknowledges God's power to give by petitioning him. And yet thanksgiving is a "greater duty" than prayer because while prayer merely acknowledges the potential, thanksgiving praises the actual; it offers thanks for gifts that have already been given. Notice that Donne doesn't actually say that the point of thanksgiving is to acknowledge *what* has been given. His formulation does not refer to the gift at all; instead, thanksgiving acknowledges "*that* God hath given" (emphasis mine). What thanksgiving acknowledges here is the act of giving itself, or rather, considering the perfect tense that Donne uses, the fact that there is givenness.[7] In other words, thanksgiving has more devotional import than petitionary prayer because by acknowledging givenness, it does more to praise God's glory.

CHRISTIAN THANKSGIVING

While much in Donne's argument is characteristically idiosyncratic, there is also a good deal that he takes from classical and Christian discussions of thanksgiving. Let me open up here a brief excursus on how these traditional conceptions of giving thanks differ from our everyday sense of the act. Thanking is one of the most ordinary acts of everyday life: I say thanks upon buying a coffee, receiving a gift, or even as a recipient of a mundane but kind gesture, such as someone holding the door for me. These are very different transactions, and "thanks" means something different in each case. When money is part of the exchange, "thanks" seems little more than a superadded gesture, a phatic confirmation of my knowing participation in an economic transaction. In response to a gift or a favor, "thanks" means significantly more: it is an acknowledgment of what I received, perhaps an implicit promise that I will eventually return the gift or the favor. This is not to say that I will give back the gift or that I will return the same favor; rather, the promise here is an acknowledgment of my participation in the symbolic economy of the gift.[8] The sort of classical iconology that appears for instance in Raphael's *Three Graces* represents this economy by depicting how three apples are passed around. As medieval and early modern mythographers explain, behind this depiction there is a sense of moral obligation not only to return the gift, but in general to maintain its circulation.[9] The act of thanking has a unique function in this symbolic economy: it expresses the acknowledgment of one's duty to maintain the cycle of the gift.

Large gifts, however, pose a challenge to this paradigm. The problem with a large gift is that it is potentially beyond the means of the receiver to return it and thus such a gift threatens to break the continuity of giving,

receiving, and returning. In such cases, the act of thanking gains in significance, but meanwhile its meaning changes: no longer a simple promise to
reciprocate, thanking is now a praise of the giver's magnanimity. This confla-
tion of thanking and praising is particularly evident in classical antiquity.
Primary among the meanings of the term *gratiarum actio* in the Roman
Empire was the rhetorical category of thanksgiving speech given on a festive
occasion, such as a military victory, an imperial anniversary, or the inaugu-
ration of a successful candidate into public office. Pliny the Younger, for instance, gave his speech of thanks for the consulship he received in 100.[10] Like
the later authors of the collection *Panegyrici Latini,* he used the occasion of
receiving public office to give thanks not only for the particular benefit of the
public office, but for the imperial *praesentia* itself, for the gift of the emper-
or's very person that Pliny describes as the source of all particular benefits.
In Pliny's performative act, thanksgiving for a particular benefit becomes an
occasion to offer thanks for the very person of the benefactor, and the act of
thanking for the gift turns into a praise of the giver.

This metamorphosis of thanksgiving into praise is neither rare nor accidental; it is a possibility inherent in the logic of thanking. In the case of
large gifts, thanksgiving is charged with a double task: it has simultaneously
to acknowledge the interruption of the gift's "natural" cycle and to reinstate
it by replacing a return gift with the symbolic gift of the praise itself. It is
as praise that thanksgiving does in fact return the gift, or rather replaces
the concrete act of returning with the purely symbolic act of giving thanks.
Moreover, insofar as "gifts" are defined as gifts for their participation in the
circle of giving, receiving, and returning, the gift that cannot be returned
is realized as a gift *only* with the act of thanksgiving, which symbolically
reinscribes the gift into the circle. In this specific sense the inherent logic
of thanksgiving is at odds with the act's temporality. Rather than simply
acknowledging a given gift, the act of giving thanks constitutes the gift by
naming it. In the same way, unmixed praise establishes the large gift as a
particular kind of gift, as unreciprocable gift.[11]

If we now turn to Christian conceptions of thanksgiving, we notice a
similar tendency to move from the individual act of thanking toward a general act that conflates thanking with praise. At first sight, discrete acts of
thanksgiving seem more obvious: the Greek *eucharistia* and the Latin *gratiarum actio* denote a number of different liturgical and devotional acts, from
a prayer said at the Eucharist, to the Eucharist itself, which is seen as a form
of thanksgiving, to the last part of the Catholic mass, which is at times desig-
nated as the thanksgiving part.[12] There are parallels in devotional contexts, as

well: based on a Pauline passage in the first letter to Timothy, prayer is often seen as consisting of four parts: beside supplication (*deēsis,* or want, need), address as prayer (*proseuchē,* or prayer toward), and intercession (*enteuxis,* meeting or audience), the fourth category is thanksgiving (*eucharistia*).[13] In the case of these discrete acts of giving thanks, thanksgiving might be described as occasional, in the specific sense that it responds to a particular gift and is accordingly bound to a particular context, to a particular time and place within devotional life. But for every use of "thanksgiving" in this limited, occasional sense, there is a corresponding use with a considerably broader meaning. While the last part of the mass is marked as the thanksgiving part, Christian authors also call the entire mass a *gratiarum actio.* The same is true for prayer; while in Timothy *eucharistia* is marked out as one kind (or one part) of prayer, elsewhere both Paul and other Christian authors use *eucharistia* as a synonym for prayer as such. Thanksgiving shifts register from the particular to the general, from the localized, individualized act of giving thanks for a particular gift to a general *disposition* of thankfulness that permeates a whole range of devotional activity, and which is expressed in the particular acts of thanking.

The contrast between occasional and general thanksgiving is particularly striking in the letters of Paul. In most of the letters, a formula for thanksgiving appears toward the end of the prescript and at the beginning of the main argument. The letter to the Romans, for instance, begins with the usual introductory formula (from Paul to X), and then continues with an instance of the general thanksgiving formula: "I thank my God through Jesus Christ for you all, that your faith is spoken of throughout the whole world" (Rom. 1:8). This thanksgiving formula is then expanded upon, in an act of establishing the communicative situation between Paul and his addressees. The regularity of such formulae in the Pauline corpus has prompted scholars not only to consider thanksgiving as one of the four (or sometimes five) parts of the Pauline letters' *dispositio,* but also to compare Paul's thanksgiving with the thanksgivings in Hellenistic letters and to suggest that Paul in effect only repeats some of the standard epistolographic *eucharistia* formulae of the period.[14] But whatever their source, in Paul's letters such particular formulae are accompanied by a different and much broader notion of thanksgiving. A number of times in the letters Paul uses *eucharistia* and its cognates without any subject, thereby suggesting that thanksgiving in these cases is not the act of acknowledging a particular benefit but the proper attitude toward a state of affairs that did not come about at any identifiable point in time, a condition that seems at every point to have already been given.[15]

While occasional thanksgiving is bound to a particular time and place, the particular context of the benefit received, the broader notion of thanksgiving presupposes an action that is repeated continuously. Indeed it seems that in this view, thanksgiving is regarded more as a disposition than a discrete act or series of acts.[16]

While occasional thanksgiving acknowledges an identifiable benefit, thanksgiving in the broader sense responds to a gift that is difficult to name, what Paul calls the "unspeakable gift."[17] Elsewhere in the same sermon on Psalm 6, Donne argues that the sense of thanksgiving as a duty of gratitude is one of the cultural concepts that classical antiquity shares with Christianity.[18] But while there is clear continuity between classical and Christian conceptions of thanksgiving, Christianity also represents a departure within the tradition insofar as it turns the "unspeakable gift," the gift that is impossible to return, from *an exception into the rule*.[19] Classical conceptions of the gift emphasize that at the core of gift economies, there is a fundamental tension: while the gift is presented as entirely free, in reality it carries within it an implicit but all the more forceful obligation to reciprocate it.[20] The large gifts that I described earlier in this chapter constitute an exception that reinforces the rule: they demand thanking that turns into praise and reinstates the cycle of the gift by doing so. But at the very beginning of Christianity, there is an attempt to radically interrupt the cycle, to cancel out the obligation for the rest of human history: Paul's message of grace is a message about a free gift, a gift that was not deserved, because it could not have been deserved, and will not be reciprocated, because by definition cannot be reciprocated. While in the classical conception a gift is defined by its participation in the circulation, the Christian gift is a gift exactly insofar as it interrupts the reciprocal relationship between the human and the divine ("the Law") and introduces, under the name of "grace," the event that is supposed to serve as the basis of a new life. Christ, in this sense, is the gift that represents the "unspeakable gift" of God's grace and provides a new paradigm of the gift.

The reason behind thanksgiving's significance, Donne has suggested, is that by acknowledging "that God hath given," it "contributes more to God's glory."[21] This notion is itself Pauline. In 2 Corinthians 4, Paul observes: "For all things are for your sakes, that the abundant grace might through the thanksgiving of many redound to the glory of God."[22] The act of giving thanks for the benefits received becomes, in the case of the unspeakable, already given gift, an act that is responsible for maintaining the cycle between God's grace and God's glory: the acknowledgment of the gift in its impossibility to be returned is what redounds to the glory of God. Thus, giving thanks for the gift becomes praise of the *doxan theou*, the glory of God. It is by entering circulation that the gift becomes a gift; and it is by thanksgiving that the gift can enter circulation, which is why thanksgiving is the very purpose of God's giving: "In every thing give thanks [*eucharisteite*] for this is the will of God in Christ Jesus concerning you."[23] Far from being an isolated liturgical or devotional ritual, thanksgiving here appears as a synonym for devotion itself. Since God's gifts, primarily the sacrifice of his son, but also creation, that is, "givenness" as such, are gifts that cannot be returned, the duty of the Christian can only be to acknowledge that a gift has been given. This acknowledging of the fact of givenness as a gift that cannot be returned is a telos of Christian life as a life of religious practice; it is a goal toward which devotion strives.[24]

When the early modern rhetorician Henry Peacham introduces the category of *eucharistia* or *gratiarum actio* with two quotations (one from Cicero and another from the Bible), he explains that "this forme of speech is used much with acknowledging the benefites received, and the unworthinesse of the receiver. . . . Sometime it is joyned with a confession of the unablenesse of the receiver to requite the giver, after the example of David, where he saith: 'What shal I give unto the Lord for all the benefites towards me? or, for all the benefites which he hath bestowed upon me?' (Psa1.16)."[25] Confession of one's unworthiness to receive the gift and praise of the giver's glory are two aspects of the same act. It is no accident that Peacham cites the Psalms as an example. The enormous popularity of the Psalms in the early modern period is often explained by reference to their affective range that includes the *de profundis* despair of the penitential psalms as well as the festive joy of thanksgiving.[26] But this explanation neglects what was evident for the early modern Christian, that ultimately *all* the psalms are hymns insofar as their final goal is to praise God's glory and to give thanks for the manifestations of his grace.[27] All other affects that they express, from despair to hope and joy, are merely ways in which their speaker attempts to reach the devotional state from which praise and thanksgiving become possible. The reason Donne can discuss thanksgiving in a penitential psalm is that thanksgiving is inscribed into the devotional movement of every psalm independent of the psalm's particular theme.

When Donne in the sermon suggests that thanksgiving is more important than prayer, his claim is firmly rooted in this tradition of thanksgiving; he refers to thanksgiving in this general sense as a telos of devotion, as the duty of acknowledging the divine gift. Donne's last passage on the matter offers an astonishing image that figures the life of the Christian as a machine created for the very purpose of giving thanks:

> God looks for nothing, nothing to be done in the way of exact recom-
> pence, but yet, as he that makes a Clock, bestowes all that labour upon
> the severall wheeles, that thereby the Bell might give a sound, and that
> thereby the hand might give knowledge to others how the time passes;
> so this is the principall part of that thankfulnesse, which God requires
> from us, that we make open declarations of his mercies, to the winning
> and confirming of others (6:42).

Life cannot return the gift of its creation to the creator; it can only acknowledge the gift and praise the giver. And this acknowledgment of the gift and praising of the giver, in turn, is itself part of the mechanism of creation, of created life. Donne suggests that we should see human life itself as a clockwork of grace that was made by God. The simile, like Donne's metaphysical conceits, is at odds with its subject: while the clock's hands indicate the passing of time, the thanksgiving machine of devotion must ring the sound of eternity.[28] The ambiguity of the "winning and confirming of others" indicates the dual purpose of devotion: devotion must point at eternity to win further gifts, and yet it must remain legible for people living in the *saeculum* to stir their devotions.[29] Thanksgiving is a telos of a devotion that both participates in a symbolic gift economy and constantly strives to transcend it. The human creature is a thanksgiving machine: it is created to give thanks for its creation and to praise the creator, and it works properly when it accomplishes this double task.[30]

THE END OF THE POEM

From this notion of thanksgiving as a telos inherent to devotional life we might already gather an answer to Donne's question of why the psalmist "deferred so primary a duty, to so late a place, to so low a roome, to the end of the Psalme?" The reason for this deferral, we might surmise, is that thanksgiving is a telos that other devotional acts, including the prayers of repentance and supplication that precede it in Psalm 6, strive to realize. It is this telic conception of thanksgiving that gives us the appropriate context to understand Donne's point about the end of the poem: "It is easie to observe, that in all Metricall compositions, of which kinde the booke of Psalmes is, the force of the whole piece, is for the most part left to the shutting up" (41). It is curious that this passage, which has been evoked time and again in Donne scholarship and beyond, has not convinced scholars to give more consideration to thanksgiving in Donne's devotional poetry.[31] Taken in itself, what Donne says here about the end of the poem is not particularly remarkable; it hardly amounts to more than saying that the end of the poem is always important. What makes it significant is that he says it in the context of thanksgiving: by drawing a parallel between thanksgiving's role in devotion and the end of the poem, Donne suggests a poetics in which thanksgiving is the end of the devotional poem.

Why does Donne evoke poetry in this particular place? In lyric poetry, the end is a chronotopic necessity: since "metricall compositions" take place in time and space, and since their very existence is based on measuring the time and place that they occupy, they *must* come to an end in order simply to be what they are, to work as poems. Thanksgiving, on the other hand, is not a chronotopic but a kairotic end: a devotional act ends in thanksgiving if and when it is fully realized, when it reaches a desired ideal. Instead of being a necessity, thanksgiving in the general, non-occasional sense is a difficult telos that may or may not be achieved by any given devotional act, including formal acts of thanksgiving. By invoking poetry to explain why thanksgiving comes last in the psalm, Donne makes thanksgiving an end of the devotional poem. In the psalm, and consequently in devotional poems of thanksgiving, the two senses of ending, the purely chronotopic end of the "metricall composition" and the kairotic telos of devotion are brought together so that the poem's end becomes the telos of devotion, the place where thanks are to be given. This merging of devotion and poetry, thanksgiving and the end of the poem amounts to a strong if unusual theory of devotional poetry.

When the task of acknowledging "that God hath given" is assigned to the end of a poem, the chronotopic end becomes kairotic as well: the place and time that is the end of the poem is now also the "right" place and time for thanksgiving to take place. In rhetoric, this kairotic chronotopos is referred to as *locus*. *Locus* is where something occurs, where something can be found (which is why in the *ars memorativa* the word acquires the specific sense of the place where memory and thinking find their material). One of the most prominent appearances of the term *locus* in the Christian Bible is in Hebrews 12:17, where, speaking of Esau, the text states: "When he would have inherited the blessing, he was rejected: for he found no place of repentance,

though he sought it carefully with tears." What the King James Bible translates here as "place of repentance" is *poenitentiae locum* in the Vulgate, which
in turn is a translation of the Greek *metanoias topon:* it is a place for a person
to change his or her mind, to repent, to convert, the place Petrarch describes
as the "miglior luogo" where we would like to return from the vagaries of the
Canzoniere.[32] The content of this locus, the *metanoia* (repentance or conversion), is for now less important for us than its formal structure: as the
context of Hebrews 12 makes clear, *locus* in this passage signifies the right,
kairotic place and time for an event that Esau sought but couldn't find.[33]
It means opportunity. Esau's devotion consisted in an attempt to *find* this
locus, and his devotion failed when the locus proved to be inaccessible for
him.[34] Esau's devotion was seeking the locus of repentance; the devotional
process that Donne is interested in is a *search* to find the locus of thanksgiving, the time and place where thanksgiving becomes possible.

The word Hebrews uses for Esau's failed attempt to find the locus of
repentance is *heuriskō*; the Vulgate translates it with the verbal form of *inventio.* When the task of "inventing" the locus of thanksgiving is assigned
to what Donne calls a "metricall composition," we see a preliminary response
of how a poem might reinvent the given as gift: the devotional poem is simultaneously an attempt to create and to discover the locus of thanksgiving.
The poem itself is the *created* artifice, built of the material of poetry, that defines the time and space within which the speaker of the poem has to *find* the
locus of thanksgiving, the gratitude that he needs in order to be able to give
thanks. The movement of the devotional poem, its unfolding toward this locus, is a *ductus,* a directed movement that is inherently teleological, striving
toward a definite goal, toward the locus of thanksgiving—though without
any guarantee of actually reaching it.[35] This account of the telic character
of the thanksgiving poem offers a preliminary definition of the devotional
poem: the devotional poem is a technology that uses the directed movement
of the poem (*ductus*) to reach its end in the *locus* of thanksgiving. The goal of
thanksgiving poetry is to reinvent the given as gift in the sense of inventing
the locus where the given might be attended, acknowledged, and thanked.[36]

Donne's last words on the poem in this sermon remind us that as an
attempt to give thanks, the devotional poem embodies the tension between
regular gift exchanges, on the one hand, and the challenge of the "unspeakable gift," on the other: "The whole frame of the Poem is a beating out of a
piece of gold, but the last clause is as the impression of the stamp, and that
is it that makes it currant" (41). The thanksgiving poem is the money that
the devotional poet coins in order to repay the received gift; and the end

of the poem is a confirmation of the poem's value as thanksgiving, thereby making it "currant," enabling it to contribute to God's glory. Of course, the direct comparison between coins and poetry has a degree of provocation to it. Much of Elizabethan and Jacobean poetry used the rhetoric of the gift in rather unsubtle ways; prefaces of Spenser and Jonson to their patrons remind their addressees that the poetic gift they are about to receive carries in it an inherent obligation to be reciprocated.[37] Donne preferred manuscript circulation of his poetry partly because he was eager to present his poems as genuinely free gifts that required no reciprocation, and partly, one assumes, to increase the value of his poem-coins by emphasizing their exclusivity. In this sermon, Donne would seem to admit that poems *are* coins. And yet in the case of thanksgiving, and consequently in the case of devotional poems, this money is worth absolutely nothing: "But *Amor Dei affectus, non contractus,* The love of God is not a contract, a bargaine, he looks for nothing againe, and yet he looks for thanks, for that is nothing, because there is nothing done in it, it is but speaking; *Gratias dicere, est gratias agere,* To utter our thanks to God, is all our performance of thankfulnesse" (42). Although the passage begins by emphasizing that thanksgiving is "nothing" when compared with the "infinitenesse" of God's gift, Donne quickly rephrases the point: thanksgiving is nothing because it is only by being nothing that it can acknowledge the free gift that wouldn't be free if thanksgiving were more than a mere nothing. Thanksgiving is the "nothing" that God looks for; it is the act that establishes the circulation of the gift by doing nothing with the gift—apart from merely acknowledging it in words. If the divine gift interrupts the logic of exchange—if the divine gift, in other words, is an event that is supposed to turn the entire logic of exchange upside down—then the response to that exchange can only be a "nothing." When Donne suggests that the act of giving thanks is "nothing," he is not saying that one is required to reciprocate God's gift as best one can, even though such reciprocation will always remain nothing when compared to the infinity of the original gift. Instead, a properly enacted thanksgiving requires that one attend to the very unreturnability of the gift, to the fact that any attempt to reciprocate will actually amount to a refusal of acceptance. Thus the "nothing" that is thanksgiving at the end of the poem is not a repayment that merely appears to be "nothing" in comparison with the infinitely greater divine gift. It is a "nothing" because it is only by being nothing that it can properly acknowledge the totality that it acknowledges.[38] Far from being a spontaneous "ejaculation" (as devotional poems are in *The Temple*'s famous subtitle), thanksgiving is an act that requires the most delicate balance of uttering words attentively, without imposing them on the gift as names.[39] Devotion, in this cast, is the carefully designed "machinery" capable of making such an utterance possible.

I suggest, then, that thanksgiving is key to the problem that I discussed at the beginning of chapter 1, the problem of how poetry and religion might be compatible, or how we could imagine a poetic invention of the religious given. When poetry becomes the machine of thanksgiving, and when thanksgiving becomes the kairotic goal of poetry, the goal toward which the poem is striving is the invention of a place or *locus* where givenness might be attended to and acknowledged as grace. At the heart of the task or "duty" of thanksgiving, there is a paradox: one must acknowledge the given without allowing this acknowledgment to suggest the possibility of reciprocation, which would prevent it from being acknowledged as "free." It is because of this difficulty that genuine thanksgiving must remain "nothing" as an action, that it becomes an action apt to acknowledge the given only by doing nothing with it, by leaving it there at the end of the poem, as reported speech, apparently uninvented. Paradoxically, in devotional poetry "doing nothing" with the given is the goal of the poem's invention, the specific task that is assigned to the end of the poem. Yet this "doing" nothing is in fact a rather complex action because it involves a transition from the mere given to the gift. In this sense the poem is a reinvention of the given as a gift, and as such it must be able to not change the given in any way except for preparing its perception as a gift. What this preparation requires is the subject of the next chapter. Before addressing it, however, let's return to "Death be not proud" to see how Donne's poem might be seen as a thanksgiving poem following Donne's account of the devotional poem remarkably closely.

THANKSGIVING IN "DEATH BE NOT PROUD"

At first, Donne's sonnet appears to have little to do with thanksgiving: it is a poem that belligerently challenges a personalized death in the hope of a future victory. Behind the mockery of death, the poem contains a vigorous eschatological expectation. But is there any sense of thanksgiving in the poem?

Statements of thanks and declarations of past or future victories are frequent companions both within Christian traditions and beyond. The dominant sense of *gratiarum actio* in Roman society was the *supplicatio*, a series of thanksgiving festivities decreed by the senate following a significant military victory.[40] In fact, the mockery of death in Paul's letter is itself followed by a *supplicatio,* a thanksgiving for victory: having "proven" the resurrection of the dead, Paul concludes 1 Corinthians 15 with these words: "The sting of death is sin; and the strength of sin is the law. But thanks be to God, which giveth us the victory through our Lord Jesus Christ." Thanks are to God, and thanks are for Christ both as a giver and as a given, for the given victory.

Indeed, when Donne introduces the subject of his sermon, he defines it in terms of a "thankfull sense of victory": "A man perchance may be safe in a Retrait, but the honour, the victory, the triumph lies in enforcing the enemy to fly. *To that David come here, to such a thankfull sense of victory.*" Up until this point, I have not discussed the particular lines of Psalm 6 with which Donne is most concerned. It is time to listen to how these lines announce a victory, with the understanding that it is here that Donne locates David's thanksgiving:

> Depart from me, all ye workers of iniquity; for the Lord hath heard the voyce of my weeping.
> The Lord hath heard my supplication; the Lord will receive my prayer.
> Let all mine enemies be ashamed and sore vexed: let them returne and be ashamed suddenly.
>
> ————————
>
> (Psalm 6.8–10)

In fact, the end of the psalm does not really declare a victory; one might describe it more accurately as inviting victory and expecting it. Later in the sermon Donne decides that the grammar of "Let all mine enemies be ashamed" is not composed of cursing words (*imprecatoria*) but "words of prediction" (*praedictoria*), and he further specifies that these words do not belong to the speaker but were in fact "pre-prophesied" by the Scriptures (55). In other words, and precisely as in the final couplet of "Death be not proud," the end of Psalm 6 announces a future defeat of the enemy by reiterating the given words of the Scriptures. In neither case are the reiterated words explicit words of thanks; and, as in the case of the psalm, Donne specifies that thanksgiving consists in "a thankfull sense of victory," which is expressed in David's "manner of declaring God's mercy."

"Death be not proud" is a devotional poem in the sense I have suggested to understand this category: a poetic "machine" with the aim of inventing the *locus* of thanksgiving. Accordingly, the end of the poem, the proclamation of Death's future death is, precisely and in itself, thanksgiving. Or rather it is *supposed* to be thanksgiving: whether it really *is* thanksgiving depends on whether the poem has succeeded in preparing the speaker for seeing the Pauline doctrine not simply as a given, preexisting, and abstract doctrine, but as a gift, something that is being given personally to him. Which is also to say that now a new question emerges: how do we know if the poem has succeeded in doing so? Indeed, what would the conditions of such a success be? Or to put it in broader terms: what does the preparation for thanksgiving require? This is the subject of the next chapter.

3

DISTRACTED PRAYERS

Here are three things, especially to be considered in the
true seeking and calling upon God: The first is Preparation,
before we call upon God in Prayer; The second is Attention
in Prayer; The third and last is, Thanksgiving after Prayer.

John Norden, *A Poor Mans Rest*[1]

IN THE PREVIOUS CHAPTER, I ARGUED that "Death be not proud" is a
thanksgiving poem in two senses of the term. First, it is a poem in which
the goal of the devotional-poetic labor is to invent the locus of thanksgiving. Second, it is a potential proof of the Pauline doctrine of the resurrection in that its purpose is to invent the given doctrine as a gift. This teleological account of the poem as aiming at thanksgiving raises the question:
how could the poem achieve this double task, the task of creating the place
of thanksgiving where the given might be seen as a gift of grace? This question of inventing grace is not a theological problem but a phenomenological one. The transition from the given to the gift isn't a matter of imputed
grace, but of moving from one kind of perception to another. The Eucharistic transformation of the bread into the body of Christ is certainly the most
spectacular instance of recognizing an X as Y, a given piece of bread as *charis anti charitos*, Christ's body as God's gift to mankind. But it is not the only
one. The challenge to any act of thanksgiving in devotion is to recognize the
divine gift in what is already given. The task of preparing for thanksgiving
is to make this recognition possible.

When Donne introduces the subject of thanksgiving in the sermon
on Psalm 6, he offers a preliminary division of his argument: "we shall first
consider *Davids* thankfulnesse," he writes, "and then, secondly, we shall see
his reason, upon which he grounded this confidence."[2] After the previous

chapter's focus on thanksgiving, my concern now is with what Donne calls David's "reason, upon which he grounded his confidence." Donne suggests that David's reason is his prayer, indeed the success of his prayer:

> And then, secondly, we shall see his reason, upon which he grounded this confidence, and this spirituall exultation, which was a pregnant reason, a reason that produced another reason; *The Lord hath heard my supplication, the Lord will heare my prayer;* upon no premises doth any conclusion follow, so logically, so sincerely, so powerfully, so imperiously, so undeniably, as upon this, *The Lord hath, and therefore the Lord will.*[3]

David's thanksgiving is an expression of his confidence that his prayer has been heard. Donne identifies this confidence with gratitude, with "the thankfull sense of a victory" that enables David to dismiss his enemies, the very same sense that allows the speaker in "Death be not proud" to challenge and ultimately dismiss death. What Donne describes as his second concern is the "reason" for David's confidence, which is to say, the very foundation of this victorious sense of thankfulness and its expression in the act of thanksgiving. This reason, this foundation of thanksgiving is prayer in the limited sense as "precation" or petition, as an elemental devotional act aiming to solicit God's favor. Prayer may turn into thanksgiving if it succeeds at obtaining God's favor, if it affords the praying subject an experience of divine grace. Prayer is the preparation, the act of invention that is responsible for creating and finding the locus of thanksgiving and the act may lead to seeing the given as a gift. Therefore all the previous queries of this book can now be summarized in a single question: if the possibility of giving thanks depends on prayer's success, what are the conditions of a successful prayer?

In order to answer this question, this chapter takes a temporary departure from Donne's poetry and turns to dramatic and theological accounts of prayer. The reason is that we are searching for the very criteria upon which we can decide whether "Death be not proud" may be seen as a successful prayer and thus a successful preparation for thanksgiving. We cannot extract such criteria from the poem itself. It is possible to critique "Death be not proud" according to aesthetic or theological principles, but we do not yet know how to evaluate it as a devotional act. This is why in the first section of this chapter I turn to the most famous early modern dramatization of prayer, Claudius's monologue in the third scene of Act 3 in Shakespeare's *Hamlet*. In this section, I argue that in the scene Shakespeare stages Claudius's devotional failure as a failure of the king's devotional attention. In the second section, I examine the possibility that attention might be a condition of efficacious prayer by looking at Christian theological and devotional accounts of attention in prayer. In the last section of the chapter, I read one of Donne's letters to show how Donne is not only aware of the difficulties of attention in prayer, but he also thinks about ways of overcoming them in the act of writing.

WHEN PRAYER FAILS

The third scene of Act 3 in *Hamlet* is best known not for what happens in it but for what doesn't.[4] The prince finds Claudius alone and praying, and yet does not kill him but defers the murder until "a more horrid hint" (3.3.88).[5] This deferral has invited speculation about Hamlet's character for centuries.[6] Yet murder is not the only missing action in the scene; also absent is a prayer that is evoked in words and gestures, yet does not actually take place. Like Esau, who "found no place of repentance," Claudius seeks but cannot find it. We see the king preparing to pray in words; we see him fall on his knees, silent, performing the physical gestures associated with prayer. But when the prince leaves, Claudius rises again and exclaims: "My words fly up, my thoughts remain below. / Words without thoughts never to heaven go" (3.3.97–98). The king admits that his prayer has failed.

But why *does* Claudius's prayer fail? The question rarely gets asked in the scholarship. Part of the reason is the dramaturgical effect of this prayer, the way in which it redirects attention from itself to Hamlet's own hesitations, and the way in which it gives a hint of divine assent to Hamlet's pursuit of revenge. Claudius's prayer must fail, both in order keep the villain for the rest of the plot and to add a further layer of complexity to Hamlet's character. But there is another reason, and this is Claudius's own confession that "I am still possessed / Of those effects for which I did the murder" (3.3.53–54). While Hamlet's delay may appear mysterious to us because we know that Claudius does not, in fact, pray, Claudius' failure to pray seems comprehensible: he doesn't ultimately pray because he is still attached to the "effects" of the murder, "my crown, my own ambition, and my queen" (3.3.55). The standard account of the scene posits the cause of Claudius's failure in his lack of sincerity: the king, it is assumed, didn't really intend to repent in the first place. Insofar as Claudius does not give up his attachment to the "effects" of the murder, he does not sincerely repent; and because he does not sincerely repent, the prayer remains a mere performance of the external signs of prayer.[7]

Ramie Targoff's account of the prayer scene in *Hamlet* is illuminating here because in explaining why Hamlet could assume that Claudius was in fact sincerely praying, it helps to articulate the related question of why Claudius's prayer failed.[8] Targoff argues that while Hamlet's reasons to postpone the murder may seem to us as mere rationalizations of the prince's habitual hesitation, contemporary audiences would have found them entirely adequate. These audiences, Targoff suggests, were encouraged to pray by performing the external gestures of prayer.[9] She argues that belief in the transformative force of devotional performance was an increasingly central view within the developing Church of England in the late sixteenth and early seventeenth centuries.[10] Such a confidence in performance and habit meant that the boundaries between a sincere internal state and external performance were more fluid than they might seem to us; rather than expressions of an internal state, the words and gestures of prayer were seen to potentially create a sincere internal state of devotion. Thus, insofar as Claudius was performing a prayer, in the eyes of the seventeenth-century audience Hamlet appeared entirely justified in assuming that Claudius *was* praying, that Claudius was in the state of grace, and that therefore if murdered, he would have avoided damnation.[11]

Targoff's account raises, however, a crucial question: if the external performance of prayer may lead to an internal state of devotion, and therefore to sincere prayer, then why does Claudius fail to pray?[12] To suggest that Claudius nevertheless doesn't pray sincerely would only obscure this question because within this scene Claudius does *not* appear insincere in any obvious sense.[13] Indeed, this scene is marked by Claudius's most sincere moment in the play: this is the first time he explicitly confesses to the murder of Old Hamlet. His contrition and confession, combined with an apparently firm faith in the power of grace and prayer pose the question: if Claudius seems to do and think everything in accordance with early modern views about devotion, then why does Shakespeare nevertheless present the prayer as a failed one?[14] Given that Claudius's soliloquy is, as Targoff argues, an attempt to pray, and given that this attempt appears both adequate by the period's standard and sincere in the context of the play—the question that emerges is not simply the question of why Hamlet accepts it at face value (Targoff's question), but also, to put it in provocative terms, why God does not.

A brief conceptual clarification is necessary here. Claudius's soliloquy in the scene comprises a number of devotional acts such as meditation, contrition, confession, and, toward the end of the soliloquy, a petition for grace. While each of these individual devotional acts may carry different meanings in different contexts, there is a sense in which they may be seen in a hierarchical order, constituting different stages of devotion.[15] Generally speaking, when conceived of as a dynamic process, devotion consists of *preparatio* and *actio,* and each devotional act serves as the preparation for the next action.[16] Thus meditation may be seen as preparation for the acts of repentance and prayer, repentance may be seen as preparation for prayer, and prayer may be seen as preparation for thanksgiving.

This progressive hierarchy is not, however, absolute. Authors of theological treatises and devotional manuals often suggest different divisions, and even those who accept the same categories may order them differently. The more we notice this diversity of particular devotional hierarchies, the more important the general distinction between *preparatio* and *actio* becomes. The tendency to order devotional acts suggests that these acts are always relative to each other—that is, the same act can be either *preparatio* or *actio,* depending on the particular context. One can pray in order to be able to give thanks; or one can meditate in order to be able to pray. In fact, the same action can be both *preparatio* and *actio;* one can pray to prepare for prayer.[17]

Act 3, Scene 3, of *Hamlet* is also a problem of devotional action and indeed of action as such.[18] I argued, in the previous chapter, that the act of thanksgiving required a foundation, a preparation; and I suggested that for the mechanisms of this preparation we needed to look at the devotional act of prayer. But Claudius's attempt to pray demonstrates that prayer itself may require preparation. What Ramie Targoff calls "the performance of prayer" in the scene is in fact devotional preparation that is supposed to bring the king to the *actio* of prayer.[19] And because the soliloquy is preparation for prayer, the question it raises is why, if his preparation is adequate, Claudius would not be able finally to pray. It seems that the king's predicament is that he cannot arrive at an ultimate decision that would lead to action; he is, in other words, stuck in preparation. Indeed, the very notion of preparation implies the possibility of infinite regress, the need to prepare for preparation, and so on; and thus it raises the question of how to leave behind preparation, how to begin the appropriate devotional action.[20]

This is why the fact that Claudius offers various explanations for devotional failure does not erase our questions about his failure but only adds to their urgency. Targoff's account helps us to see Claudius's soliloquy in terms of an attempt to reach the internal state of devotion that would be the basis of prayer. If we then recognize that Claudius addresses the obstacles to his prayer even as he is struggling with these very obstacles in trying to pray, it follows that we need to consider everything that Claudius says in the soliloquy as part of his prayer. And this recognition suggests that we need to see the significance of his prayer's failure, not in the reasons that the king offers, but despite the fact that he offers them. Everything that the king says ought to be seen as part of his preparation for prayer, as fulfilling a role in bringing Claudius closer to the *actio* of prayer.

Let us look at the soliloquy from this perspective. As preparation for prayer, the soliloquy begins with Claudius's declaration that although he does have the intention to pray, his "guilt" is stronger. But of course one prays in order to be relieved of guilt (if by "guilt" Claudius means his own feeling of guilt),[21] or to be forgiven for guilt (if he means by "guilt" the fact of the crime)—and Claudius is fully aware of this:[22]

> What if this cursèd hand
> Were thicker than itself with brother's blood,
> Is there not rain enough in the sweet heavens
> To wash it white as snow? Whereto serves mercy
> But to confront the visage of offence?
> And what's in prayer but this twofold force,
> To be forestallèd ere we come to fall,
> Or pardoned being down?
>
> ————————
>
> (3.3.43–50)

Divine mercy is to "wash it white as snow" no matter whose blood it is, or how long since the crime has been committed. Prayer, in turn, is to ask for the divine mercy that alone can "confront the visage of the offence," that alone can change the significance of that which has already happened. Simultaneously offering his confession of the crime and his contrition for it, Claudius also expresses faith that divine mercy can absolve the sinner from any sin. Of course, the line between faith in grace and confidence that one's devotional action would itself bring about salvation is a delicate one. If Claudius would go on trusting the "twofold force" of his prayer; if he were entirely confident that his actions could save him ("Then I'll look up. / My fault is past"), he might appear to fall into superstition.

Instead, Claudius sinks further into despair over his own sinfulness. A new doubt halts him: does prayer have the force to evoke mercy when the crime is not a matter entirely past? This question, which Claudius raises with remarkable precision, leads to a deeper confession of and contrition for his sin, that is, a more profound understanding of the significance of his crime in the larger scheme of devotion and salvation:[23]

> But, O, what form of prayer
> Can serve my turn? 'Forgive me my foul murder'?
> That cannot be; since I am still possess'd
> Of those effects for which I did the murder,
> My crown, mine own ambition and my queen.
> May one be pardon'd and retain the offence?
>
> ⸻
>
> (3.3.51–56)

What was initially an abstract confrontation between "guilt" and the "intent" to pray is now rearticulated with concrete referential content. Claudius cannot pray because he is "still possess'd / Of those effects for which" he murdered Old Hamlet. The reason his "guilt" cannot be a mere past matter, the reason it emerges as a counter-intention to his intent to pray is that by still desiring the "effects" of his crime, Claudius still has the very intention that led him to murder old Hamlet, and indeed this intention might force him to commit further crimes. It is as if he were still committing the murder, every day, by wanting and enjoying the queen and the crown, and in this sense the crime is a present sin.

At this point, Claudius finds himself in an existential and devotional predicament. He has taken two main steps toward genuine repentance: contrition and confession. He has recognized the extent of his past and present sin; he has understood the soteriological significance of his sin; and meanwhile he has retained his faith that full repentance, sincere prayer would obtain for him God's mercy. But in order to achieve this full repentance, in order to turn his *preparatio* into *actio,* his soliloquy into prayer, what is required of him is that he stop intending the murder, stop desiring the queen and the crown. He would, in other words, have to genuinely repent not only his past actions but also his past and present motivations.

As before, Claudius shows not only candor in confessing his crimes and intentions but also precision in articulating the resulting theological and devotional predicament. If he still goes on with his attempt to pray, it is because he is now praying *in order to be able to repent;* that is, he is now attempting to prepare for repentance.[24] In other words, he prays in order to be able to pray. His gloss on the matter still retains some of his scholastic precision, but the Protestant mood is now dominant:

> Try what repentance can. What can it not?
> Yet what can it when one cannot repent?
> _____
>
> (3.3.65–66)

The circularity implied in the passage is both the soliloquy's most important theological statement and the turning point in Claudius's preparation for prayer. Claudius needs to repent in order to be able to pray, and yet he needs to pray in order to be able to repent. At this point the problem he is facing is not merely his personal predicament. Rather, Claudius recognizes the problem that is at the core of early modern Christianity: the limit of personal agency in devotion. For the problem of how to leave preparation and engage in action, the Christian answer is "grace"—indeed, grace is the very name for the moment when one becomes able to decide and act.[25] Grace, in this sense, is what opens up the circularity of devotional preparation, as Donne himself points out in one of the *Holy Sonnets*:[26]

> Yet grace, if thou repent thou canst not lacke.
> But who shall give thee that grace to begin?[27]

Repentance is the condition of asking for grace, and yet repentance requires grace. If repentance has grace, then it "can" achieve anything; if it has no grace, then "one cannot repent," then one cannot even begin the *actio* of repentance or prayer. What both Claudius and Donne describe is the devotional aspect of the theological question of how to prepare for grace— the theological question the Reformation conceptualized in the *sola gratia* formula.[28] If theology's claim is that salvation is possible only by grace, in devotion this claim may be paraphrased as devotional action being possible only by grace.[29] In fact, it is in the realm of devotion that the formula *sola gratia* becomes an acute problem, a problem of praxis: since repentance and prayer are petitions that request the very thing that they depend upon in order to make their requests, logically speaking they appear to be impossible actions. Or rather, they appear to be impossible *as* actions. What the formula *sola gratia* indicates is the transition from human *preparatio* to divine *actio,* that is, from action to event. When salvation or prayer itself depends on grace, human agency is partially suspended, giving room for the expectation that prayer, like salvation, would *happen* by virtue of grace.

This requires a revision of our earlier formulation about *preparatio* and *actio.* For the preparation for prayer to reach the threshold of actual prayer, it must become action not so much in the modern sense of the term (controlled by agent) as in the sense of being assisted by a transcendent power. The action of prayer in this sense is a passion of prayer as well. One of the traditional definitions of prayer sheds light on this distinction. Lancelot Andrewes's formulation in *the Institutiones Piae* is exemplary: "Prayer (as a Father well saith) is a familiar conference with GOD. By it, we talke with him (as it were) face to face."[30] Andrewes's definition echoes the ancient view that prayer is a conversation with God: the actuality of prayer depends on whether God is an active partner in the conversation, whether he hears and listens to the prayer, and whether he responds to it.[31] The form of Claudius's attempt to pray reflects this definition. In the seventeenth century, soliloquies are devotional monologues such as meditations or prayers.[32] The Latin term "soliloquium" became popular in the Middle Ages, partly due to a devotional collection entitled *Liber soliloquiorum animae ad deum,* which was usually attributed to Augustine.[33] But the precise meaning of the term is neither prayer nor meditation. Coined by Augustine in the *Liber soliloquiorum,* the original meaning of soliloquy is a philosophical and theological preparation for prayer, a thinking consideration of what is required to enter into a colloquy with God.[34] Claudius's speech is soliloquy in the original sense of the term: it is a thinking dialogue with the self to consider what is necessary to address God, which leads to the recognition that without grace the threshold of actual prayer cannot be reached.

This explains the sudden change of tone in Claudius's soliloquy after the passage on the circularity of repentance. Until this question, the soliloquy has been a meditative *preparatio* for prayer, that is, a psychologically deliberate and theologically accurate, rational consideration of the difficulties of prayer as action, in terms of guilt, forgiveness, and repentance. This meditation comes to a sudden halt when Claudius recognizes that the repentance that he must perform in order to be able to pray itself implies a circle; that it is logically impossible as action and can only be completed if God joins the conversation. After this recognition, the soliloquy undergoes a radical transformation both in tone and content. The rational, meditative discourse is left behind; Claudius is not thinking about how to pray, but prays in order to be able to pray:[35]

O wretched state, O bosom black as death,

O limèd soul that, struggling to be free,

Art more engaged! Help, angels! Make assay.

Bow, stubborn knees; and, heart with strings of steel,

Be soft as sinews of the newborn babe.

All may be well.

———————

(3.3.67–72)

Begging both the angels and his own body, Claudius no longer thinks of prayer as an act that he would perform but as something that would happen to him, performed by divine agents. With the preparation for prayer having run into the impossibility of prayer, the king now tries to overcome the original conflict between "guilt" and the "intent" to pray by abandoning decision and requesting supernatural intervention. The first quarto's version of Claudius's final cry, which reduces the above quoted six lines to two, shows that contemporaries did not fail to notice the petition of grace at the end of the king's soliloquy:

Most wretched man, stoope, bend thee to thy prayer.

Aske grace of heaven to keepe thee from despaire.[36]

If Claudius still fails to pray, as he himself admits after emerging from his silent prayer, it is not because he didn't intend to pray or because he hasn't sincerely tried. It is because he has not received the divine grace that he prayed for, the divine grace that he would have needed to be able to *really* pray.

This might look like a dead end for an investigation to discover in Claudius's soliloquy a model for devotion. The purpose of a poetics of prayer is to analyze the mechanisms of devotional acts within the boundaries of language; it aims to describe linguistic phenomena that are available for direct observation. But poetics here runs into the monopoly of theology. According to the kind of theology that is implied in Claudius's soliloquy, the only way the king's prayer could have been successful is if it had received grace, and consequently the key to its failure could not have been any flaw within the prayer itself—it must have been the absence of grace. Why the king did not receive grace seems to fall outside the scope of analysis. It might be that Claudius is a reprobate, a victim of what early modern Protestants called double predestination.[37] But without the play offering any further hints about Claudius's soteriological fate, this remains a theological and metaphysical speculation.

Of course, in a sense even the assumption that the king's prayer has failed is a speculation: after all, we do not know if the prayer has *really* failed. We only know that *if* it has, then it must have done so because of the absence of grace. And we assume that it failed because the character Claudius has told us that it did. This is important because it necessitates a reformulation of the original question: what we need to ask isn't *why* Claudius' prayer fails, but *how* the king knows that his prayer has failed.[38] This is where we can move on to a phenomenology in the proper sense. While in theological terms we cannot go beyond the assumption that if Claudius's prayer fails, it is because of the lack of grace, the soliloquy suggests that Claudius has a particular experience of this failure. It is this negative devotional experience, or rather Claudius's account of it, that demands priority over any theological question. And indeed, the words stand there at the end of the scene all too conspicuously: "My words fly up, my thoughts remain below / Words without thoughts never to heaven go." These words hold the key to the issue of devotional efficacy; perhaps the reason they have not attracted much scholarly attention is precisely their transparency. The king suggests that throughout his prayer, he has remained distracted. His guilt, his attachment to the queen and the crown, all of those factors that he has characterized as obstacles to his prayer turn out to be obstacles insofar as they distracted him from his prayer. The reason Claudius knows his prayer hasn't been successful is that he has not been able to attend to the words of his prayer.

If Claudius's failure consists in distraction, why is it so tempting to assume that the king's error is insincerity? Indeed, why is it that early modern commentators would themselves insist on intention as the condition of successful prayer? Partly this is a matter of translation. Until well into the early modern period, the Latin *intentio* and many of its vernacular cognates (including both the English "intention" and "intent") are often used as synonyms of attention in the general sense of "stretching toward." The distinction that emerges between the two concepts has to do with a conception of attention as the general human disposition (or ontological condition) of perpetual "tending toward" something, while associates intention with a modality, often a volitional, concentrated version, of this tending toward. The notion of intention as will or desire is an early development; but for a long time this sense of intention as resolution remains bound up with a notion of attention.[39] Take the following account of prayer by Thomas Becon:

Prayer, after the common definicion of the Doctors, is a lyftinge up of
a pure mynde to God, wherein we aske somewhat of hym. What other
thynge meaneth this worde, lyftynge up, than to shewe that who soever
entendeth to praye, must utterly seclude and put out of his herte all
vayne cogitacion and wordly thoughtes, all carnall fantasies, all ungod-
lye ymaginacions, to conclude al such thynges as might make the herte
of hym that prayeth to crepe upon the grounde, to alienate and estraung
his mynde from the meditacion of celestiall and devyne matters? . . . In
prayer ther is not so much nede of the voyce as of the thought, nor of the
stretchyng out of the handes as of the intencion of the mynde.[40]

Becon's passage is representative of early modern accounts of prayer in emphasizing the "intencion of the mynde" as a condition of prayer that is more
crucial than the physical gestures or the words associated with it. But it is
also helpful in demonstrating that this "intencion" has little to do with sincerity as an affect. It is instead bound up with the concept of attention: the
contrast Becon sets up at the end between "the stretching out of the handes"
and "the intencion of the mynde" works because of the common Latin root
of *intendere* and *attendere* (transmitted to English through the Old French
entendre and *atendre*) meaning the stretching, the tending of the mind. Notice that Becon goes from interpreting the "lyftinge up of a pure mynde to
God" as the seclusion of all distractions to "the intencion of the mynde":
the mind is pure, its intention is fully set on prayer if all distractions have
been eliminated.

Writing almost two decades after the first performances of *Hamlet*, a
little-known devotional author, John Norden, published a devotional man-
ual by the title *A Poor Man's Rest*. Norden is better known as a cartographer,
and it seems that he wrote devotional treatises mainly to supplement his
earnings. His contribution to the vast literature of early modern English devotion would hardly stand out were it not for one small difference: where
other devotional authors would describe religious hypocrisy as an error of
intention, Norden consistently uses the term "attention." In *A Poor Man's Rest*,
he divides devotion into three main parts: preparation for prayer, petitionary prayer, and thanksgiving after prayer. In the second, central part of the
treatise, Norden posits attention as the condition of genuine prayer. It is not
enough, he argues, to perform the external signs of attentiveness: "It doth not
follow, that although the eye be fixed on any certaine object, or be shut, that
therefore the heart is rightly set on God."[41] While one performs the external
signs of prayer, the heart might be "wandring in the fields of Corne" or for

that matter "over-come with pride, plotting revenge." Such prayers cannot become efficacious because they are "made with an extravagant heart," and as a result "be they in words never so holy they are imputed unto us as sin."[42] Norden's account sheds light on the difference between moral and religious interpretations of devotional failure. When we characterize Claudius's failure to pray as a failure of his *intention,* it's tempting to assume that Claudius's error is his desire for Gertrude and the crown, the causes and the "effects" of his original sin of killing his brother. But if following Norden we describe it as a failure of attention, it becomes clear that the problem with the king's attachment to Gertrude or the crown isn't a sin because it goes against human or divine law but because it distracts Claudius from his prayerful turn to God.[43]

Norden's account also helps us see that a concern with distraction is there in Claudius's soliloquy from the very beginning. Torn between his "guilt" and his "intent" to pray, the king is paralyzed at the very beginning of the scene, "like a man to double business bound, / I stand in pause where I shall first begin, / And both neglect." The problem with guilt isn't that it cannot be forgiven—it can. Nor does it pose some sort of metaphysical obstacle to devotion. Guilt is a problem for the same reason the king's thinking about Gertrude or Denmark is: it distracts him from the prayer that would require exclusive attention. As Jeremy Taylor puts it, "Remember that it is a great undecency to desire of God to hear those prayers, a great part whereof we do not hear our selves. If they be not worthy of our attention, they are far more unworthy of Gods."[44] When the king admits his failure at the end of the scene, he shows full awareness of this: it isn't that he cannot believe in the power of prayer, in divine mercy, or in the possibility of his own salvation. It's "just" that he finds himself incapable of focusing on the prayer he would very much like to perform.

ATTENTION IN VOCAL AND SILENT PRAYER

If Claudius's prayer fails insofar as the king remains distracted, does this mean attention would have made his prayer successful? This question leads us beyond the boundaries of the play, to a broader issue: does attention to the words of prayer guarantee prayer's success? This is a question that often exercised medieval and early modern devotional authors, particularly on the Catholic side. Theologians developed a sophisticated vocabulary to discuss the question of just how much and what kind of attention the priest must pay to the words of his prayer while reciting the Sunday vespers.[45] On the surface, distinctions between material, literal, and spiritual attention, or between virtual and habitual attention, served to elucidate questions of whether the priest's attention must have been sustained or only present at the beginning of the prayer, and so on.[46] In surveying the debates, one gets the impression that at least one purpose of this sophisticated vocabulary was to justify a considerable deal of leniency: most discussions agree that the priest cannot be expected to pay sustained attention to his prayer, they claim that distraction cannot be fully escaped in human devotion, and that therefore attention cannot be seen as a condition of prayer. Yet the very persistence of these discussions shows that attention was thought to be generally relevant to prayer. What should we make of this seemingly ambivalent attitude toward the question of attention in prayer?

The difference between vocal prayer (*oratio vocalis*), on the one hand, and silent or mental prayer (*oratio mentalis*), on the other, is key in this context. Early modern discussions tend to agree about the difficulty of maintaining one's attention to the words of vocal prayer, and at times they question if such sustained attention is even necessary. But when it comes to silent prayer, they unequivocally claim that attention for this kind of prayer is essential. Take the Dominican Domingo de Soto's 1533 discussion of the question, "Utrum ad solvendum canonice divinum officium requiratur attentio," "whether in performing the duty of reciting the Divine Office requires attention."[47] After discussing the difficulties of maintaining attention in vocal prayer, de Soto makes a startling claim: "In mental prayer, where attention is the prayer itself, it is meaningless to ask whether the prayer requires attention."[48] It's as if we are reading an early version of Malebranche's claim that attention is "natural prayer," except that instead of "natural" de Soto speaks of "mental." This isn't an accident, and if we now go back to de Soto's source, Thomas Aquinas's discussion of devotional attention in the *Summa Theologiæ*, we will understand both the relationship between "natural" and "mental" prayer, and the reason de Soto and others insist on the role of attention in silent prayer.

In what is probably the most extensive discussion of attention's role in devotion, Aquinas confronts the question head on: "Is attention necessary for prayer?"[49] The first three considerations suggest that prayer, indeed, requires attention: prayer cannot be "in spirit" if it is not attentive; prayer cannot be an ascent of mind to God if it is not attentive; and prayer is sinful if the mind wanders away with the words of the prayer.[50] After these initial considerations, however, Aquinas decides that attention is in fact *not* absolutely necessary for prayer, indeed, if it were necessary, we could never pray efficaciously: "Because of the weakness of human nature, the human mind cannot long remain aloft, and thus by the weight of human weakness the soul is brought down to the level of inferior things. Thus, when the mind of one praying ascends to God in contemplation, it quickly wanders because of weakness (2a2æ. 83, 13).[51] In Aquinas's view, fallen human nature is simply not capable, and thus cannot be expected, to maintain the kind of attention that meritorious prayer would seem to require. This, of course, suggests not so much that attention is not necessary, but that it is not possible. Specifically, what Aquinas doubts is that human attention would be capable of *sustained voluntary* attention for the duration of an entire *vocal* prayer. It is the *oratio vocalis* that raises the question of how is one to attend to the words and their meanings as they address God throughout the entire temporal duration of prayer; and Aquinas's view is that such sustained attention is not possible and therefore cannot be required.

What complicates this summary is that Aquinas's discussion of attention in vocal prayer is preceded by another section on prayer, a section in which Aquinas addresses the prior and more fundamental question of whether prayer should be vocal at all. In this section, Aquinas makes a rather different claim about the relationship between attention and prayer. Since God doesn't need the medium of language to hear our prayers, vocal prayer would seem unnecessary. Nevertheless, Aquinas argues that vocal prayer may be useful under two conditions. First, in the case of public prayers it may stir devotion in those who witness the prayer (though, he adds, one should not pray in order to be seen by others). Second, using words in private prayer may have the potential benefit of stirring up one's own devotion:

> Individual prayer need not be vocal, yet the voice is sometimes used in this prayer . . . in order to excite interior devotion whereby the mind of the person praying is raised to God, because through external signs, whether words or deeds, the man's mind is moved to apprehend and consequently to desire. Hence, Augustine says that by *means of words and other signs we arouse ourselves more effectively to an increase of holy desire.* Hence, in individual prayer words and other signs should be used in so far as they help to arouse the mind internally. (2æ2a. 83, 12)[52]

This is a statement that speaks to the period's view about the role of exercise in devotion. Based on the Aristotelian notion of *habitus,* it understands religious practice as a way of conditioning the worshipper's inner devotion. Indeed, this is the view whose traces Ramie Targoff discovers in the devotional writings of the early modern Church of England. But Aquinas adds a qualification: "If these signs impede or distract the mind, as often happens in those whose mind is sufficiently prepared for devotion without signs, they should not be used."[53] This is a crucial comment because it sheds light on the hierarchical relationship between vocal and silent prayer, and thus on attention's role in both. Vocal prayer is allowed insofar as the words it employs do not distract, by their sound or meaning, the mind from devotion; insofar as it serves as preparation for this "devotion without signs." In other words, vocal prayer is subordinated to the purposes of mental prayer, which Aquinas considers a purer mode of devotion. This explains why, when in the subsequent section on attention Aquinas finally addresses the question of attention's objects, he says at least one kind of attention *is* in fact necessary for prayer: "Three kinds of attention are possible in prayer. One kind attends to words, lest one err in pronouncing them, a second attends to the sense of the words, and the third attends to the end of the prayer, namely to God, and to the thing for which we are praying. This last kind of attention is most necessary and even the weak-minded are capable of having it."[54] The distinction operating in this passage is what later theologians label as one between material, literal, and spiritual attentions. Aquinas suggests that even in vocal prayer, spiritual attention, the attention to "God and to the things for which we are praying," is in fact necessary. At the same time, material attention to the sound of words and literal attention to the meaning of words are necessary only insofar as they support this last kind of attention, which is both the most necessary and the most possible, so that "even the weak-minded are capable of having it." What distinguishes this last type of attention from the previous two is of course the fact that it is supposed to attend to someone or something absent: "to God, and to the thing for which we are praying." In other words, Aquinas's point is that voluntary attention to the words of one's prayer is not necessary for prayer's efficacy, but a different, *intransitive* attention whose object is not present to the senses (either because it is a transcendent being, "God," or because it is a future object or event, "the thing for which we are praying") is. Insofar as mental prayer is the most direct, most immediate turn to God, vocal prayer ought to serve its purposes; and insofar as mental prayer is an act of attention, it is the goal that even the potentially distracted acts of vocal prayer are supposed to pursue. The effort of attention that is mental prayer is both the easiest and the highest kind of prayer; the easiest insofar as even the "weak-minded are capable of having it," and the highest insofar as it means attending "to God, and to the thing for which we are praying."

Aquinas's discussion is helpful not only in clarifying the relationship between vocal and mental prayer but also in shedding light on the distinction between attention and intention. Even in mental prayer, attention cannot be long sustained, Aquinas argues. To use a later scholastic distinction, *actual* attention that is sustained at every moment of prayer is not required. What is necessary is a kind of attention that is either virtual or habitual: "To realize this effect [of merit], attention throughout prayer is not required, because the force of the original intention [*vis primæ intentionis*] with which one begins prayer renders the whole prayer meritorious."[55] Sustained actual attention is not required in prayer; but what is necessary is a first, voluntary application of the mind to the prayer's end. As long as this original act of attention, which Aquinas repeatedly calls *intentio,* is not willfully revoked later, it makes the prayer meritorious. Sustained attention to the words of the prayer is neither possible nor necessary for prayer, although it can serve as a preparation for genuine prayer. But this genuine prayer consists in a single, concentrated act of attention.

The distinction has to do, of course, with the discrepancy between human and divine temporality in Christianity: the temporal unfolding that the words of the prayer require is irrelevant for the eternal being that is God. Therefore what this eternal being requires is not attention throughout the prayer, but a single original act of attention, an "intention." What Aquinas calls "intention" in these passages is simultaneously an act of resolution to turn to God and the turn itself; indeed, the "undistracted turn to God" consists in the very resolution to do so. In this sense, "intention" is an act of will. But it has little to do with sincerity as a psychological affect; it is instead an act of attention and it cannot be understood without the notion of a holy attention because genuinely *intending* something implies *attending* to the purpose that God has chosen for the individual. Making a devotional decision, in this sense, is finding out what has already been decided. Like the two senses of *inventio,* intending and attending are the two facets of the same act.[56] The transient and intransitive attention gathered in the initial intention of prayer does not make prayer efficacious, and it does not force God to listen to and respond to one's petitions. But according to Aquinas, it is necessary for prayer's success in creating at least the possibility of prayer successfully addressing God.

"THE FIRST RISING"

If intransitive attention is at least one of the conditions of efficacious prayer, what purpose do words serve in prayer? Obviously, this is a crucial question for any discussion of *oratio vocalis,* and an even more urgent problem for the question of devotional poetry. As we have seen in Aquinas's discussion, words might contribute to prayer insofar as they stir up the devotions of the praying subject, or when they help convey a devotional example to others. Yet on a more fundamental level, they pose a risk: if prayer as such requires an initial act of undistracted, voluntary, intransitive attention, then the emergence of words threatens to dissolve and scatter this initial act of attention. In the next chapter, I will look more closely at how this challenge is taken up by Donne in the practice of poetry. Before doing so, however, I want to show that Donne grappled with this very problem in conceptual terms as well. My point isn't about reception history. Donne was certainly familiar with Aquinas and even with de Soto; however, the goal of this concluding section of the chapter isn't to argue for influence but to show that the problem both Aquinas and Donne tried to articulate was more fundamental than the theological disputes that define confessional differences would allow us to see.[57] In the context of a seemingly casual letter to his friend Henry Goodyer, Donne offers a brilliant and remarkably precise discussion of how thanksgiving, prayer, attention, and words relate to one another.[58]

As in many of his forty-eight letters to Goodyer, Donne begins with an *in medias res* meditation on letter writing and friendship.[59] According to the testimony of his letters, Donne was fascinated with both questions, but I would argue that above all he was invested in what letters and friendship had in common. Comparable to the way that sexual intercourse in the *Songs and Sonets* articulates both the self's boundaries and the openings on these boundaries, the idea of two friends exchanging letters allows Donne to think time and again about the question of what might carry the self beyond its limits, how the self might transcend itself.

In this particular letter, the general theme of the self's potential to go out of itself is discussed in the particular context of grace and prayer. In the opening sentences, letter writing itself is discussed in terms that recall the context of prestation gift against which grace is defined:[60]

> I send not my Letters as tribute, nor interest, not recompense, nor for
> commerce, nor as testimonials of my love, nor provokers of yours, nor to
> justifie my custome of writing, nor for a vent and utterance of my medita-
> tions; for my Letters are either above or under all such offices; yet I write
> very affectionately, and I chide and accuse my self of diminishing that
> affection which sends them, when I ask my self why: onely I am sure that
> I desire that you might have in your hands Letters of mine of all kindes,
> as conveyances and deliverers of me to you, whether you accept me as a
> friend, or as a patient, or as a penitent, or as a beadsman, for I decline no
> jurisdiction, or refuse any tenure.[61]

In chapter 2, I noted Donne's refusal to allow his poetry to enter the circulation in which both monetary units and prestation gifts participate. Something similar is being emphasized in this passage. The first few lines, driven
by an ecstasy in which negative grammar turns into a negation of the self,
accumulate these negations to preempt thinking about the letter in terms of
a gift that might require any sort of reciprocation. In this systematic decon-
struction of the idea that writing a letter is part of an exchange, letters first
seem to be reduced to nothing at all; the letter is *not* something, *nor* something else. But just when letters would seem to be reduced to this nothing,
they also emerge as intended to be everything that a person might be able
to give—that is, they appear as gestures that deliver the person in all his
personae to the other. A letter, in this presentation, is a gift whose integrity
is guaranteed by the sender's intention to be fully given over to the other.

Despite being depicted as a free, non-prestation gift, the letter does
contain a kind of request to be reciprocated; it invites the kind of giving
that it performs. But this invitation is different from the demand that gift
exchange can imply. Both letters and friendship belong to the circulation
of that special kind of gift which is called grace, and which is defined by its
resistance to the regular circulation of the gift. In the three sentences that
follow, friendship is figured as a matter of grace, this time in the sense of a
gift that demands a kind of waiting that is without expectation: "I would not
open any doore upon you, but look in when you open it. Angels have not,
nor affect not other knowledge of one another, then they lift to reveal to one
another. It is then in this onely, that friends are Angels, that they are capable
and fit for such revelations when they are offered."[62] Knowing one's friend is
entirely at the discretion of the friend; to be friends with someone is to be
waiting for the other's grace of revealing himself for one's "capable and fit"
attention. Conceived in terms of grace, the idea of friendship introduces a

distinction between two modes of attending: the old theological sin of the kind of *curiositas* that brought about the fall of the first human couple on the one hand, and the intent waiting, that is, the attentive *vigilantia* that characterizes the ascetic concept of prayer on the other. The first, curious attending led to the fall from grace; the second, patient but vigilant attending is the condition of asking for grace, the condition for regaining grace.

Indeed, as the reference to angels already indicates, in the rest of the letter Donne is moving away from the issues of letters and friends, and toward the theologically motivated, but not exclusively theological question of how to ask for grace; of how to pray. Even if a kind of attention that resembles *curiositas* appears in friendship, it is in the service of the higher order action of prayer. In the next sentence, Donne fashions himself as Goodyer's beadsman: "If at any time I seem to studie you more inquisitively, it is for no other end but to know how to present you to God in my prayers, and what to ask of him for you; for even that holy exercise may not be done inopportunely, no nor importunely."[63] Early modern typologies of prayer oftentimes began with a twofold distinction: prayer as petition and as thanksgiving. The first kind of prayer, petition, is a general category itself that includes three types of petition; Lancelot Andrewes calls these "precation" (petition for a benefit), "deprecation" (or "removal of some evil"), and "intercession" (which is essentially a petition for a benefit for someone other than the petitioner).[64] Yet what is distinguished in theory may appear indistinguishable in cultural and religious practice. Even as he turns from the matters of letter writing and friendship to the issue of intercession, Donne remains interested in all these actions insofar as they are instances of *gratiarum actio* in the broadest sense, as action of grace. Actions of grace are actions that can reach completion only in and by an agent who is transcendent to the self; letter writing, friendship, and prayers for grace are all such openings toward someone else. What Donne is mainly concerned with is the "opportune" way of performing such a *gratiarum actio* (as I noted in chap. 2, opportunity is a term that translates the Greek *kairos*). While *curiositas* is inquisitive attention that is driven by the expectation of a gift, the vigilant attention that is associated with *gratiarum actio* is a receptivity that allows one to find that which is given to it by someone else (a door is opened and a revelation is provided by an other, be it an angel or a friend). How such vigilant attention works, and how prayer might be performed "opportunely" are thus related issues, and together they constitute Donne's main concern in the rest of letter.

That these issues are not exclusively Christian receives emphasis early in the letter when Donne's first survey of how to ask "opportunely" finds

Greek examples. We saw that in the sermon on Psalm 6, Donne emphasized that "even naturall and morall men," that is, even non-Christians
and particularly the ancient Greeks and Romans, are "acquainted with the
duty of gratitude, of thanksgiving."[65] This time the Greeks are called on as
witnesses to the difficulty of asking: "I finde little errour in that Grecians
counsell, who saies, If thou ask any thing of God, offer no sacrifice, nor ask
elegantly, nor vehemently, but remember that thou wouldest not give to
such an asker: Nor in his other Countriman, who affirms sacrifice of blood
to be so unproportionable to God, that perfumes, though much more spirituall, are too grosse."[66] Throughout Donne's transhistorical train of thought
that leads from Erasmian epistolary exercises to Senecan meditations about
friendship as the site of grace and to Greek views about prayer, the form of
his discourse is apophatic.[67] Letter writing is "neither tribute nor recom-
pense"; prayer ought to be neither elegant nor vehement; and for an address
to God, the burning of incense is as inadequate as blood sacrifice itself.
Even the concept of the "opportune" can only make an appearance by virtue
of a double negation: the "holy exercise may not be done inopportunely,
no nor importunely." Donne's insistence on apophasis in describing or at
least circumscribing the right way of asking for grace emphasizes that aspect of *gratiarum actio* that I called patient but vigilant attention: the action of asking as a non-action, a way of turning even the seemingly passive
but nevertheless active attention of *curiositas* into an attentive receptivity to
something or someone else. This chain of apophatic statements eventually
leads to the non-apophatic statement of the ultimate *gratiarum actio*: "And
that advantage of nearer familiarity with God, which the act of incarnation gave us, is grounded upon Gods assuming us, not our going to him."[68]
Christ as the incarnate God is *charis anti charitos,* grace upon grace (John 1:16),
and this grace upon grace is here referred to as God's own act of making
friends with mankind. This divine act of grace is both the foundation and
the paradigm for the human act of asking for grace: "And, our accesses to
his presence are but his descents into us; and when we get any thing by
prayer, he gave us before hand the thing and the petition."[69] What is essential to all actions of grace, that they can only be completed by another
agent, becomes a manifest paradox in the Christian context. Divine grace is
not merely a completion of the act of asking for grace by another agent; it is
the foundation of the very act itself; and indeed the act of asking for grace,
insofar as it is "opportune," is already the gift itself.[70] But what does being
"opportune" mean for this paradoxical act?

Donne seems to approach the question of devotional opportunity, or what I called in chapter 2 the kairotic locus of thanksgiving, in the traditional terms of an "opportune" time for devotion in the liturgical sense. He admits the significance of the "canonique hours," the rite that devises a systematic correspondence between devotion and the passing of time, thus making the experience of time and devotion mutually dependent on each other. But the liturgical instructions of the Book of Common Prayer do not offer a solution for that broader question of "opportune" time for prayer that springs from the discrepancy between human temporality and divine eternity. A successful prayer is successful even before it begins precisely because its success lies not in the temporal action of the person who prays but in the eternal divine grace that has granted its success. In order for a prayer to be "opportune," this discrepancy between human time and divine timelessness must be somehow surpassed. Donne's first suggestion in this direction erases the theological distinction between prayer and thanksgiving:[71]

> I am farre from dehorting those fixed devotions: But I had rather it were bestowed upon thanksgiving then petition, upon praise then prayer; not that God is indeared by that, or wearied by this; all is one in the receiver, but not in the sender: and thanks doth both offices; for, nothing doth so innocently provoke new graces, as gratitude.[72]

If God is neither "indeared" nor "wearied" by petitions and thanksgivings, why does Donne attribute both here and in the sermon on Psalm 6 more significance to thanksgiving than to prayer? The notion that thanksgiving might be used as petition to "provoke new graces" is not uncommon in the early modern Protestant devotional literature.[73] But in Donne's letter, it receives a particular emphasis: thanksgiving appears as an attempt to transcend secular temporality from within the practice of devotion. It is a devotional act that aims to reunify that which is always-already unified in the "receiver" (that is, in an eternal divinity) but is fragmented by secular temporality within the petitioner. In this sense, thanksgiving is both the highest manifestation of devotional praxis, and at the same time an audacious trick, a human invention that attempts to transcend the very conditions of any human activity by mimicking the paradox of grace, by creating a self-simultaneity that parallels that eternity of grace.

But though thanksgiving in this sense has primacy over other devotional actions in addressing God, it still faces the challenge of being

performed "not inopportunely." It still has to find the locus within time
from where it could speak to the divine that dwells outside of time. Above
I suggested that for Aquinas, as for many other medieval and early modern
theologians, this problem was deeply intertwined with the matter of language. Aquinas follows an older tradition when he distinguishes between
silent and vocal prayer, between *oratio mentis* and *oratio vocalis*. He then
dedicates a separate section to the latter, because it is mainly the vocal
prayer, the prayer that uses sounds and words, that raises the question of
temporality and thus the question of distraction. As soon as prayer is uttered, the devotional act becomes an entity within time and space; it gains
a body, a *res extensa,* a thing that extends in time and space. And as soon as
prayer becomes a *res extensa,* it becomes an entity that carries in itself the
possibility of distraction as bodies carry their weight: "I would also make
short prayers then extend them, though God can neither be surprised, nor
besieged: for, long prayers have more of the man, as ambition of eloquence,
and complacencie in the work, and more of the Devil by often distractions:
for, after in the beginning we have well intreated God to hearken, we speak
no more to him."[74] One should not mistake "shortness" as a devotional virtue for mere temporal brevity. Even if in practice Donne agrees with the
theological tradition that advises concision in devotion, behind this tradition there is a view that places the ideal prayer in the realm of pure potentiality. Aquinas called this potentiality "intention"; intention was his word for
that concentration of attention that transcends the temporal distractions of
the speech act of prayer by preceding it. Donne characterizes this "intention" as the "first rising" of prayerful thought or language:

> Yea words which are our subtillest and delicatest outward creatures, be-
> ing composed of thoughts and breath, are so muddie, so thick, that our
> thoughts themselves are so, because (except at the first rising) they are
> ever leavened with passions and affections.[75]

It is telling that the very sentence that points out the "inopportune or im-
portune" character of human language for *gratiarum actio* is itself a set of
hypotaxes that are on the verge of breaking down and giving in to a paratactic equilibrium. Even the seemingly weightless words are too heavy to reach
up to God; even the thoughts themselves are infected by the gravity of time.
The only moment that is protected by a parenthesis in this chaos of a sentence (and one recalls that Donne once called human temporality itself a
"parenthesis in eternity") is the exception, the sole exception of the "first

rising."[76] This first rising is vigilant attention in the most literal sense: it is the turn toward God, vocally or silently, in its very first moment of coming into being; a moment of wakening attention that cannot yet be distracted because it has no extension at all. Indeed, readers of Donne recognize this "first rising" in all of Donne's poetry, from the *Songs and Sonets* to the *Holy Sonnets,* so many of which begin in a key of awakening, where language is at its freshest, at its most tender moment. Where could one go from this beginning? In the letter, Donne ends by contrasting attentive intention with distracted extension:

> Even this Letter is some example of such infirmitie, which being *intended* for a Letter, is *extended* and strayed into a Homilie. And whatsoever is not what it was purposed, is worse; therefore it shall at last end like a Letter by assuring you I am—[77]

If this and the previous paragraph may be taken as Donne's view on the matter, he indeed comes close to Aquinas's position: since actions of grace are exposed to human distraction when they enter temporality, they need to be kept brief, not so much in the sense of taking up little space and time, but in the more radical sense of being limited to the intention of the agent. It is only in the concentrated attention within the intention of the agent that an action of grace may exist, in that timeless moment that fades away as soon as the action would appear to take place in the world of time and space. If Donne left the letter unfinished on purpose, the irony is palpable: since the execution is necessarily thwarted by distraction, the writing of the letter as a *gratiarum actio* is here "completed" by being left incomplete, by returning to the beginning, by creating a circle, but a circle with an opening. If thanksgiving is a human invention that tries to imitate the circularity of divine attention by thanking for that which it also asks for, Donne's letter plays with the same sense of translating the self-simultaneity of eternity into the self-simultaneity of a linguistic utterance that breaks down so that it can return to its own beginning.

4

ATTENTION EXERCISES

But the attentive man
Saw the face of God.

Friedrich Hölderlin, *Patmos*[1]

The preoccupation with technique is already the effect
of what it opposes. Unbeknownst even to some of its
promoters, the creation of mental constructs (imaginary
compositions, mental voids, etc.) takes the place of attention
to the advent of the Unpredictable.

Michel Certeau[2]

AS A TURNING OF ONE'S ATTENTION to God, vocal prayer's challenge is that the very words it contains threaten to scatter the attention that may have existed in the original intention to pray. This is the threat Donne articulates in his letter to Goodyer, and this is the challenge he seeks to outmaneuver when instead of completing the letter he circles back to its beginning. The starting point of this chapter is the admission that this problem isn't exclusive to vocal prayer but pertains to devotional poetry as well. In fact, it is even more acute there because in poems language is deployed in ways that tend to call attention to itself (when Aristotle in the *Rhetoric* warns against using poetic language in orations, his argument is that rhymes distract the audience's attention from the orator's rhetorical proofs).[3] This raises the question: what is attention's role in devotional poetry? Is attention nevertheless a condition of the devotional poem's success? Does it have any role in poetry at all?

The key to answering this question is the recognition of the degree to which vocal prayer and indeed a wide range of devotional practices from meditation to spiritual exercises are preparations of attention for silent prayer. At first, this might sound counterintuitive, for two reasons. First, in the previous chapter we saw that silent prayer's attention was characterized by Aquinas as easy or natural so that even "the weak-minded are capable of having it." Second, *oratio mentis* itself is often associated with meditations and spiritual exercises. The answer to both of these objections lies in the distinction between silent prayer in general and a specific subcategory of silent prayer, the so-called pure prayer, in particular. While the defining element of silent prayer (including meditations) is the absence of vocalization, the most radical ideals of pure prayer demand stripping one's attention from all objects, including vocalized or mental words, physical or visualized images, and even abstract thoughts.[4] This ideal of pure prayer is where the notion of a holy attention first emerges. However, perfect prayer is a contentious ideal, and throughout its vexed history it has often been relegated to the margins of Christian orthodoxy along with other Platonizing conceptions of devotion. My interest in this chapter isn't in tracing it in mystical or heterodox practices, but in understanding how this seemingly radical ideal has influenced rather more mundane forms of devotion, including vocal prayer. To put it bluntly, I am interested in how pure prayer and its ideal of a holy attention may help us explain why one is expected to be attentive in prayer at all, which in turn will be essential to assessing attention's role in devotional poetry. This is why in this chapter I don't follow a linear chronology but go back and forth between late antique and medieval asceticism and monasticism, on the one hand, and early modern Protestant and Catholic discussions, on the other. In the first section, I show how Donne's rather skeptical discussion of attention in prayer relies on ascetic assumptions about spiritual perfection. In the second section, I look at early modern revivals of the ascetic ideal of holy attention. In the third and fourth sections I return to Donne's Holy Sonnet "This is my Playes last Scene" to show the degree to which Donne's poem follows early modern models of attention exercises—and to point out how it also departs from them.

HOLY ATTENTION

In one of his funeral sermons, Donne describes the difficulties of concentrating in prayer:

But when we consider with a religious seriousnesse the manifold weak-
nesses of the strongest devotions in time of Prayer, it is a sad consideration. I throw myself downe in my Chamber, and I call in, and invite God,
and his Angels thither, and when they are there, I neglect God and his
Angels, for the noise of a Flie, for the ratling of a Coach, for the whin-
ing of a doore; I talke on, in the same posture of praying; Eyes lifted up;
knees bowed downe; as though I prayed to God; and, if God, or his Angels
should ask me, when I thought last of God in my prayer, I cannot tell:
Sometimes I find that I forgot what I was about, but when I began to forget
it, I cannot tell. A memory of yesterdays pleasure, a feare of tomorrows
dangers, a straw under my knee, a noise in mine eare, a light in mine eye,
an any thing, a nothing, a fancy, a Chimera in my braine, troubles me in
my prayer. So certainly is there nothing, nothing in spirituall things,
perfect in this world.[5]

The passage comes as the denouement of an argument that Donne develops to show that no act of prayer can be considered perfect in itself. In
the course of making this point, he first discusses two supposedly "heretic"
approaches to prayer: one is taken by the "Cathari" (that is, the Cathars),
who "thought themselves so pure, as they needed no forgivenesse," and the
other by the Catholic Church, which makes "merchandise of prayers by way
of exchange." The "heresy" these two views share in common is the attribu-
tion of too much power to human agency. The Cathars believe that spiritual
perfection is humanly possible, and that once it is achieved, the individual
is no longer in need of divine grace. Meanwhile, the Roman Catholics believe that prayer is a *quid pro quo* between the individual and God, as if the
actions of humans and the divine were comparable. But having dismissed
these two views, Donne proceeds to argue that even those who pray with
the "strongest devotions in time of Prayer" are bound to fail. The last illusion of spiritual perfection is the illusion that a completely undistracted act
of prayer is possible. The passage explains why such prayer is in fact impossible: no matter how determined one is to focus on prayer, the distractions
are so manifold—coming from past, present, and future—and so powerful, that the original intention to focus on the prayer and on God melts
away and the mind finds itself scattered among its many engagements with
the world.

To emphasize the inescapability of distraction, Donne focuses on the
mundane: "A memory of yesterdays pleasure, a feare of tomorrows dangers, a straw under my knee, a noise in mine eare, a light in mine eye, an

any thing, a nothing, a fancy, a Chimera in my braine." Removed from the noise of the world into a "Chamber," one becomes all the more vulnerable to even the slightest of distractions conveyed by the body or produced by the mind itself. The experience is frequently addressed in early modern devotional handbooks and manuals of prayer, which themselves echo late antique and medieval discussions of the distractions the monks battle in their everyday practices. Donne argues that the inevitability and therefore familiarity of distraction in prayer shows that perfection in devotion is beyond the power of human creatures. The silent yet crucial assumption behind this argument, however, is anything but mundane: it suggests that if one *were* able to get rid of all distractions, one would or at least could achieve spiritual perfection.

This assumption depends on a notion we would not expect to appear in a Protestant sermon: the idea of a holy, perfectly undistracted attention in what is sometimes called pure prayer (*pura oratio*). In its most direct positive formulations, the idea of holy attention suggests that in leaving behind all distractions one finds oneself capable of knowing God and becoming god-like.[6] The idea haunts Christianity for a long time, censured time and again and yet recurring in contexts as different as the hesychasm of the Eastern Orthodox and Catholic traditions or the French quietist movement in the seventeenth century. Indeed, its influence expands beyond the boundaries of religion, as illustrated for instance by Hölderlin's *Patmos,* which I quoted in one of the epigraphs to this chapter. But for the origins and the most explicit articulations of the concept of a pure, holy attention, we have to go back to the early centuries of Christianity. The idea of a holy attention first emerges in the period bookended by two authors in particular, the Church Father and theologian Clement of Alexandria, who worked at the end of the second and the beginning of the third century, and the Christian theologian-turned-monk Evagrius of Pontus, who lived in the second half of the fourth century.

Both Clement and Evagrius posit attention as a condition of pure prayer. For both of them, however, prayer is a broad category encompassing far more than just concrete speech acts addressed to God. First of all, prayer is theology (and theology is prayer) insofar as prayer's ultimate goal is to know God in the act of *gnōsis*.[7] Second, in this striving to know God, prayer isn't a discrete act. In the chapters on prayer in the *Strōmateis,* Clement describes the gnostic as someone who, following the Pauline admonition from 1 Thessalonians 5:17, prays unceasingly and transforms his entire life into an act of prayer.[8] This lifelong, unceasing striving to know God by addressing and praising him in prayer is what Clement describes as the Christian's "undistracted turning to God."[9]

The definition of prayer as "undistracted turn to God" bears out Greek and Latin philosophical influences in two ways. The notion of attention as stretching toward is indebted to Pythagorean and Stoic notions of tone (*tonos*), in the sense of a stretched-out cord that resonates in response to its environment.[10] For the Stoics, this notion of *tonos* was akin to what we might call an ontological principle; from the human being to the physical universe itself, entities were seen to work according to the principles of tonal movement.[11] (A Christian echo of this idea appears in *The Merchant of Venice* when Lorenzo claims that Jessica's melancholy response to music is in fact a sign that "your spirits are attentive," a comment that follows directly upon his request that Jessica "listen" to the music of the spheres and therefore means, in this context, that the now Christian Jessica's soul is attuned to the harmony of creation).[12] Second, the notion of *prosochē* (attention or attentiveness) emerged in Stoic philosophy as an ethical value, a condition of good life. It implies a disposition, a constant vigilance, rather than attention to something concrete. Stoic meditative exercises such as Marcus Aurelius's *Meditations* are in part exercises to cultivate this virtue of attentiveness.[13] Both the ontological and the ethical notions of attention are crucial for understanding the idea of undistraction that informs Clement's definition of prayer. Behind this definition, there is an understanding of human beings as beings whose ontological condition is a tending-toward, a being stretched-toward. Attention in this sense is not a human faculty, nor something that humans do; it is a modality of human existence.[14] Clement's account suggests that the essence of Christian devotion consists in the act of directing one's entire being toward God, which God in turn rewards with the gift of increased attention.[15] His account replaces the Stoic ethical concept of *prosochē* with a fundamentally different, religious concept: attentiveness as the undistracted turn to God is not, in this religious conception, a virtue that serves as the condition of the good life. It is, rather, both the condition and the reward of one's devotion to God.[16]

Neither Clement nor Evagrius suggests that this striving toward God will necessarily lead to knowing God. The telos of prayer is instead the condition they describe with the term *apatheia*. Today *apatheia* is familiar mostly as the Stoic ideal of being free of all passions.[17] While this definition is relevant for the *Strōmateis,* in Clement's conception of gnostic prayer *apatheia* appears in a broader sense as freedom not only from the passions but from all distractions, from any aspect of the world that would hinder

the turn to God. The Desert Fathers in the third and fourth centuries inherit this conception, and when in the late fourth century Evagrius system-
atizes their ascetic teachings, he describes *apatheia* as freedom from all
"images."[18] What first appears as a form of iconoclasm, however, is in fact
an emphasis on attentiveness. For Evagrius, devotion is a progressive teleological movement that begins with a turning away from the world in
order to withdraw into oneself. Once the distractions of the world are shut
out, the monk encounters a new set of challenges: his own memories and
expectations that revive the world and its distractions within the monk's
mind. With further work and experience the monk may acquire the habits that help him overcome these inner distractions. But if he succeeds, he
may face another challenge: thoughts that might seem to come from God.
Apatheia is the state that prepares the monk for this last set of distractions.
For Evagrius, it is a state in which the monk is free not only from all perceptions of the world, not even just from all memories and expectations but
also from any and all thoughts. And yet this state of perfect prayer, while
it is without thoughts and thus without distractions, isn't without thinking.
On the contrary: "Undistracted prayer is the mind's highest intellection."[19]
Apatheia isn't equivalent with knowing God; it is, however, the closest the
monk can get to preparing himself for attending on the possibility of God
making himself known to him.

If we now return for a moment to Donne's sermon, we can see how
the ascetic ideal of a holy attention is implied in Donne's argument: even
as Donne argues against the possibility of perfect spirituality, he does so
by relying on the ascetic idea that a perfectly undistracted, holy attention
would result in perfect devotion. In this sense, the ascetic ideal of a perfect
attentiveness haunts Donne's account. At the same time, we must remember that Donne's purpose in this passage is to emphasize the *impossibility* of
either pure attention or spiritual perfection. In so doing, Donne echoes the
critique that Protestant Reformers often voiced against the ascetic ideal of
apatheia.[20] In fact, the critique itself goes back to much earlier precedents in
Christianity, and a brief look at the first contexts will help us see its original
motives. Soon after the Evagrian ideals became known in the West, they
came under severe criticism by some of the most influential theological and
devotional authors of the time, including Jerome and Augustine.[21] Jerome's
critique was particularly devastating because it implied *apatheia* in the Origenist and Pelagian controversies of the period. In a famous letter, Jerome
argued that Evagrius's ideal of *apatheia* means that the monk would have to
become either a stone or God.[22] The problem with impassibility for Jerome

was that it suggested that man could overcome his fallen nature and thus his need of grace already in this life. In the *Confessions,* Augustine articulates a less explicit but more sophisticated philosophical and devotional critique that doesn't focus on *apatheia* as emotional indifference but on pure attention. The details of Augustine's critique are too complex and important to be treated here, and I will return to them in chapter 6. For now, in order to give a sense of their historical impact, let me focus on how Augustine's analysis agrees with Jerome's objections by denying the possibility of a perfectly undistracted attention in life. The core insight of Augustine's account is that in the logic of human attention, it's the discrete acts of attention that are responsible for the continuous accumulation of distraction—the more we attend to something, the more we are distracted from everything else, and the more the self becomes scattered in the world. For this reason, while acts of attending contain vestiges of a perfect spiritual existence, they also reveal man's irreducibly fallen nature.[23] This skeptical view about the possibility of a pure, holy attention is what Donne echoes in his sermon.

ATTENTION EXERCISES

Despite the Protestant reformers' distaste for ideals of spiritual perfection, and despite the widely embraced Augustinian *skepsis* about fully avoiding distraction in prayer, exhortations to attentiveness are pervasive in the early modern period. In the previous chapter, we saw how earlier theologians including Aquinas held ambivalent views about whether attention was necessary in prayer. No such ambivalence appears in the devotional literature of the post-Reformation era. Catholic and Protestant authors are alike in tirelessly urging their audiences to be vigilant in their devotions. Take, for instance, Luther's famous letter to his barber. Perhaps the most poignant passage of the letter is when Luther uses the barber's own trade as an example to highlight the importance of attention in prayer:

> It seems to me that if someone could see what arises as prayer from a cold and unattentive heart he would conclude that he had never seen a more ridiculous kind of buffoonery. But, praise God, it is now clear to me that a person who forgets what he has said has not prayed well. In a good prayer one fully remembers every word and thought from the beginning to the end of the prayer. So, a good and attentive barber keeps his

thoughts, attention, and eyes on the razor and hair and does not forget how far he has gotten with his shaving or cutting. If he wants to engage in too much conversation or let his mind wander or look somewhere else he is likely to cut his customer's mouth, nose, or even his throat. Thus if anything is to be done well, it requires the full attention of all one's senses and members, as the proverb says, "Pluribus intentus, minor est ad singula sensus"—"He who thinks of many things, thinks of nothing and does nothing right." How much more does prayer call for concentration and singleness of heart if it is to be a good prayer![24]

The somewhat sinister comparison aside (what would be the parallel of the customer's throat in prayer?), the goal of the letter is clear: Luther's purpose is to make the trade of prayer understandable and available to the layman. His comment about the necessity of remembering every word and thought of the prayer from beginning to end echoes traditional, pre-Reformation discussions of attention in prayer, the most famous of which is Augustine's in Book XI in the *Confessions*. Considering that many such traditional accounts conclude by dismissing the necessity of attention in prayer on theological and philosophical grounds, it is remarkable that in this rather less theoretical passage Luther insists on the importance of maintaining attention in devotion.[25]

Indeed, in stressing attention's devotional importance while omitting the theological complications around it, Luther's letter is typical of the ways in which sixteenth- and seventeenth-century Protestant discussions of devotion translate traditional and often complex views into laymen's terms. In discussing prayer in *Holy Living*, for instance, Jeremy Taylor recycles scholastic concepts of actual and habitual attention.[26] In a section titled "Remedies against wandring thoughts in prayer," he suggests that "when you have observed any considerable wandring of your thoughts, binde your self to repeat that prayer again with *actual* attention" (294, emphasis mine), and adds, "It helps much to attention and actual advertisement in our prayers, if we say our prayers silently, without voice, onely by the spirit. For in mental prayer, if our thoughts wanted, we onely stand still; when our minde returns, we go on again, there is none of the prayer lost, as it is, if our mouths speak and our hearts wander (295)." The stark contrast we noted in the previous chapter between vocal and silent prayer in terms of their requirements of attentiveness is here transformed into a practical distinction that allows the reader to see silent prayer simply as a better way of sustaining attention. Taylor's passage is indebted not only to scholastic typologies of devotional attention but also to discussions of distraction in monasticism. But Taylor's target audience is neither priests nor monks; *Holy Living* is addressed to lay people as well as to the clergy.

In fact, while in pre-Reformation discussions of attention tend to focus on private devotion, in the sixteenth and seventeenth centuries such discussions often included public devotion as well. For instance, when in mid-sixteenth-century England Protestants and Catholics debated whether the language of public devotion should be Latin or the vernacular, they were particularly concerned with the question of the churchgoers' attention. Protestant authors argued that holding the service in English would allow lay audiences to understand the meaning of what they heard and thereby support their attention to the service. A Catholic response objected that attention to the liturgy would be in fact detrimental because it would distract the audience from their private devotions during mass.[27] The implications of this debate for the sixteenth-century attitudes toward public devotion have been explored by others; for my purposes, it is sufficient to note how, while in these debates Catholics and Protestants disagreed about what the object of devotion should be, they shared an investment in attention itself as devotional common denominator.[28] In one of the most influential Catholic handbooks of prayer, Luis de Granada, an author Donne knew well, went so far as to suggest that attentive thinking rather than faith was the main challenge and therefore primary objective for post-Reformation Christianity:[29]

> Prayer (to define it properly) is a petition wee make unto almighty God, for such things as are appertayning to our salvation. Howbeit, prayer is also taken in another more large sense; to wit, for every lifting up of our heart unto God. And according to this definition, both Meditation and Contemplation, and every other good thought may be called Prayer. And in this sense we do now use the word, because the principal matter of this Booke, is of Meditation and Consideration of things appertaining to Almighty God, and of the principal mysteries of the Catholike faith. The very thing that moved me to treate of this matter, was for that I understood, that one of the principall causes of all the evils that be in this world, is the lack of Consideration; according as the Prophet Jeremy signified, when he said: All the earth is destroyed with desolation, because there is none that thinketh with attention upon the things appertaining unto God. Whereby it appeareth, that the very cause of our evils, is not so much the want of faith, as the want of due consideration of the mysteries of our faith.[30]

Granada's book is of course part of the counter-Reformation movement's attempt to respond to Protestantism on the level of individual devotional practices. Indeed, one might see in Granada's emphasis on attention a characteristically anxious Catholic response to the increasing decentralization of Christian religious life in Europe. Granada's description in which "all the earth is destroyed with desolation" is likely a Catholic vision of the fragmentation of Christianity, due, in Granada's view, to a lack of attention paid to those elements in Christianity that would keep it "Catholic" in the sense of being both universal and subject to the Church.[31] What in Granada's view would help recreate the lost unity is neither faith nor the knowledge of faith's objects; it is instead "the due consideration" of the mysteries of faith, as if the individual's recollection of his attention could somehow remedy the scattering of the church.[32] Granada relies here on an extraordinarily broad understanding of prayer, one that also includes meditation, contemplation, and spiritual exercises. It is in all of these acts of devotion, he suggests, that Christians should pay more attention to the very foundations of their faith; indeed, all of these acts *are* ways of paying attention to such foundations.

How do we explain that despite the post-Augustinian skepticism about perfect attentiveness, these accounts insist on the importance of attention in devotion? What are we supposed to make of the seeming tension between the theological pessimism about attention, on the one hand, and the devotional exhortations to attentiveness, on the other? To answer these questions, it is necessary to return briefly to the aftermath of Jerome's and Augustine's critiques of the Evagrian ideal of *apatheia* and pure prayer. The writings of John Cassian in particular help illustrate the two-sided development of theological marginalization and devotional integration. As the first major author of Western monasticism, Cassian was significantly influenced by Evagrian ideas, to the degree that some scholars see his *Conferences* and *Institutions* as milestones in Christian history precisely because these texts turn the Evagrian ideals into practical instructions, while upholding Jerome's and Augustine's objections.[33] Both *apatheia* and the Evagrian metaphysical underpinnings of the concept are missing from Cassian's texts: the devotional life of the monachos is no longer conceived of as a striving toward the actual and achievable telos of *apatheia* or toward the *gnōsis* of divine nature. At the same time, Cassian does not dispose of the ideal of ascetic attention but makes it an internal principle of monastic life—without implying that a perfectly undistracted, apathetic attention is possible for any monk to achieve. Take the opening pages of the *Conferences,* which focus on the question of what the true end of the monk's life is. The first answer is that the goal of monastic life is the kingdom of God. But at this point, Abbot Moses elaborates:

> The end of our profession indeed, as I said, is the kingdom of God or the kingdom of heaven: but the immediate aim or goal, is purity of heart, without which no one can gain that end: fixing our gaze then steadily on this goal as if on a definite mark, let us direct our course as straight towards it as possible, and if our thoughts wander somewhat from this, let us revert to our gaze upon it, and check them accurately as by a sure standard, which will always bring back all our efforts to this one mark, and will show at once if our mind has wandered ever so little from the direction marked out for it.[34]

It has been argued that what Cassian calls "purity of heart" is the equivalent of the Evagrian ideals of pure prayer and *apatheia*.[35] Even if there are similarities between the two ideals, the differences are just as striking. Monastic life is grounded in the renunciation of the world in the pursuit of godly life, and in this it resembles the Clementian "undistracted turning to God." But this initial turn away from the world is only the beginning of a lifelong battle against distractions. The complete lack of distraction that the Clementian and Evagrian ideas of *apatheia* suggest is in Cassian's account emphatically impossible: "To cling to God unceasingly and to remain inseparably united to him in contemplation is indeed, and as you say, impossible for the person who is enclosed in perishable flesh. But we ought to know where we should fix our mind's attention and to what goal we should always recall our soul's gaze."[36] The ascetic ideal of holy attention here becomes a regulative ideal of "purity of the heart": though unachievable, it is nevertheless an aspiration that the monk must follow in all of his actions.[37] By shifting emphasis from a general search for the kingdom of God to the problem of how to keep this telos of monastic life in focus, the *Conferences* effectively define the battle between attention and distraction as a central concern of monasticism. It is not in the power of the monk to eliminate distractions from his life, but it is a matter of his will to battle them when they come, and indeed to live a life that is a permanent cultivation of attention, a habitual rejection of any distraction.[38] In this sense monastic life is a continuous exercise in the art of attention: reading the Scriptures, saying one's prayers, or chanting psalms are all exercises in which attention is trained to hold onto an object in a sustained fashion. To put it schematically, while in Clement and Evagrius *apatheia* as intransitive attention is the real, achievable condition of the spiritual perfection, in Cassian's monastic model holy attention becomes a regulative ideal: it is a goal that is beyond the monk's reach, and yet a goal that influences all of the monk's activities, turning them into a continuous prayer in the specific sense of attention exercises.[39]

If we now return to early modern exhortations for attentiveness in prayer, it is useful to remember that the sixteenth- and seventeenth-century rallying of Christianity that we customarily divide into Protestant reformation and Catholic counter-reformation was in another sense a collective revival and popularization of devotional techniques formerly known to and practiced primarily by monks and the clergy. Moreover, this expansion of ascetic and monastic religious practices beyond the walls of churches and monasteries had gone back centuries before the Reformation; the *devotio moderna* movement in particular had its roots in the twelfth century.[40] The Reformation, in many ways a break with medieval Catholicism, was in this particular sense a continuation of reform movements that began within Catholic devotional life. The eradication of traditional forms of devotion, such as auricular confession, increased a sense of personal responsibility in one's religious life: a new demand for devotional technologies fostered the translation of ascetic and monastic ideals into more quotidian devotional goals. The early modern popularization of ascetic and monastic modes of devotion brought with it a new emphasis on holy attention. A key text in this development is Ignatius of Loyola's *Spiritual Exercises,* which entails an idea of attention as a regulative ideal of devotion.[41] Written to help lay people make a decision by seeking out God's will, Ignatius's book offers an experience of monastic life condensed into a month's time. The problem of attention lurks behind this premise: not only does the practitioner have to leave behind the distractions of the world to enter the exercises, but the very goal of the exercises is to free him of what Ignatius calls *affecciones desordenadas,* the distractions that stand in the way of recognizing God's will.[42]

Indeed, to understand how deep the affinity between the Ignatian exercises and the idea of holy attention runs, we need to look at the text's quiet but significant appropriation of the ascetic ideal of *apatheia.* Some context is necessary. Five years after the publication of the Latin *Exercitia spiritualia,* the Dominican theologian Tomás Pedroche launched an attack against Ignatius on the basis that the book contained heretical teachings. Pedroche's charges were serious because they alleged a similarity between Ignatius's use of the concept of indifference and the pronouncements of the Spanish *alumbrados,* a loose group of mystics in Spain.[43] The *alumbrados* had been condemned as heretics on the ground that they believed a perfectly sinless state and a union with God was possible for the believer.[44] Ignatius had already been accused of sympathizing with the *alumbrados* while he was studying in Salamanca.[45] Pedroche now claimed to have discovered one of the main tenets of the *alumbrados* within the *Spiritual Exercises:* he suggested that the principle of indifference implied in Annotation Fifteen was evidence for Ignatius's sympathy with the *alumbrados*'s notion of spiritual perfection.[46]

Pedroche's attempt to tie the Ignatian exercises to the heresy of perfect prayer eventually fell flat, not the least because of Jerónimo Nadal's *Apología,* in which Ignatius's disciple successfully defended the orthodoxy of the *Spiritual Exercises.*[47] Even today, Pedroche's criticism might appear either a misunderstanding or a deliberate misreading of the *Exercises.* Yet for the affinities that I am trying to highlight here, Pedroche's case is instructive because it sheds light on the connection that Loyola's contemporaries detected between the *Spiritual Exercises* and the traces of the ideal of holy attention. To understand this connection, we need to revisit the main object of Pedroche's criticism, the notorious fifteenth annotation. In the annotation, Ignatius offers a surprising recommendation to the spiritual director who oversees the exercitant: "The director of the Exercises ought not to urge the exercitant more to poverty or any promise than to the contrary, nor to one state of life or way of living more than to another."[48] A few reminders are in order here, both in order to understand this passage and to appreciate how unexpected the imperative it contains is within the context of the *Spiritual Exercises.* Ignatius's exercises aim at a concrete, practical goal: they are to help the exercitant make a decision. Although such a decision may be part of anyone's life in any given life situation, and thus Ignatius emphatically keeps the exercises open to virtually anyone, the paradigmatic case is when a young man of talent is about to decide whether entering the Society of Jesus is the right course of action for him. This is why it is surprising that at the very outset of the exercises Ignatius should discourage the director of the exercises not only from urging the exercitant to poverty but "to one state of life or way of living more than to another," including such fundamental Christian ascetic values as "continence, virginity, the religious life, and every form of religious perfection" (6). Why would urging the exercitant to make these choices be at odds with the ideal of decision? Why does Ignatius think that the exercitant should be *indifferent?*

Since the observation is about the director rather than the exercitant himself, we might assume that what is at stake is that the decision must be authentic in the sense of belonging to the exercitant. The decision cannot be made for the exercitant by someone else but by him alone; insofar as a decision is a matter of will, it should be only an act of the exercitant's own will. But this interpretation is based on a notion of authenticity that is fundamentally different from the one that is relevant to Ignatius's text. It is true that in this passage Ignatius wants to emphasize that the decision cannot belong to the director. But later in a parallel passage, one that first deploys the term "indifferent," he makes clear that the decision cannot really belong to the exercitant either: "I must be indifferent, without any inordinate attachment, so that I am not more inclined or disposed to accept the object in question than to relinquish it, nor to give it up than to accept it" (75). The principle of indifference that connects these two passages is central to the conception of the *Spiritual Exercises*.[49] It suggests that alongside the director of the exercises and the exercises themselves, even the exercitant is only an instrument in the process because the will that the decision belongs to isn't ultimately his but God's. Insofar as the exercises are to prepare the individual for making a decision, the preparation they contain is about making the exercitant capable of recognizing the divine will. This is why Ignatius consistently describes the self as an instrument and the task of the exercises as an act of calibrating this instrument as precisely as possible.[50] The model that Ignatius develops is one in which the director and the exercitant work together to achieve a state of mind that suspends all of its "attachments"— word that Ignatius uses as an umbrella term to include any preexisting motive that could influence the decision—be they intellectual preconceptions or emotional inclinations. The *Spiritual Exercises* offer a method of tuning the exercitant's attention in order to help him leave behind all potential and actual distractions so that he can attend to what should be the sole factor of his decision: the divine will concerning any matter.

At this point, we may begin to realize that Ignatius's concept of indifference is indebted to the ascetic notion of *apatheia,* and perhaps we will even start to understand why Pedroche might have associated Annotation Fifteen with the heresy of perfect prayer. To be sure, one might object (as Nadal did) that indifference is not the ultimate goal of the exercises. Ignatius himself is careful to demarcate the territory within which the principle of indifference is valid:

> Outside the Exercises, it is true, we may lawfully and meritoriously urge all who probably have the required fitness to choose continence, virginity, the religious life, and every form of religious perfection. But while one is engaged in the Spiritual Exercises, it is more suitable and much

better that the Creator and Lord in person communicate Himself to the
devout soul in quest of the divine will. (6)

This should go without saying: the ideal result of the exercises is, on the
contrary, when the exercitant does develop a strong and authentic commit-
ment to a particular position, such as poverty. The indifference that Ignatius
urges appears to be a *temporary* suspension of one's attachments, and its
purpose is to enable the exercitant to go through the exercises and finally
discern the divine will that his own decision needs to reflect. In this sense,
the attention that Ignatius wants the exercitant to achieve has an object,
and its object is an affective discernment of the divine will. Yet insofar as
this divine will itself is not in the control of the exercitant, the state that
the exercises themselves are aimed to create is a formal and intransitive attentiveness, a state of mind independent of what its particular object might
eventually become (when in 1530 Ignatius was summoned to Rome, he was
suspected of both *alumbradismo* and Lutheranism, the latter on account of
his emphasis on grace).[51]

The first principle of the *Spiritual Exercises* further clarifies the role of
indifference in the process of the exercitant's preparation:

> Man is created to praise, reverence, and serve God our Lord, and by this
> means to save his soul. The other things on the face of the earth are cre-
> ated for man to help him in attaining the end for which he is created.
> Hence, man is to make use of them in as far as they help him in the attain-
> ment of his end, and he must rid himself of them in as far as they prove
> a hindrance to him. Therefore, we must make ourselves indifferent to
> all created things, as far as we are allowed free choice and are not under
> any prohibition. (12; my emphasis)

This passage, which echoes the traditional distinction between using and
enjoying developed by Augustine in *De doctrina Christiana,* is where Ignatius establishes the principles that one has to keep in mind while navigating
through the exercises. Here the meaning and relevance of the concept of indifference is expressed most concisely. Indifference as a dispositional ideal
toward each created entity is the condition of discovering the difference
that the very same entity might make in terms of the exercitant's devotion
to God. Suspending one's "inordinate attachments" to any given matter is a
way of discerning how this given matter might play a role in the "attainment

of man's end." The attention that the initial act of indifference purified and formalized is afterward placed under the most systematic and rigorous training: in a series of exercises, attention is first directed at a select number of divine themes (soteriological and biblical), observed and pondered in a sustained, disciplined fashion; then it turns to the exercitant's self so that the affective responses that the exercitant has to these initial meditations can be discerned. If we recall that attention in medieval and early modern psychology is an act of the will, we recognize that the ideal of a holy attention marks not only the beginning but also the end of the Ignatian exercises insofar as they are exercises at all.

While Ignatius's integration of indifference with a concept of a pure, formalized attending provoked the criticism of Pedroche, one might speculate that the extraordinary success of the *Spiritual Exercises* had something to do with the way in which Ignatius's work made the monastic art of holy attention available to a broader, partly lay audience.[52] The art of holy attention was especially well suited to answer the needs of a post-Reformation public. As that which "wait[s] to put on the divine image," holy attention is a passive receptivity to divine grace. But at the same time it is available for active cultivation, and as a result devotional acts from prayer to meditation may be seen as the labor of purging attention from distractions. Attention promises a possibility of negotiating human acts of devotion with divine grace as the limit of such actions, a way of mediating between Catholic conceptions of devotional labor and the Protestant emphasis on grace.[53] As a passive disposition nevertheless available for active cultivation, attention offers a model of the kind of agency that the post-Reformation era was looking for: one that assumes a degree of volition without in any way competing with divine grace. It is no accident that after Ignatius, the rare explicit conceptualizations of this ideal of devotional attention belong to authors who came from a Catholic background but who, much like Donne himself, eventually engaged with Protestantism for personal or vocational reasons. Writing from the Reformation capital of Calvinism, and responding very much to what he saw as the Catholic and Protestant divide threatening the unity of Christianity, the Catholic Francis of Sales was one of them. In the influential *Traicté de l'amour de Dieu,* the bishop of Geneva defines contemplation as "no other thing than a loving, simple and permanent attention of the spirit to divine things." Punning on the French "attente," he defines indifference as a voluntary disposition involving both waiting and attending (much the way Donne does in *La Corona*):

The soule in this indifferencie, that willeth nothing, but leaves God to will what he pleaseth, is to be saied to have her will in a simple expectation; since that to expect, is not to doe, or act; but onely remaine exposed to someever. And if you marke it, the expectation of the soule is altogether voluntarie, and yet an action it is not, but a mere disposition to receive whatsoever shall happen, and as soone as the events themselves are once arrived and received, the expectation becomes a contentment or repose; Marry till they happen, in truth the soule is a PURE EXPECTATION [*l'ame est une simple attente*], indifferent to all that it shall please the Divine will to ordaine.[54]

More explicitly than any other devotional author in the period, Sales argues that indifference as *attente* is the best model of devotional action because it is a disposition that is voluntary without becoming an action. *Attente,* modeled on the ancient concept of a vigilant, indifferent attention, here becomes the paradigm of devotion by avoiding two pitfalls: assuming too much human agency, thereby denying the relevance of divine grace, and assuming an entirely passive human disposition that makes devotional action impossible. In Sales, the theological critique of the notion of undistracted prayer becomes the very reason attention can emerge as a spiritual ideal: indifference as attentive waiting is the model of a devotional action that complies with the paradox of grace because it prepares for divine grace without taking any action to solicit it.[55]

POETRY AS ATTENTION EXERCISE

If my account of holy attention's early modern conceptions in the previous section has merit, we are now in a position to articulate a hypothesis. The hypothesis goes like this: Holy attention in the sense of a perfectly undistracted, intransitive attention is a feature of *pure* prayer. The words of *vocal* prayer are initially seen as mere distractions from this perfect, silent attention. And yet, once holy attention is transformed into a regulative ideal of religious action in general, the relationship between vocal prayer and pure prayer may turn upside down and the words of vocal prayer can become instruments of turning one's active, transitive, and voluntary attention into the devotional disposition of holy attention. Such exercises may never achieve their goal of a perfectly undistracted attentiveness. They may not be intended to achieve this goal either. Nevertheless they structurally entail the ideal of a holy attention insofar as they require attention at all. In other words, we might see vocal prayer and by extension devotional poems as exercises aiming to cultivate and prepare their authors, readers, and reciters for the disposition of holy attention.

Let us then return to Donne's Holy Sonnet "This is my Playes last Scene" to see how the poem may bear out this understanding of devotion as an exercise of attention. At first, Donne seems an unlikely person to write poetry in the mode of spiritual attention exercises; after all, if the idea of a holy attention was already marginalized in medieval Catholicism, in the post-Reformation English Protestantism that Donne sought to inhabit, the cluster of ideals that go back to asceticism (including the ideals of pure prayer, holy attention, *apatheia* or indifference) were considered particularly suspicious. Indeed, the curious reception history of "This is my Playes last Scene" suggests that the poem itself struggles between Catholic devotional models and Protestant ideals. The poem has been cited in twentieth-century scholarship as paradigmatic for both Catholic and Protestant interpretations of Donne's devotional poetry. In *The Poetry of Meditation,* Louis Martz quotes the poem as evidence of a strong Ignatian influence on Donne's poetics.[56] In Barbara Lewalski's *Protestant Poetics,* the same poem appears as proof that Donne's poems dramatize the Calvinist doctrines of "justification and regeneration in language often remarkably precise."[57] At first, the poem seems to bear out both of these interpretations. As I showed in the Introduction, the poem's beginning resembles the techniques familiar from the Ignatian spiritual exercises:

> This is my Playes last Scene, here heavens appoint
> My Pilgrimages last Mile, and my race,
> Idely, yet quickly run, hath this last pace
> My Spanns last inche; my Minutes last pointe.[58]

Martz suggests that one of the main techniques Donne adopted from the Ignatian exercises is the so-called *compositio loci,* an effort to place oneself in a scene that has soteriological implications. Such a scene might come from the Bible, or it might be a scene from one's own life. In "This is my Playes last Scene," the abrupt, immediate beginning familiar from Donne's love poems is turned into an exercise of devotional deixis: the referent of the initial "this" is presumably the speaker's own death, and the next four lines are his attempt to imagine this death.

On the Ignatian model, a meditation should now continue to the next two stages: first, to the intellect that seeks to understand the meaning of the images provided in the *compositio loci,* and then to the will that is supposed to respond affectively. Indeed, the poem ends with what Martz calls an affective petition to God, or what we can simply call prayer. But the prayer is set in conspicuously Protestant language:

> Impute me righteous thus purg'd of evill,
> For thus I leave the world, the fleshe, and devill.

In this final couplet, Lewalski's Protestant reading gains traction. In invoking the Book of Common Prayer, the poem's last line is a direct quotation from a Protestant devotional text. But even more importantly, the penultimate line's "Impute me righteous" is a conspicuous reference to the Protestant doctrine of justification only by grace. Indeed, the Protestantism of the poem is further emphasized by the strained temporality that the word "thus" creates: if the two "thus"s refer back to the very devotional acts of the poem, the last line's meaning is that even after all the work that the speaker has performed, sin *still* infects the self, and it can only be removed by God's intervention.

How are we to read a poem that begins by performing Catholic spiritual exercises but ends with a Protestant prayer? Commenting on the discrepancy, Richard Strier argues that the final lines' "Reformation vocabulary does not correspond to the vision presented; the matter will not take this print," and adds that in general in the *Holy Sonnets* we see "Donne's deep inability to accept the paradoxical conception of a regenerate Christian."[59] Strier's comment voices the unease we might feel about the fact that the poem's concluding Protestant prayer does not seem to follow from the poem's inventions. It is as if, to return to the term I used earlier in this book, the couplet were simply reiterating a given without earning the right to this reiteration either devotionally or poetically.

But now let's see if reading the poem as an exercise of attention might shed light on how the end might actually follow from the beginning. In Martz's view, the poem's beginning as a poetic version of the Jesuit *compositio loci* is supposed to be an attempt to *imagine* death. But the way the speaker offers images for death is odd: as if not satisfied with any one of them, he goes through many, perhaps too many, images:

> This is my Playes last Scene, here heavens appoint
> My Pilgrimages last Mile, and my race

> Idely, yet quickly run, hath this last pace,
> My Spanns last inche; my Minutes last pointe.[60]

A play's last scene, a pilgrimage's last mile, a race's last pace, a span's last inch, a minute's last moment: the quick movement from one image to another makes each of them feel transient. Donne's efforts in this poem go toward thinking the last moment without images, measured instead by the bare temporal and spatial extension of the self, by the extremities of the "me" who speaks. Pace Martz, by the end of the fourth line when the speaker identifies the reference of the first "this" as a mere "last pointe," it seems that what the stanza has achieved is not an act of imagining the "this," but an act of forcing attention to hold onto the "last pointe" as an infinitesimal, incomparable, and therefore unimaginable entity.

What Donne is trying to achieve in this poem isn't incompatible with the technique of the *compositio loci*. A seventeenth-century comment on the *compositio loci* sheds light on this: "Now by means of this imaginary scene we confine our mind within the mystery upon which we intend to meditate, so that it may not wander hither and thither, just as we confine a bird in a cage, or put jesses on a haw so that it remain upon the fist."[61] The purpose of images here is to confine attention, to limit the temptations of distraction to a minimum. But the poetic trap of Donne's sonnet is all the more intriguing because it involves the acknowledgment that the mystery that it tries to ponder, the mystery of one's own death, cannot really be imagined. Donne uses poetic devices to strip attention from all images, from all content, and indeed, by the last line, from all extension, spatial and temporal (does a minute's very "last pointe" still have duration?) The function of language and poetry here is not to create an internal reference and help the reader imagine it, but to systematically manipulate and finally entrap the reader's attention in order to offer a momentary experience of undistraction.

The issue isn't that Martz was wrong in identifying Jesuit influences in Donne's poetry or in discovering the technique of *compositio loci* in this particular poem. It's that by concentrating on ostensible structural parallels between the Ignatian exercises and Donne's poems, he lost sight of the deeper ways in which Donne's poems share the goals (rather than the exact methods) of Ignatian spiritual exercises. Much like Donne's poem, the official Directory of the Society of Jesus warns against placing too much confidence in the *compositio loci*: "Touching this place-representation, one must diligently beware of spending too much time over its construction; and one must avoid excessive forcing of the head. The chief fruit of the meditation is not here; it is merely the road or means to the fruit itself."[62] In the very first stanza of "This is my Playes last Scene," Donne observes this instruction: he relies on the technique of *compositio loci* only in order to use the technique against itself, as it were. In the first four lines of the poem it seems that the "fruit" or goal of this technique is a pure, undistracted, holy attention. We might even notice that the poem's movement away from images and toward attention resembles the ascetic ideal of prayer we encountered in the previous chapter. Evagrius's iconoclastic ideal of *apatheia* is particularly relevant here: like ascetic prayer, Donne's poem begins as an exercise in imagining death only to move toward thinking the last moment of the self without imposing any images on it.

DWELLING IN DISTRACTION

But how do we get from this initial attempt to prepare for an undistracted turn to God to the actual, final prayer of the poem? Sticking to the hypothesis that the words of the poem aim to prepare and maintain attention, we would expect that the poem's next eight lines continue this kind of ascetic work of focusing on the thought of a bare lastness. Yet the poem does not stop at the end of the first quatrain to attend to the lastness or further increase the intensity of attending to it, but opens up a new "last" moment by reiterating the formal structure of the first quatrain. To paraphrase Paul Valéry's comparison between diving and attending, it is as though the first quatrain had been the diver's attempt to go underwater, but now the same diver ran out of breath and suddenly had to come back to the surface of the water.[63] The poem's second quatrain, its "and" at the beginning, is like a long-awaited gasp, like taking breath after being underwater for too long. It is as though the poem tried to pay attention to lastness too intensively:

> And gluttonous death will instantly unioynt
>   My body and Soule, and I shall sleepe a space,
>   Or presently, I know not, see that face
> Whose feare allredy shakes my every ioynt.

The poetic images and conceits that seemed to disappear by the end of the first quatrain here return: an impersonated, vulture-like Death is imagined preying on the dying speaker, and the theatrical image of Death disjointing body and soul is followed by imagination doing the work of theology in speculating about the fate of the dead.[64] All of a sudden, the theatricality of the first stanza is back, and with it, a scattered attention trying to follow imagination's rush to figure a disjointed body and soul, as well as a third entity who will either be asleep or face divine judgment.

If the second quatrain signals the return of the poetic and then theological imagination, and the locus of attention that the first quatrain seemed to have approached now disappears among the images of an afterlife, the third quatrain takes both imagination and the scattering of attention to a whole new level:

> Then as my Soule, to' heaven her first Seate takes flight,
> And earthborne body in the earth shall dwell,
> So fall my Sins, that all may have their right,
> To where they'are bred, and would presse me, to hell.

The theological hesitation of the second quatrain is gone here; in its place, there emerges the image of a fantastic salvation machine where soul, body, and sin duly report back to their "right" places. There is, indeed, something disturbingly mechanical about this process where the soul, the body, and sin all follow their supernatural course as if in a system of transcendent gravity and antigravity, only to leave the "I" of the poem hovering somewhat hesitantly in the last line, not quite knowing yet which of the three entities it will eventually join. The scattering of attention that began in the second stanza is here completed by a scattering of the self itself: dispersed in the process of imagining judgment, it is not body, not soul, and especially not a union between them. It is from this confusing and fanciful eschatological image that we are suddenly pulled back to the poem's last two lines and their direct address:

> Impute me righteous thus purg'd of evill,
> For thus I leave the world, the fleshe, and devill.

With this, we are back to Strier's comment: there is something amiss here. Even though the poem's first stanza seemed to follow the logic of words being instrumental in manipulating and preparing attention for prayer, the two middle stanzas went in the opposite direction as if to deliberately distract the speaker from his initial goal—and yet the prayer arrives at the end as if it had nothing to do with the poem's competing movements, as if it were spoken by a different person. While the poem's first stanza carefully purged itself of images, the last couplet seems to spring from an unprepared, sudden and altogether more violent rejection of poetic invention as such. Moreover, the couplet seems to be confused about its own statement: if the poem's previous twelve lines did succeed in performing the work of purging, then why ask for imputed grace? And if they didn't, then why add, *after* the request for grace, "thus purg'd of evil?"

In order to see more clearly what Donne is trying to achieve, it will be useful to compare "This is my Playes last Scene" with a different, Puritan poetics of grace.[65] Expanding on Lewalski's insights that Protestant poetry abandons poetic inventions in order to rely exclusively on biblical sources, Roland Greene has called Anne Lock's sonnet sequence *Meditations of a Penitent Sinner* the beginning of a Puritan poetics.[66] According to Greene, Puritan poetics resisted the then-emergent notion of *inventio* as poetic creation and instead tended to be "materialist," that is, relying and emphasizing its reliance on received matter both in terms of poetic form and semantic content. Greene cites Lock's fourth sonnet as an example of the Puritan conviction that *inventio* is not only sinful but also impossible because the ultimate author of the poem can only be God. The sonnet is based on a single line of Psalm 51, which appears in the margins of the *Meditation* in Lock's translation as "For I knowledge my wickednes, and my sinne is ever before me":

> Have mercie, Lord have mercie: for I know
> How much I nede thy mercie in this case.
> The horror of my gilt doth dayly growe,
> And growing weares my feble hope of grace.
> I fele and suffer in my thralled breast
> Secret remorse and gnawing of my heart.
> I fele my sinne, my sinne that hath opprest
> My soule with sorrow and surmounting smart.
> Drawe me to mercie: for so oft as I
> Presume to mercy to direct my sight,
> My Chaos and my heape of sinne doth lie,
> Between me and thy mercies shining light.
> What ever way I gaze about for grace,
> My filth and fault are ever in my face.[67]

Needless to say, even this poetry cannot completely abandon poetic invention; traces of Lock's style are apparent throughout the poem. But how should
we characterize this style? Lock's poem seems closer to what has been called
maniera: if style deliberately emphasizes *inventio* as the individualization of
poetic matter, *maniera* leaves poetic matter, that which is given before the
poem begins, visible in its materiality.[68] In Lock's poem, "the free gesture of
the writer [il libero gesto dello scrittore]" is replaced by a deliberate attempt
to suppress style and emphasize manner, to restrain *inventio* and allow the
given text of the psalm come to the fore instead. The form of this poetry
serves the purpose of emphasizing the given biblical text; indeed, Lock's poetic solutions make the return to the biblical and theological sources seem
simultaneously repetitive and inevitable. The frequent repetitions of individual words and phrases (especially, and not accidentally, "mercy"), often
immediately following each other ("Have mercy, O Lord, have mercy"; "daily
growe, / And growing weares"; "I fele my sinne, / my sinne that"), together
with Lock's insistence on assonances and consonances and her unrestrained
use of alliteration ("My filth and fault are ever in my face"), all create a sense
of inevitability to this repetitive tendency. Lock's "improper" language is not
glossolalia but ordinary language spoken as though it were glossolalia, me-
chanically, moved forward not by semantic relations but by the reiterative
occasions of the syntactic and phonetic facade of language.

While in Petrarchism the sonnet sequence is an opportunity of narrative development, in Lock's hands it becomes a framework in which the
reader can repeat time and again the back-and-forth movement between
the "heinous gylt of my forsaken ghost" and the "cry for mercy to releve my
woes" (63). As a result, it is not so much that there is no modulation in the
sequence but rather that modulation itself is repetitive. The sonnet form in
Lock's sequence becomes a penitential device, a technology in which the
turn, the *volta,* is not so much a figure of conversion emerging within the
poem but rather an ever-present possibility, an axis between "grace" and
"face" so that whenever one appears the other is simultaneously evoked and
eventually uttered.[69] "Grace" has a virtually inevitable connection with its
rhymes; whenever "grace" appears, one of its regular rhyming pairs ("case,"
"pace," "face," and "deface") inevitably follows, and vice versa.[70] The last couplets in the *Meditation of a Penitent Sinner* tend to be a summary of this
monotonous modulation between the two extensities of penitence. Indeed,
Lock's sonnet here ends with the self returning from the improper, with the
speaker's gaze finding its own face where it was seeking grace.

What is the point of this poetry? Here Lewalski's account is illuminating. At the time of working on *Protestant Poetics,* Lewalski would not have known Anne Lock as a poet.[71] It is a testament to her insight that virtually every aspect of the theory of biblical poetics is borne out in Lock's *Meditations.* First published in 1560, Lock's sonnet sequence appeared as an appendix to Lock's translation of five sermons by Calvin. The connection between the sermons and the sonnets is in part formal: they both cite and elaborate on specific biblical passages. Indeed, in describing the sequence as a "Paraphrase upon the 51. Psalme of David," Lock associates the poems not only with psalm translations but more generally with biblical paraphrases.[72] But there is also a deeper, theological and devotional affinity between the two parts of the volume. As Lock explains, "I have added this meditation followyng unto the ende of this boke, not as parcell of maister Calvines worke, but for that it well agreeth with the same argument."[73] The argument of Calvin's sermon turns doctrine into a *religious ethic:* it stresses the imperative of acknowledging all afflictions as just punishments for sinfulness and seeing any good exclusively as a result of divine mercy. If Calvin's sermons are already about applying doctrine to life, Lock's sonnets take this agenda one step further by using the sonnets as an exercise in habituation. Lock's sonnet sequence is a meditation in the specific sense of affective exercise: in merging Calvinist doctrine and the voice of the Psalmist, Lock creates a poetics that is in the service of internalizing doctrine as a habit of the mind.[74]

The difference between Lock's Puritan poetics and Donne's achievement in "This is my Playes last Scene" is thus both aesthetic and devotional. While in Lock's poem "grace" and its rhymes are linked consistently in order to establish their association in the mind of the reader, in Donne's poem the prayer for grace emerges out of the forgettings, distractions, and errors of the poem, as if by accident, though a carefully prepared one. Let us look again at the two middle quatrains of the poem:

> And gluttonous death will instantly unioynt
> My body and Soule, and I shall sleepe a space,
> Or presently, I know not, see that face
> Whose feare allredy shakes my every ioynt.
> Then as my Soule, to' heaven her first Seate takes flight,
> And earthborne body in the earth shall dwell,
> So fall my Sins, that all may have their right,
> To where they'are bred, and would presse me, to hell.[75]

The path leading out of the derailed imaginative exercise that these lines represent and to the concluding couplet's prayer emerges with the recognition of what the speaker has forgotten during the first three quatrains. While in Lock's poems words like "face," "race," "space," or "face" would be automatically followed by "grace," Donne's poem omits the word and instead asks for the unnamed favor in the poem's final petition. But if the final petition is literally a recollection of grace from within the poem's body, it is also a recollection of a scattered self from the previous quatrains. In the whirlwind of salvation that the third quatrain depicts, the self too has remained unaccounted for. Stripped of all its constitutive parts, the "me" of the poem after the end of the third quatrain recognizes that grace has remained absent throughout the poem and responds to this recognition by voicing a petition. As we saw earlier, in order for this prayer to be genuine, the "me" would already have to possess grace. When "This is my Playes last Scene" ends with the given, the question is whether this given is given to the speaker—or whether it is merely a given that exists prior to and independent from the speaker. This is why we need to realize that it is the very absence of the self that pulls the speaker back from the speculative imaginations of the two middle quatrains into the "this," the now of the poem. This absence is what motivates the speaker to abandon the imaginative exercises and turn to an altogether different speech act, a petitionary prayer: "Impute *me* righteous, thus purg'd of evill" (emphasis mine). That is: the speaker has purged himself of all the evil he could imagine as part of a poetic and devotional exercise, but this process of imaginative purgation has made his need for grace only more evident.

In Lock's sonnet sequence, the function of poetry is to engrave doctrine into the mind of the poems' reader. The two aspects of Calvinist doctrine are already *given*, literally so in the sermons that precede the poems in the 1560 volume. The "self" that speaks and reads must recognize in herself the cause of her afflictions, and simultaneously she must recognize God as the sole source of salvation.[76] The poems are designed to turn these imperatives into automatisms of the mind, and they do so by using them as automatisms of the verse. In Donne's poem, in contrast, the "I" of the speaker and the grace of God are the two entities that remain forgotten until the very end of the poem. Rather than reliable substances, they are elusive objects of the poem's quest and they become all the more elusive in the course of this quest. Doctrine in Donne's poem is not immediately available either, the way it is in Lock's, but rather emerges out of the poem's paradoxical movements. This is not to suggest that in Donne's poem the speaker in some way merits grace:

though the petition for mercy could not appear in the closing couplet without the wanderings in the previous twelve lines, it emerges not because but in spite of these lines. Between the "Catholic" opening and the "Protestant" closing, Donne creates an experimental poetics that affords the reader occasional revelations through the cracks and crevices of language, that searches for attention by building edifices of distraction.

It seems, then, that the attempt to apply the basic insight of a poetics of attention on "This is my Playes last Scene" is leading to mixed results. The poem's beginning and end do work in a way that confirms some of the insights that theology offers about thanksgiving and devotional attention. In the first quatrain, the poetic devices are used in a self-deconstructing manner so that by the end of the fourth line the initial work of imagination is replaced by an intense effort of attention. Poetry begins to consume itself in order to provide support for the effort of attention; words as potential sites of distraction are sacrificed so that they can become instruments of attention. The last couplet, in turn, is a *gratiarum actio,* a petition for grace that turns away from the previous three quatrains of the poem, toward an unnamed but implicitly addressed God whose grace can alone impute righteousness. If attentiveness is the condition of prayer, and therefore of *gratiarum actio,* it seems that Donne's poem begins by inclining toward the production of attention, but, as if exhausted by the effort to concentrate, in the second quatrain it lets attention scatter and imagination "distend" toward new images. Or it is as though the increasing state of attentiveness at the end of the first quatrain itself had evaded the poem's attention, and thus the poem swerved away from this brief instant of attentiveness toward a returning display of poetic and theological imagery. It is as though the Puritan grace machine that works so flawlessly in Lock's sequence has been sabotaged by an unruly poetic imagination that decided to make fun of the machine itself, only to be redirected to devotion by the end of the poem. Donne's poem, it seems, comes to its final petition for grace not because of the poetic work that precedes it but in spite of it, not out of a concentrated attention but from distraction. If in the *Holy Sonnets* Donne does follow holy attention as a regulative ideal of religious practice, it seems he is equally keen to depict the ways in which the speakers of the poems become distracted from the initial search for attention. What should we make of this emphasis on distraction? This is the question I address in the next chapter.

EXTENTUS

Do not flatter yourself that you can succeed without the outmost effort of attention; and attention's greatest achievement will be to discover that which exists only at its expense.

P. Valéry[1]

IF "THIS IS MY PLAYES LAST Scene" is an exercise of attention, what should we make of the poem's dwelling in distraction? In order to answer this question, I return here to Augustine's contribution to the tradition of holy attention. There are two reasons for this. First, Augustine's account of why distraction is inevitable is the single most influential chapter in the history of Christian thinking about holy attention. Second, Augustine was also one of the most important sources for late medieval and early modern lyric poetry, particularly lyric sequences and devotional poems. His influence for poets from Petrarch to Donne has been much discussed.[2] What has mostly escaped critical consideration, and what I want to show in the following pages, is that Augustine was influential for lyric poetry precisely as a thinker and practitioner of attention.[3]

In the first two sections of this chapter, then, I focus on the development of Augustine's thinking about attention and distraction from the *Soliloquies* to the *Confessions*. Augustine comes to doubt the possibility of a pure, undistracted attention in human life on philosophical and theological grounds. But he doesn't abandon the ideal; instead, he projects the possibility of holy attention into the future of the resurrected body. In the third and fourth sections, I discuss how late medieval and early modern poets seek to translate this dual Augustinian heritage into poetry. I suggest that while Petrarchist poets associate lyric poetry with the Augustinian scattering of the self, Donne creates poetic intimations of what a postresurrection state of attentiveness might feel like. Insofar as we will begin to look at how Donne invests in the resurrection, this chapter is also a transition from the Platonist ideal of pure attentiveness to a more characteristically Donnean, embodied understanding of attention.

THEOLOGY AS PREPARATION FOR
PRAYER: THE SOLILOQUIES

One of Augustine's most central claims in the *Confessions* is his admission that "distentio est vita mea"—"my life is distraction."[4] This exclamation toward the end of Book XI is neither a chance utterance nor a hyperbolic expression of repentance. Behind it, there is an entire philosophy of life as distraction, of distraction as the human condition. We mustn't forget that Augustine makes this claim as part of a conversation: "ecce, distentio est vita mea." Or rather, since we cannot know if there is an actual conversation, and since in the paragraph Augustine speaks in the vocative, it is more accurate to say that the thought that life is distraction occurs in the context of an attempt to address God in a prayer. How might this affect the meaning of Augustine's claim? In *De interpretatione*, Aristotle notes that prayers cannot be interpreted as true or false because they do not contain propositional statements—a comment that invites a comparison between prayer and poetry.[5] Does this mean that "my life is distraction" cannot be seen as a propositional statement? How are we to read such a statement, or any statement, when it occurs in the context of an address?

These are crucial questions to ask and to keep in mind for the following pages because most of Augustine's remarks on attention appear not in his theological, pastoral, or exegetical texts, but in two unusual, highly experimental works in which addresses play a crucial role. The two works are the *Soliloquies*, written around 386 or 387, and the *Confessions*, written roughly ten years later. Although Augustine himself becomes only gradually aware of the ultimate purposes of these experiments with genre and style, what ties the two works together is that they both seek to articulate the relationship between philosophy and Christian religion, between thought and devotion, between, we might say, propositional statements and prayerful address. In both, Augustine poses fundamental philosophical and theological questions about human and divine nature. But in both, the challenge is how these inquiries, and the knowledge they might yield, relate to devotion. Is the knowledge of God the ultimate purpose of Christian life? Or is such knowledge a means toward addressing and praising God? Is there, indeed, a difference between knowing God and addressing him?

In both texts, Augustine's goal is not so much to articulate a theoretical answer to these questions as to develop a way of speaking in which thought and devotion find their proper relation to each other, as if to see what constellation they would want to form if they had their own will. The two titles refer to new genres, two new ways of speaking both philosophically and devotionally: the terms "soliloquy" (a new coinage) and "confession" refer to different stages (both temporally and hierarchically) of the same project. My contention in the following two sections is that the reason Augustine's remarks on attention appear in these two works is that he placed attention at the juncture of philosophy and religion, thought and devotion.

In order to see how Augustine's ideas about attention develop, let me first turn to the earlier text, the *Liber soliloquiorum*.[6] Augustine identifies the text as a philosophical treatise with a twofold subject: "the first treats the soul; the second, God."[7] At first sight, this description does not seem to match the actual content of the book. Augustine's discussion in the text includes a number of classical philosophical topics such as the questions of truth and falsity, fictions and the ontology of semblance, whereas God never really becomes the subject of the discussion, presumably because Augustine left the book unfinished. Still: why claim the soul and God as the text's sole subjects?

The answer to this question has to do with the form rather than the content of the *Soliloquies*. In casting his argument as a dialogue between himself and Reason, Augustine follows the Platonic tradition of dialectics and Cicero's own philosophical dialogues. Yet by calling the dialogue "soliloquy," Augustine also departs from this philosophical tradition. The name plays on "colloquy" not just in the sense of any conversation, but a conversation with God—one of the earliest and most pervasive definitions of prayer. This raises an interesting possibility: perhaps Augustine identifies God and the soul as the two central subjects of the *Soliloquies* because they are the two entities who converse in prayer as a colloquy. This would mean that the inquiry about the nature of God and the soul is a means toward a different end, the end of prayer as a conversation between God and the soul. In other words, the philosophical purpose of knowing God and the soul would in fact be subordinated, by the form of the soliloquy, to the devotional goal of prayer.

But how would soliloquy as a form prepare for prayer as a colloquy? When decades later in the *Retractations* Augustine recalls the writing of the *Soliloquies,* he explains that his method was to write in an "as-if" mode, "as if there were two of us—Reason and I—whereas I was by myself."[8] In the later *Confessions,* where Augustine's purpose is explicitly devotional, his writing employs different voices that now appear, now retreat; some have entities assigned to them (Reason, soul, especially the Psalmist's *anima mea*), some appear only as evanescent gestures and near-imperceptible shifts in tone and register. In the *Liber soliloquiorum,* in contrast, the form is far more straightforward: as an "as-if" mode, the soliloquy is an imitated conversation, a literary experiment that tends toward prayer without being fully conscious of its own tendency. It is a *mimetic* form that tries to prepare for prayer as conversation by creating a conversation in the absence of another voice. It is preparation not only in the sense of seeking knowledge about God and the soul but also in the sense of trying to invite a real conversation by performing a feigned one.

In contrast to recent usage of the term "performance," the goal of describing soliloquies as mimetic preparations for prayer here is not to erase the division between soliloquy and colloquy, between a feigned conversation and a real one, but on the contrary, to allow the question of how one gets from preparation to action to emerge more sharply. This is a question that I touched upon in chapter 3 when I discussed Claudius's failed prayer. Although the term "soliloquy" does not receive its modern theatrical sense until the nineteenth century, Claudius's monologue in *Hamlet* is a real soliloquy in the original, Augustinian sense of the term. Left alone, the king prepares for his (presumably silent) prayer by meditating about the conditions of prayer in a dialogical form, going back and forth between the necessity and the impossibility of praying for forgiveness. As we saw, Ramie Targoff argues that Hamlet does not consider the possibility of Claudius's devotional failure because in the early seventeenth-century devotional context the performance of prayer was seen as continuous with prayer itself: "There were no absolute divisions between sincerity and theatricality, inwardness and outwardness within the early modern English church."[9] This argument goes against a wealth of early modern witnesses who insist on a distinction between sincerity and the lack thereof in devotion; between right and wrong ways of addressing God, between failed and successful prayer. It also goes against the scene itself, in which the king tells the audience that his prayer did, in fact, fail. But most importantly, it goes against the logic of prayer. We recognize this last point most clearly if we consider prayer, as I suggested in the Introduction, simultaneously as a mimetic action and as an action of grace. Augustine's soliloquy is a mimetic action in that it performs an as-if conversation; it prepares for prayer by imitating the form prayer would presumably take. It is, at the same time, an action of grace in the sense that all this performance can do is prepare for its subject by inviting it, as it were: the soliloquy can only become a colloquy if God decides to engage it. Let me return to the example of sleep for a moment. The act of falling asleep is a mimetic action insofar as it involves a series of gestures and exercises that invite sleep by imitating it—we assume the position we think we are in when we sleep, we breathe the way we think we do when we sleep, and so on. In this sense, the mimetic, preparatory actions to fall asleep are all "secular prayers" that try to "invite" sleep by performing it.[10] At the same time, sleep is also an action of grace in the sense that we cannot make ourselves fall asleep (induced sleep aside): sleep is a grace, it comes when it wishes. Yet, and this is the crucial point for my current concern, there is obviously a difference between the performance of sleep and sleep itself. The fact that we can prepare for sleep does not erase the division between preparation for sleep and sleep itself, but on the contrary, it intensifies the question of how one gets from preparation to action, from performance to actuality.

Soliloquies, in this specific sense as mimetic actions of grace that attempt to invite the event that would complete them, are similar to that class of entities that Augustine in a crucial section of the *Liber soliloquiorum* defines as the type that "tends to exist and does not succeed [*aut omnino esse tendit et non est*]."[11] This is a peculiar category in Augustine's text because it is added as a third to the previously articulated distinction between the "fallax" and the "mendax." The *fallax* are false things insofar as they resemble other things in order to deceive others. The *mendax* are also false, but they resemble without intention to deceive, and it is notable that Reason identifies literature (comedy and poetry) as *mendax* in this sense. When Reason introduces the third category of things that tend toward existence but do not succeed, Augustine is at first surprised, particularly since Reason explains that comedy, poetry, art, as well as mirrors and shadows can belong in this third category, so it is not clear how this third category would be different from the category of the *mendax*. It becomes clear only later that while the distinction between *fallax* and *mendax* is based on the intention of those who create them, in the case of the third category Augustine is interested in the ontology of representation. A poem is written in order to resemble something, and insofar as it aims to resemble its subject for a particular purpose though without wanting to deceive its audience, it is *mendax,* a fable, a mimetic artifact. But a poem is also something that resembles its subject but does not become it; in this sense it always only "tends" toward its subject but never quite reaches it. The implicit stake of the *Soliloquies,* then, is whether the pretense of conversation between Reason and Augustine remains a captive of this third category, a representation that tends toward its subject without being capable of reaching it, or whether it can become a colloquy with God. This is why Augustine invents a new form, and this is why the subject of the fictional dialogues is God and the soul.

But the experiment of the soliloquies, both as an inquiry for knowledge about God and the soul and as a preparation for prayer, runs into one major obstacle from the beginning: the challenge of distraction. The character of Reason is aware of the problem, and he addresses it in his description of the genre of the soliloquy:

AUGUSTINE: I have nothing to say and I am ashamed of my previous too hasty assent.

REASON: It is nonsensical for you to be ashamed, as though we had not chosen this manner of discussion for this very reason. Because we are speaking to ourselves alone, I chose to call it by the title of Soliloquies, a name which is, to be sure, a new one and perhaps an awkward one, but one which is quite suitable to indicate its purpose. Since, on the one hand, truth cannot be better pursued than by question and answer, and since, on the other hand, hardly any one can be found who is not ashamed to be defeated in an argument, with the result that it almost always happens that a subject for discussion which is well begun is driven out of mind by the unruly noise of self-opinion, accompanied also by wounded feelings which are usually concealed but at times evident—for these reasons it was my pleasure to seek the truth with God's help in peace and propriety by questioning and answering myself.[12]

The new genre of the soliloquy follows the Platonic tradition of dialectics; Reason's assumption that "truth cannot be better pursued than by questions and answers" indicates the extent to which Augustine at this point in his life still sees antique philosophy as the main framework for thinking. But the problem with the Platonic method of conversation, Reason suggests, is that talking with others may cause distraction, much in René Girard's sense of mimetic desire: once an other is present, the subject focuses not on truth but on the interaction and its impact on the ego. Hence the new genre and the new name: soliloquy is an attempt to keep the dialectical method of conversation without the potential distraction that the presence of another speaker would cause. It is not difficult to recognize in Reason's explanation echoes of the ascetic ideal of holy attention: Reason assumes that leaving behind all distractions is the condition of the search after truth, and he also seems to believe that such eschewing of distraction is actually possible. Yet the difficulties of the new genre and its requirement of solitary attending are indicated by the semicomical comment in which Reason claims the invention of the new term for himself: "Because we are speaking to ourselves alone," Reason declares, "I chose to call it by the title Soliloquies." The shifting personal pronouns in the sentence reveal that the problem shared by the new genre and the ideal of a holy attention is a problem of agency.

Indeed, Augustine himself articulates the problem:

> Even though I have been tormented within the last few days by a severe toothache, and was not permitted to meditate on anything save what I had already perchance learned, and although I was completely prevented from studying, for which I need all my attention [*ad quod mihi tota intentione animi opus erat*], nevertheless it seemed to me that if the light of truth had appeared to my faculties, I would not have felt that pain, or at least I would have borne it as though it were nothing.[13]

The passage simultaneously expresses Augustine's faith in the possibility of a completely undistracted attention and his frustration about the reality of not experiencing it. From the beginning, he is an unruly partner in the conversation; at times he rushes enthusiastically to conclusions, while at other times he is overwhelmed by the difficulty of the subject, often to the degree of tears and physical pain. Though there aren't others present, and thus Augustine should be able to search for truth "in peace and propriety," it is now his own self, and indeed his own body, that proves to be an infinite supply of distractions.

In Book II, Reason grows increasingly more impatient with Augustine's inordinate behavior, often punctuating his philosophical arguments with variants of the same exhortation: "Nunc attende! [Now pay attention.]"[14] Seemingly to no avail: Augustine continues interrupting him, at times to express his enthusiasm, at times to complain. More and more, it seems that their search after truth is failing. Yet all of a sudden, in chapter 13 of Book II, Reason declares that they had reached the conclusion they had been looking for: "What we were seeking had been found" [*Illud igitur quod quaerebamus inventus est*]. The reader might feel that he has overlooked something because it is not clear what finding Reason refers to, but it turns out Augustine too has missed the crucial moment: "What are you telling me?" [*Quid narras?*] When Reason insists that their thesis, the immortality of the soul, has been proved, Augustine is still in doubt and asks him to repeat the proof. Reason agrees, but now he warns Augustine in the harshest terms he has used to date: "I shall do what you evidently desire but pay the strictest attention" [*Faciam quod te velle video, set attende diligentissime*].[15]

What follows is a series of arguments about Truth, the body, and the soul. Toward the end of these arguments, Augustine still seems to be in doubt, but now Reason declares unequivocally that "the soul is, therefore, immortal." The reason he gives, though, has little to do with the previous philosophical arguments about mortal bodies and immortal mathematical truths; instead, it is a spectacularly circular argument:

> Believe your reasons, believe the Truth. It proclaims that it dwells within you, that it is immortal, that its dwelling place can be taken from you by no death of the body. Turn away from your shadow, return to yourself; there is no death for you except you lose sight of the fact that you cannot die [*avertere ab umbra tua, revertere in te; nullus est interitus tuus, nisi oblitum te esse quod interire non possis*].[16]

This is a puzzling passage. At this point in the dialogue, Reason and Augustine are still searching for evidence of the soul's immortality. Reason now claims that this evidence consists in the immortality of truth. But this is an odd, singular kind of evidence, because if we can believe Reason, it is proof only insofar as (indeed as long as) Augustine holds onto it as truth. It is a proof that as a proof does not exist without the thinking subject's attention to it. The immortality of truth constitutes the immortality of the soul in the very action of being attended to: "there is no death for you unless you lose sight of [forget, turn away from, cease to attend to] the fact that you cannot die."

Here, at the end of the investigation, it seems as though knowledge, faith, and attention have collapsed into one another, into a single act of circular, self-referential attention that is depicted as capable of constituting a foundation for philosophy *and* theology. Throughout the conversation, the dialectical search after truth has been hindered by Augustine's serial distractions, and Reason has repeatedly warned him to be more attentive. Attention has been a means toward an end, a condition of a solitary dialogue. In Reason's concluding passage this hierarchy between knowledge and attention, in which attention appears to be in the service of pursuing knowledge, is reversed. It is now in the act of attending that knowledge becomes possible at all; and the kind of knowledge that Reason propagates can only exist insofar as the foundational act of attention is sustained. Attention is no longer a mere instrument in the progress towards knowledge; it is, rather, the foundation without which knowledge remains impossible, and a telos in which knowledge finds its fulfillment.

Such an emphasis on attention is puzzling indeed. If Reason's claim is a philosophical proposition, it is difficult to make sense of: how could immortality consist in a momentary act of attending? It will be helpful to return here to the observation that in the *Soliloquies*, Augustine's goal is to find a new form that merges philosophy and devotion. If this is the case, then the questions about God's nature and the soul's are not purely philosophical questions but questions about prayer—that is, the question about the soul's immortality is not an ontological question about the soul's nature, but a devotional question about how the soul might find itself capable of addressing God, how it might find in itself the essence of immortality that would enable it to speak to God. Then Reason's claim is not a proposition about the soul's nature, but an exhortation: if you believe in your own immortality, and if you attend to the thought of your immortality, then you will become capable of addressing God.

The bewilderment that this passage may provoke in the reader is then a proper reflection of Augustine's own struggle to find language for a new, Christian philosophy, a philosophy in which propositional knowledge is subordinated to devotion, and devotion itself becomes a form of knowledge. Augustine never finished the *Liber soliloquiorum;* after two books, the dialogue abruptly ends. It is possible that Augustine's reason for abandoning the project was his growing dissatisfaction with Platonism and in particular with the Platonist theory of knowledge as recollection. Yet it is striking that within the extant work, the main reason Augustine's character cannot advance in knowledge is that he keeps getting distracted by his own self, and particularly by his own body. These two reasons, Augustine's rejection of Platonism and his character's permanent distraction, may in fact be closely related. Reason's brief but momentous sentence about immortality is a final expression of the paradox of the soliloquies: the truth of soul's immortality here is something that the subject cannot simply *recall,* as he should be able to within a Platonist framework, but something that he has to hold onto in a voluntary act of attention. And this voluntary act of attention to the truth of one's immortality is in fact what human immortality consists in.

The structure of this argument leaves Platonism behind and approaches the Pauline argument about resurrection in 1 Corinthians 15 that I explored in chapter 1. Indeed, Reason's call to belief at the beginning of the passage invokes Paul's own exhortation to faith in the resurrection. The small sentence signals the difficulty of this transition from Platonism to devotion. It also foreshadows the rise of a new, Christian philosophy in the seventeenth century—Descartes's own invocations of attention echo Reason's argument very closely.[17] For my purposes, it suffices to note that the passage, and indeed the entire text of the *Soliloquies,* shows that at this point in his intellectual development, Augustine had not yet completely abandoned the ascetic ideal of a holy attention. Despite the recurrent distractions throughout the text, and despite the experiment's ultimate failure, the notion that a completely undistracted, voluntary act of attention is within the reach of the subject informs the dialogue from Reason's first definition of the new genre to his last "proof" of the soul's immortality.

As we move on to the *Confessions,* it is worth noting that when in the *Retractions* Augustine recalled his experiment in the *Soliloquies,* he criticized those passages in the book that seemed to invoke associations with the ideal of a voluntary holy attention. "I certainly do not approve," Augustine writes in the *Retractions,* "of what I said in the prayer: 'O God, who has willed that only the pure will know the truth."[18] Augustine clarifies that such purity is in fact not a necessary condition of knowledge. Even more strikingly, Augustine disagrees with his own former claim that "the soul is already happy in the knowledge of God." Such happiness can only exist, for the incarnate human being, in the form of hope. Too much emphasis on fleeing the body, not enough emphasis on Christ: this is the essence of Augustine's retrospective self-critique. As we will see momentarily, these are the principles that inform Augustine's second and most sustained engagement with the question of devotional attention in the *Confessions.*

CONFESSION AS DISTRACTION

The *Liber soliloquiorum* is one of Augustine's early texts from the period when he is still developing his theology and devotional theory in the context of a Platonist philosophy. When later in his life he returns to the question of attention and distraction in devotion, Augustine's perspective is considerably different. The *Liber soliloquiorum* bears the marks of an experiment:

it is part of Augustine's ongoing attempt to articulate Christianity within the framework of an essentially Platonist philosophy. In merging the two discourses, Augustine, perhaps involuntarily, also exposes their conflicts, while we get only brief hints about what a new, Christian philosophy would look like. Insofar as the *Confessions* represents another stage in the same experimental process, it is distinguished from the *Liber soliloquiorum* by Augustine's recognition that Platonism is not fully appropriate for articulating Christian devotion. If the Platonic theory of knowledge as recollection is one of the primary reasons for this incompatibility as Augustine perceives it, the obvious novelty of the *Confessions* is the explicit consideration of devotional attention, and a strong interest in how an embodied attention may partake in devotion. In the following, I show that this new concern prompts Augustine to develop not only a new account of attention, but a poetics of attention—that is, a phenomenological account of how attention relates to linguistic utterances, motivated by the question of what it would mean to attend to God.

Though often interpreted as a philosophical and theological discussion of temporality, Book XI of the *Confessions* returns time and again to questions of reciting verse.[19] Augustine quotes Ambrose's hymn ("Deus creator omnium") to think about how we perceive the difference between short and long syllables.[20] Toward the end of the book, he invokes the experience of reciting a psalm in a final version of his argument:[21]

> I am about to begin a psalm that I know [*Dicturus sum canticum, quod novi*]. Before I begin, my expectation alone reaches over [*tenditur*] the whole: but so soon as I shall have once begun, how much so ever of it I shall take off into the past, over so much memory also reaches: thus the life of this action of mine is extended [*distenditur*] both ways: into my memory, so far as concerns that part which I have repeated already, and into my expectation too, in respect of what I am about to repeat now; but all this while is my marking faculty present at hand, through which, that which was future, is conveyed over, that it may become past: which how much more diligently it is done over and over again, so much more the expectation being shortened, is the memory enlarged; till the whole expectation be at length vanished quite away, when namely, that whole action being ended, shall be absolutely passed into the memory.[22]

Augustine argues that in reciting a known psalm, the mind is stretched out between a remembered past and an expected future, which confirms his

previous suggestion that time is the "distention" of the soul.[23] Here and in
the other passages that refer to poetry, it seems as though verse provides
Augustine with a laboratory to conduct a philosophical and theological experiment about the human experience of time. Indeed, in the most influential accounts of this passage, Augustine's use of poetry is set aside as non-
specific and purely instrumental.

But in reading this passage, one must also remember that Augustine began the *Confessions* by doing exactly what he imagines doing now: attempting to recite a psalm he knew.[24] In fact, the *Confessions* began with a *gratiarum actio,* a thanksgiving praise: *Magnus es, domine, et laudabilis valde:*
"Great art thou, O Lord, and greatly to be praised."[25] This first address to
God, which, as Augustine's commentators note, is wholly unusual of Latin
prose and characteristic only of poetry, could be not only the beginning
but the end of Augustine's confession. It seems to perform everything that
a *confessio laudis* is required to do: it addresses God to acknowledge and
praise his magnanimity in words that are God's own.[26] This praising of God
is the purpose of creation, "for thou hast created us for thyself."[27] Augustine
could stop here. Instead, he proceeds to ask a number of difficult questions:
"Grant me, Lord, to know and understand what I ought first to do, whether
call upon [*invocare*] thee, or praise [*laudare*] thee?" The temporal order that
an address to God should follow is Augustine's first concern; the second is
the relationship between *theologia,* the knowledge of God, and prayer, the
call upon God: "Which ought to be first, to know [*scire*] thee, or to call upon
[*invocare*] thee? But who can rightly call upon thee, that is yet ignorant of
thee? for such an one may instead of thee call upon another."[28] Within a
few sentences, the first, in medias res, direct address to God gives room to
questions and hesitations. The *Confessions* begins with Augustine's attempt
to address God, but almost immediately, this attempt of address turns into
a meditation about the question that Augustine wanted to but never ended
up asking, the question of how one would need to know God in order to
address him. The meditation on reciting verse in Book XI is then not just
philosophical thinking about time using poetry as an accidental example; it
is rather Augustine's attempt to come to terms with what he has been doing
all along.

In Book I, the hesitation between addressing God in prayer and seeking to know God theologically leads to the confessions proper, the ten long
books of Augustine narrating his life. To be sure, the narrative is not independent from the initial prayer. Toward the end of his first train of thought,
Augustine still insists that the purpose of his text is to address God: "Thee

will I seek, O Lord, calling upon thee; and I will call upon thee, believing in thee" (3). But based on the previous recognition that invoking God requires at least some knowing of God, Augustine sets out to find God in himself: "Since therefore I also am, how do I entreat thee to come into me, who could not be, unless thou wert first in me?" (5). The narration of the life is simultaneously a search for God and a confessional call upon God: throughout the first ten books, Augustine keeps addressing his discourse to the *Domine* of the first address. But as he is nearing the end of his narration in Books X and XI, the initial questions about what it would mean to speak to God return with renewed force. In Book X, Augustine focuses on memory; Book XI concentrates on time and attention. In both, the central question is how humans who live in time, in distention, could call upon a God that exists in eternity. Toward the end of Book XI, Augustine seems to come to the recognition that as a human being he cannot in fact do anything to actually address God—he can only hope that God listens to him. And immediately following this recognition, he declares his entire life a *distraction*: "ecce distentio est vita mea."

If life is a distraction, what is it a distraction from? The first answer seems to be that it is a distraction from that first act of praise that began the *Confessions*. Indeed, Book XI begins with a commentary on the act of narrating life:

> Canst thou that art the Lord of all eternity, be ignorant of what I say unto thee? Or dost thou see in relation to time, that which passeth in time? Why then do I lay in order before thee so many narrations? Not to this end I do it, that thou mayest come to know them upon my relation; but thereby I stir up mine own and my readers' devotions towards thee, that we may say all together: Great is the Lord, and greatly to be praised [*Magnus dominus et laudabilis valde*].[29]

The passage seems to be clear enough, and in making a point about the discrepancy between the temporality of human devotions and divine omniscience, it echoes a traditional theological concern about prayer.[30] If God knows everything that has ever existed or is going to exist in time, why should humans perform prayer at all? What is it that they could tell God? What is it that prayer could actually do? But here it is worth considering Augustine's reasons to focus on verse in all his examples about time. It is the recurrent references to poetry that make it clear that neither omniscience nor experience is the real issue here. If they were, using a poem as an example would make little sense, for "to repeat a psalm that I know" conflates precisely those categories that Augustine would need to keep separate: the distinction between memory and expectation, but also and more importantly the distinction between divine omniscience and the temporality of human experience. If I can have the whole psalm in front of me ("*in totum expectatio mea tenditur*"), then in this particular respect and in terms of knowledge I am like God, who similarly has the totality of time in front of him.

But Augustine uses verse as example to erase this difference between human and divine knowledge so that he can focus on another, for his purposes vastly more important distinction:

> Certainly if there be any mind excelling with such eminent knowledge and foreknowledge [*scientia et prescientia*], as to know all things past and to come, so well as I knew that one psalm; truly that is a most admirable mind, able with horror to amaze in that nothing done in the former, or to be done in the after ages of the world, is hid from him any more than that psalm was to me whenas I sang it; namely, what and how much of it I had sung from the beginning, what and how much was there yet unto the ending? But far be it from us to think, that thou the Creator of this universe, the Creator of both souls and bodies; far be it from us to think, that thou shouldest know better what were past, and what were to come. Far, yea, far more wonderfully, and far more secretly dost thou know them.[31]

There is a *quantitative* difference between the divine modality of knowing and human knowledge, but this is not the subject of Augustine's discussion; it is the *qualitative* difference that he wants to establish. If there were divine *attentio,* the difference between it and human attention would have nothing to do with the amount of knowledge that God has. The real difference would be that God would know everything *and* that He could pay attention to everything at the same time. In fact, in *De civitate Dei* Augustine comes close to actually attributing to God something that we could call omni-attention:

> It is not that there is any difference in God's knowledge according as it is produced by things not yet in existence, by things now or by things that are no more. Unlike us, He does not look ahead to the future, see the present before him, and look back to the past. Rather he sees events in another way, far and profoundly different from any experience that is

familiar to our minds. For he does not variably turn his attention [*cogi-tatione*] from one thing to another. Hence all events in time, events that will be and are not yet and those that are now, being present, and those that have passed and are no more, all of them are apprehended by him in a motionless and everlasting present moment. . . . Nor does it make any difference whether he looks at them from present, past or future, since his knowledge, unlike ours, of the three kinds of time, present, past and future, does not change as time changes. . . . Neither does [God's] atten-tion stray from one subject to another [*intentio de cogitatione in cogita-tionem transit*] . . . for he knows events in time without any temporal acts of knowing of his own.[32]

This is the contrast that Augustine wants to emphasize by using poetry as his main example throughout the discussion: the totality that exists for God in an eternal self-simultaneity would be the timeless subject of his total at-tention. Human attention works fundamentally differently. There are, Au-gustine argues, "three things done" in the mind in all of its operations: "it expects [*expectat*], it marks attentively [*adtendit*], it remembers [*meminit*]; that so the thing it expecteth, through that which it attentively marketh, passes into which it remembereth" (*Confessions* 2:277). Augustine here sets aside the issue that attention must select its object even within the present; for him, it is troubling enough that attention seems to be responsible for dividing the divine unity of temporality into a scattered succession of con-stantly passing moments. Questions of multitasking have little to do with Augustine's concerns: for him, even if one were able to attend to every-thing that there is in any given moment *spatially,* attention would still be responsible for the *temporal* scattering of the self. The present moment that is always passing and that in passing constitutes a transition between future and past is here blamed on a fallen, human attention. It is because of this attention to the present that the self is simultaneously and constantly dis-tracted from its own presence by the past and the future: "The life of this action of mine is extended [*distenditur*] in both ways, into my memory . . . and into my expectation" (2:277).

Not only is human attention incapable of the undistracted turn to God that the ascetic authors before Augustine would require of prayer, but here it appears to be the very reason human creatures are distracted from God. The act of attending to the present is the very act that scatters the self into time and thus makes him ontologically different from God, incapable of ad-dressing God. Human attention is what replaces the eternal divine presence

with the ceaselessly passing present of time, and thereby turns the self into
scattered, stretched-out existence between the past and the future. By the
end of Book XI, we realize that even the first act of praising God was already a distraction *from* God. The single sentence of the *confessio laudis* is
already too distracted, too distended to accomplish the task of devotion,
the thanksgiving which ought to be entirely simultaneous with itself in a
single act of attention: "confitear tibi quidquid invenero in libris tuis, et audiam vocem laudis" [let me confess unto thee whatsoever I shall find in
thy books, and let me hear the voice of praise].[33] In the actual act of praise,
words and their sound all follow each other in a sequential order: it is as if
by our acts of attention we were forced into speaking a language that operates in a frequency fundamentally different from God's. In fact, Augustine
goes even further: distention in the sense of temporal stretching-out and
scattering is characteristic not only of vocal prayer but even of silent prayer.[34]
Since the source of distraction is attention itself, the example of how we are
constantly producing distraction in the process of reciting a psalm emerges
as a paradigm for human existence:

> What is now done in this whole psalm, the same is done in every part of
> it, yea and in every syllable of it; the same order holds in a longer action
> too, whereof perchance this psalm is but a part; this holds too through-
> out the whole course of man's life, the parts whereof be all the actions of
> the man; it holds also throughout the whole age of men, the parts whereof
> be the whole life of men.[35]

If human acts of prayer and human existence itself are always-already distended and unable to perform the undistracted turn to God that ascetic devotion would require, then what is left for human devotion to do? What is
the labor that the *Confessions* itself is designed to perform?

    We saw that at the beginning of Book XI, Augustine answered this
question in part by referring to the public function of devotion: "Why then
do I lay in order before thee so many narrations? Not to this end I do it,
that thou mayest come to know them upon my relation; but thereby I stir
up mine own and my readers' devotions towards thee, that we may say all
together: Great is the Lord, and greatly to be praised [*Magnus dominus et
laudabilis valde*]."[36] Augustine returns to the very phrase he used when he
began the *Confessions;* yet the lapse of time between the two utterances of
the *confessio laudis* modifies the praise. The initial "magnus es, domine,
laudabilis valde" was an invocation addressing God in the vocative. The

following ten books were, to cite John Stuart Mill's characterization of poetry, "overheard" speech: Augustine never addresses his readers but keeps the vocative *domine* throughout the narrative of his life.[37] In Book X, as Augustine returned to the questions of what it means to call upon God, the direct addresses to God became less frequent. But it is only now, in Book XI, that the initial vocative is, temporarily, suspended. In a negative and implicit apostrophe, Augustine reiterates the laudation but without the vocative: "Magnus dominus et laudabilis valde"—"Great is the Lord, and greatly to be praised." These two repetitions frame Augustine's life story; a private address and a public praise. The life, its narrative: at once an attempt to find the *confessio laudis* that is simultaneously spoken and heard, that is being given, and the *distentio* that makes this mission impossible by keeping the given and being perpetually separate. What ten books ago was a personal, direct address to God is now a public praise in the third person. We cannot hope to address God directly, Augustine suggests; but we still are obliged to praise him, not in hope of meriting his response, but "to stir up mine own and my readers' devotion to thee." By defining the labor of devotion in creating a paradigmatic affect that can be imitated both by the self and by others, Augustine here creates a precedent that is echoed by generations of Christians after him. We saw Aquinas make the same point about vocal prayer; and we saw Donne suggesting that the point of praise is to "make open declarations of his mercies."[38]

But while at the beginning of Book XI Augustine seems to suggest that this is the only labor devotion can hope to perform, at the end of the same book he makes a statement that is different both in tone and in content. Returning from the temporary apostrophe and from talking to his human audience, Augustine begins speaking to God again:

> But because thy loving kindness is better than life itself, behold, my life is a distraction [*ecce distentio est vita mea*], and thy right hand hath taken hold of me, even in my Lord the son of Man, the Mediator betwixt thee that art but one, and us that are many, drawn many ways by many things: that I may apprehend him in whom I am also apprehended, and that I may be gathered up from old conversation, to follow that one, and to forget what is behind: not distracted but attracted, stretching forth not to what shall be and shall pass away, but to those things which are before: not, I say, distractedly but intently [*non distentus, sed extentus, non secundum distentionem, sed secundum intentionem*], follow I hard on, for the garland of thy heavenly calling, where I may hear the voice of thy praise,

and contemplate these delights of thine, which are neither to come, nor to pass away.[39]

"*Non distentus, sed extentus, non secundum distentionem, sed secundum intentionem,*" not distended, but extended, not according to distention, but according to intention. This passage is notoriously difficult to interpret.[40] The Christological emphasis that was missing from the *Soliloquies* is evident. The meaning of *intentio* appears to be relatively straightforward as well: if *distentio* is the scattered modality of *attentio*, *intentio* is a recollection, an attempt to bring together the scattered fragments of the self in singular efforts of attention. After Augustine, it is standard to distinguish *attentio*, the act of the intellect, from *intentio*, the act of the will; the distinction appears in this passage in nuce. But how does that which is *extentus* stand in contrast with *distentio*?[41] Scholarship on Augustine calls attention to the possible mystical connotations of *extentus;* if we interpret the prefix "ex-" as intensification, an *extentus* act could be like an act of attention except more durable, more focused, more capable of comprehending God.[42]

The source of Augustine's sentence is the Vulgate translation of Paul's letter to the Philippians: "Brethren, I count not myself to have apprehended: but this one thing I do, forgetting those things which are behind, and reaching forth unto those things which are before [*quae ante sunt, extendens me*]. I press toward the mark for the prize of the high calling of God in Christ Jesus."[43] While Book XI of the *Confessions* might be read as Augustine's critique of the ascetic ideal of pure prayer, it is in the Pauline concept of *extentus* that Augustine nevertheless leaves a vestige of holy, intransitive attention in the *Confessions*. In discussing the practical goal of monastic life as "purity of heart" in the sense of always keeping the mind focused, Cassian cites the same Pauline passage in the *Conferences:*

> Thus, indeed, the end of our chosen orientation is eternal life, according to the very words of the Apostle: "Having your reward, indeed, in holiness, but your end in eternal life." But the scopos is purity of heart, which has not undeservedly been called holiness. Without this the aforesaid end will not be able to be seized. . . . When he was teaching us about our immediate goal the same blessed Apostle significantly used the very term "scopos" when he said: "Forgetting what is behind, but reaching out to what is ahead, I press on to the goal, to the prize of the heavenly calling of the Lord." . . . Whatever therefore can direct us to this scopos, which is

purity of heart, is to be pursued with all our strength, but whatever deters us from this is to be avoided as dangerous and harmful.[44]

Cassian reads the "mark" (in the Vulgate, *destinatus,* and *skopos* in the Greek) of Paul's passage as purity of heart, and he understands Paul's verb "press toward" (*diōkō* or *persequor*) as expressive of the monk's lifelong effort to concentrate on this goal. Insofar as in Paul's passage these two terms, the "mark" and the "press toward" are parallels of the "before" (*emprosthen* and *ante*) that is the object of the self-extending (*epekteinō* and *extendere*), in Cassian's interpretation Paul's passage describes the monastic pursuit of leaving distractions behind and focusing on the immediate goal of the purity of the heart.

If, in the *Confessions, secundum intentionem* is one modality of *attentio,* a modality of bringing together that which is *distentus,* scattered by an act of will, *extentus* gestures in the opposite direction: it is a modality in which the self branches out so that it can hold onto a totality much like God does but without actually having this totality in front of it. The key of the passage is Augustine's use of the word "ante." The *extentus* tending that Augustine envisions leaves the past, the "life as distraction" behind, in order to focus on the before, the *ante* that is after the future, in front of the present. The *ante* is the eternity of God, the eternity of life in God, and God himself. But if we go back to Paul and look at the context, we find that more accurately it is the resurrection. The verses leading to the passage that Augustine quotes are as follows:

> Yea doubtless, and I count all things but loss for the excellency of the knowledge of Christ Jesus my Lord: for whom I have suffered the loss of all things, and do count them *but* dung, that I may win Christ, And be found in him, not having mine own righteousness, which is of the law, but that which is through the faith of Christ, the righteousness which is of God by faith: That I may know him, and the power of his resurrection, and the fellowship of his sufferings, being made conformable unto his death; If by any means I might attain unto the resurrection of the dead. Not as though I had already attained, either were already perfect: but I follow after, if that I may apprehend that for which also I am apprehended of Christ Jesus (13: 8–12).

Paul explains his own devotion as a pursuit of the *gnōsis,* the knowledge of Christ, and indeed as the pursuit of knowing Christ in his resurrection. But at the end of the passage Paul warns that by this he does not mean that he has actually reached this knowledge, which would imply spiritual perfection; it means only that he pursues this goal of knowing the resurrected Christ. This is what Paul describes, in the verse that follows immediately, as a stretching toward a before.

The problem of human *attentio* in Augustine's account is that it does not have temporal extension, that in any given instant it can only mark a temporal singularity.[45] But while *attentio* is singular, the phenomena that the body is exposed to, and the phenomena that the body experiences as multiplicity can only be "processed" by *attentio*, can only be attended to in temporal sequence.[46] Precisely because attention is incarnated and yet has no extension, *attentio* is inseparable from *distentio*; in order to attend to the multiplicity of phenomena, attention has to move, but as soon as it is in movement, it also has to make selections; indeed, it is nothing but this moving and selective stretching toward that which it has selected. In this process of moving and selecting, attention is inevitably distracted from everything else; insofar as it holds onto an aspect of the totality of phenomena, it always has to leave out an infinite number of phenomena, to which it cannot attend, just as it cannot attend to the totality of phenomena either. *Attentio* and *distentio*, attention and distraction, are two aspects of the same movement of consciousness, which also explains why God cannot have attention in the proper sense of the word: in God there would be no *distentio*, no distraction, only a pure, self-simultaneous, timeless act of attention.

For Augustine's devotion the implication is that instead of a truly extended attention, there is only hope and desire, a longing to leave behind distraction and to know God—emphasis being on the fact that this could never become more than desire.[47] If the movement of *attentio* could be *extentus*, if it could open up and become capable of holding onto a totality without having one in front of it, then it would not produce distraction—then it would be a perfectly intransitive, holy attention. But this would be possible only in a different kind of body, akin to the Pauline spiritual body of the resurrected. Insofar as the human, incarnate *attentio* is not capable of transcending temporality, for human beings there is no such thing as "extentio," a state of attentiveness that corresponds to the divinity, but there is only a movement that is *extentus*, an *affectio*, a moving forward driven by the desire to apprehend as one is apprehended.[48] The object of *this* kind of longing is the *ante* that Augustine establishes carefully to point to that which is after the future, before the past, and in front of the present, always beyond the reach of *expectatio, memoria,* and *attentio*.[49] This *ante*, transcendence itself, is the direction of the hands in Donne's thanksgiving clock; it is the eternity that for postlapsarian consciousness can exist only as an object of longing.

"CROWN OF PRAYER AND PRAISE"

Augustine's engagements with the idea of a holy attention are deeply ambivalent. In theological terms, both the *Soliloquies* and the *Confessions* assert that a perfectly undistracted, pure attention is beyond the reach of the incarnate, fallen human being. But this propositional claim about holy attention's impossibility is countered by Augustine's vocative utterances that continue to aspire to pure attention in the context of devotion and indeed make such attention the foundation and the goal of their own acts as prayers. In the *Soliloquies,* this appears in the idea of a circular attention, which turns out to be intransitive in that its object, the immortality of the soul, exists only insofar as the very act of attending constitutes it. In the *Confessions,* attention under the sign of the vocative has the potential to be *extentus* and intransitive insofar as it does not attend to something already existing but to the future that is also the past, that is, the dimension of the transcendent. Such *extentus* attention is exempt from the dialectic of attention and distraction that Augustine draws up in the *Confessions* because it does not have an object and therefore does not produce distraction—it is instead an intransitive act of waiting for its own objects, ultimately the second coming and the resurrection.

These are lofty ideas, and it is remarkable how little space Augustine dedicates to them, and how hermetic his writing tends to become when he describes them. It is likely that for doctrinal or pastoral reasons (and perhaps for both), he found it more appropriate to emphasize the ubiquity of distraction than to engage into speculations about holy attention. But after Augustine, this ambivalence about the possibility of holy attention becomes a productive tension, nowhere as centrally as in lyric poetry. The reasons for holy attention's relevance for lyric poetry are partly historical, partly formal. The influence of Augustine's *Confessions* on the most important late medieval lyric sequence, Petrarch's *Canzoniere,* is partly responsible for the early modern lyric's investment in questions of attention and distraction. But the formal reasons are even more important. The most obvious characteristic that prayer and lyric poems have in common is their unapologetic use of address and apostrophe. Since these are the speech acts that raise, for Augustine, questions of attention and distraction, it stands to reason that lyric poetry's own use of address and apostrophe leads poets to ask similar questions, often in strikingly Augustinian terms.

Let me return here for a moment to the poem I discussed in the Introduction, *La Corona.* Though likely earlier than the *Holy Sonnets,* the seven poems of Donne's sonnet crown already engage in a poetics of address and attention that echo Augustine's discussions. I now quote only the relevant lines of the proem:

> The ends crown our works, but thou crown'st our ends,
> For at our end begins our endless rest;
> This first last end, now zealously possessed,
> With a strong, sober thirst, my soul attends.[50]

I suggested in the Introduction that the problem the proem contemplates is what could a poem do toward redemption if Christ's sacrifice has earned salvation for mankind. The speaker's answer to this question carries the echoes of Augustine's meditations on attention. If redemption is already given, the task of the poem is to help the soul to attend to this already given redemption. The meaning of "attending" as "waiting" is relevant here, but only insofar as it overlaps with the intransitivity of holy attention. In other words, the attending that is the task of the poem can be characterized as waiting only if we dissociate waiting from a future event. Donne is very precise about this: what "my soul attends" is not just salvation or the resurrection, but the "first last end," an oxymoron that in this context simultaneously refers to *all* the divine works of redemption, be they in the past, present, or future tense. The "first last end" is in other words Donne's own formula for what Augustine called the "ante" of an *extentus* attention: it is God's incarnation in Christ, it is the crucifixion, it is Christ's resurrection, his ascension, but it is also the speaker's own resurrection and redemption, which can only happen through his attention to all of the mysteries of redemption.

This explains why in the following six sonnets Donne produces a peculiar blend of theological statements and prayerful addresses. Each of these subsequent sonnets is dedicated to one of the mysteries, from the annunciation to the resurrection and the ascension. But instead of making propositional statements about these mysteries, Donne's speaker weaves them into an intricate web of constantly shifting addresses. In the course of the six sonnets, the speaker addresses his own soul, the Virgin Mary, God, and Christ, in such quick succession that at times he himself seems confused about the addressee of his speech act. The result is a labyrinth of apostrophes, which envelops and metabolizes the theology of each of the mysteries. Indeed, at the end when the poem returns to its initial address, the naming of the poem itself turns out to be a proposition that depends on all the other acts of prayer in the sequence: the crown of sonnets can be properly called a "crown of prayer and praise" only if the poem's previous addresses were successful, "if thy holy Spirit, my Muse did raise."[51]

In mixing theology and address, Donne of course relies on various devotional practices, from a generic sense of meditation and contemplation to the specific practice of praying the rosary. Indeed, the poem's invocation of the rosary is surely relevant to the poem's investment in answering the circular paradox of grace by creating its own, poetic circle. But from an Augustinian point of view, *La Corona* is fascinating because it shows how the poem's success, indeed its very existence as a devotional poem (a poem of "prayer and praise"), depends on whether the addresses it performs succeed in calling on their addressees, which in turn means that it depends on whether the speaker's attention manages to hold onto the "first last" as the only source of the works of redemption. In other words, it depends on whether or not Donne's poem achieves the kind of holy or *extentus* attention that Augustine envisions in the *Confessions*.

Does it? Indeed, could it? Is it intended to? I suggest that the answer at least to this last question is yes: in *La Corona* and in the *Holy Sonnets* Donne rather audaciously experiments with a poetics whose ultimate aim is not only to cultivate attention or to depict the struggle with distraction, but to actually achieve a state of intransitive attention. This objective sets Donne's poetry apart from virtually all of its precedents. While poets from Petrarch to Philip Sidney are perfectly aware of Augustine's account of attention and distraction, insofar as they transform Augustine's account into a poetics, they produce an aesthetics of distraction. Let me illustrate this point by taking a brief look at Petrarch's and Sidney's poetry, before returning to Donne's devotionally rather more ambitious efforts.

POETICS OF DISTRACTION: PETRARCH AND SIDNEY

It is often suggested that in following Augustine, Petrarch also fundamentally transformed Augustine's religious thought. According to one of the most influential articulations of this view, in Petrarch's hands "the thematics of idolatry [is] transformed into a poetics of presence."[52] But this transformation appears less significant if we translate "idolatry" into distraction and "presence" into intention; in other words, if we read Petrarch's *Canzoniere* as a poetic performance of the Augustinian attempt to overcome distraction in acts of attention. In this reading, the poems of the *Canzoniere* will be seen as individual attempts to regather the poet's shattered world into the intention of the poetic act itself. The success of such acts is always and necessarily transient ("un breve sogno"), hence the *Canzoniere*'s double achievement: thematically and theologically, it reinforces the Augustinian thesis that life is distraction and offers a chronicle of Petrarch's serial distractions, the poems themselves; while poetically and aesthetically it constitutes a monument for the author by recording the traces of his intention.

The quest to overcome the scattered attention that Augustine calls distention is manifested most clearly in Petrarch's "l'avaro che 'n cercar tesoro," the miser who collects and recollects not only his own history but the history of the world, mythological and political, into the singular poetic acts of attention of what Petrarch originally named *Rerum vulgarium fragmenta*.[53] The *l'avaro*, the miser, who is of course the poet himself, uses poetry to overcome the distention, the fallen state of being in flesh and in time. Every poem is an attempt to reassemble the world that was shattered into fragments in the moment of the speaker's encounter with Laura, the moment of *innamoramento*. The paradox of the *innamoramento* is similar to the paradox of Laura: like Laura, who is both a sign of Christ and an idol distracting the poet from Christ, the *innamoramento* is both a poetic fiction of the fall and an intimation of redemption. But what the poems do isn't a Platonic recollection of the *innamoramento*. Instead, every poem is an immense effort of attention, an intention to create a kaleidoscopic totality in which the given, the pieces of a broken mirror, are used to rebuild the mirror so that attention can return from a state of distraction by attending to an image of eternity to which Petrarch dedicates the name (*senhal*) "Laura."

Sonnet 190, the famous "Una candida cerva" is a programmatic poem in allegorizing both the quest and its necessary failure:

> Una candida cerva sopra l'erba
> verde m'apparve, con duo corna d'oro,
> fra due riviere, all'ombra d'un alloro,
> levando 'l sole a la stagione acerba.

Era sua vista sí dolce superba,
ch'i' lasciai per seguirla ogni lavoro,
come l'avaro che 'n cercar tesoro
con diletto l'affanno disacerba.

"Nessun mi tocchi" al bel collo d'intorno
scritto avea di diamanti et di topazi.
"Libera farmi al mio Cesare parve."

Et era 'l sol già vòlto al mezzo giorno,
gli occhi miei stanchi di mirar, non sazi,
quand'io caddi ne l'acqua et ella sparve.

[A white doe on the green grass appeared to me, with two golden horns, between two rivers, in the shade of a laurel, when the sun was rising in the unripe season.

Her look was so sweet and proud that to follow her I left every task, like the miser who as he seeks treasure sweetens his trouble with delight.

"Let no one touch me," she bore written with diamonds and topazes around her lovely neck. "It has pleased my Caesar to make me free."

And the sun had already turned at midday; my eyes were tired by looking but not sated, when I fell into the water, and she disappeared. (Translated by Robert Durling)]

A tempting reading of this poem is that the speaker's falling into the water is a moment of baptism. Since Sonnet 190 is the last poem in the *Canzoniere*'s first part (in the Giovanni form), it makes sense to assume that the end of the poem is indeed indicative of a thematic division.[54] But another possibility is that the poem is paradigmatic not because it is different from the previous attempts, but because it sums up the quest itself. The poem is a *hysteron proteron*: it foreshadows Laura's death, an event that has not happened yet within the sequence of the sonnets. The way in which this foreshadowing is signaled is through typology: by invoking the *Noli me tangere* scene from John 20:17, Petrarch uses the association between Laura and Christ to indicate that the doe's earthly presence, much like Christ's after the resurrection, is only a sign referring beyond itself to God. The hallucinatory force of the vision suggests that the miser feels and knows that he is supposed to attend; yet he doesn't understand that the sight he is looking at isn't what he is supposed to concentrate on. This is why the poem ends with what today is called "directed attention fatigue," and which early moderns knew by the name "lethargy": when his concentration wears out, the miser falls into the water, shattering the very image he didn't know how to attend to. The last line invokes the Narcissus-myth: the miser's quest fails not only because he didn't know how to attend, but also because he was really attending to himself all along.[55]

Every poem in the *Canzoniere* is an attempt of the speaker to gather his scattered existence into a single act of intention. Confirming Augustine's account of attention's dialectic production of distraction, every poem is also a "failure": even if they individually succeed as acts of intention, they at the same time necessarily perpetuate the distention they were supposed to remedy. The *Canzoniere* itself is thus a chronicle of the speaker's chronic distraction. This is one of the reasons the book begins with a poem that calls the collection "rime sparse," scattered rhymes: the book as a collection is a work that imitates Augustine's *Confessions* in collecting a scattered self into the artificial unity of the book. To paraphrase Freccero's thesis, Petrarch transforms the Augustinian thematic of distraction into an aesthetic of scattering.

The Augustinian thematic of distraction becomes even more emphatic in Protestant poetry. But while in Petrarch's *Canzoniere* distraction is the byproduct of poetic intention, in Protestant devotional poetry distraction emerges as a figure of poetic authority or lack thereof. Take the first poem in the Sidney psalter:

> He blessed is, who neither loosely treads
>   The straying stepps as wicked Counsel leades;
> Ne for bad mates in way of sinning waiteth,
>   Nor yet himself with idle scorners seateth:
> But on God's law his heart's delight doth bind,
>   Which night and day he calls to marking mind.
>
> He shall be lyke a freshly planted tree,
>   To which sweet springs of waters neighbours be,
> Whose braunches faile not timely fruite to nourish,
>   Nor withered leafe shall make yt faile to flourish.

So all the things whereto that man doth bend,
Shall prosper still, with well succeeding end.

Such blessings shall not wycked wretches see:
    But lyke vyle chaffe with wind shal scattred be.
For neither shall the men in sin delighted
    Consist, when they to highest doome are cited,
Ne yet shall suffred be a place to take,
    Where godly men do their assembly make.

For God doth know, and knowing doth approve
    The trade of them, that just proceedings love;
But they that sinne, in sinnfull breast do cherish;
    The way they go shal be their way to perish.[56]

This is an odd poem: after the first three sestet's complex but confident adaptation of the psalm's parallelisms, the limping fourth stanza breaks the poem's symmetry. When Mary Sidney revised the poem, she must have thought it was unfinished because she erased the last stanza and replaced the jarred, dilated third one with a more concise rendition of the Psalmist's last three lines:

Not so the wicked, but like chaff with the wind
Scattered, shall neither stay in judgment find
Nor with the just, be in their meetings placèd:
For good men's ways by God are known and gracèd.
But who from justice sinfully do stray,
The way they go, shall be their ruin's way.[57]

Mary Sidney's version is far more elegant than her brother's, and insofar as it gives a better impression of the psalm's parallel structure it may also be characterized as a more accurate translation. But it overlooks the very poetic innovations that in Philip Sidney's version highlight the speaker's concern with Petrarchism and distraction. When in the proem to the *Canzoniere*, Petrarch describes his own poems as "rime sparse," he merges a reference to Augustine's *distentio* with a play on the first psalm's depiction of the sinner as "the chaff which the wind driveth away." In Philip Sidney's rendition of the same psalm, this association between sin, distraction, and poetic form becomes the poem's leitmotif. The first stanza distinguishes between the godly and the sinner both thematically and formally. The godly is characterized by his *skopos:* he "neither loosely treads" but constantly "calls to marking mind" God's law. Sinners, in contrast, stray, wander off, become distracted. Influenced by French poetry, Sidney figures this distinction between attentive godliness and distracted sin through the use of feminine rhyme. The stanza begins and ends with masculine lines describing the godly; but as we move into the stanza's center, the feminine lines express the speaker's own straying away from the godly *skopos* and dwell in the act of imagining the wicked.

Such distraction remains neatly contained in the first two stanzas: the feminine rhymes and the straying they voice are framed and controlled by the strong, masculine lines with which each stanza begins and ends. But in the third stanza, the containment comes under threat. The wicked are no longer safely contained in the weak middle parts but break out of their imprisonment and contaminate the entire stanza. Notably, this contamination happens precisely in the stanza that paraphrases the Psalmist's line about the wicked as "chaff," which Sidney renders as scattering: "lyke vyle chaffe with wind shal scattred be." As if understanding the association between sin and distraction only now, the speaker utters the middle feminine lines with a hesitation and a jarring enjambment: "For neither shall the men in sin delighted / Consist, when they to highest doome are cited." The intriguing solution of rendering "stand" as "consist" gives voice to the speaker's anxiety about himself becoming distracted; an anxiety that concerns both the spiritual coherence of the subject, and the poetic coherence of the sequence.[58]

It makes sense, then, that Sidney adds a last, seemingly fragmented stanza to his translation, a stanza in which the feminine rhymes that until this point have occupied the middle position within each stanza are no longer answered and controlled by masculine lines. The virus of distraction has spread to the end of the poem; the final condemnation of the wicked is uttered in weak lines, with fading attention, a fading away that was foregrounded by the poem's growing anxiety about distraction and its gradual loss of focus. The continuity between Petrarch's and Sidney's poetics is clear: both accept the Augustinian thesis that fallen life *is* distraction. But the differences are just as important: while in the *Canzoniere* the serial distractions of the poem are recorded as monuments of Petrarch's poetic glory, in Sidney's psalm translations it is poetic authorship itself that creates and spreads distraction onto its biblical materials, so that poetic form becomes a figure of distraction, condemning its own author.

BEYOND DISTRACTION

Donne, while clearly aware of these precedents, seeks to accomplish something devotionally rather more ambitious in his poems than either Petrarch
or Sidney: instead of illustrating the theology of distraction by poetic *spar-
gimento,* he uses poetic form to dissolve authorial intention into attention.[59]
To understand this, it will be helpful to remember that Donne's religious
lyric was part of a shift from a "biblical" to an "authorial" religious poetry in
the late sixteenth and early seventeenth centuries. Most sixteenth-century
English poets from Thomas Wyatt to Philip Sidney kept their secular love
lyric strictly separate from their religious poetry. Indeed, sixteenth-century
English Petrarchism rarely features the kind of obsession with transcendence that permeates the *Canzoniere;* if and when English poets invoke religious themes in their love poetry at all, they tend to turn them into matters
of ethics. The reason isn't that sixteenth-century English poets were less
concerned with religion than Petrarch, of course; the outpouring of religious verse by the very same authors demonstrates the opposite. But characteristically, the majority of sixteenth-century religious verse belongs to
the category of biblical poetry in the concrete sense that it features mostly
metrical translations and paraphrases of scriptural texts. One might sum-
marize this Protestant biblical poetry in the principle that the poet may
address God only in God's own words: it is a poetry of the given. As we saw
in Sidney's case, a central problem of biblical poetry is therefore poetic form:
since form is the only obvious *inventio* that the poet adds to the given matter,
it is the main locus of anxiety about the potential incompatibility between
religion and poetry.

If in this sense much of sixteenth-century poetry observed a division
absent in Petrarch's *Canzoniere,* by the late sixteenth and early seventeenth
century poets such as Henry Lok and Barnabe Barnes moved away from
this model and began to write authorial religious poetry, that is, poetry
that can no longer be described as mere metricalization or paraphrasing
of biblical materials (though it continues to rely on the Scriptures to a far
greater extent than Petrarch's poetry). Donne's religious poems belong to
this trend. Indeed, if we compare Donne to earlier religious poets, one difference is that despite the variety of Donne's religious poetry, he seems to
have avoided biblical poetry rather consistently. Donne's "Lamentations of
Jeremy" comes closest to the Protestant exemplars of biblical paraphrases,

though Donne's verse translation builds mainly on the Jewish-Italian Immanuel Tremellius's Latin version. Affinity with the Psalms in tone and content of course pervades Donne's devotional poems. In the *Holy Sonnets* and in the hymns, the speakers perform the kind of intimate yet inhabitable personae that we associate with the Psalmist; and Donne's poem on the Sidney psalter testifies to his investment in psalm translations and public devotion. Yet none of Donne's devotional poems is intended for public worship, and it is remarkable that Donne, virtually alone among the great religious poets of the English Renaissance, never tried his hand at translating the Psalms.[60] With the possible exception of the "Lamentations," all of Donne's religious lyrics are authorial poems.

This explains why Donne's *Holy Sonnets* differ from Petrarch and his English followers. If in Petrarch poetic intention always results in *distentio,* and if in Sidney poetic form is always-already distraction, in Donne's poems distraction is an integral part of the poems' striving to attentiveness. A brief comparison with Petrarch's style will be helpful here. One central conceit of the *Canzoniere* is that each poem in the sequence is an act of the poet's intent seeking to overcome the *distentio* caused by original sin, figured in the sequence as the *innamoramento.* Hence the emphasis on style, on the propriety of form; hence the scarcity of enjambments, the perfection of meter, the consistency of diction: every poetic institution in the *Canzoniere* is subordinated to this purpose of overcoming distention in a sudden effort of intention. These individual efforts are then gathered together in the sequence that creates a monument for poetry by documenting the speaker's serial failure to collect his attention.

Donne's *Holy Sonnets,* in contrast, tend to dwell in distraction. One of the most conspicuous signs of this dwelling is the way the *Holy Sonnets* hesitate between poetry and prose. Jean-Claude Milner has argued that the main criterion for distinguishing poetry from prose is the *possibility* of enjambment.[61] It is a precarious criterion, for it might imply that poetry is most poetic when it has no enjambment at all (that is, at the maximum *potentiality* of enjambment), or on the contrary, it might suggest that poetry is most poetic when it is always on the verge of erupting into prose (that is, when it contains the maximum actuality of enjambment without becoming prose itself). Then again, one might argue that the difference is not between more and less poetry but between two different kinds of poetry; that precisely in this lies the contrast between style and *maniera,* between classicism and mannerism in poetry: maximum distance from prose on the one side, maximum proximity to prose on the other. In this scheme, much of

Petrarch's poetry would fall on the side of style and classicism, despite his many occasional mannerisms. The poems of the *Canzoniere* develop a style that is the signature of their author; every particular feature of this style reflects the intention of the author, indeed his intention as a poet, his poetic authority to bring about a poetic world. The *Canzoniere*'s poeticity manifests itself in creating and maintaining a maximum distance from prose; the lack of enjambment, the virtuoso formal solutions, the abundance of poetic devices all serve to celebrate the intention of poetry. The poems of the *Canzoniere* are at the maximum distance from prose, from the *distentio* of postlapsarian temporality, because they seek to overcome this *distentio* by every available means, so that they can look at the mythic moment of falling in love, the *innamoramento,* not only as a figure of the original sin (*peccato originale*) but also as potential redemption. The *Holy Sonnets* are in contrast on the side of *maniera:* of maximum proximity to prose, in a recurrent deviation from poeticity, with a repeated release of individuality and the ownership of the language that they speak. It is not only that there is not a single Holy Sonnet in which enjambment would not play a crucial role; even more generally, these poems are always on the verge of erupting into prose. The sequence itself modulates between more and less prosaic poems. Poems that resonate with the tender lyricism of the *Songs and Sonets* are exceptions:

> I ame a litle World, made cunningly
> > Of Elements and an Angelique Spright,
> > But blacke Sin hath betrayd to endles night
> My Worlds both parts, and Oh both parts must dy.[62]

Other poems, in contrast, are cast in legal terms and maintain a hypotactic syntax that is in odd dissonance with their poetic form and religious sense. It is not simply that matters of redemption are discussed in terms of economic transaction, which, as we have seen in chapter 2, is not uncommon either in the period or in Donne's poems and sermons. The following address to God is remarkable for the explicatory precision that defines the syntax and pervades the tone:

> Father, part of his double interest
> > Unto thy kingdome thy Sonne gives to me;
> > His ioynture in the knotty trinitee
> He keepes, and gives me his death's Conquest.[63]

In another poem, Donne needs only four lines to create a legal puzzle; the speaker and God were, are, or will be in various legal relationships with one another, and the quatrain's syntax is entirely subordinated to the purpose of expressing these relationships with juridical precision:

> As due by many titles I resigne
> > My selfe to thee (O God): first I was made
> > By thee, and for thee, and when I was decayde
> Thy blood bought that, the which before was thyne.[64]

This tendency to approximate prose within the limits of the sonnet is reinforced by Donne's notorious metrical difficulty. Part of the difficulty is constituted simply by the large number of monosyllables followed time and again by bi- and trisyllabic, often Latinate words. But it is also that the lines that are expected to follow the rules of iambic pentameter depart from it so often that they force us to reset our expectations,[65] resulting in what has been called Donne's "hovering accent," a habitual hesitation of emphasis that reemerges over and over again in the poems.[66]

This result, however, is paradoxical in that it simultaneously brings verse in proximity to prose and, by the same gesture, keeps it apart from prose. The effect of the metric irregularities, the resulting hovering accent, or the frequent enjambments is that neither sound nor sense alone is allowed to dictate the rhythm of attention; or rather that whenever either of the two begins to dictate, the other soon cuts in. Hence the ambiguous character of the movement of the *Holy Sonnets*; sometimes this movement is explicitly hesitant, pausing; sometimes it runs fast but with a rhythm that at one point suddenly, for no obvious reason, breaks down and gives room to a wholly different one.

Some of the most interesting poems in the group are those that begin by inviting attention to look in a certain direction, seemingly without hesitation, almost ecstatically, and then to even intensify the invitation, calling on attention to follow—only to be suddenly arrested, as if something had been forgotten, something so significant, so decisive that the poem cannot go on in the same vein and must find another course to reach its end. The Holy Sonnet in which this poem-long hesitation is perhaps the most conspicuous is the eighth sonnet in the Westmoreland sequence. With this poem, we are returning to the theme of the resurrection of the dead:

At the round Earths imagind corners blow
>   Your trumpets Angels, and Arise Arise
>   From Death you numberles infinities
Of Soules and to your scattered bodyes go,
All whome the Flood did and fyre shall overthrow
>   All whome Warr, dearth, age, agues, tyrannyes,
>   Dispayre, Law, Chance, hath slayne . . .[67]

This is a mimetic-performative enactment of the tumult at the Last Judgment; the ecstatic, apocalyptic tone, the way the paratactic urgency of the first call is further intensified and reaches its climax in the last two lines' long asyndeton all fit in with the notion of *compositio loci*. The initial address to the angels shift to a general address to all participants of the general resurrection, and the work of attention dissolves into the act of imagining the actors of the Last Judgment.

In "The End of the Poem," Giorgio Agamben uses Milner's thesis about enjambment to ask how the poem can end as a poem if, as seems to be the case, the last line cannot contain the possibility of enjambment. He sees in the poem a "theological conspiracy about language": "The poem is like the *katechon* in Paul's Second Epistle to the Thesalonians (2:7–8): something that slows and delays the advent of the Messiah, that is, of him, who, fulfilling the time of poetry and uniting its two eons, would destroy the poetic machine by hurling it into silence."[68] The end of the poem in Agamben's essay has a strange eschatology that delays the apocalypse, the final judgment that would reconnect sounds and sense; instead, it seeks to maintain a certain hesitation between them even in the silence that follows the last word of the poem.[69] Something similar happens in Donne's sonnet; after the two-quatrain long, resounding invocation for the dead to rise, for the Last Judgment to begin, the speaker suddenly changes his mind:

> . . . and you whose eyes
Shall behold God, and never tast deaths wo.
But let them sleepe, Lord, and me mourne a space . . .

The poem's parataxis reached its climax in the enumeration of the dead according to the cause of their death, in three lines of sheer asyndeton. But here the ecstasy of the paratactic invocation breaks down, and gives room to a hypotactic argument. It is impossible to see immediately what has brought about the breakdown; we see only the result, the sudden change of form and tone; as in the case of "This is my Playes last Scene," we can only sense that there must have been a *volta* because of its apparent impact on the poem. It is as though something had just occurred to the speaker, a hitherto re-pressed thought, which has led to the abandonment of the invocation and a sudden shift of address from all the participants of the resurrection to God. No longer seeking to imagine the resurrected, the speaker now attends to God and asks for his special grace. What could have caused the apostrophe, what might we find behind the poem's *volta?*

In the context of the poem the call on those who "never tast deaths wo" seems to be an anomaly, for the paratactic invocation that turned into an enumerative asyndeton began as a call for the dead. It is as though the poem had been carried away by its own form, the paratactic form moving toward the last three lines' asyndetons, and in this ecstatic enumeration included a category that does not really belong there—the category of those who are not dead yet and who can therefore hardly "arise." The *volta* occurs right after this anomaly; as if the speaker had noticed the anomaly, and his notic-ing of the anomaly had forced him to attend to a different idea. The *volta* and the new address to God in this sense emerges out of the discrepancy between form and content; the impetus of the parataxis performed, carried out the tumult of the dead, and included, as if by accident, the living, includ-ing the self.

The discrepancy between form and content calls attention to that other discrepancy that is the central subject of every Holy Sonnet: the discrepancy between common grace and special grace.[70] As the parataxis fades away and gives room to hypotactic syntax and to something that looks very much like a syllogism, though may not actually be one, special grace becomes the son-net's theme leading up to the last couplet:

> For if above all these my Sins abound
> Tis late to ask abundance of thy grace
>   When we are there: Here on this lowly ground
> Teach me how to repent, for that's as good
> As if thou hadst Seald my pardon with thy blood.

Given Donne's fascination with Psalm 6, it is safe to assume that the inspira-tion for this argument comes from the penitential psalm, and it is therefore important to point out that in the psalm the argument for the delay of judg-ment is based not on a petition for grace, but on thanksgiving: "For in death

there is no remembrance of thee: in the grave who shall give thee thanks?"
Yet the kind of *gratiarum actio* that Donne's sonnet ends with is nevertheless a petition for grace, one of the most explicit in the entire sequence. In
the "mourning space" that leads up to the *gratiarum actio,* we may recognize the echoes of a passage from Romans:

> For as by one man's disobedience many were made sinners, so by the
> obedience of one shall many be made righteous. Moreover, the law entered, that the offence might abound. But where sin abounded, grace did
> much more abound: That as sin hath reigned unto death, even so might
> grace reign by righteousness unto eternal life by Jesus Christ our Lord.
> (Rom. 5:19–21)

Notice in Paul's passage the contrast between the hypotactic appearance and
the actual argument: the latter is based not on logical subordinations but on a
number of parallelisms. In other words, the order of words is hypotactic, but
the order of thoughts is paratactic: the one disobedient bringing about many
sinners is juxtaposed with the one obedient imputing righteousness on many;
sin abounded and grace abounded, sin reigned unto death, grace reign unto
life. The entire passage has the appearance of logic, and the order of faith.

Donne reiterates elements of the Pauline passage, and he inserts them
in a form that imitates the Pauline hypotaxis. Let me quote the lines again
so that we can pay attention to the syntax:

> For if above all these my Sins abound
> Tis late to aske abundance of thy grace
> When we are there: Here on this lowly ground
> Teach me how to repent, for that's as good
> As if thou hadst Seald my pardon with thy blood.

If in Paul's passage the hypotactic rhetoric is in contrast with the parallelisms of faith that the hypotaxis conceals, in Donne's sestet hypotaxis serves
to formulate the request that stands in stark opposition with the octave's
enumeration. Once the self emerges out of the movement of distracted attention in the octave, it claims all attention to itself. "Tis late to aske abundance of thy grace" is followed not by a trochee ("*When* we are there") but
by the regular iamb ("When *we* are there"): the argument is that the time
that separates the living self from the "numberles infinities" of the dead
needs to be increased because "by the obedience of one shall *many* also

made be righteous" but not the one, not the one whose sins abound "above all these." Standing together at the Last Judgment may gain a pardon for the many, for the "we," but it cannot gain a pardon for the one—especially if that one is the one who is the one added to the "numberles infinities."

Thus the ending couplet claims not that Christ did not actually give his blood for mankind, but that "teaching" the speaker "how to repent," that is, providing the speaker with the special grace that he needs in order to repent, is like a personalization of Christ's sacrifice, it is as though the sacrifice were reiterated now with the sole goal of pardoning the speaker: "As if thou hadst Seald my pardon with thy blood."

But for our purposes the question remains the *how:* how did the poem earn the right to ask for this special treatment, this special grace? What has led to the direct address to God? What is the poem's argument, in this very specific sense of the word? The *gratiarum actio* is introduced by five lines that have the appearance of an argument; beginning right after the *volta* and its "let them sleepe, Lord, and me mourne a space," the speaker now turns away from the dead and attends to the living instead, or rather to the one living being that is speaking right here, right now. The argument that leads to the *gratiarum actio* begins with a conditional; repentance and, in turn, the grace that one needs in order to be able to repent are recognized only insofar as this conditional provides the ground for their recognition. Yet this conditional is puzzling. The speaker has to ask for grace here, while still alive, and before the Last Judgment, seemingly only "if above all these my Sins abound," which is also to say, *because* "above all these my Sins abound."

What does the deictic "these" refer to? The previous lines did not really include sins, the enumeration focused instead on common causes of death; we could perhaps name "Dispayre" as sin from a Christian perspective, but that would still not be satisfying as a reference for the deictic "these." Is it possible that "these" refers to the tumult of the dead that the parataxis enumerated? That would seem to be a category mistake. But perhaps we *should* look at it as a category mistake, as a strange instance of misspeaking, a technique Donne often uses as a moment of grammatical impropriety that suddenly refocuses the scattered attention of the poem. Here the deixis unveils, not previous sins, not even the tumult of the dead, but rather the "these"-ness of the octave, the parataxis, the asyndeton itself. If so, then "these" refers to the words themselves, the words of the poem, the wordiness of the poem; it is the moment when the speaker realizes that he has more sins than words in his poem.

Within one poem, then, we have two cases of "misspeaking." First, carried away by the paratactic structure, the speaker includes the living, and thus himself, among the dead that he calls on to rise; this discrepancy between form and content, the inattentive collapsing of the living with the dead, "wakes up" the speaker from the dream of the poem's imagination of the Last Judgment. The second instance of "misspeaking," however, is intentional: the "above all these" is the awakened speaker's recognition of his previous dream and of the fact that he needs to repent. Repentance, and thereby the devotional conversion that is expressed by the poem's *volta*, is thus prepared by the poem's own mistakes. We might recall, then, that "metanoia," conversion and repentance, are also rhetorical categories; indeed this is how Puttenham defines the trope, which he also calls "The Penitent," in the *Arte of English Poesie*:

> *Metanoia:* Otherwhiles we speake and be sorry for it, as if we had not wel spoken, so that we seeme to call in our word againe, and to put in another fitter for the purpose: for which respects the Greekes called this manner of speech the figure of repentance: then for that upon repentance commonly followes amendment, the Latins called it the figure of correction, in that the speaker seemeth to reforme that which was said amisse.[71]

One way to think about the *Holy Sonnets* is not as lyric poems but as dramatic soliloquies, each of them spoken by a character with distinct style, on a distinct theatrical stage. The characters can range from the merchant-lawyer who uses legal jargon to negotiate about divine matters, to the penitent sinner who submits himself completely to God, to the millenarian enthusiast who calls for the Second Coming. In each poem, the character receives the given, the form and the content and even its own character, and begins to perform them. The performance tends to follow the formal structure of Ignatian meditation, and in each case it serves the goal of making the given present so that it can become the subject of attention; the poem always begins as the enacting of the given for an unnamed audience. But in each case, this performance breaks down, and if we recall Augustine it is not too difficult to conceptualize this failure. In each case, the givenness of the given escapes attention because the poem distends and thereby scatters attention, which thus fails to reach the singularity it would need to become devotional attention.

Indeed, the sudden withdrawal from the apocalyptic tone in the poem occurs right after another Pauline line. Those whom the poem names by their "eyes," those who "Shall behold God, and never tast deaths wo," are the subjects of Paul's "secret thing" in 1 Corinthians 15, just a few verses before Paul announces the death of Death: "Behold, I shew you a secret thing; We shall not all sleep, but we shall all be changed, In a moment, in the twinkling of an eye at the last trumpet; for the trumpet shall blow, and the dead shall be raised up incorruptible, and we shall be changed" (1 Cor. 15:51–52). One of Paul's most apocalyptic passages, this announcement promises that the end of the world, the last judgment, and the resurrection will arrive so soon that some of those who are alive at the time of the announcement will witness it alive. In one sense, then, Donne's poem was actually right: the resurrection will affect everyone, dead and alive in the same way. But in another sense, the poem's mistake becomes all the more visible when compared with the Pauline passage. For if the poem was supposed to call forth the resurrection, it shouldn't have *imagined* the many, the scattered, the dead, but instead it should have *attended* to the "twinkling of an eye" itself; it is this "twinkling of an eye" that contains the "last trumpet" and the "secret thing." The "twinkling of an eye" is a moment of imperceptibly small extension; yet it is long enough for the body to shed its flesh and change into its new, incorruptible form.

This is what escaped, and indeed necessarily escaped, the attention of the poem from the very beginning; instead, the poem must have distended in time so that it could enlist the multiplicity that the apocalyptic last moment would entail. In this consisted the poem's own sin; and this is why "above all these" does, in fact, refer back to previous sins—the sins of the poem itself. By now, it should be also clear that the "mourning" here refers to the sins for which the self, recalled from distraction, is repenting; but that these sins are also coextensive with the dead of the octave: mourning thus means mourning sins, mourning the dead, but also mourning and creating the space that separates the time of the living from the time of the dead. Augustine says of death that it is nothing but flesh falling off the bones; what "above all these" does to the poem is to tear off the flesh of words from the skeleton of the octave's syntax to create the "twinkling of an eye," the moment of death that concentrates attention and forces it into the "mourning space," the *locus penitentiae* of the poem.

At the core of the poetics of the *Holy Sonnets,* then, there is a moving discrepancy between form and content, between sound and sense. Every Holy Sonnet begins by performing the given, by giving form to the given. But this form always turns out to be slightly inadequate and it does not subject the given to attention in its givenness but rather distracts from it. The poems then dwell in this distractedness like Augustine's *Confessions* dwells in sin before conversion. In this, they are different from Petrarch's intentional poetics. But they are also different from Sidney's figuring of poetic form as distraction: in Donne, distraction is the substance out of which a new, intransitive attention can emerge. Precisely in the distractedness, in the flesh of the poem, the givenness of the given might emerge from behind the content and the form of the sonnet, making itself the subject of another sort of attention. It is a process of unfolding; that which at the beginning of the poem was folded in within the given is gradually teased out, unfolded by the moving layers of sound and sense so that in the end it might emerge as the gift that the act of thanksgiving longs to acknowledge. In the *Holy Sonnets*, Donne creates an experimental poetics that afford the reader the occasional experience of an *extentus*, intransitive attention that emerges not out of the poet's intent but through the cracks and crevices of language, out of the very distraction that words create.

6

SARCASMOS

IN THE PREVIOUS CHAPTER, I ARGUED that in the *Holy Sonnets*, Donne follows an Augustinian-Petrarchan poetics by fashioning the poem itself as flesh and thus as a source of distraction. But one curiosity of the *Holy Sonnets* is that in them, Donne's speakers often not only encounter distraction but seem to deliberately seek it out and, we might say, indulge in it. We have seen this in "At the round Earths imagind corners," and earlier in "This is my Playes last Scene," in which after the first quatrain's effort to produce attentiveness the following two quatrains of the poem carried the act of imagining the process of salvation to an extreme, to a point where the images became fantastical and the self scattered. Surely, Donne might want us to remember theological considerations such as Augustine's suggestion that "of earthly bodies . . . the philosophers affirm cannot dwell in the heavens, because whatever is earthly is drawn back to earth by its own natural weight."[1] But in the context of the poem's particular movement, one feels tempted to ask: Is this still entirely serious? It is one thing to accept, as Donne does following Augustine's suggestions, that distraction is inevitable, that it is the other of human attention and therefore an inherent aspect of devotion; but it is quite another to dwell in this distraction, to insist on the images that a seemingly uncontrolled imagination produces. When sins, the soul, and the body travel through the air, toward hell, heaven, and the earth, we might begin to wonder whether or not we are subjected to a mockery of salvational literalism, and we might surmise that the apparent distraction in the poem is ironic.

Indeed, in Donne's secular poetry, and particularly in the *Songs and Sonets*, scholars have long noticed a tendency of carrying "a given idea, a metaphor, or assertion out to its logical extreme," suggesting that when this logical extreme is reached the idea becomes its own ironic parody.[2] In the context of the *Songs and Sonets,* there is much to support this interpretation. The *Songs and Sonets* are among the most virtuosic poems of late sixteenth- and early seventeenth-century England, poems that proudly display their poetic *inventio.* And *inventio* in the *Songs and Sonets* is the very opposite of the *inventio* of Lock's Puritan poetics: if Puritan poetry tends to underplay the sense of *inventio* as poetic creation in order to emphasize its sense as finding, as allowing the Scriptural material to appear, in the *Songs and Sonets inventio* seems to point toward paradigms of poetic originality. Donne's love lyrics fight and mock and transcend not only conventional Petrarchist tropes and figures but also their anti-Petrarchist counterparts. In virtually every aspect, these poems seem to present themselves in opposition to poetic traditions; everything that is given is either avoided in them or, if it does get integrated, it is also subverted, mocked, and hyperbolized. And when the *Songs and Sonets* turn to givens, now a Petrarchist metaphor, now a Christian doctrine, carrying them to their extreme conclusions where their logical absurdity may become conspicuous, readers embark on a hermeneutics of irony.

There is no space to discuss the legitimacy of irony as a guiding principle in interpreting the *Songs and Sonets* here, although one might note that while in certain poems irony seems evident, it is perhaps not as central to the *Songs and Sonets* as one would think on the basis of the impression that scholarly literature on these poems provides. At any rate, attributing a similarly central role to irony in the *Holy Sonnets* poses obvious problems. As poetic exercises that aim to give thanks and to praise God, what could they mock? How would irony have a role in their devotions?

Yet it is also true that the *Holy Sonnets* lack the humble, self-abasing attitude of Lock's sonnets. Donne's poems reiterate Christian doctrines with a devotional promiscuity (most strikingly displayed when Donne claims religion is most true when "She's embrac'd and open to most Men"), which has led to debates not only about the specific theology of these poems but also about whether or not we should take their theological assertions seriously. While there is a tendency toward the mechanical in the *Holy Sonnets*—that is, toward reiterating the given and reaching the *gratiarum actio* with a teleological automatism—it is also true that often a sense of bitter mockery accompanies the devotional mechanisms. In this chapter, I suggest that this bitter mockery is Donne's version of the rhetorical trope early moderns called "sarcasmos."[3] While today *sarcasmos* is identified as a kind of irony, in early modern rhetoric it was seen as a more independent trope that might or might not be used ironically. What was crucial for *sarcasmos* was its particular function in mocking the body, or more accurately the flesh, *sarx*. The goal of this chapter is to show how Donne uses *sarcasmos* to mock the poem's own body as the flesh that distracts. This is crucial: while in the previous chapters I concentrated on the Platonizing, intellectual, and spiritual aspects of both devotion and Donne's devotional poetry, the trope of *sarcasmos* in the poems signals Donne's deep investment in the materiality of both the human and the poetic body. *Sarcasmos* plays a central role in the poetics of the *Holy Sonnets:* it is the figure that incarnates inattention in a poetic *Stimmung* or mood, thereby allowing the poems' speakers to attend to their own distractions.[4]

IRONY AND *SARCASMOS*

The seventeenth Holy Sonnet in the Westmoreland sequence has long been both a favorite and a much-debated poem for reasons that have a lot to do with the question of irony. The poem is traditionally considered to have been written on the occasion of (or in remembrance of) the 1617 death of Donne's wife, Anne More. Given the scarce personal references in the *Holy Sonnets,* readers and critics alike have embraced this opportunity to speculate about Donne's sentiments toward his wife. Some have considered Donne a cynical opportunist who, once he discovered that his marriage was an obstacle to his worldly career, instead of the advantage that motivated him to arrange the marriage in the first place, couldn't wait to get out of wedlock. Others have suggested that on the contrary, from all the available evidence, Donne seems to have had only tender feelings for his wife until the end of her life, and indeed long after her death.

Neither of these views can enlist much evidence. Aside from a few brief personal comments in the letters and some less personal ones in the sermons, as well as an epitaph Donne wrote on August 15, 1617, we only have the poems themselves. Despite the scarcity of evidence, or perhaps because of it, scholars have been keen on finding clues for Donne's "real" feelings for Anne in this particular Holy Sonnet. But the attempts encountered the poem's own resistance to such quests, and for a reason that is highly relevant for us. Donne's poem is a thanksgiving poem for Anne's death, but the thanksgiving seems hardly won and bitterly resented.

The sonnet begins with a quatrain that scholarship has traditionally identified as a reference to Anne's death:

Since She whome I lovd, hath payd her last debt
     To Nature, and to hers, and my good is dead
     And her Soule early into heaven ravished,
Wholy in heavenly things my Mind is sett.[5]

As usual in the *Holy Sonnets,* the symbolic scenery of the poem is set with
striking immediacy and with a hint of ambivalence. Personal pronouns
dictate the quatrains' rhythm, the poem bouncing between "She" and "I"
as though between two walls. The rhythm creates a space of mourning.
In the tradition of the *Vita Nuova* and Petrarchism, the quatrain vacil-
lates between divine and earthly love. Yet the oscillation is telic, and the
mourning eventually emerges as an intentional attitude; the poem is tending toward the divine, even while looking back at "She." If the poem is
about Anne More, it seems that her death is already transformed into a
Neoplatonic-Christian opportunity to look beyond the distractions of the
world, which included the living Anne More, and to focus attention on the
transcendent.[6]

Yet the second quatrain shows that this turn to the transcendent is not
as easy as the first quatrain suggests: instead of looking at those "heavenly
things" that his mind is supposed to be set on, the speaker returns to the
time when "she" was still alive. In almost didactic terms, an explanation
follows to see "she" as a mediatrix whose earthly presence already induced
a conversion in the speaker. But the conversion, the "turn toward God" was
not yet fully undistracted; "she" who helped the speaker turn his attention
toward the divine source was also an obstacle to reaching it, like the river's
flow that creates resistance to the swimmer who wants to move upstream:

Here the admyring her my Mind did whett
     To seeke thee God; so streames do shew the head,
     But though I have found thee,' and thou my thirst hast fed,
A holy thirsty dropsy melts mee yett.

The water imagery of the quatrain (the foretaste of grace from the pun on
"whett" to the streams, and the "holy thirsty dropsy") uses the traditional
identification of the holy water with divine grace to continue the first quatrain's passionately ambivalent devotional movement.[7] The whole movement is, in fact, passionate in the proper early modern sense, full of tears
and humors, liquids that seem to want to overflow the limits of the poem's
body. With all its emphasis on passion, however, the poem is entirely in

accord with a Neoplatonist poetics in which the beloved is an earthly vestige of divine grace, turning the lover to God.

With the third quatrain, we witness a change in both the tone and the content of the poem. On the one hand, these are the lines in which the former description fluctuates into active devotion, culminating in the poem's final thanksgiving: the speaker wants to understand Anne's death as a sign of God's love for him. These are the lines in which the hitherto theoretical-descriptive register of the poem gives room to the devotional acknowledgment of God's grace. On the other hand, however, in this process of actively turning toward God with a *gratiarum actio,* the poem's former teleological and watery devotional movement is suddenly interrupted by an entirely different mood. No gestures, no expressions accompany the remaining lines that contrary to the flowing, watery quality of the first quatrain, focus on argument, distinction, division. It is as though the speaker had found himself in a new mood:

> But why should I begg more Love, when as thou
>> Dost woe my Soule for hers, offring all thine:
> And dost not only feare least I allow
>> My Love to Saints and Angels things divine
> But in thy tender iealosy dost doubt
> Least the World, fleshe, yea Devill putt thee out.

The poem asks a question ("Why should I ask for more of your love, God?") and answers it ("For you have already given me abundant signs of your love by forbidding idolatry and taking her away from me"). This is both a formal volta and a conversion ending in a thanksgiving. If the first two quatrains described the speaker's quest for more divine grace, the last lines express the recognition that divine grace *has been given*—in the form of her death.

The content of these lines is orthodox in theological terms and conventional in the poetic tradition: it brings together an Augustinian-Petrarchan poetics with the God of love in the Gospels by using the notion of the jealous God of the Exodus. Yet the orthodoxy is excessive, the use of poetic convention mechanical, and the question overtly rhetorical. If spoken by a character in a play, the slightest sneer would be enough for the audience to interpret the closure ironically. All the excessive theological and poetic appropriateness would become a sign of the speaker's scorn for the propositional content of the closure; the more hyperbolic his thanks were, the louder the audience would hear a bitter complaint about his loss that subverts the devotional thanksgiving.[8]

But in "Since She whome I lovd," there is no such gesture. The poem's final tone is sustained in a harsh, bitter mood but without creating or even allowing a position outside of the poem's unease with its own language. Without a gesture, without such an outside position for irony, the poem's closure seems mechanical and almost inhuman. Prompted by this unsettling impression, critics have been keen to find the reason of the closure's ambivalence in Donne's own mood, in his struggle and partial failure to find consolation for his loss in Christian religion.[9] There is of course a danger in this: when we begin to speculate about Donne's personal feelings because we cannot make sense of the mood that we find in the poem, we submit to our own sense of what is proper and what is improper in emotions; or to our own desire to see in the poem the kind of humanity and indeed humanism that we value. More importantly for the purposes of this book, such a going-beyond the poem to the author's real or imagined feelings would mean abandoning our central question, the work of the poem in devotional poetry. For here the bitter mood that pervades the poem's devotion seems very much to belong to the poem itself, independent of whether it helps or obstructs the devotional goal of the poem. If we want to develop a theory of devotional poetry of thanksgiving, we need to investigate this mood that in "Since She whome I lovd" seems to run counter to the mechanisms and goals of prayer and thanksgiving. We need to investigate the possibility of *sarcasmos* as bitter, even hostile mockery that at the same time resists ironic interpretation.

BITING INTO FLESH

Hamlet is the most iconic speaker of sarcastic language in early modern literature. From the moment he first appears on the stage to address his mother and Claudius, his utterances are infused with a bitter irony. Were he to speak merely ironically, without the bitterness, no one at the court would find him "particular"; sixteenth-century ideals of courtly self-conduct, *sprezzatura* and its derivatives all use linguistic and behavioral codes in ironic ways.[10] Yet, while these ideals employ irony as an instrument that moderates and mediates the self in society, Hamlet's irony is excessive and hostile; it is sarcastic irony that seizes on an expression or implication in the other's remark and turns it upside down in an insulting manner, aggressively mocking the speaker and his or her discourse simultaneously.[11]

But on occasion, Hamlet's verbal abuses resist ironic interpretation altogether. Only moments before the end, when Laertes asks for a foil, Hamlet responds with what seems to be a final instance of his usual sarcastic wit:

> I'll be your foil, Laertes. In mine ignorance
> Your skill shall, like a star i'th' darkest night,
> Stick fiery off indeed.
>
> ---
>
> (5.2.192–195)

"You mock me, sir," Laertes reacts, puzzled by Hamlet's apparent humility or insulted by what he assumes to be Hamlet's real meaning behind the words. He, along with the audience and the scholarship, assumes that Hamlet's remark is consistent with his earlier discourse: it seizes on "foil," turns its meaning upside down,[12] and then praises his enemy's skill in ironic terms that imply his contempt for Laertes. Of course Laertes has every reason to think that Hamlet's remark mocks him. How could he believe that the prince, who has self-righteously judged everything and everyone throughout the play, and who has attacked him viciously in Ophelia's grave, would now suddenly change tone in such a dramatic fashion and humble himself in front of his enemy, calling himself his enemy's advantage (one of the meanings of "foil" in this case). For Laertes and for the audience, the hyperbole that casts their coming duel in cosmic terms suggests the opposite of what it says: instead of expressing tranquil and humble resignation, it mocks Laertes under the guise of praising his skills as a swordsman. And yet Hamlet refuses Laertes' charge with unusually plain language: "No, by this hand."

Scholars have proposed that we imagine here an insulting physical gesture that would accompany the words.[13] The suggestion is speculative but it sheds light on the conditions of irony: an aggressive physical gesture would unequivocally indicate the remark's irony and thus cleanse all potential ambiguities from it. While no *physical* gesture is indicated in any of the *Hamlet* texts, one can take the cosmic excess of praise in Hamlet's remark as a *linguistic* gesture that invites ironic interpretation. Such an interpretation would also invite us to connect Hamlet's remark with his "provocative mood" throughout the play; indeed ironic interpretation has a close association with psychological readings.[14] The most consistent (or the most exaggerated) ironic hermeneutic is what Paul Ricoeur has called the hermeneutics of suspicion, that is, Freudian psychoanalytical theory; it is no wonder that psychoanalysis found in Hamlet a model of the psychoanalytical subject, a character more Oedipal than Oedipus himself; no wonder, indeed, that it interpreted Hamlet's sarcastic discourse as an expression of his unconscious, narcissistic, and cannibalistic desire to punish both the source of his disappointment (that is, his mother) and the rival who has seized her (Claudius).[15]

But what if we simply believe Hamlet? What if we simply accept the prince's denial that he was joking? What if we suppress the speculative impulse that Hamlet's character evokes and take Hamlet's words at their face value; that is, listening to what they say instead of what they might mean? What if, in other words, we read this passage as poetry, not in the sense of focusing on its formal characteristics but by assuming that the words *contain* the "provocative mood" *in themselves,* instead of assuming that they express the mood of a speaker? The remark's internal excess would of course still remain operative; and as a result, we would have a figure reminiscent of what scholarship used to call "the metaphysical conceit," and which Helen Gardner described as follows: "A conceit is a comparison whose ingenuity is more striking than its justness, or, at least, is more immediately striking. All comparisons discover likeness in things unlike; a comparison becomes a conceit when we are made to concede likeness while being strongly conscious of unlikeness."[16] To be sure, Hamlet's remark is not particularly ingenious, nor is it elaborate the way metaphysical conceits are considered to be. If Gardner's description is still relevant here, it is because even despite the conventionality of the simile between skill and stars, the comparison seems devious; it is because Laertes and most critics are reluctant to concede likeness, remaining "strongly conscious of unlikeness." For them, Hamlet's words will gesture toward the opposite of what they say. The comparison between Hamlet's "ignorance" and the "darkest night," between Laertes' skill and the star that suddenly explodes into this darkness and illuminates the night, will appear not as ingenuous, but as a conventional figure taken to such an excess that this very excess becomes a sign indicating the irony of the remark. Metaphysical conceits provoke disbelief: Hamlet's overt and hyperbolical simile raises suspicion on the parts of Laertes and the audience; instead of "conceding likeness," they suspect a foul play on words.

If, however, one approaches the simile with faith in it, if one does concede likeness and delves into the possibilities embedded in Hamlet's remark, rather than staying outside it in the position of irony, the simile opens up and its metaphorical foundation becomes visible. For the simile that compares ignorance with night and skill with a shining star is grounded in an implicit but no less excessive figure, one that lacks the connecting "like" and therefore emerges as a simple metaphor. Hamlet's "I'll be your foil" sets up this metaphor: while the sense of foil as advantage prepares the comparison between ignorance and skill, the literal meaning remains operative, indicating that Hamlet is speaking about the duel.[17] What in the simile appears as Hamlet's "ignorance" and "darkest night" is in a metaphorical sense Hamlet's own flesh, the flesh that Laertes' "skill" and "star," and ultimately his sword, will penetrate.

Once again prophetic, Hamlet does not mock Laertes: his target is the flesh itself. The exchange recalls the initial words of his very first soliloquy in 1.2: "O that this too too solid flesh would melt, / Thaw and resolve itself into a dew" (1.2.129–130). But the flesh that he mocks now, at the end of the play, is no longer the flesh of his own body only—it is flesh in the figurative, Christian sense, the flesh that pulls one back to the world, the flesh that Hamlet, Laertes, and even the very words they exchange all share. Regardless of whether his intention was to mock and insult Laertes, his words now mock themselves, their own semblance.[18] Behind this semblance of the hyperbolical simile, they establish a metaphorical level that will soon become literal; for only a few moments later Laertes' sword does indeed penetrate Hamlet's flesh and staunch the flow of his verbal wit. Hamlet's mockery is laden with apocalyptic expectations, and the seemingly excessive cosmic simile becomes an expression of a personal apocalypse, a revelation that both anticipates and requires the destruction of the flesh.

Renaissance rhetoricians were intensely aware of this aspect of the trope that they called *sarcasmos*.[19] They insisted on the "biting" potential of *sarcasmos* and emphasized its etymon, the Greek *sarx* (flesh), to suggest that *sarcasmos* is so excessively aggressive that it could penetrate the flesh. In this, they relied on the classical rhetorical tradition that saw in *sarcasmos* a bellicose trope, an expression to provoke the enemy. But while for the classical tradition the enemy to be provoked was the epic enemy in war-like situations (and thus examples for the trope were usually taken from Homer and Virgil), Christian writers began to find *sarcasmos* in the Scriptures.[20] Indeed, one of the commonly cited passages in the Bible was the Pauline mockery of death that Donne reiterates at the end of "Death be not proud": the resounding address "O death, where is thy victory? O death, where is thy sting?" was seen as a Christian version of the classical trope of *sarcasmos*.[21]

I suggest that the difference between classical and Christian *sarcasmos* goes beyond the use of different examples. Christian writers used *sarcasmos* to attack a new, Pauline enemy: flesh (*sarx*) and everything that flesh stood for. *Sarcasmos* emerged as an expression of an *ēthos,* of the Christian attitude toward the world that lives and exists according to the flesh (*kata sarka*).[22] It became an implicit element of the Christian style.[23]

THE RHETORIC OF *SARCASMOS*

Classical and early modern rhetoric saw *sarcasmos* as a trope; although various accounts differed in their exact classification, in most of the cases *sarcasmos* was considered as a type of both *allegoria* (that which means something other than what it says) and *ironia* (that which means the opposite of what it says).[24] Yet there is no classical or early modern definition of *sarcasmos* that would explicitly say that *sarcasmos* implies something different from, let alone the opposite, of what it says.[25] What they emphasize instead as the *differentia specifica* of *sarcasmos* is what we might call an attitude, the attitude that *sarcasmos* expresses or embodies. Thus one of the most widely accepted definitions describes *sarcasmos* as "hostilis inrisio cum amaritudine" (hostile and bitter derision);[26] another characterizes it as "plena odio" (full of hatred);[27] yet another calls attention to its "severity" and to the fact that despite being a type of mockery and derision, it does not incite laughter.[28]

Readers of Elizabethan literature are familiar with the attitude expressed by *sarcasmos.* Take the case of one of the most influential poems of the period, "The Lie," often attributed to Sir Walter Ralegh.[29] In contrast to the popularity it enjoyed at the time, today the poem is often glossed over as a conventional courtly satire. Indeed, after the valedictory first lines ("Go soule the bodies guest / Upon a thanckles arrante"), the poem begins to mock the court and worldly ambition in general:

> Say to the court it glows
>> And shines like rotten wood,
> Say to the church it shows
>> What's good, and doth no good:
>>> If church and court reply,
>>> Then give them both the lie.

Tell potentates, they live
    Acting, by others' action;
Not lov'd unless they give;
    Not strong, but by affection.
      If potentates reply,
      Give potentates the lie.

Tell men of high condition,
    That manage the estate,
Their purpose is ambition;
    Their practice only hate.
      And if they once reply,
      Then give them all the lie.

The poem sustains this self-identity as courtly satire until the fourth stanza. But then in the fourth and fifth stanzas a movement appears that seems to probe the limits of this identity. Until now, the "soule" has been sent to belie people of ambition and institutions of hierarchy; now, it is sent to challenge "zeale," "love," "time," and "flesh." The change is registered first on the level of logical mood: what seemed to be a particular negative (the scorn of particular agents and institutions of the world, beginning with the court), is now replaced by an increasingly abstract and universal negative. Even as this ominous movement toward a seemingly unjustified excess on the logical level continues ("age," "honor," "bewty," even "charity" are among those to be challenged) and the poem transgresses the genre of courtly satire, it remains within the secular and sacred traditions of *contemptus mundi*. Yet the insistence with which the poem repeats and extends its initial conceit becomes more and more conspicuous. The imperatives follow one another with increasing frequency:

Tell zeale it wanttes devotion
tell love it is but lust
tell tyme it meedes but motion
tell fleshe it is but Dust.

By this point, the poem shows a conspicuous reluctance to moderate its own bitterness and hostility; it commands the "soule" to provoke everything and everyone in the world. It is as though once the poem releases its hostility, it cannot take it back; like an infection, the poem's *sarcasmos* spreads quickly not only from one signified to another but suddenly to every signified, bringing the whole poem to the brink of collapse. What differentiates "The Lie" from the poetry of the High Renaissance is not the subject matter, but this conspicuous lack of moderation: the poem exhibits a stubborn, bitter insistence with which it repeats its conceit through twelve stanzas, perduring in time for seven stanzas after it dismissed "time" for the fact that "it meedes but motion."

It is as though the poem were motivated by a resentment that does not originate in a particular object but rather uses the poem *to seek out* an enemy that could help its articulation.[30] Early modern responses to the poem show that contemporaries took an acute interest in the poem's excess, even if they did not consent to the poem's use of it. Among the number of poems responding to "The Lie," many turn the central conceit of the poem against itself; one response changed the refrain:

> If Rawhead this denye
> Tell him his tongue doth lye.[31]

Another one charged:

> The lyes thou gave so hott
> Returne into thy throate.[32]

All these satiric responses recognize that "The Lie" is just one step away from becoming a mockery of itself: if everything and everyone is a liar, then why would the poem itself remain an exception? They call attention to the fact that "The Lie" has the potential of collapsing under the burden of its own conceit, not unlike the paradox of the liar.[33]

But of course "The Lie" is neither paradoxical nor ironic. Its excess does not become another sign, transcending, questioning, and ultimately replacing the meanings within the poem. In irony, excess questions the sign by becoming a sign itself, thus creating a quasi-grammatical structure in which that which is said is countered by its opposite which is not said (but which appears in the index of the excess); the nature of irony is such that the linguistic utterance always manages to contain itself in this way. But with the excess of "The Lie," no such quasi-grammatical shift emerges; the excess seems to remain unwarranted.

This is why, when we read early modern texts like "The Lie" and notice their hostile attitude, we cannot rely on our own understanding of sarcasm.

In its most common meaning today, sarcasm suggests a crude and hostile use of irony. While sociolinguistic and psychological studies offer a more sophisticated understanding of sarcasm, they still insist on its fundamentally ironic character, suggesting that in sarcastic expression the message is accompanied by an implicit metamessage that rejects and derides what is explicitly said. For early modern commentators, by contrast, the *differentia specifica* of *sarcasmos* was its association with hostility and bitterness, *even if*, as in "The Lie," *sarcasmos* does not emerge as ironic. For them, *sarcasmos* was primarily an overt and provocative mockery of the enemy. In Philip Melanchthon's words, *sarcasmos* was the winner's mocking of the defeated ("cum victor victum irridet");[34] and in Julius Caesar Scaliger's opinion it implied the derision of dead flesh.[35] As mockery, *sarcasmos* was seen as an expression so biting that it could pierce the flesh ("Sarchasmos . . . dicitur a sarchos quod est caro quia talis derisio penetrat usque ad interiora carnis").[36]

None of these definitions implies any necessary connection between irony and *sarcasmos,* despite the classical categorization of *sarcasmos* as a type of *ironia* in the sense of an opposition between words and their meaning.[37] Indeed, a number of Renaissance commentators took note of this divergence and pointed out that *sarcasmos* had no ironic implications but could simply be taken to mean what it said.[38] For the same reason, the place of *sarcasmos* in rhetoric was problematized as well; at least one commentator argued that *sarcasmos* was not a trope at all but simply an inelegant way of saying what it meant.[39] *Sarcasmos* is the polar opposite of *charientismos,* the trope of grace, of *charis,* that expresses the unpleasant in pleasant terms.[40] *Charientismos* dresses up an unpleasant meaning in graceful expression. If Renaissance *charientismos* seeks to hide an insulting sense behind pleasing words, *sarcasmos* makes the words all the more insulting to provoke the enemy. This *sarcasmos* is what defines the tonality of "The Lie," and it explains why the poem ends by setting the soul against all else, that is, against flesh and dissembling (and flesh *as* dissembling). For only the soul can resist the dagger of *sarcasmos:*

> Soe when thou hast as I
> Commaunded thee done blabbinge
> Althoughe to give the lye
> Deserve noe lesse then stabbinge
> Stabbe at thee hee that will,
> No stabbe thy sowle can kill.

This end of "The Lie" is a reminder that in its most influential sense in Christianity, flesh (*sarx*) is different from the body (*soma*).[41] Paul's eschatology implies the final destruction of flesh even while it promises the resurrection of the body: the body is the given mode of existence for every created being, while flesh is the mode of fallen, temporal existence, in the state of disgrace. Unlike the body, the flesh cannot be redeemed; it can only be destroyed. Accordingly, it is not the body but flesh that stands in opposition with the soul. The *sarcasmos* of "The Lie" expresses this Pauline hostility toward flesh and everything that flesh stands for. The poem sends out the soul to mock and provoke the world according to the flesh in the most bitter and aggressive way possible: its relentless *sarcasmos* is the expression of an apocalyptic Christian *ēthos*.

The classical trope of *sarcasmos* fulfills a specific role in Christian literature: potentially, at least, it becomes the expression of a Pauline *ēthos*, of the Christian rejection of the flesh and everything that flesh stands for. The relentless hostility, the non-ironic, bitter, and seemingly uncontrolled antagonism of poems like "The Lie" is an expression of the Christian's total rejection of the world *kata sarka*, according to the flesh. Since flesh is not redeemable, it must be destroyed, and *sarcasmos* is the linguistic-rhetorical equivalent of the war that Christianity was waging on the flesh. "The Lie" is Christian mockery of the flesh in this sense; indeed, there is an old scholarly view that debates the traditional ascription of the poem to Sir Walter Ralegh explicitly on the basis that the poem's excess must be the expression of the writer's Puritan zeal, inconsistent with Ralegh's distaste for Puritans.[42]

This may not be a valid point; Hamlet, who is hardly a Puritan, attacks flesh in a similarly aggressive way throughout the play.[43] Donne himself uses *sarcasmos* as mockery of the flesh a number of times in his poetry. The most famous example is of course the *Anniversary* poems that mourn the young Elizabeth Drury's death in the most hyperbolical terms possible. Despite Jonson's charge that the poems are blasphemous because of their excess, the *Anniversaries* are consistently Christian: they present the young girl as life-giving divine grace, the world's animating soul, and contrast her with the world's body that becomes a decaying, rotting "lump of flesh" in the absence of the young girl's grace. Flesh, and not body. This may explain why critics have had so much trouble identifying the structure of "The Anatomy of the World," or even its main subject.[44] The poem's very conceit is that it anatomizes the world's flesh rather than its body. The poem is an extended instance of *sarcasmos*; like the biting trope, it cuts into the flesh of the world, and while continuing the bizarre examination of the "lump of flesh," it repeatedly expresses its disgust over what it sees, and indeed what it smells. Darwin once argued that the reason sneering and nasality can express disgust and contempt is that they suggest, metonymically, the speaker's physical reaction to a revolting taste or smell.[45] The response to such sensations is an immediate attempt to get rid of the source of the sensation; therefore the gestures and expressions that normally precede the actions that the body would take, from the voluntary and controlled gesture of spitting to the involuntary vomiting. Sneering and nasality can thus be gestural indices of extreme *sarcasmos,* suggesting that the speaker is disgusted by the taste and smell of his own words:[46]

> But as in cutting up a man that's dead,
> The body will not last out to have read
> On every part, and therefore men direct
> Their speech to parts, that are of most effect;
> So the worlds carcasse would not last, if I
> Were punctuall in this Anatomy.
> Nor smells it well to hearers, if one tell
> Them their disease, who faine would think they're well.

(ll. 434–442)[47]

But while "The Lie" and—albeit in a different sense—even the *Anniversaries* use *sarcasmos* to mock the world *kata sarka,* according to the flesh, once we turn back to the *Holy Sonnets* we face a curious puzzle. "The Lie" is hyperbolical in its conceit and bitter in its attitude; yet once we identify the poetic persona, the speaker of the poem (a devout Christian) and his enemy (the world *kata sarka*), the rhetorical excess and the sarcastic mood become functions of the poem's Christian *ēthos* toward the world. We have seen that Donne's poem "Since she whome I lovd" displays a similar sarcastic mood. But oddly enough, in this poem the sarcastic mood is not directed at an external enemy, something outside the poem that could be identified as "flesh." Rather, in "Since she whome I lovd" it is the devotion itself that appears sarcastic. Indeed, as I will show, in the *Holy Sonnets* devotion generally does not express itself in bitter and hostile *sarcasmos* toward the world *kata sarka;* instead, it seems as though devotion itself were expressed in bitter and hostile terms. What or who is the target of this devotional *sarcasmos*? God? The speaker? Or the poem itself? What role does *sarcasmos* fulfill in these poems? How does (or doesn't) *sarcasmos* contribute to the devotional work of poetry in the *Holy Sonnets?*

THE POETICS OF *SARCASMOS* AS MOOD

As a thanksgiving devotional poem, every Holy Sonnet uses the sonnet form to drive itself toward its *volta* and closure; that is, toward a poetic conversion and the ensuing grace. Devotion and the work of the poem coincide in them; it is the poetic rhythm of turn and completion that becomes the substrate of devotion. Yet in the *Holy Sonnets* this simultaneously poetic and devotional movement is performed in a sarcastic mood that seems to question its genuineness; the words are spoken as though they were in quotation marks, not really belonging to the speaker, similar to what I have called earlier, using Agamben's phrase, the expropriating language of *maniera.* The poem's mood (its *Stimmung*) does not seem to be in accord with its devotional movement; it is as though the instruments of the *Holy Sonnets* were not properly tuned to play the music of devotion. Insofar as *sarcasmos* belongs to the poem, insofar as it therefore constitutes at least part of the poem's work, the question is, how does it relate to the poem's devotion? Does it contribute to devotion, or does it, on the contrary, subvert and misdirect devotion?

Earlier I suggested that *sarcasmos* in the Christian context may become the expression of a Christian *ēthos,* the Pauline hostility toward flesh and what "flesh" stands for, the world *kata sarka.* It is now time to articulate the implications of this view with more theoretical-rhetorical precision, in terms that refer us back to the theme of chapter 1 and specifically the Aristotelian rhetorical theory of proofs, *pisteis,* one of which is *ēthos* in the *Rhetoric.* Let us recapitulate the Aristotelian argument, now focusing not on the inartificial proofs, the subject of chapter 1, but on the artificial proofs or what Aristotle calls *pisteis entekhnoi.*[48] At the beginning of Book I, having defined rhetoric as "the faculty (*dunamis*) of discovering the possible means of persuasion in reference to any subject whatsoever," Aristotle turns to the "proofs" or "means of persuasion" (*pisteis*) that rhetoric may employ. There are two kinds of such *pisteis:* artificial (*entekhnoi*) and inartificial (*atekhnoi*). Inartificial *pisteis* exist independent of the oration; they are "witnesses, tortures, contracts, and the like." Aristotle does not give much consideration to these in the *Rhetoric;* he focuses on the second category,

those artificial *pisteis* that are constructed by the speaker through his ora-
torical performance. These have to be "invented" by the orator in the sense
of creating, and therefore they are the proper subject matter of rhetoric as
a *technē*. The artificial *pisteis* fall under three categories: "The first depends
upon the moral character [the *ēthos*, what Latin commentators would call
habitus or *mores*] of the speaker, the second upon putting the hearer into a
certain frame of mind [which Aristotle himself would later call *pathos*], the
third upon the speech [*logos*] itself, in so far as it proves or seems to prove."[49]

The third category, the speech or argument (*logos*) itself, need not concern us here. Aristotle's focus discussing this particular sense of *logos* is on
that aspect of what is said that we might call logical. The two kinds of *pisteis* that belong to *logos* in this restricted sense are the example and the en-
thymeme (or the "rhetorical syllogism"). What connects these two kinds of
logos is that they have a basically logical relationship to the subject matter
of the speech or legal process; they contribute to the process of persuasion
through this logical (or pseudological) connection. In contrast, *ēthos* and
pathos concern exclusively the *relations* between the speaker, the audience,
and the *logos*. The crucial point that Aristotle makes here, in the *Rhetoric*'s
discussion of *ēthos* and *pathos,* is that both of these categories belong to
what he calls artificial proofs or *pisteis*. *Ēthos* is not the orator's ethical character, already existing before the oration. Rather, it is the character that the
orator constructs for himself in his oration. The *Rhetoric* is quite insistent
on this point: in the course of his speech act, the orator makes a *pistis* out of
himself because "moral character . . . constitutes the most effective means
of proof." Not in his person, but in his rhetorical persona, the orator himself
becomes a proof, a *pistis*. The same applies to *pathos*. By *pathos*, Aristotle
does not mean the general disposition of a given audience. Rather, *pathos*
is the disposition in which a listener finds himself in response to the orator's performance, the mood that the orator's performance induces in the
audience. *Pathos* is thus the other side of the same relationality that itself is
constructed in and by the oration.

Rhetoric is concerned with *ēthos* and *pathos* insofar as they are two
sorts of *pistis*. Together, rhetorical *ēthos* and *pathos* constitute a dynamic
relationship between the speaker and the listener; this relationship is the
space in which that which is being said can unfold. Although the orator
must have a working knowledge of psychology to be able to determine what
ēthos would work best with a given audience, and what *pathos* should prepare the audience best for the *logos* that he is delivering, neither *ēthos* nor
pathos is a psychological concept. As two types of *pistis,* they are rhetorical

categories; and we should add that as categories existing exclusively in the relationship between the speaker, the audience, and what is being communicated by the speaker toward the audience, they are phenomenological categories as well.

When later, in Book II, Aristotle returns to the matter, he makes a crucial point about the relationship between *ēthos* and *pathos*: "The emotions (*pathē*) are all those affections which cause men to change their opinion (*metaballontes diapherousi*) in regard to their judgments, and are accompanied by pleasure (*hēdonē*) and pain (*lupē*)."[50] Although in a crucial sense this is still *pathos* from the point of view of rhetoric, in that it is construed by the orator, the *pathos* that Aristotle defines here is not any longer just the rhetorical *pathos*. It is in accordance with the *Metaphysics,* where Aristotle defines *pathos* as that which permits movement or change, or as the change and movement itself. The *pathē* are those emotions that drive people to move away from their former decisions or judgments, ultimately from their former *ēthos;* or they are these movements themselves turning away from a former *ēthos* and toward a new one.

Now, even though later in the *Rhetoric* Aristotle allows style to be associated with *ēthos* or *pathos* (contributing to the tradition that associates *pathos* with tragedy and *ēthos* with comedy),[51] he is generally quite consistent in using *ēthos* for the speaker's expressed attitude and *pathos* for the audience's solicited mood. This distinction may appear to be a problem for a discussion of *ēthos* and *pathos* in poetry. The notion of a "speaker" is itself deeply ambiguous in poetic discourse in a way that goes beyond the ethical-pragmatic function of the orator's character in his performance. More importantly, "audience" as an external listener is by definition absent; even if we are able to specify the historical audience of a given poem, such as a patron or a coterie circle in the case of Donne's poetry, a lyric poem may still require that we read it as though it spoke to its actual audience only by coincidence, as though it were, to invoke again John Stuart Mill's dictum, "overheard" speech.[52] Nowhere is this absence of human audience more conspicuous than in devotional poetry. At least since Augustine's *Confessions,* devotional discourse (prayer, meditation, confession) operates on the structural assumption that any human audience that may witness it would do so only by coincidence. We need to emphasize that this is a structural assumption in the sense that it does not speak to the actual readerly practices of devotional poetry; rather, it refers to the poems' own demand that they be read as though they had been addressed to God.[53] How can we speak of *pathos* in devotional poetry, then? How could we apply the rhetorical category of *ēthos* and *pathos* in the context of a poetry that is addressed to absent audiences?

What may appear to be a problem here is in fact the most instructive part of Aristotle's theory for the interpretation of poetic mood. In meditation, prayer, and thanksgiving, which are all specific kinds of rhetorical performances, the speaker and the listener coincide: they *happen* to be the same person.[54] Rhetoric and poetry here diverge: if devotion is different from an ordinary rhetorical performance in that the speaker and the listener coincide in it, poetry performing devotion is different from both in that the speaker and the listener exist, as in rhetoric, only as functions of the linguistic utterance itself, but they also coincide, as they do in meditation. When poetry becomes the vehicle of devotion, as a rhetorical performance it induces a mood in its own speaker within the poem, which is also to say that *pathos* in the context of devotional poetry is not the pathos of an external audience but the *pathos*, the mood of the poem's speaker.

But what does it mean to talk about the mood of a poem? We are accustomed to think that a poem may express an attitude or a mood—but could a poem have its own mood? The answer is that it couldn't, as long as we think of mood as psychological category, a temporary disposition. If, however, we move away from the psychological terminology toward a phenomenological one, we may describe mood as the self's relatedness to the world and to itself. This phenomenological description allows us, in turn, to apply the term for poetry. "Poetic mood" is like the subjunctive in grammar:[55] it is the way in which a poem is related to itself and to its propositional content, the content of the poem being the poem's "world," different from the world of the poem's author.[56] This poetic mood may be expressed by the poem's poetic speaker, although it does not have to be; but when it is in the voice, in the tone, of the poetic speaker that the mood manifests itself, it still belongs to the poem, we still need to talk about it as "poetic mood" because it has no direct relationship with the author's psychological disposition. What I have suggested in the previous passages is that this phenomenological approach to poetic mood is in fact inherent in classical rhetoric and may be best investigated in the terms that classical rhetoric has for what I have called attitude and mood, as *ēthos* and *pathos*.[57]

Insofar as *sarcasmos* is defined by the bitterness, hostility, and biting mockery of expression, it belongs to those aspects of speech that Aristotle discusses in terms of rhetorical *ēthos* and *pathos*, under the general category of producing artificial (*enteknoi*) proofs. In what follows, I will read the *Holy Sonnets* in terms of poetic *ēthos* and *pathos*. By poetic *ēthos*, I mean the way in which the poem relates to its propositional content and to itself; in "The Lie," *sarcasmos* is poetic *ēthos* in that it performs the speaker's ethical position toward "the world," that is, the world *kata sarka* that the poem invents as its own reference. By poetic *pathos,* in turn, I mean the way in which the poem finds itself related (disposed) to itself, *including* its own *ēthos.* Poetic *pathos* emerges in the poem as the poem's response to its own discourse; it is the mood in which the poem finds itself upon hearing itself, which may be (but does not have to be) expressed in the tone, in the voice of the poem's speaker. While in "The Lie" and generally in Christian discourse *sarcasmos* is the expression of an *ēthos,* that is, of an attitude toward the world *kata sarka,* my suggestion in the following is that *sarcasmos* in the *Holy Sonnets* belongs to the movement of a poetic *pathos,* the poem's "found" disposition toward itself. In "Since She whome I lov'd," the speaker of the poem begins by a theological interpretation of "her" death; but when the poem turns into a thanksgiving for her death, this thanksgiving is performed in a sustained sarcastic mood, a mood that is not directed at any external "world" but remains self-referential, belonging to the poem, to the poem's speaker.

If Aristotle's theory of *pathos* as the condition of change, of moving from one *ēthos* to another, is applicable to the *Holy Sonnets,* we can expect *sarcasmos* to have an essential role in the devotional movement of these poems: we can expect *sarcasmos* to fulfill the role of precipitating movement in the specific sense of a turn. Until this point, we have been thinking about the condition of thanksgiving, the "undistracted turning toward God" as a unidirectional "stretching toward," the work of attention; it is this linear, progressive work of attention that we were trying to find in the *Holy Sonnets.* But by doing so, we have avoided the issues of repentance and conversion as movements of turning; we have avoided the meaning of "turning" in the phrase "undistracted turning toward God" as a turning away from something and toward something else. And yet it is of course this sense of turning as a devotional apostrophe that is essential to Christian devotion; as Donne notes in the sermon on Psalm 6, "naturall and morall men are better acquainted with the duty of gratitude, of thankesgiving, before they come to the Scriptures, then they are with the other duty of repentance, which belongs to Prayer."[58] If *sarcasmos* in the *Holy Sonnets* is a poetic mood, the poem's finding itself in a certain disposition toward its own utterance, this *sarcasmos* must have a role in the turning away and the turning toward. As a *pathos*-proof, *sarcasmos* may be the condition of moving from one *ēthos* to another, and we might already assume that this means a movement from a *kata sarka* *ēthos* toward a different, devotional, thanksgiving *ēthos,* and that therefore the movement consists in turning resentment at the world into thanksgiving for the given gift.

SARCASMOS AND RESENTMENT

"Since She whome I lovd" is something of an exception within the *Holy Sonnets*. While the majority of the *Holy Sonnets* refrain from any personal references to Donne's secular life and address instead either one of the persons of the Trinity or the *anima mea* known from the Psalms, this poem seems to be dedicated to the memory of Donne's wife. Then again, such a reference does not necessarily mean that the poem is *about* Anne More. Rather, "She" becomes, already in the first quatrain, the world *kata sarka*, according to the flesh, an implication made explicit by the last couplet's "World, flesh, yea, Devill." Indeed, one of the meanings of Paul's *kata sarka* is the attitude toward the world based on relations of the flesh (what we would today call blood relationships): family, tribe, nation, race.[59] *Kata sarka* is an *ēthos,* an ethical and one might say ethnic attitude toward the world.

There is only one other *Holy Sonnet* in which such a *kata sarka ēthos* appears explicitly in the form of family relationship. It is the tenth poem in the Westmoreland sequence, and it begins by invoking "my fathers soule":

> If faythfull Soules be alike glorified
>> As Angels, then my fathers Soule doth see
>> And ads this even to full felicitee
> That valiantly'I hells wide mouth orestride.

As in "Since She whome I lovd," here too the first quatrain imagines the dead and immediately begins mediating the *kata sarka ēthos* with another, *kata pneuma* or spiritual attitude. In fact, the "fathers Soule" serves the purpose of dramatizing the theological material of the poem. Probably derived, if only indirectly, from Aquinas's discussion of angelic knowledge in the *Summa Theologiæ,* the poem's material is what we might call theological epistemology; it asks, with Aquinas, whether or not the elect may possess a capability of seeing spiritually, face to face, or *kata pneuma* even those who are still in the flesh, that is, living in their earthly bodies.[60] By focusing not simply on the elect in general but "my fathers Soule" in particular, the poem transforms this abstract theological material into a personal drama.

Insofar as this dramatization of theology is concerned, the critical response to the poem has been favorable: critics have praised the way Donne
uses poetry and specifically the sonnet form to perform and enliven the
theological material. But hesitation and puzzlement follow when the closure of the poem becomes the topic. Until the last couplet, the poem maintains and even heightens the drama of the first quatrain by mingling the
theological material with issues of theatricality and interpretation, dissimulation and sincerity:

> But if or Minds to these Soules be discride
>> By Circumstances, and by Signes that bee
>> Apparant in us, not immediatlee
> How shall my Minds whight truthe to them be tride?

To be sure, the personal stakes of the drama have become less clear in this
second quatrain, where the speaker's own question about how his soul might
be accessible to the dead ("How shall my Minds whight truthe to them be
tride?") becomes a rather abstract derivative of the general theological-
epistemological question. But even though logically speaking the personal
question seems derivative, the bitter tone of the poem is becoming more
emphatic, and in the third quatrain the speaker sounds increasingly resentful at the sheer thought that transcendence may not imply full transparency, that the dead may not have direct access to the soul of the living:

> They see Idolatrous Lovers weepe and mourne
>> And vile blasphemous Coniurers to call
>> On Iesus Name, and pharasaicall
> Dissemblers feigne devotion . . .

And here, in the middle of line 12, the poem suddenly turns away from all
these dramatic and resentful questions toward a doctrinal imperative, which
it utters without any sign of the anger and resentment of the previous lines,
in a tone of absolute devotional submissiveness. The way the sonnet's *volta*
overlaps with this conversion-like turn to theological doctrine and devotional submission is exceptionally unequivocal:

> . . . then turne
> O pensive Soule to God; for he knowes best
> Thy true griefe, for he put it in my brest.

By this last couplet, the poem seems to have abandoned the dramatization of its matter and turned to a different mood of utterance. The *volta* does not seem to follow from, much less complete the previous three quatrains; rather, it seems to interrupt them to reiterate a theological doctrine in a different, declarative, and as some critics have noted, suspiciously mechanical way. Once again, the conclusion is conventional and utterly orthodox: no matter what individual theologians had thought about the kinds of knowledge that angels or the elect might have had, they all agreed with Aquinas that "solus Deus cogitations cordium cognoscere potest," that it is only God who has direct access to the human mind. How does poetry relate here, in the closure of the poem, to the theological content that is reiterated in it? In other words, what is the poem's mood toward the theology of the last couplet?

From the beginning, the poem does more than just dramatize theology; it also uses grammatical mood to transform Aquinas's epistemological question into an ontological one. In asking the question of whether the elect can see face to face, or *kata pneuma,* even in the world of flesh, the sonnet begins by envisioning the consequences of a positive answer. In fact, the answer is emphatically positive, thanks to the poem's use of its grammatical mood:

> If faythfull Soules be alike glorified
> > As Angels, then my fathers Soule doth see
> > And ads this even to full felicitee
> That valiantly'I hells wide mouth orestride.

The first quatrain is a single conditional sentence, but a very special one. The protasis is in the present subjunctive ("If faythfull Soules *be* alike glorified"), which should introduce an apodosis in the future indicative to make up a future hypothetical. Instead, the present subjunctive is followed by three rapid present indicatives ("doth see," "ads," and "orestride.") The "valiant" tone of the last line, indeed the triumphant mood (now in the dispositional sense) of the whole quatrain, is partly the result of this slight grammatical gesture, for the omission of the future tense gives the hypothetical a greater sense of the possibility being real.

What the quatrain's grammatical moods perform appears on a thematic level as well. Despite the poem's usual interpretation that sets theatrical performance against sincerity, dissembling against the "Minds whight truthe," the first quatrain, the supposed alternative world of "sincerity," is very much

a theater itself. It is a theater where the audience, the angels and the elect—
including "my father"—are able to see everything because from their perspective, as it is given to them, the theater of the world is entirely transparent.
"Hells wide mouth," while standing for the medieval "world, flesh, and the
devil," that is, temptation in general, is also a common piece of stage scenery
in medieval and Renaissance mystery plays. The hero who "valiantly" avoids
the gaping abyss is very much an actor gracefully dancing around the hell-
mouth of the stage to please the elect and particularly his "fathers Soule."

When the second quatrain raises the opposite possibility, that even the
elect would see *kata sarka* or by way of signs, the confident *ēthos* of the first
quatrain disappears and the present subjunctive is continued in the gram-
matically appropriate future indicative:

> But if or Minds to these Soules be discride
>> By Circumstances, and by Signes that bee
>> Apparant in us, not immediatlee
> How shall my Minds whight truthe to them be tride?

It is only in this quatrain that the "minds whight truthe" emerges; it is not
an interior state that had existed before the poem's thought experiment began but a product of this experiment. In the first quatrain's transcendent
and transparent theater of the world, there was no "minds whight truthe,"
for the very distinction between exterior and interior, genuine and counterfeit, did not exist. The white truth emerges only as a result of the possibility
that the elect may not have a fully transcendent, *kata pneuma* perspective;
it is, indeed, a *reaction* to this possibility, a resentment of this possibility.

Moreover, it seems that the possibility that even the elect may see *kata
sarka* cannot be contained within the quatrain, nor within the limits of mere
possibility. It overflows the quatrain's limits and constitutes another reality, which in turn is expressed with a now unrestrained resentment against
the dissemblers of the world who make use of the very lack of transpar-
ence that the speaker resents. If the transcendent audience of angels and the
dead cannot see *kata pneuma,* then they will not see through dissembled
devotion:

> They see Idolatrous Lovers weepe and mourne
>> And vile blasphemous Coniurers to call
>> On Iesus Name, and pharasaicall
> Dissemblers feigne devotion.

The first quatrain's modified subjunctive present returns here with a similar ontological effect, but this time the effect lasts longer. Once again, the future tense has disappeared and the merely possible emerges as reality. But there is more to it: it seems as though this emergence of a new possibility, and out of this possibility a new world, is irrevocable. It seems as though once the poem uttered the possibility that even the elect may not see face to face, *kata pneuma,* the world of dissembling emerges not simply as a real world but as the only possible world.

What is the reason behind this loss of alternative worlds in the poem? And what is the result of it? One might think of Hamlet's own encounter with his father's ghost here to see that the grammatical moods of the poem perform quite closely the poem's poetic mood, that is, the ways in which the poem is given to its world. When Hamlet first meets with the Ghost, his reaction is enthusiastic; his "O my prophetic soul!" expresses the revelation that his inarticulate resentment toward Claudius has now gained form and reason, and he swears to "sweep to my revenge" valiantly, like Donne's speaker in the first quatrain. For like Donne's speaker, the encounter with his father's Ghost lifts Hamlet out of the world and allows him to see the world as a transparent theater, *kata pneuma,* as it is. But once the Ghost leaves, Hamlet gradually sinks back into a world whose dissembling he is now aware of without being able to transcend it; he is part of the world that he despises. This is why Hamlet is not a classical hero but a character of resentment (and this is why the *Mouse-trap* will be his solution; he must use dissembling against dissembling).[61]

In the same way, the speaker of Donne's poem is allowed, in the first quatrain, to see the world and himself from the assumed transcendent perspective of his "fathers Soule." The audience as elect is constitutive of the actor who valiantly dances on the stage because the actor sees himself through their eyes; he is valiant because they see him as valiant; he is given to himself valiantly, as it were. Once, however, this transcendent perspective fades away, what remains there is the sense of an irrevocable loss; therefore the insistence of his "Minds whight truthe" in the second quatrain and the sudden and almost uncontrolled, bitter outburst against the world of dissemblers; like Hamlet after being left behind by his father's Ghost, the speaker of the poem can only bitterly insist on his truth and complain against the world in sarcastic manner.

What the poem's movement across its three quatrains produces, both on a thematic and on a grammatical-performative level, is a poetic mood of resentment. Out of the conflict between two ethical attitudes, *kata sarka* and *kata pneuma,* in the poem's first quatrain, a new mood is born, a movement away from the *ēthos* of the beginning and toward the *pathos* of resentment, based on the recognition of and reaction against the fact that the perspective of the speaker is never the transcendent one of the imagined "Angels" but that of someone who is thrown into a "dissembling world," a world in which the opaqueness of the flesh does not allow sight to penetrate behind itself; it is the flesh that sees and is seen. The poem's resentment is both produced and found by the poem: the contrast between sincerity and dissembling is a contrast that the poem produces in its thinking-performative process, but it is also a contrast that in turn produces its own reality, and the poem's second and third quatrains express, in their mood, the speaker's reaction to this produced-found, invented reality.

If we now turn to the closure of the poem, we realize how mistaken we were about the abruptness of the final couplet's theology, and how mistaken we were about the poem's mood going against its devotional movement. The last couplet is not, as many scholars have argued, a direct quotation from Aquinas but rather a paraphrase with a subtle but crucial change:

> ... then turne,
> O pensive Soule to God; for he knowes best
> Thy true griefe, for he put it in my brest.

In Aquinas, the turn to God in the philosophico-theological argument occurs because only in God do substance and attribute, making and knowing fully coincide—therefore it is only God who can know perfectly, unburdened by the discrepancy between the inside and the outside. But Donne's God in this Holy Sonnet is not a maker of man but a maker of "thy true griefe." On the purely theological level, by this change the poem ties together Aquinas's doctrine with the Reformation thesis of *sola gratia;* "true griefe" is the genuine penitence, which both Augustine and Luther see as the sign and result of divine grace. God's grace creates "true griefe" and gives it to the sinner.

Within the poem, however, this theological point is articulated in a breathtakingly daring way: for the "true griefe" is directly tied to the resentment that the poem performed and indeed produced in the previous three quatrains. "Then turne," the conversion that appears in the sonnet's *volta,* is the turn from this resentment to the "true griefe"; it is not a turn *away* from the resentment but rather a willing dwelling in this resentment, a decision to attend to this resentment. Insofar as there is a conversion in the poem, it consists in the totalization of resentment, in turning toward and attending to the pathos of *sarcasmos* as a mood in which a person can utter his *gratiarum actio*. As a mood of expression, *sarcasmos* is grounded in the totalization of resentment, in the recognition that the flesh is the way a speaker is given to himself, that the only perspective one is given is the perspective of the *kata sarka*.

SARCASMOS AND INCARNATION

We approached the poem with the expectation that the *pathos* of *sarcasmos* may be part of the poem's devotional movement, its "turning undistractedly toward God." We assumed that insofar as this turning is not only a tending-toward, a work of attention, but also a conversion, a turning away from something and a turning toward something else, *sarcasmos* might have a role in the turn away from a *kata sarka ēthos* toward a devotional, spiritual attitude. Yet what we have seen in "If faythfull Soules" is in a sense the exact opposite of this expectation: while *sarcasmos* as a *pathos*-proof does create a conversion-like movement, a turning away and turning toward, the turn that it induces and accompanies is not away from the *kata sarka* perspective but rather a turning-back toward the flesh and toward the mood of finding oneself in the flesh, imprisoned by the flesh. The *pathos* of the poem is a sustained, totalized resentment, a resenting of the flesh that is not turned-away-from but attended-to by the poem through the poem's dwelling in the mood of *sarcasmos*. How can such an insistence in *sarcasmos* be part of Christian devotion?

In order to answer this question, let me turn to that *Holy Sonnet* which, uniquely in the sequence, takes *sarcasmos* as its conceit and thematizes it. The thirteenth *Holy Sonnet* begins with these ruthless lines:

> Spitt in my face ye Iewes, and pierce my side,
>   Buffet, and scoffe, scourge, and crucify mee.

Since Martz's study of the influence of Christian meditation on seventeenth-century poetry, it has been customary to assume that these two lines correspond to the first stage of the Ignatian practice of meditation. The initial *compositio loci* is supposed to provide the imagination with such a vivid representation of a sacred scene that the meditating person could feel as if

she were present there; it is a technique of (a primarily spatial) presentifica-
tion. Martz in fact lists this sonnet among no more than four poems that,
in his estimation, fully and directly adopt the structure of Jesuit meditation.
But he avoids the question of what exactly constitutes the "sacred scene"
that these lines represent, presumably because he takes it for granted that
the scene is the Passion of Christ. Yet even if we temporarily disregard the
fact that the poem does not describe but command or provoke, it remains
at once a dispersed and narrowly construed representation of the Passion:
two verbs in the first line, four in the second, all violent imperatives evoking
not a scene but a series of actions culminating in the crucifixion, and addressing not the imagination but "ye Iewes."

Representing the Passion as a series of events and actions unfolding
in time is a familiar genre; we might think of the iconology of the *Via Crucis* or Way of the Cross that recalls the Passion *through* the representation
of fourteen distinct moments from Christ's condemnation to his death to
the deposition. Poems like George Herbert's "The Sacrifice" follow this
model: Herbert's poem begins with Judas's betrayal of Christ and dedicates
a stanza for every significant moment of the Passion until the crucifixion
and Christ's death. Such a comparison helps us see that each of the six verbs
that Donne's poem introduces in rapid, quasi-asyndetic succession, evokes
a particular moment within the Passion. "Spitt in my face" may refer either
to Jesus's trial by the High Priests (cf. Matt. 26:67 and Mark 14:65) or to his
mock coronation by the Roman soldiers (Mark 15:19); "buffet" may evoke
these same scenes (cf. Luke 22:63–63, John 18:33, and John 19:1–5). On the
other hand, "scourge" and "pierce" refer to clearly identifiable events: Jesus is
scourged at Pilate's order by Roman soldiers (cf. Matt. 27:29, Mark 15:17–19,
and John 19:1–5), and the piercing of Jesus's side appears only in John's gospel
at 19:34, where a Roman soldier, traditionally identified as (Saint) Longinus,
inflicts the wound in Christ's side.

But the comparison also calls attention to an obvious difference: while
the iconology of the *Via Crucis* is essentially narrative (so much so that early
Franciscan texts required only fourteen crosses with no figural depiction
of the events), Donne's poem disrupts the narrative order of the Passion.
This is obvious in the first line where the beginning (assuming that "Spitt in
my face" refers to the mocking scene at the Sanhedrin) is juxtaposed with
the end (Longinus's stab). Instead of beginning a narrative, the first line
constitutes a sort of a cornice for the Passion; marking the beginning and
the end, it frames the ensuing details. It is therefore worthwhile to mention another medieval and early modern genre relevant for Donne's poem,

the so-called *Arma Christi*. The *Arma Christi* is "a pseudo-heraldic design depicting the Instruments of the Passion."[62] Unlike the *Via Crucis,* where emphasis is on the narrative unfolding, the *Arma Christi* offers the very materiality of the depicted objects for meditation through imagination and affectionate response. Often in gruesome ways, it depicts both Scriptural and apocryphal objects associated with the Passion, among them the thorns of Christ's mock crown and the vernicle.

Along with the spatial emphasis of the *compositio loci* and the temporal succession of the *Via Crucis,* the *Arma Christi* offers a useful comparison because of its focus on materiality and the body, also crucial for the Donne poem. As in the *Arma Christi* depictions, where the instruments metonymically invite the spectator to recall the body of Christ and the wounds that the various instruments have inflicted on it, in Donne's poem too each of the verbs implies physical harm or mental insult. Moreover, *Arma Christi* representations, both verbal and visual, often include an idiosyncratic element that Donne's poem reiterates: the figure of a Jew spitting at Christ. Consider the anonymous *Gloryous Medytacyon of Ihesus Crystes Passyon,* which depicts this moment of the Passion in a grotesque woodcut and explains it in verse:

> The Iewes that spytte lord in thy face
> All thou suffred and gave them grace
> That I have offended or ony man me
> Forgyve it lorde for thy pyte.[63]

The six verbs in the first two lines of the *Holy Sonnet*—spit, pierce, buffet, scoff, scourge, and crucify—evoke not individual moments but a single *aspect* of the Passion. Consider the way the first line's hissing consonants and closed, high vowels—"*Spitt in my face ye Iewes, and pierce my side*"—morph into the deeper and altogether darker tone of the second line. What these verbs and their progression evoke is a kind of abasement that is so extreme that it does not stop at the skin (spit, buffet) but tears it up (scourge) and penetrates into the flesh (pierce). What they evoke is not the Passion in general or its particular details; they focus on a single aspect of the Passion, the crucifixion as extreme, penetrating mockery and humiliation; the crucifixion as *sarcasmos.*

While classical tradition saw in *sarcasmos* an epic trope, Renaissance commentators found in *sarcasmos* a trope befitting the Christian style; as I have mentioned, examples were increasingly drawn from the Bible, and the most common example that Christian commentators used to illustrate *sarcasmos* was the crucifixion itself, and specifically the way the crucified Christ was mocked by the Jews and/or Romans. Two lines were particularly often quoted. The first was the "Ave rex judeorum," that is, the mocking of Christ as "King of the Jews," usually attributed to the Roman soldiers at the crucifixion. The second, more common example was the "Si Filius Dei es, descende de cruce," that is, the provocative "if you are the Son of God, descend from the cross."[64] The first to find *sarcasmos* in the Scriptures seems to be the Venerable Bede, who already associates it with the crucifixion and particularly the mocking request to Christ to descend from the cross: "Sarcasmos est plena odio atque hostilis inrisio, ut: 'Alios salvos fecit, se ipsum non potest salvum facere; si rex Israel est, discendat nunc de cruce, et credimus ei' [Sarcasm is a mockery, which is filled with hatred and hostility, as in (Matt. 27:42): 'He saved others; himself he cannot save. If he is the King of Israel, let him now come down from the cross, and we will believe him"]."[65]

After Bede, this episode remains the most frequent biblical example for *sarcasmos* in medieval and early modern discussions. Melanchthon uses both classical and Christian examples; thus he quotes Virgil ("En agros et quam bello Troiane petisti, Hesperiam metire iaces"), the standard passage from Matthew 24 ("Si filius Dei es descende de cruce"), and, somewhat unusually, the Psalms ("Speravit in domino eripiat salvum faciet eum, quoniam vult eum").[66] In the English context, both Sherry and Peacham use the example. For Sherry, the definition of *sarcasmos* is a mocking of the enemy: "Sarcasmus. Amara irrisio is a bitter sporting a mocke of our enemye, or a maner of iesting or scoldinge bytynglye, a nyppyng taunte, as: The Jewes saide to Christ, he saved other, but he could not save hym selfe."[67] Peacham's *sarcasmos* refers back to Christ's visit to the temple in Jerusalem: "An example of the Holy Scripture. . . . Thou which does destroy the Temple, and build it again in three dayes, have thy self and come down from the crosse. Another: He saved others, him selfe he cannot save. Let that Christ the king of Israel come down now from the crosse, the wee may see and believe him." He carefully adds: "These examples of the Jewes against Christ are here set down to teach the forme of this figure, and not to confirme the abuse."[68] We should also note that a number of commentators point out that *sarcasmos* is not necessarily a verbal expression; it can also be a simple gesture, and there is a whole iconography of such examples, once again using the Jews as a main example.

Although these examples were usually quoted from the Gospels, Melanchthon's discussion of *sarcasmos* in *Institutiones Rhetoricae* offers an exception: it cites the standard "Si filius Dei es, descende de cruce" from Matthew side by side with Psalm 21's "Speravit in domino eripiat salvum faciet eum, quoniam vult eum."[69] This is an important exception. Read by Christian exegetes as a prophecy of the Passion, Psalm 21 (22 in the Masoretic text) is particularly focused on mockery:

> All they that see me laugh me to scorn: they shoot out the lip, they shake the head saying, he trusted on the LORD that he would deliver him: let him deliver him, seeing he delighted in him. . . . For dogs have compassed me: the assembly of the wicked have inclosed me: they pierced my hands and my feet. I may tell all my bones: they look and stare upon me. They part my garments among them, and cast lots upon my vesture. But be not thou far from me, O LORD: O my strength, haste thee to help me. Deliver my soul from the sword; my darling from the power of the dog. (7–20)

The psalm verses focus on a theme familiar from "The Lie": the mocking crowd of bestial beings (in addition to dogs, lions and unicorns also appear) abuse the speaker's flesh, but even though they manage to penetrate it, they cannot get to the soul (*anima mea*), which the speaker offers to God for salvation. Specific details like the shaking of the head, the piercing of the flesh, and the anger of the dogs regularly appear in definitions of *sarcasmos*.

Sarcastic mockery is central to both Psalm 21 and to the Gospels' depiction of the Passion. The ascription of sarcastic mockery to Romans and Jews in the Gospels and in the Christian tradition may be therefore best understood as a function of the Christian typological or figural interpretation of the Psalms.[70] Indeed, to understand the exceptional significance of sarcastic mockery for Christian devotion, we need to return to one of the most influential sources interpreting Psalm 21 as a psalm about the Passion of *Christus totus*. In a collection of exegetical and homiletic texts on the Psalms, which were known after Erasmus as *Enarrationes Psalmos*, Augustine interprets Psalm 21 as "spoken in the person of the crucified one, for here at its beginning is the cry he uttered while he hung upon the cross. He speaks consistently in the character of our old self, whose mortality he bore and which was nailed to the cross with him."[71] When this assumed mortality meets the mockery of the crowd, Augustine explains that the derision was only a matter of lips and flesh: "All those who watched me sniggered at me: they laughed at me, all those onlookers. They mouthed at me and wagged their heads. They spoke not in their hearts, but only with the lips. They wagged their heads in mockery, saying, He put his hope in the Lord, so let the Lord rescue him; let him save him, since he holds him dear! These were words, yet only mouthings."[72] This emphasis on mockery according to the flesh (*kata sarka*) is a polemic against the "carnal attitudes" of the Jewish people, which Augustine develops parallel with the increasingly direct identification of the *Corpus Christi* with the Church.

In the second, homiletic exposition on the same psalm, which Augustine assumedly preached on Good Friday, his concern is with remembering:

> The Lord's passion happened only once, as we know, for Christ died only once, a just man for the unjust. And we know, we hold as certain, we maintain with unshakable faith, that, rising from the dead, Christ will never die again, nor will death ever again have the mastery over him. Those are the words of the apostle Paul. Yet to ensure that we do not forget what was done once, it is re-enacted every year in our liturgical commemoration of it. Does Christ die every time his passover is celebrated? No, yet the yearly remembrance in a sense makes present what took place in time past, and in this way it moves us as if we were actually watching our Lord hanging on the cross, but watching as believers, not mockers [*non tamen irridentes, sed credentes*].

At the same time, Augustine also continues his polemic with the mockers of the *Corpus Christi*. This time, his target is not the carnal attitude of the Jews, however, but the Donatists, who mock Christ by putting the Church in danger of a schism. In the context of the debate, mockery becomes a condition of ritual remembering:

> Or perhaps he is still being mocked? Yes, and today it is not with the Jews that we should be angry, for they at least jeered only at a dying man, not a reigning King. Who is it who still tries to mock Christ? I wish there were only one of them, or only two, or at any rate a countable group! But no, all the chaff on his threshing-floor mocks him, and the wheat groans to hear its Lord derided. This is what I mean to groan over now, together with you, for this is the time to lament. The Lord's passion is being commemorated: it is a time for groaning, a time for weeping, a time for confessing and imploring God's help.[73]

What the Jews of the Gospel and the Donatists have in common, according to Augustine, is that their devotion is literal or *kata sarx*, according to the flesh. In the case of the Jews, this means that they find the incarnation and especially the crucifixion a scandal (in Paul's famous words, a "stumbling block," a *skandalon*) because it contradicts their ancient beliefs about the Messiah; in the case of the Donatists, Augustine's criticism is that the Donatists insist on a literal faith when they do not accept "sinners" into the Church.[74]

Psalm 21 and its emphasis on mockery are especially important for Christian interpretations of the Gospel because one of Christ's last utterances on the cross, the often-quoted "Why has Thou forsaken me?" ("Eli Eli lama sabachthani?" in Matthew and "Eloi Eloi lema sabachthani?" in Mark) is itself a quotation from Psalm 21. In what is often interpreted as Christ's most solitary moment in the Gospels, a moment where he fully assumes and understands the human condition, the son of God cries out by quoting the Psalms. Seventeenth-century religious writers had their own interpretations of this scene. When, for instance the Puritan John Andrewes, an early seventeenth-century "circumforanean theologaster," differentiates between four distinct kinds of meditation, he defines the "spiritual meditation" as that in which the "the godly mind seeth and rightly considereth what the Passion is." This spiritual essence of the Passion, Andrewes explains, is expressed when "Iesus cryed with a lowd voice saying Eli, Eli, lama sabachthani, my God, my God, why hast thou forsaken me?"[75] Andrewes finds in this cry the essence of the Passion insofar as Christ's utterance is a paradox: for "God had indeed forsaken him," and yet "this lowd crying voice was not of the feare of death, should not hee that saveth all men, be able to save himselfe?" It is in the very moment of being forsaken by God that Christ was able to address him as the God of humankind: Christ's recitation of the psalm's words are the words of faith that are found in the moment of greatest resentment.[76]

If the moment of Christ's crying out to God is the essence of the passion, it presents a particular problem for devotion. There's a paradox here. On the one hand, insofar as this is the moment when God is finally fully incarnated *as a human,* it is a moment of the greatest proximity between God and humans. On the other hand, precisely because it is God whose sacrifice is now complete, Christ's cry is a singular and inimitable act of the divine. The sequence of the first three poems of Herbert's *The Church*—the middle, lyric, and properly devotional part of *The Temple*—highlights this paradox. The opening poem, "The Altar," introduces the following poems as an appropriation of Christ's sacrifice on the altar that is Herbert's poetry itself, offering the altar of poetry as the poet's response to the divine sacrifice:

O let thy blessed SACRIFICE be mine,
And sanctifie this ALTAR to be thine.[77]

But the next poem, "The Sacrifice," immediately reveals the difficulties in this idea of devotional poetry as response to Christ's sacrifice. In attempting to give a poetic account of Christ's sacrifice, Herbert engages in an experiment that is entirely unique in *The Temple*: "The Sacrifice" is the collection's only poem that is spoken by Christ himself. But if in this sense the poem is an *imitatio Christi,* the refrain concluding all but two of the sixty-three quatrains is a challenge to those human readers and speakers who would want to engage in Christ's imitation: "Was ever grief like mine?" Throughout the first fifty-three stanzas, the Christ-like speaker keeps posing this challenge to the reader. But then, the fifty-fourth stanza breaks the pattern:

But, *O my God, my God!* why leav'st thou me,
The sonne, in whom thou dost delight to be?
My God, my God————
                    Never was grief like mine.[78]

In "The Sacrifice," the gospels' "Why has Thou forsaken me?" is the moment when the possibility of *imitatio Christi* becomes the most difficult to imagine. As the sacrifice is fulfilled, Christ's grief appears no longer simply a challenge to humans; it is now a positively singular event with no precedent, thus raising the question of its imitability. Though the next few stanzas seem to regain the original refrain and ask, for eight more times, "Was ever grief like mine?" this is just a temporary recovery, and the poem concludes with Christ's death, which leads to the refrain insisting on the sacrifice's singularity:

But now I die; now all is finished.
My wo, mans weal: and now I bow my head.
Onely let others say, when I am dead,
                    Never was grief like mine.[79]

"The Sacrifice" thus ends with a statement that invites the reader to see the following poems as attempts to say that Christ's grief was singular, to respond to the sacrifice as singular. What response could possibly be appropriate to an absolutely singular gift? In theory, the answer is of course thanksgiving, and the next poem in *The Temple* is "The Thanksgiving." But while in this poem Herbert returns, once again, to the experience of being forsaken by God ("My God, my God, why dost thou part from me? / Was such a grief as cannot be"), "The Thanksgiving" isn't a proper thanksgiving poem but rather a poem that expresses the speaker's utter helplessness in searching for an appropriate answer: "Then for thy passion—I will do for that—/ Alas, my God, I know not what."[80] The rest of *The Church* consists of poems that try to find the appropriate voice to respond to the sacrifice that received its fullest expression in Christ's cry for help to God.

Like Herbert's "The Sacrifice," Donne's sonnet also appears to be a poetic *imitatio Christi,* at least at the beginning:

> Spitt in my face ye Iewes, and pierce my side,
>   Buffet, and scoffe, scourge, and crucify mee:
> For I have sin'd, and sin'd: and humbly hee
>   Which could do no iniquity hath dyde.

A complex drama of identification and difference is unfolding in this first quatrain. The first two lines evoke the Passion indirectly, by addressing the persecutors of Christ: for all we know, these two lines could be spoken by Christ himself. But then the rest of the quatrain reveals the irreducible difference between the sinful speaker and Christ. The paratactic and onomatopoeic character of the first two lines makes way for the hypotaxes of the third and fourth lines; the enjambment draws ambivalent attention to the contrast between "hee" and "mee," and the ambivalence grows with the internal rhyme "iniquitie" in the last line. The identity of the first two lines falls apart and the speaker reemerges as different, indeed irreducibly different from the original subject of the Passion. Now the first two lines appear as a failed *imitatio Christi* that failed because it took imitation literally and the speaker pretended to actually be Christ. The speaker suddenly finds himself on the other side of the initial division:

> But by my death cannot be satisfy'de
>   My sins; which passe ye Iewes impietee:
> They killd once an inglorious, but I
>   Crucify him dayly, beeing now glorifyde.

In the course of the theatrical penitence that Donne's poem performs, not only in the first two lines in fact but throughout the first two quatrains, mockery and the Passion seem to be different aspects of the same event,

just as martyrdom and persecution are different aspects of the same identity. But what in Augustine is part of polemic, in Donne's poem receives an
unexpected turn:

> And Iacob came clothd in vile harsh attyre
> > But to supplant and with gainfull intent:
> God cloth'd himselfe in vile Mans flesh, that so
> He might be weake inough to suffer wo.

Relying on typology, critics have always read Jacob in these lines as a *figura*
for Christ. I would like to suggest that the more important issue here is
the relationship between dissembling and *sarcasmos*. Before Jacob's figure
would direct attention forward to the sacrifice of Christ, it invites us to look
back on the speaker's initial *imitatio Christi*. Jacob put on his brother's attire
to deceive Isaac so that he could assume the role of the blessed one. In a
similar way, the self-directed address in the poem seeks to assume the role
of Christ as an object of *sarcasmos* in order to gain God's grace. This act,
when compared to the divine act of self-humiliation, is ironic affectation
that betrays rather than hides its intent. The model of *sarcasmos* is God's
own act:

> God cloth'd himselfe in vile Mans flesh, that so
> He might be weake inough to suffer wo.

God's ultimate *sarcasmos* is the incarnation itself: he created flesh to sacrifice it, gave it so that it can be taken away.

Reformation theologians routinely sought to distinguish between "flesh"
in John 1:14's "The word became flesh" (*ho logos sarx egeneto*) and the Pauline
meaning of *sarx*. Commenting on the sentence, Calvin notes:

> The worde *fleshe* is of greater force to expresse his minde, then if hee had
> saide that he was made man, His meaning was to shew unto howe vile
> and base an estate the sonne of God came downe from the lightnesse of
> his heavenly glory, and all for our sake. When as the Scripture speaketh
> of man contemptuously hee calleth him fleshe. Therefore albeit there is
> so great difference betweene the spirituall glory of the woorde of God,
> and the rotten dregges of our fleshe, yet notwithstanding the sonne of
> God did abase hymselfe so muche that hee tooke upon him this flesh
> which is subiect to so great miserie. But flesh is not take in this place for

the corrupt nature, (as Paule doth oftentimes take it) but for the mortal man; although it doth by contempt signifie his frayle & brittle nature.[81]

For Calvin, "flesh" in John is different from the "corrupt nature" that according to Calvin Paul means by *sarx*. But even Calvin suggests that the evangelist uses *sarx* to emphasize the "rotten dregges" and "vile estate" that the incarnation implies; that it is to refer to humanity "contemptuously." In Donne's poem, the distinction between these two senses of flesh becomes imperceptible. In the sonnet, God assumes flesh so that he can become subject to the mockery of the crucifixion. The incarnation is God's own *sarcasmos*: it is a willing appropriation of the hostile mockery of the flesh in the crucifixion.

In a sermon preached at St. Paul's on Easter in 1623, Donne returns to the spitting, buffeting, and scoffing of Christ:

> It is more, that the same Jesus, whom they had crucified, is exalted thus, to sit in that despised flesh, at the right hand of our glorious God; that all their spitting should but macerate him, and dissolve him to a better mold, a better plaister; that all their buffetings should but knead him, and presse him into a better forme; that all their scoffes, and contumelies should be prophesies; that the *Ecce Rex, Behold your King;* and that *Rex Judaeorum, This is the King of the Iews,* which words, they who spoke them, thought to be lies, in their own mouthes, should become truths, and he be truly the King, not of the Jews only, but of all Nations too.[82]

The victory of Christ, Donne argues in this passage, consists in appropriating the sarcastic mockery of his enemies and turning it into the truth of Christianity. By assuming Christ's person in the first quatrain, the speaker in Donne's poem performed an *imitatio Christi* that was the opposite of this act of appropriated mockery: instead, it was an act of spiritual dissimulation. In "Spitt in my face," we witness the speaker recognizing the false *ēthos* of his devotion as he understands the true *pathos*, the true passion of Christ. Insofar as the *Holy Sonnets* speak the discourse of grace sarcastically, they offer an idiosyncratic *imitatio Christi*: like God in the incarnation, they mock the human flesh not from without but from within, as the given human condition.

7

THE SPIRITUAL BODY

The distraction fit.

T. S. Eliot[1]

THE FIRST CHAPTER OF THIS BOOK began with a question: what is the proof of the proclamation that stands at the end of Donne's "Death be not proud," the proclamation that "Death shalbe no more?" What makes the speaker of the poem so confident in death's death? The final couplet of Donne's poem relies on one of the most widely cited examples of *sarcasmos* in early modern rhetoric, Paul's mockery of death at the end of the fifteenth chapter in the first letter to the Corinthians: "O death, where *is* thy sting? O grave, where *is* thy victory?" The question of what allows Donne's speaker to proclaim the death of death thus has a precedent in Corinthians, where Paul himself has to prove that the general resurrection will occur. I have argued that in Paul's letter the locus from where death could be taunted was provided by Paul's concept of faith. In turning the Greek rhetorical notion of *pistis* into a central religious ideal of Christianity, Paul changed the meaning of the term: *pistis* for him no longer meant either proof or the belief that proofs can induce but a faith that is its own proof.

Paul's "proof" for the resurrection is thus faith itself, and the "argument" of the letter to the Corinthians is Paul's demonstration of what it means to believe in the resurrection. In following Paul's letter closely, Donne invites us to see the work of the poem as a poetic *pistis,* a proof that emerges out of the poem's own work. I have argued, in the course of the preceding five chapters, that this work of poetic *pistis* consists of two parts. First, it is the labor of *ending* the poem with the given: since the telos of devotion is thanksgiving, the end of the poem is the locus where the given is supposed to be perceived as a gift, giving rise to the act of thanksgiving. Second, in order to prepare for this thanksgiving, the other part of the poem's labor is to do *nothing* to the given but acknowledge it as a gift. I have sought to show that this labor is one of attention: at the center of Donne's poetics in the *Holy Sonnets*, there is an effort to create a movement in which attention emerges out of the fissures of language and the gaps of distraction, so that it can attend to the given as a gift that is being given to it in the present. What is a work of *pistis* in Paul's letter to the Corinthians becomes the labor of poetic attention in Donne.

But there is, in Paul's letter, one final obstacle that the Corinthians face before they can accept the possibility of the general resurrection, before the faith in Christ's resurrection can turn into a mockery of death: "But some man will say, How are the dead raised up? and with what body [*sōma*] do they come?" (35). It seems that Paul's audience, willing to believe in Christ's resurrection and probably longing to believe in the general resurrection as well, is still reasonably skeptical of the sheer logical possibility that the body, metaphysically the source of corruption and empirically the clearest evidence for it, could be recollected from the grave and made alive once again. The seemingly technical question of how the body could be resurrected is the last stumbling block of faith. The answer that Paul provides in the letter to the Corinthians becomes one of the most influential and most debated ideas in Christianity. He suggests that the resurrected body will be a different body from the body of flesh: it will be a spiritual body (*sōma pneumatikon*).

In this last chapter, I suggest that the spiritual body is also the last question of Donne's poetics of attention in the *Holy Sonnets*. It happens to be the case that Donne was personally fascinated with the doctrine of the resurrection of the body; indeed, perhaps no other Christian doctrine intrigued him as much. To his modern readers, this can be an uneasy surprise. On the one hand, we see Donne as a relentless skeptic; a Christian, sure, but also a genuinely experimental mind willing to put even the most fundamental orthodoxies of Christianity to the test in his secular and even in his devotional poetry. Donne is neither a dogmatic nor a mystic Christian, and sometimes we might feel inclined to imagine him as someone who thought of religion as a culture more than anything else. On the other hand, Donne seemed to have absolutely no doubt about the one doctrine of Christianity that to the modern mind can appear the most fabulous, most irrational, and least acceptable, not because of its ethical or social consequences, but for its sheer ontological and biological impossibility.[2] One might solve this apparent contradiction by appealing to Caroline Walker

Bynum's point that the doctrine of the resurrection of the body is one of
the main sites for Christians to explore questions of identity and the self
for almost two millennia, and there is no question that Donne's interest
in the idea was fueled by his investment in the integrity and continuity of
the self. In what follows, however, I am far more interested in the question
of how the idea of the resurrection and more particularly the idea of the
resurrected, spiritual body might have influenced Donne's poetics in the
Holy Sonnets. I show that much as Donne was intrigued by the spiritual
body as the earthly body's potential successor, he was equally interested in
how this earthly existence might include hints of the spiritual body, and
how such hints might be reproduced in poetry. This is why the question
of the spiritual body is not only the last step for Pauline faith, but also the
last step for Donne's idiosyncratic devotional poetics. Reading "Death be
not proud" in relation to the spiritual body will help us recognize what
kind of proof the poem is: as in Paul's letter, where the idea of a spiritual
body is a proof for the possibility of the resurrection and not for its fac-
tuality, Donne's poem is an attempt to prove that the Pauline doctrine is
possible—or that it would be possible, if the poem's holy attention could
be sustained.

My discussion in this chapter has three parts. In the first, I offer a brief
account of the Christian concept of the spiritual body and Donne's lifelong
interest in it. In the second, I suggest that there is a connection between
Donne's interest in the spiritual body and his poetics of attention in the
Holy Sonnets. I show that for Donne, the difference between the spiritual
body and the body of flesh isn't that the former is less material but that it
is capable of a pure, entirely undistracted, holy attention. This is why for
Donne experiences of attention foreshadow the experience of being in the
resurrected body. But even more important for my purposes, this is why the
devotional poem can become a proof of the resurrection only insofar as it
becomes a figure of the spiritual body by generating an experience of full
attentiveness. In the last section, I return to "Death be not proud" to show
how the poem enacts this poetics of an attentive spiritual body.

IMAGINING THE SPIRITUAL BODY

Let's start by looking at the passage where Paul introduces the idea of a
spiritual body:

Thou fool, that which thou sowest is not quickened, except it die: And that which thou sowest, thou sowest not that body that shall be, but bare grain, it may chance of wheat, or of some other *grain:* . . . So also *is* the resurrection of the dead. It is sown in corruption; it is raised in incorruption: It is sown in dishonor; it is raised in glory: it is sown in weakness; it is raised in power: It is sown a natural body; it is raised a spiritual body. There is a natural body, and there is a spiritual body [*sōma pneumatikon*]. (36–44)

The suggestive organic metaphors aside, Paul's discussion of the spiritual body in this passage is not an attempt to *imagine* what the resurrected body might be like. Paul's implied audience is asking the question: How is it possible that the body, dead and decomposing, might somehow be recollected and made whole again in the final resurrection? How might we imagine this possibility? The concept of the spiritual body answers this question not by actually explaining what a resurrected body might be like, but by pointing out the limitations of the question itself. Those who ask the question are "fools" in the specific sense that they let their minds set limits to their faith. This is why the "spiritual body" is a deliberate oxymoron: it is Paul's provocative way of reminding his audience that God's ways are not always compatible with human reason, and that therefore the Corinthians should not allow their imagination set limits to their faith. The concept of the spiritual body in this sense is a sheer placeholder, a rhetorical figure that tells Paul's audience, "There are more things in heaven and earth . . . Than are dreamt of in your philosophy." It is an invitation, not to imagine the resurrected body, but to have faith in its possibility.

Of course this hardly set a limit to Western imagination. Bynum's work has shown the astonishing range of theological, literary, and artistic speculations that Paul's suggestion about the resurrected body has produced in Western Christianity and its critics, and she pointed out the degree to which such speculations were motivated by anxiety about the self's identity with the body.[3] Donne was an eminent participant in this tradition. On Easter day in 1623, he preached to the audience at St. Paul's:

For when the Apostle argues thus, *If Christ be not risen, then is our preaching in vaine, and your faith in vaine,* he implies the contrary too, *If you believe the Resurrection, we have preached to good purpose: Mortuum esse Christum, pagani credunt; resurrexisse propria fides Christianorum:* The Heathen confesse Christs death; to beleeve his Resurrection, is the proper

character of a Christian. . . . All the Gospell, all our preaching, is contracted
to that one text, *To beare witnesse of the Resurrection.*[4]

Faith in the resurrection is for Donne "the proper character of a Christian," both because it is what sets them apart from those who acknowledge
Christ's death but deny his resurrection, and because it encapsulates Christian faith in general. In the same sermon, Donne goes on to speculate about
the resurrected body and takes a largely Tertullianist positon, insisting on
the corporeality of the resurrected body.[5]

Indeed, resurrection is one of the few Christian doctrines with which
Donne had a lifelong concern, long predating his career in the Church of
England and accompanying him till the end. Some of the love poems treat
the matter lightly; in "The Relique," Donne depicts a gravedigger who fan-
cies a "bracelet of bright hair about the bone" of the corpse of the speaker
as a device that is supposed to bring together the lovers for one last ren-
dezvous "at the last busie day," as they are trying to recollect their body
parts for the resurrection.[6] Other poems in the *Songs and Sonets* figure the
resurrection far more seriously, as for instance "A Valediction forbidding
mourning," where resurrection is the central conceit of the poem and the
answer to the question of why separations (of the body and the soul, and of
the lovers) are only temporary (hence the poem's seemingly odd reference
to the female lover's soul growing "erect" when reunified with the speaker's
soul: the pun is on *anastasis,* resurrection in the sense of rising, growing
erect). Indeed, resurrection is one of the two most important religious concerns that Donne turns into poetry in the *Songs and Sonets:* if many of the
misogynist poems are explorations of faith and belief, the love poems that
read the most earnestly are virtually always thought experiments about the
soul and the body, and about their separation and reunification. Oftentimes
Donne insists both on the physical continuity between the earthly and the
resurrected body, and on the seeds and signs of the spiritual body being already present in the earthly body, particularly when eroticized.[7] The question of the body is less explicit in the devotional poems, but occasionally
it appears there, too, most explicitly in "Batter my hart" where the speaker
evokes again the etymology of the eschatological erection by asking God to
assault him so that he can "rise, and stand":

> Batter my hart, three-persond God, for you
>   As yet but knock, breathe, shine, and seeke to mend;
>   That I may rise, and stand, orethrow me . . .[8]

When toward the end of his life, Donne commissioned an engraving depicting him in his shroud as he expected to be found at the resurrection, he concluded this lifelong concern with the resurrection of the very body in which he knew himself.

Two poems are worth citing in more detail here because in them, Donne speaks not so much about the body after a general resurrection, but about bodies that appear to be spiritual bodies or something akin to it here on earth, perceptible to living human beings. In this sense, these poems are Donne's most intriguing efforts to *imagine* the spiritual body—or rather, as the case is, to have someone else imagine it for him. The first poem is "Resurrection, Imperfect," a poem whose title often invites questions. The problem traditionally raised about this poem is whether Donne left it unfinished, a question motivated partly by the title and partly by the "Desunt cætera" that follows the poem in the 1633 *Poems by J. D.*[9] Another possibility, however, is that the "imperfect" in the title refers not to the poem, or not only to the poem, but to the body that is the main subject of the poem, a body that is already resurrected but is not yet *entirely* spiritual—hence, its resurrection is "imperfect." The poem is about Christ's resurrection; Donne imagines that someone is present at the scene to witness when Christ, and emphatically Christ's body, rises from the grave. Donne concludes the poem with a speculation about what this spectator might have seen (or what he might have thought he saw):

> He would have justly thought his body a soul,
> If not of any man, yet of the whole.[10]

Of course, the couplet is a pun insofar as it suggests that Christ's body, which is to say God's grace incarnate in a human body, is the life-giving soul of the entire world.[11] But behind the pun, there is a fascination with the question of how this soul-like grace-body would appear to human sense organs. This is the very question, the nagging doubt that Paul's invention of the spiritual body, a form as unrelated to the earthly body as the wheat stalk to its seed, is meant to displace, and it is typical of Donne to have it both ways: while the poem actually ends up describing Christ's body on its way to becoming a spiritual body, Donne disowns this fantasy by attributing it to the "credulous pietie" of the spectator, who foolishly thinks he is be able to see a soul with his eyes. Still: what in Paul is an oxymoron that resists imagination becomes in Donne's poem a body that actually looks like a soul; and this apparent spiritual body is singularly interesting because it is a body that appears here, on earth, within the *saeculum,* that is, within the interim time between Christ's first and second coming. In this proper sense of the word secular, Donne's subject here is a secular spiritual body, an imperfectly resurrected body, and the poem is particularly delightful because in it we see Donne not being able to resist the temptation and trying to imagine the spiritual body instead of simply believing it.

A few years after Donne's death, in 1638, an English translation of Juan de Valdés's *Hundred and Ten Considerations* was published with George Herbert's preface.[12] Valdés's work includes a chapter on resurrection, in which Valdés talks about a body that is like the resurrected body, but is still a living, earthly body. Valdés calls this secular spiritual body "vivified": "I use to call Mortification an imperfect death, and *vivification* an *imperfect resurrection.* And I understand, that such shall be the resurrection in eternity, as the Vivification is in the present; I would say, that the glory of the resurrection shall answer to the perfection of the Vivification." (Emphasis mine.)[13]

In positing a continuity between vivification and the resurrection, Valdés's passage is part of a long tradition of thinking about ascetics, monks, and saints as partially resurrected and living in a spiritual body while still alive on earth; the Clementian and Evagrian notions of impassibility were among the early articulations of this idea. Of course, Donne in "Resurrection, Imperfect" is talking about Christ, who, after all, *was* resurrected according to the Christian gospel, whereas Valdés's point is about actual devotional techniques available to any practicing Christian. But the point is that Valdés and Donne both fantasize about how bodies that are still here on earth might become similar to the spiritual body

Elsewhere, Donne's thought experiments go beyond imagining resurrection within Christian lore altogether. The *Second Anniversary* contains Donne's most interesting attempt to conceive of a body that is not quite earthly though not quite heavenly either. The poem is famous for its hyperbolical praise of a dead child, Elizabeth Drury: Donne depicts her as the grace whose incarnation is the world itself, as the vivifying soul of the entire world. Her passing means that the world becomes a soulless corpse, a lump of lifeless flesh that quickly starts to decay and loses its articulation. As I suggested in chapter 6, the dominant mood of the poem is *sarcasmos;* Donne focuses on describing the rotting away of flesh. All the more arresting is a passage that refers to Drury's living body:

. . . We understood
Her by her sight, her pure and eloquent blood
Spoke in her cheekes, and so distinctly wrought,
That one might almost say, her bodie thought.[14]

As in the case of Christ's half-resurrected body, the question the passage raises is not what this "thinking body" might mean (philosophically, theologically), but what it might look like. Donne's conceit here is that Drury's body is simultaneously an actual human body of flesh and a Christ-like "quickening spirit" of the whole world, grace incarnate. Yet in these lines the focus lies more on the appearance of this grace, of the quickening spirit on Drury's face, "in her cheekes," in the way her body expressed itself and made a display of grace. Something similar occupies Donne here as in "Resurrection, Imperfect," but this time there is no resurrection implied: here it is a body that does and does not belong to the earth; a body that is still a body, but is already spiritualized to the degree that it tends toward eternity. A thinking body that appears strikingly like the spiritual body.

ENACTING THE SPIRITUAL BODY

I have focused on these two poetic examples rather than on the many other instances where Donne talks about the resurrected body in his sermons not so much to catch Donne in the act of imagining the unimaginable, but in order to suggest that in his poetry, Donne was interested in what we might call a *secular* spiritual body—that is, a spiritual body that exists in time. My real concern in this chapter is not with images of the resurrected body, be they theological or poetic. Rather, I am interested in that other, very different attitude toward the resurrection that is less invested in imagining what the resurrected might look like than it is in practices that are aimed at preparing the body for the resurrection; that is, practices that follow Paul not by simply believing in the possibility of the spiritual body but by seeking to prove its possibility by enacting it, however imperfectly. Such practices can vary widely. Bynum argues that "the raised and glorified body of which monks, nuns, poets, and schoolmen spoke in the twelfth century was described in words borrowed from Jerome and Augustine. As in the fifth century so in the twelfth, the resurrection body *was* the body of the saint."[15]

Cults of relics and saints, ascetic and monastic practices, the mystics' arousal of desire: all these may be seen as efforts to make the earthly body prepared for the resurrection, to ensure continuity between the physical and the spiritual body, to begin the victory over death while still alive. Insofar as the Pauline spiritual body is a transformed body, a body that has entirely left its corrupt flesh behind, it is of course a metaphysical-theological notion, an abstract concept whose only existence is based on its contrast with what actually exists, the body *kata sarka*. But the difference between theology and devotion is always in the fact that distinctions that are rigid, gaps that seem unbridgeable in theology, become, in devotion, objects of desire and places of experimentation. Such experiments are not only a feature of monastic and mystical practice; that is, at the extreme and intensified forms of religious life. They can also be found in institutions as quotidian as prayer and thanksgiving, particularly once monastic life in the strict sense is replaced by a more general sense of spirituality available outside the monasteries. Practices of devotion acknowledge that the spiritual body is beyond reach and, nevertheless, search for traces of the spiritual body in the experiences of the physical one. Insofar as a gesture in prayer, a symbolic movement of the body in liturgy, a modulation of the voice in the singing of a psalm is an attempt to open the body for divine grace, the search for signs of the resurrected body inheres in devotion.

As we saw in the sermon above, Donne was consistently emphatic about the corporeality of the resurrected body. But for him, the question that had utmost priority was whether the self here on earth and the self beyond would be somehow identical with each other; whether there would be fundamental continuity between them. Belief in such continuity might rely on two notions. The first is indeed the theological view that the resurrected body is corporeal, that it inherits, at least to some degree or in some form, the flesh of the very body we inhabit here on earth. The second, however, is a devotional attitude: it is the pursuit of discovering an affinity with the spiritual body in the very body that one lives in. Much as in his sermons and in his theology Donne insisted that the resurrected body would inherit the physical identity of the earthly body, he was also deeply invested in secular experiences that might foreshadow the postresurrection experience of being in the spiritual body. A famous passage from one of Donne's sermons at Lincoln's Inn provides an example. As one of the oft-anthologized passages from the sermons, it is usually excerpted without its immediate context, prompting various misinterpretations, so allow me to quote it a bit more extensively here:

Shall I imagine a difficulty in my body, because I have lost an Arme in
the East, and a leg in the West? because I have left some bloud in the
North, and some bones in the South? Doe but remember, with what
ease you have sate in the chaire, casting an account, and made a shilling
on one hand, a pound on the other, or five shillings below, ten above,
because all these lay easily within your reach. Consider how much lesse,
all this earth is to him, that sits in heaven, and spans all this world, and
reunites in an instant armes, and leg, bloud, and bones, in what corners
so ever they be scattered. The greater work may seem to be in reducing
the soul; That the soule which sped so ill in that body, last time it came
to it, as that it contracted *Originall sinne* then, and was put to the slavery
to serve that body, and to serve it in the ways of sinne, not for an Ap-
prentiship of seven, but seventy years after, that that soul after it hath
once got loose by death, and liv'd God knows how many thousands of
years, free from that body, that abus'd it so before, and in the sight and
fruition of that God, where it was in no danger, should willingly, nay de-
sirously, ambitiously seek this scattered body, this Eastern, and Western, and Northern, and Southern body, this is the most inconsiderable
consideration; and yet, *Ego,* I, I the same body, the same soul, shall be
recompact again, and be identically, numerically, individually the same
man. The same integrity of the body, and soul, and the same integrity
in the Organs of my body, and in the faculties of my soul too; I shall be
all there, my body, and my soul, and all my body, and all my soul. I am
not all here, I am here now preaching upon this text, and I am at home
in my Library considering whether *S. Gregory,* or *S. Hierome,* have said
best of this text, before. I am here speaking to you, and yet I consider by
the way, in the same instant, what it is likely you will say to one another,
when I have done. You are not all here neither; you are here now, hearing me, and yet you are thinking that you have heard a better Sermon
somewhere else, of this text before; you are here, and yet you think you
could have heard some other doctrine of downright *Predestination,* and
Reprobation roundly delivered somewhere else with more edification to
you; you are here, and you remember your selves that now yee think of
it, this had been the fittest time, now, when every body else is at Church,
to have made such and such a private visit; and because you would bee
there, you are there. I cannot say, you cannot say so perfectly, so entirely
now, as at the Resurrection, *Ego,* I am here; I, body and soul; I, soul and
faculties.[16]

The habit of citing particularly eloquent passages from Donne's sermons stripped of context has made this passage famous on two different accounts. The second half of the passage tends to appear alongside Donne's other meditations on devotional inattention, often as an example of Donne's modern, subjectivist sensibility. Influenced by Logan Pearsall Smith's 1919 *Donne's Sermons: Selected Passages,* for instance, T. S. Eliot in his essay on Lancelot Andrewes quotes it from "I am here speaking to you," and then uses it as an illustration of Donne's fundamentally distracted sensibility, in contrast to Andrewes's unconditional absorption in the object at hand.[17] The first half of the passage, about the ease with which God is supposed to recollect the scattered parts of the body in the resurrection, is in turn a favorite of modern scholarship focusing on Donne's religious beliefs, in this case his belief in the resurrection of the physical body.[18] The result of this practice of disconnecting two parts of the passage is that the connection between them is missed, an unfortunate oversight leading to ignoring the very argument that Donne is building here. Donne's text in the sermon is Job 19:26: "And though, after my skin, wormes destroy this body, yet in my flesh shall I see God." The Job passage allows Donne to ask the question that is so crucial in Paul's letter to the Corinthians: if the body after death is scattered into infinite pieces, how are we supposed to accept that it will be eventually resurrected? But where Paul offers the idea of a spiritual body as a placeholder for the possibility of the resurrected body and thus the ultimate piece of the proof that death will die, Donne provides an entirely different argument by reminding his audience of their permanent distraction. To question that God would have any difficulty recollecting the body parts into a new whole is ridiculous, Donne claims. The far bigger question, Donne adds, is how the *soul* could possibly be gathered back together from its permanently scattered state: "The greater work may seem to be in reducing the soul." What follows is one of Donne's characteristically intimate addresses, one of those memorable moments when Donne momentarily suspends preaching and begins a conversation with the audience:

> I am not all here, I am here now preaching upon this text, and I am at home in my Library considering whether S. *Gregory,* or S. *Hierome,* have said best of this text, before. I am here speaking to you, and yet I consider by the way, in the same instant, what it is likely you will say to one another, when I have done. You are not all here neither; you are here now, hearing

me, and yet you are thinking that you have heard a better Sermon somewhere else, of this text before.

Even in sheer rhetorical terms, this is brilliant: by addressing their distraction, Donne revitalizes his audience's attention. But there is more to it: the
philosophical and theological point Donne is making in reminding his
audience that he and they share the same condition of distraction (and the
passage feels so close to Augustine's discussion in the *Confessions* that one
feels tempted to use the term *distentio*), is twofold. On the one hand, he
confirms the Augustinian point that human life is permanent distraction,
that the self cannot ever be fully whole until the resurrection. Not only is
the spiritual body continuous with the earthly self; it is only in the spiritual
body that the self can call itself Ego in the full sense of the term. But in describing the scattering of the self in secular time through the experience of
distraction, Donne smuggles in another point as well: the soul is scattered
all over space and time, *and yet occasionally we do experience attention*—not
perfect attention, not the kind of attention that the sight of God that the Job
passage refers to involves, but attention in the sense of *some* gathering of the
self nonetheless. The effect of the passage, in other words, is the revelation
that given our inherent and seemingly irresistible tendency to be distracted,
any experience of attentiveness is something of a miracle foreshadowing the
full recollection of the self in the resurrected body. Donne does not make
this point, to be sure, but having offered the counting of shillings and pen-
nies as an example of how easy it is to re-collect physical objects, can we
imagine that his audience would not fancy that in the very act of attending to Donne's words, they are experiencing a presentiment of being in the
resurrected body?

   If in the sermon Donne suggests that even everyday, secular experiences of comparative undistraction foreshadow the experience of being in
the resurrected body, in his devotional poetry he goes much further in trying to produce a more intensive version of the experience of attention. Let
me return here for a moment to Valdés's distinction between mortification
and vivification. The mortification of the body is of course a well-known
concept of Western asceticism and monasticism. Valdés defines it as "imperfect death" in the sense that it is a preparation for death, and he distinguishes it from "vivification," which he considers an "imperfect resurrection" that will be perfected in the resurrection of the body. I want to suggest
that these two aspects of the same devotional movement can be translated
into the terms of attention and distraction. The mortification of the body

is the systematic suppression of actual and even possible distractions; the fully mortified body would be, to use again the ancient ascetic concept, an apathetic, impassable body. Vivification, on the other hand, corresponds to a body that is inhabited by an attention so pure that it spiritualizes the entire body. A vivified body is a body that is moved by its own attention much as sanctified bodies are moved by grace alone.

The emphasis on the expressive character of Drury's body, its ability to function as if it were an eloquent and *wrought* language, is already a hint that Donne is interested in the spiritual body in a way that goes beyond imagining versions of it in poetry and prose. In addition to imagining versions of the spiritual body, and in a sense even in opposition to imagination as such, I suggest, Donne used poetry as a devotional technology to create the spiritual body—that is, to create the poem itself as a secular spiritual body, but also to make both the author and the readers of the poem spiritual bodies for the duration of reading the poem. The "thanksgiving machines" that I described in chapter 2 are, in this sense, poetic engines whose purpose is to create a secular *sōma pneumatikon,* a spiritual body that has physical (spatio-temporal) extension and yet appears capable of the kind of undistracted or "holy" attention that is necessary for asking and receiving grace. Of course, it is by creating the *sōma pneumatikon* that the poem could also lead to thanksgiving; if the *sōma pneumatikon* is the final defeat of death, it is also the foundation of the sense of gratitude and the act of thanksgiving which rely on this final victory, as both Psalm 6 and Paul's first letter to the Corinthians make clear. Although the suggestion that the *Holy Sonnets* are devotional-poetic engines to create a secular *sōma pneumatikon* may sound provocative, in one sense this thesis simply follows from the theology of devotion: if the efficacious petition for divine grace requires that the petitioner and the petition itself already have grace, then both are, indeed must be, spiritual bodies, extended in physical time and space, and yet spiritual insofar as they are "in grace"—whatever this being in grace might mean. And of course the question is precisely this: what does this grace mean? What would the "spiritual" refer to in Donne's poetic *sōma pneumatikon?*

GRACE AGAINST DEATH

From the beginning of his career, Donne was interested in the idea that there might be a level of attention so absorbing, so intense, that it turns the body itself from a source of distraction and temptation into an organ of attention—thus transforming it into an erotic and at the same time spiritual and even immortal body. Donne's eroticization of attention has precedents. The Greek verb *egeirein* (to awaken and to raise, erect, resurrect) and noun *anastasis* (resurrection) are terms that figure the resurrection of the dead by using both the physical image of rising and the mental state of awakening, vigilant attention. Augustine plays on these terms when he describes the attention that prayer requires:[19]

> It is said that the brothers in Egypt have certain prayers which they recite often, but they are very brief, and are, so to speak, darted forth rapidly like arrows [*raptim quodammodo iaculatas*], so that the alert attention [*ne illa vigilanter erecta*], which is necessary in prayer, does not fade and grow heavy through long-drawn out periods. By this practice they show quite well that, just as this attention is not to be whipped up if it cannot be sustained, so, if it can be sustained, it is not to be broken off too quickly. Prayer is to be free of much speaking, but not of much entreaty, if the fervor and attention persists.[20]

The point here is not to read any erotic intent into Augustine's thinking about the attention that is required for prayer as "erecta" but to recognize the shared gendered and physical nature of the figures that describe both the resurrection and devotional attention.

The same tissue of associations appears at the end of Donne's "The Good-Morrow" with the line, "None doe slacken, none can die." The central conceit in "The Good-Morrow" is that falling in love is a kind of awakening that reverses the effects of the Fall:

> And now, 'Good morrow' to our waking souls,
> Which watch not one another out of fear.[21]

The reversal becomes more apparent if we compare it with Milton's depiction of the Fall, where Adam and Eve:

> . . . each the other viewing,
> Soon found their eyes how opened, and their minds
> How darkened; innocence, that as a veil
> Had shadowed them from knowing ill, was gone,

Just confidence, and native righteousness
And honour from about them, naked left
To guilty shame he covered, but his robe
Uncovered more, so rose the Danite strong
Herculean Samson from the harlot-lap
Of Philistean Dalilah, and waked
Shorn of his strength, they destitute and bare
Of all their virtue: silent, and in face
Confounded long they sat, as stricken mute.

———————————

(Book XI, 1052–64)[22]

In Milton's representation of the fall, the awakening from innocence signals the arrival of shame and fear, the inevitable consequences of postlapsarian knowledge. The Fall from Eden itself was due to a slip of attention, whether willful or innocent. This single slip of *curiositas* yielded fallenness as a condition of perpetual distraction: by falling from Eden, the first human couple also fell into the Augustinian state of *distentio,* a scattering of the self and a distraction from God. Gathering attention into the erect, alert vigilance that Augustine described in the letter above is one of the ways in which ascetic and monastic authors in ancient Christianity and their heirs in the seventeenth century thought they could begin rectifying this original error.[23] According to Donne's unusual take on the alba tradition in "The Good-Morrow," the moment of falling in love is the lovers' *awakening* from their dreams of fear and shame, and this awakening allows them to attend to each other with an intensity that obliterates all other things, "But love all love of other sights controls." The poem is shot through with references to Christian religion and particularly to conversion from its first stanza, where the reference to the Seven Sleepers invokes the story of the seven Christian youth who fell asleep in a cave during the Roman persecution of the Christians but woke up after Theodosius had made Christianity the state religion of the Roman Empire. But while falling in love thus corresponds to awakening in the sense of finding oneself in a new, converted world, the end of the poem imagines the possibility that if the lovers could maintain their newly gained total attention to each other in equal measure and without "slackening," then they could overcome death.[24] "The Good-Morrow" brings two prominent tendencies of the *Songs and Sonets* together: the erotic union of two bodies as a figure for the resurrection, and the experience of attention as a foretaste of redemption.

But while attentiveness that spiritualizes the body is a central concern throughout Donne's poetry, it is the *Holy Sonnets* that turn this concern into the organizing principle of their poetics. In the *Holy Sonnets,* the poetry of attention becomes an instrument of asking and thanking for divine grace. Since in order to ask and thank for grace the petitioner has to already have it, the *Holy Sonnets* are singularly preoccupied with the circle of grace and try to use poetic language to find a way into it. But they are preoccupied with grace on the level of practice; unlike poems like the "Good-Morrow," which uses the idea of vigilance as one of its conceits, the *Holy Sonnets* do not so much speak about the issues of grace and attention as try to produce them. For these reasons, I would like to finally return to the poem with which I began this book, and which posed the question of what role poetry could fulfill in the devotional actions of asking and thanking for grace. My purpose in reading and interpreting the poem is this time entirely deictic: I will simply point out the way in which "Death be not proud" uses poetic language and devices to create an undistracted, holy attention.

Of all the *Holy Sonnets,* "Death be not proud" is the most direct engagement with Paul's first letter to the Corinthians. But at first, the spiritual body seems to be absent from the poem. It is time to quote the poem in full:

> Death be not proud, though some have called thee
> Mighty and dreadfull, for thou art not so.
> For those whom thou thinkst thou dost ouerthrow
> Dy not poore death, nor yet canst thou kill mee.
> From rest and sleepe, which but thy pictures bee,
> Much pleasure; then from thee much more must flow,
> And soonest our best men with thee do go,
> Rest of their bones, and Soules deliveree.
> Thou art Slave to Fate, Chance, kings, and desperat men,
> And dost with poyson, war, and sicknesse dwell;
> And Poppy or Charmes can make us sleepe as well,
> And easier then thy stroke, why swellst thou then?
> One short sleepe past, we live eternally
> And Death shalbe no more, Death thou shalt dy.

After Paul has explained that the resurrection is a "secret thing" that will occur in "a twinkling of an eye" and will turn the body into a spiritual body, he sums up the letter with these lines: "So when this corruptible hath put on incorruption, and this mortal hath put on immortality, then shall be brought to pass the saying that is written, Death is swallowed up into victory. O death where *is* thy sting? O grave where *is* thy victory?" (I Cor. 15: 53–55).[25] "Death be not proud" follows Paul's letter not only in the concluding taunt of death, but in the argument that leads to it. The letter is addressed to the Corinthians, who are "carnal" and "babes in Christ," meaning both that they are too focused on their own flesh and that they imagine eschatological matters in terms of the flesh, that is, literally. The oxymoron of the spiritual body challenges this fleshly imagination, as if to say: if you believe in the spiritual body, then you can overcome death, and mock it as a defeated enemy, as Paul does. The spiritual body, in this sense, is the foundation from which Paul can say that death is defeated, the basis from which he can mock death, the proof of death's future death. The poem reiterates the same mockery of death—but it doesn't speak of the spiritual body. And this raises the question: what is the poem's basis for mocking death? What might justify its claim that death will die? I suggest that the reason the poem does not mention the spiritual body is that the whole poem is an attempt to create that body as a basis from which death can be mocked. If the spiritual body in Paul's letter is the final proof for the future defeat of death, now the poem itself is meant to provide this final proof *as* a secular spiritual body, so that in the end it can announce, following Paul, the defeat of death.

In order to follow Paul's letter, the poem plays with a contrast between imagination and attention. It begins with a poetic address to Death, which is also a *prosopopeia,* a figure often called personification, the device of putting face on an abstraction, an absence, often a dead person. Here the use is paradigmatic in that Death itself is evoked, addressed. It is standard to think about *prosopopeia* in terms of imagination: when the poet addresses someone who is absent, we think that this address is the product of imagination's labor. But this emphasis on imagination does not explain Donne's poem. Imagination could not achieve what is expected from the poem: according to the Christian metaphysics of attention, the body is simultaneously the site of mortality, of death, and of distraction; indeed, the body is the site of mortality insofar as it is the site of distraction. The corollary of this metaphysics is that if attention could be directed at death itself, at distraction itself, then Death could be overcome. And this, I suggest, is what the poem is trying to do: it tries to make Death the subject of the poem's attention.

Initially, the poem's strategy is very direct: it begins by naming three accidental properties of Death—pride, might, and dreadfulness—and then proceeds to deny Death each of these qualities in the next three quatrains,

dedicating one quatrain to each. But while the poem proceeds with this literal imitation of Paul's mockery of death, a paradoxical movement emerges.
Each denial provokes death to return still more forcefully in the subsequent quatrain. Death, the poem claims, cannot kill; yet the next quatrain,
while denying that death is to be feared, acknowledges that death is mighty
enough to kill. Again, while the third quatrain claims that death is base and
a slave, it acknowledges that it is dreadful like poison and strikes heavier
than sleep. In every quatrain, the poem denies one of Death's qualities—but
the very same quality returns in the next quatrain. In other words, while the
poem is trying to pay attention to Death by focusing on its properties (its
dreadfulness, for instance), another quality slips out of the poem's attention
and thus back into the next quatrain.

Why? The answer lies in the Augustinian logic of attention: the poem's
attention, like human attention, is incarnate attention, which means primarily that the more it tends to something, the more distraction it produces
at the same time; distraction is the inevitable by-product of attending itself.
The result is that throughout the poem, death doesn't simply escape the
poem's attention, but is in fact massively produced by the poem's attention,
as the poem's own inattention. This explains what we might call the resurrection of Death in the last lines:

> One short sleepe past, we live eternally
> And Death shalbe no more, Death thou shalt dy.

Notice that it is here, in these last lines, that for the first time the poem turns
away from its initial addressee, a personalized death; and it speaks about
death in the third person ("Death shalbe no more"), as if it has already defeated death. But just as earlier when the denials of death's accidents re-
sulted in the other accidents creeping back into the poem's body, now the
ostensible final annihilation of death leads to the complete resurrection of
death: as if waking from its own dream, the poem now returns from the
apostrophe to face a fully present, personalized and capitalized death, the
Death that the poem produced for itself, as its own, personal inattention
and Death.[26]

Critics have long noted that the final twist in Donne's poem is that the
Death that the speaker claims to have defeated reappears only stronger and
more vivid in the poem's last address. The observation could lead to enlist-
ing "Death be not proud" as yet another example of Donne's fondness for
irony and ambivalence. I want to suggest, as a conclusion of this chapter

and indeed the argument of the entire book, that the end of "Death be not proud" in fact completes the task of the poem in terms of "proving" the Pauline doctrine. If throughout the poem death was invoked but always slipped out of attention, it is here, in the last line, that Death fully returns, as the paradoxical invention of the poem itself, made out of its own body, of its own dialectic of attention and inattention, and yet somehow despite its own intention. On the one hand, this means that the poem ends by resurrecting Death, by finally allowing the thought of death occurring to the speaker's full and undistracted attention. In this sense, the poem ends by giving the "gift of death" to the speaker.[27] On the other hand, however, it also means that in this final address the poem's own blind spot, the very distraction that it has produced in the previous thirteen lines, is suddenly attended to.[28] In this lies the poem's victory. The moment the poem can attend to its own distraction, it has produced an experience of pure attention. And insofar as the poem ends with an experience of pure, holy attention, it provides a practical, experiential proof for the mortality of death by showing that distraction may be overcome. By its creation of this circular, self-reflexive movement of attention, it is here that the poem overcomes the paradox of asking for grace: it finds grace in the very experience of attention with which it concludes.

CODA: THE EXTENT OF ATTENTION

All that we need to doe to make all our Perceptions evident, is only to look for such Means as can increase the Attention and Extent of the Mind.

Nicolas Malebranche[1]

ONE MIGHT ASK: EVEN IF WE accept that "Death be not proud" ends with a victory over distraction and hence over Death, what exactly is the *extent* of this victory? How far does it extend beyond Donne's poem, if at all? Does it apply to Donne's other poems? Does it remain relevant beyond Donne's poetry? Perhaps beyond poetry?

The first answer to these questions is just a reminder that the purpose of "Death be not proud" as a figure of the spiritual body is to prove only that mortality could be overcome *if* an entirely undistracted, holy attention were sustainable. This qualifies not only *what* the poem proves but what *kind* of proof the poem is: it is a proof only *if* and *insofar as* it is being attended to. From an aesthetic point of view, this means that the poem comes to life as an experiential proof every time a reader dedicates to it the extent and quality of attention the poem requires. This, perhaps, isn't particularly surprising. What is probably less expected is that this notion of a proof depending on being attended to by the subject isn't exclusive to Donne's poem, poetry, or even devotion, but reappears in early modern philosophy as well. Of course, to claim that there is continuity between Christian devotional practices and early modern philosophy is nothing new; the influence of spiritual exercises on Descartes's system, for instance, is well documented.[2] My point in the following isn't to add further support to the argument for historical continuity but to indicate how the early modern projects of devotion, devotional poetry, and philosophy had a shared interest in holy attention. Before turning to Descartes and Malebranche, then, let me show that although "Death be not proud" is a particularly complete exercise of attention, what it tries to achieve is by no means incompatible with Donne's other, seemingly less self-assertive poems. Indeed, understanding how markers of ambiguity and doubt are part of the poems' exercises will also help us recognize the ways in which Donne's poems anticipate early modern philosophy's methodological concern with attention.

MAKING DOUBT WORK

In the Introduction to this book, I argued that in *La Corona,* Donne used the phrase "first last end" as a double reference to salvation, on the one hand, and the poem's own lines, on the other. But "first last end" could also be seen as a more specific reference to a single line in the poem. As a crown of sonnets, *La Corona* ends with its first line: "*Deign at my hands this crown of prayer and praise.*" Strictly speaking, this is the poem's true first last end: it's the prayer at the beginning and at the end the poem, and it's the prayer the whole poem is a preparation for. It is therefore important to acknowledge that at the end of the poem Donne's speaker doesn't actually repeat the very same line. That is, he utters the same words at the beginning and at the end of the poem, but by the second time, the words mean something different not only because there's an entire poem behind them but because this time they constitute the second clause of a *conditional.* Let me quote the last sonnet in its entirety:

> Salute the last and everlasting day!
> Joy at th'uprising of this sun and Son,
> Ye whose true tears or tribulation
> Have purely washed or burnt your drossy clay!
> Behold! The Highest, parting hence away,
> Lightens the dark clouds which he treads upon;
> Nor doth he, by ascending, show alone,
> But first he, and he first, enters the way.
> O strong ram which hast battered Heaven for me,
> Mild lamb, which with thy blood hast marked the path,
> Bright torch, which shin'st that I the way may see
> Oh, with thine own blood quench thine own just wrath,

And if thy Holy Spirit my Muse did raise,
Deign at my hand this crown of prayer and praise.

What is the new meaning of the prayer when it is reiterated here? Recall that *La Corona* begins with a meditation on what a devotional poem is. First, it seems that insofar as the poem is a "crown of prayer and praise," its purpose is to ask for the "crown of glory" that is salvation. But it turns out that such labor is unnecessary because salvation has already been earned by Christ's own "thorny crown." The givenness of salvation could lead to devotional nihilism, but this isn't the conclusion Donne's speaker arrives at. Though salvation for humankind has been earned by Christ's sacrifice, this is only a general, abstract, and potential salvation insofar as the individual who speaks the poem's words is concerned. Therefore the poem's purpose is to translate this abstract potential of redemption into the speaker's faith in his own salvation by prayer. The proem of *La Corona* ends on a note of confidence about the possibility of this translation: "'Tis time that heart and voice be lifted high: *Salvation to all that will is nigh.*"[3]

The sonnet crown's last poem appears to confirm the speaker's confidence in the efficacy of human works toward salvation. Though Christological, the final sonnet depicts Christ not just as a redeemer but as an exemplar who offered a model for humans to follow: Christ here is the "ram which hast battered Heaven for me," and the lamb whose "blood hast marked the path." The implication should be that human works of devotion (and thus the poem itself) have the potential to follow Christ and earn salvation. Yet the poem and thus the whole sequence ends with a final twist:

And if thy Holy Spirit my Muse did raise,
Deign at my hand this crown of prayer and praise.

By leaving it open whether "my Muse" is the subject or the object of raising, the penultimate line reopens the very question the proem was supposed to answer. As a result, it throws the poem's purpose into doubt: in this final moment, it seems that once again we are confronted with the possibility that the grace the poem was supposed to solicit cannot be earned by any human works.

What should we make of this final ambiguity in *La Corona?* Robin Robbins denies that there is any ambiguity here; as he puts it, "for Christian writer and reader, there will be no doubt that 'Holy Spirit' is subject and 'my Muse' is object, as in Milton's invocation in *Paradise Lost,* I. 17–23."[4] Margaret Mauer, in contrast, claims that the point of the last sonnet in *La Corona* is to raise doubt:

> Sonnet 7 reveals the precise limits of human ingenuity. It begins with eight lines of joyous praise for Christ ascending into heaven in the company of the elect of the Old Law. It ends with a sestet in which the speaker prays that he might one day make that ascension. What it cannot do is establish a relationship between the two parts. To the extent that the mood of joy in the octet imbues the subsequent petition in the sestet with a note of confidence—"O strong Ramme, which hast batter'd heaven for mee" (7.9)—that confidence only sets up the doubt to which the melancholic spirit is vulnerable. . . . To anyone following the argument closely, "La Corona" turns abruptly at its most triumphant moment.[5]

Exceptionally sensitive to the poem's subtle moves and the modulations of the speaker's mood, Mauer frames her observations in terms of a dichotomy between certainty and doubt. Her conclusion is that Donne's poem finally undermines its own apparent achievements. By questioning devotional agency, the poem's final "if" in Mauer's reading is an admission of the limits of both devotional labor and faith in redemption. Mauer's reading thus echoes long-held views about Donne's "if" as a marker of his inability to let go of ambiguity, ambivalence, and doubt.

One of the reasons this interpretation of Donne's devotional poetry in terms of doubt is appealing is that it seems to be supported by Donne's explicitly self-reflective moments in the *Holy Sonnets*. An important example is the last, nineteenth poem in the Westmoreland sequence of the *Holy Sonnets*. It is a poem that has often invited a reading of its statements as a kind of *ars poetica* for all of the *Holy Sonnets* and perhaps for all of Donne's devotional poems. Since it is also one of Donne's most misunderstood poems, it is worth quoting here in full:

> Oh, to vex me, contraryes meete in one:
>> Inconstancy unnaturally hath begott
>> A constant habit; that when I would not
> I change in vowes, and in devotione.
> As humorous is my contritione
>> As my prophane love, as soone forgott:
>> As ridlingly distemperd, cold and hott,
> As praying, as mute; as infinite, as none.

> I durst not view heaven yesterday; and to day
>> In prayers, and flattering Speaches I court God:
>> To morrow I quake with true feare of his rod.
> So my devout fitts come and go away
>> Like a fantastique Ague: Save that here
>> Those are my best dayes, when I shake with feare.[6]

Confessional in tone and content, the sonnet seems to give support to crit-ics who see the *Holy Sonnets* as expressions of Donne's (or at least a fictional speaker's) inability to come to unconditional faith. If the poem's beginning emphasizes, with a possible jab at Catholic ideas of habit and habituation, the inconstancy of the speaker's devotions, the end seems to embrace and prioritize fear of God over any devotional labor with a bleak, Calvinistic fatalism.

But if we read the poem in the tradition of holy attention, we recognize that its end builds on a different and far more specific concern with vocal and silent prayer. The key is in the poem's second and third quatrains. Hav-ing set up a parallel between his profane love and his devotions, the speaker goes on to elaborate by stating that he has been inconstant by going from praying (in the general sense of courting the mistress or God in words) to being mute, from an excess of devotion ("infinite") to none at all. In the next quatrain, this distinction between prayer and muteness is rearticulated as a contrast between prayer and a (presumably mute) quaking fear of God. Once the poem has (almost imperceptibly, as the *Holy Sonnets* often do) mapped the idea of fearing God onto the previous concept of muteness, the stage is set for the *volta* to appear:

> So my devout fitts come and go away
>> Like a fantastique Ague: Save that here
>> Those are my best dayes, when I shake with feare.[7]

The penultimate line provides the speaker with a difficult but vitalizing truth: while the poem has been a confessional act of blaming him for not being able to sustain his prayers and falling into muteness, it now turns out that the muteness that he first identified as lack of prayer is in fact a higher level of devotion. As Lewalski suggests, Job 28:28 is relevant here: "The feare of the Lord, that is wisdome."[8] Insofar as the speaker's muteness is a result of his fear of God, it turns out to be a superior prayer because it involves knowing God in "fear and trembling."[9] Insofar as the references to "shaking"

and "quaking" echo Philippians 2:12's "continue to work out your salvation in fear and trembling," the poem ends by suggesting a continuity between vocal prayer and silent trembling: *both* turn out to be parts of the
same labor toward one's salvation, a labor that cannot earn the prize it
works toward but is necessary nevertheless. The end of "Oh, to vex me" isn't
a mere summary of the poem's list of devotional shortcomings, much less
a generic Calvinist claim about the vanity of devotional labor. On the contrary: the poem ends with the recognition that devotional labor is not only
possible but that it happens all the time, often in moments when we are the
least aware of it.

What "Oh, to vex me" *does* confirm along with all of Donne's other
devotional poems is that the holy, complete attention that devotion to God
requires cannot be *sustained* in time, that "inconstancy" will necessarily become a "constant habit." But we might want to take Donne's speaker at
his word here and consider that what might seem like a *dichotomy* between
doubt and certainty is in fact a *habit* or rather a dialectical *method*. In "Oh to
vex me," the doubting of his own constancy in devotion leads the speaker to
recognize the certainty he has of God in moments of apparent inconstancy.
If we now return to *La Corona,* we might posit that the penultimate line's
apparent doubt about the devotional efficacy of the poem is in fact a similar preparation for certainty in prayer. Mauer argues that *La Corona* ends
with the recognition that it is impossible to establish a connection between
Christ's sacrifice and the speaker's own redemption; in other words, she
suggests that the poem has failed to translate the given of Christ's sacrifice
into the speaker's personal faith in his own salvation. But the poem doesn't
end on a note of doubt. Instead, it ends on a note of a prayerful address to
God that is prepared by a conditional. Insofar as the conditional expresses
doubt, it is doubt only in the sense of being part of the preparation of eliminating any presumption, any distraction that might stand in the way of the
petition that asks God to accept the speaker's prayer.

There are many reasons *La Corona* begins and ends with the same
prayer: in addition to simply following the rules of a sonnet crown, Donne
uses this structure to recall the rosary and to symbolically overcome the
difference between linear human time and the circle of divine eternity. But
there is one more reason: *La Corona* is a prayer that also prepares for prayer;
hence it is that after the sonnet crown-long preparation for prayer, the
speaker is prompted to pray the very words that lead us back to the beginning
of the sonnet crown. The conditional in the penultimate line of *La Corona*
isn't an ambivalent conclusion but the condition of a new commencement;

it is the moment where attention is freed up for prayer to begin. The poem in this sense is Donne's most eloquent poetic figure for the circularity of attention that we saw in Augustine's *Soliloquies* and in Donne's "Death be not proud." It is also a meditation that anticipates the philosophical methods of Descartes and Malebranche. A full comparison of devotional, poetic, and philosophical ideals and uses of attention would go beyond the limits of this book. I want to nevertheless conclude by indicating how Descartes's and Malebranche's concern with attention echo some of the themes I've been tracing throughout the preceding argument.

CARTESIAN CIRCLES

One of the first and most resilient objections against Descartes's argument in the *Meditations* is a critique of the so-called Cartesian circle. In the seven sets of official objections that were published along with the Latin text of the *Meditations* in 1641, it is brought up at least three times, by Marin Mersenne, Antoine Arnauld, and the Jesuit Pierre Bourdin. For brevity's sake, I quote Arnauld's version, which is also the most incisive:

> *The only remaining scruple I have is an uncertainty as to how a circular reasoning is to be avoided in saying:* the only secure reason we have for believing that what we clearly and distinctly perceive is true, is the fact that God exists. *But we can be sure that God exists, only because we clearly and evidently perceive that; therefore prior to being certain that God exists, we should be certain that whatever we clearly and evidently perceive is true.*[10]

In the *Meditations* Descartes's goal is of course not to prove that something exists beyond doubt, but to find a criterion by which we can have certainty about the truth of a thought. The relevance of the "cogito ergo sum" is that it offers such a criterion: when—after the methodological application of doubt to all sense-perception and thought—finally the thought of the cogito appears so clearly and distinctly that I cannot *not* accept it as true, the category of "clear and distinct" itself emerges as the criterion of certainty. Arnauld's scruple is that from the *Meditations* it appears as though God is both the sole guarantee of this criterion and an idea that is itself guaranteed by the fact that it is clear and distinct.

Every time Descartes responds to this objection, his tone suggests indignation about the fact that one would ask a question to which the answer should be clear as day. This time let me quote the answer he gives to Bourdin:[11]

> I have sufficiently explained in various places the sense in which that *nothing* ought to be understood [i.e., the nothing in the statement "nothing, absolutely nothing can resist doubt unless we have proved God's existence and that he doesn't want to deceive us"]. So, for example, that as long as we attend to some truth which we perceive very clearly, we cannot indeed doubt it. But when, as often happens, we do not attend to any truth in this manner, although we remember that we have often known such truths quite well, there is none, nevertheless, of which we may not rightly doubt if we are unaware of the fact that everything we perceive clearly is true.[12]

Descartes's solution to the Cartesian circle, here and elsewhere, is to distinguish between attention and memory. Something that is "clear and distinct" is irresistibly evident even without recalling God's good intentions as long as we attend to it. But since such attention cannot be sustained ad infinitum, we need to rely on memory. That is, when we no longer attend to a clear and evident thought, we can still trust it by recalling that once we found it clear and evident—it's just that in this case we do need to rely also on the thought that God is good and doesn't want to deceive us, and that hence we can believe that the thought that we once found clear and distinct is still the same.

The answer could appear to solve the circle, were it not for the fact that when Descartes defines what he means by "clear and distinct," he once again invokes attention. The following passage is from the *Principia:* "I term that clear which is present and open to an attentive mind [*quae menti attendenti praesens et aperta est*] . . . and distinct . . . what is so precise and separate from all others that it contains in itself absolutely nothing but what is clear."[13] This curious sentence blurs the distinction between the active and the passive: truth appears at the origin of Cartesian philosophy as an event that takes place between something "clear and distinct" and a prepared, attentive mind. If the perception of something as "clear" is the foundational moment in Descartes's system, the fulcrum of this experience is attention; like holy attention in asceticism, attention in Descartes can provide certainty as long as it is sustained. The raison d'être behind Descartes's method, however, is the Augustinian insight that attention cannot be sustained.[14]

Although perfect attention provides certainty, since such attention cannot be extended either in space or time, a different, geometrical method is necessary that may provide a more reliable foundation for philosophy's goal to achieve certainty.

If for Descartes attention's unsustainability is the reason behind the need for a new method, in Malebranche's thought philosophy itself is a method to cultivate and improve attentiveness. Malebranche is known today for his occasionalism, the view according to which our actions are only the occasions of the events that they seem to bring about, whereas the sole real, efficient cause is God's will. Attention is the key to the method of this system: as an epistemological equivalent of natural causes, it is the occasion for philosophy itself, as it were, and Malebranche sought to instill a habit of attending into his readers to prepare them for the event of truth.[15] In the following, I focus on how Malebranche articulates the significance of attention for his method in the 1674 *Recherche de la Verité,* his first philosophical work.[16]

Malebranche dedicates the first five books of the *Recherche* to the many sources of errors we make in our judgments. Then, in the sixth, final book, which is dedicated to method, he finally turns to the question of how we could build a positive method, something that prevents errors as much as possible. The key to developing this method, Malebranche suggests, is a simple rule: "We must never give a full Consent [*consentement*], but to those Propositions that appear so evidently true [*évidemment vraies*], that they cannot be denied it, without feeling an inward Pain.[17] The question is: when is a proposition so evident that it cannot be denied without feeling an inward pain? That is, when is a proposition "evident" or as Malebranche elsewhere describes it in more explicitly Cartesian terms, "clear and distinct?" This is a tricky question because in the first five books, Malebranche argued that the source of all errors is applying judgment hastily and without due consideration; that is, without having a clear and distinct idea in front of us. In making this argument, he distinguished between the two main faculties of the mind, perception and will, and argued that perception can never be wrong in itself but only when the mind applies judgment to it by a hasty act of will. The problem, however, is that judgment cannot *make* things clear and distinct; ideas either appear clear and distinct in perception, or they don't. Echoing sixteenth- and seventeenth-century debates about grace, Malebranche's concern is with the question of what is left for the philosophical subject to do if the very core of philosophy, the clear and distinct perception of an idea, does not depend on the subject's agency. If certainty can only come from the ideas themselves, what is left for us as subjects of philosophical inquiry to do? Malebranche's answer is twofold: we can attend, and we can cultivate our capacity to do so: "We must then look out for Means that may hinder our Perceptions from being confused and imperfect. And because, as every one knows, nothing can make them more clear and distinct, than Attention; we must find our Means to become more and more attentive."[18] We cannot make our ideas clear and distinct if they aren't already so. In order to create certainty, what we can do is attend to them, by which Malebranche means primarily an act of the will that isn't positive but negative: we need to attend to them in the specific sense of *withholding judgment* and not allowing anything to distract us from the thought—to allow the thought to come to its own and to emerge as clear and distinct. Yet this passive disposition at the center of philosophy may be cultivated actively by a philosophy that exercises attentiveness.

The attentive reader may have noticed Malebranche's aside: *as everybody knows*. We might connect this aside to Descartes's indignant responses to Arnauld and Bourdin: for both Descartes and Malebranche, attention's role in philosophy is evident. Looking back at seventeenth-century philosophy, it is not immediately obvious why Descartes and Malebranche attributed so much potential to attention in philosophy. Today we associate attention with the mind's capacity to focus; attention is primarily a psychological, not a philosophical concept.[19] That is, if we can even call it a concept: after about three centuries of recurrent attempts to define it in philosophy, psychology, and most recently in the cognitive sciences, attention remains elusive as ever, stubbornly resisting the efforts to conceptualize it. Yet if we look at Descartes or Malebranche, one immediately striking feature of their discussions is that they never bother to define attention as a concept or even explain what they mean by it. Concerted efforts to define attention, primarily as a faculty of the mind, really begin only in the late seventeenth century and in the early eighteenth century, when thinkers from John Locke to the Abbé de Condillac seek to situate attention within a philosophy of the mind.[20] It is as if before them, thinkers like Descartes or Malebranche had known attention as something else than we do: rather than a capacity of the mind, attention in their systems is both the beginning and the end of philosophy, a disposition necessary to start thinking, and a disposition that is the result of thinking. In this book, I have tried to show that the precedent for attention's role in thinking is holy attention's role in prayer and poetry. By making attention a foundational concept in their philosophical and scientific systems, seventeenth-century thinkers such as Descartes and

Malebranche participated in the process of appropriating a religious ideal. The reason they thought attention's significance (both in its potential and in its limitations) was evident for their readers is that for them the devotional associations of attention as a practice and as a disposition were still primary. Their philosophies simultaneously enact the art of holy attention and begin the process of its secularization.

NOTES

INTRODUCTION

1. "The mind's attention is a natural prayer that we address to the internal Truth, so that it may reveal itself to us. But this sovereign Truth doesn't always answer our desires, because we do not know how to pray to it" (my translation). French original in "Conversations chrétiennes," in Nicolas Malebranche, *Oeuvres complètes* (Paris: Librairie J. Vrin, 1958), 4:14. For a discussion of the afterlife of this passage in Franz Kafka, Walter Benjamin, and Paul Celan, see Werner Hamacher, "Bogengebete," in Norbert Haas et al., eds., *Aufmerksamkeit* (Eggingen: Edition Isele, 1998), 11–43.

2. *Christian Conferences* (London, 1695), 2–3.

3. I take the term "holy attention" from the cartographer and devotional author John Norden's *A Goodlie Mans Guide to Happinesse; A Manuell of necessary Motives, holy Meditations, and godly Prayers, to stirre up the hearts of men unapt to pray; to the great Comfort of all, that with due and holy attention will practice this most godly and Christian dutie* (London, 1624). Similar terms appear in other early modern authors, and Norden could have taken the idea from Calvin's "pia attentio" (translated into French as "une estude attentive et saincte diligence" and into English as "godly attentiveness"). See *Ioannis Calvini in librum Psalmorum commentarius*, ed. A. Tholuck (Berolini: Gustavum Eichler, 1836), 2:473. Cf. *Commentaires de Jehan Calvin sur le livre des Pseaumes* (Paris: Ch. Meyrueis, 1859), 2:536, and *The Psalmes of David and Others: With M. John Calvin's Commentaries*, trans. Arthur Golding (London, 1571), 2:231ᵛ.

4. Gary Stringer, ed., *The Variorum Edition of the Poetry of John Donne, Volume 7, Part 1: The Holy Sonnets* (Bloomington: Indiana University Press, 2005), 16. (Further quotations from the *Holy Sonnets* are taken from this volume.) Compare Donne's line with Paul's "And Death is swallowed up in victory" in the KJV (see p. 248, note 29 below). For more on the specific relationship between Donne's sonnet and Paul's letter, see chaps. 1, 6, and 7.

5. On the role of affective experience in English seventeenth-century devotion, see Barbara Lewalski's account of "the application of the subject to the self" in Protestant

sermons and meditations (Barbara Lewalski, *Donne's Anniversaries and the Poetry of Praise* [Princeton, NJ: University of Princeton Press, 1973], 73–107 and 142–73), and Richard Strier's discussion in *Love Known: Theology and Experience in George Herbert's Poetry* (Chicago: University of Chicago Press, 1983), 143–47. On the importance of *sapientia experimentalis* in the post-Reformation era in general, see Susan E. Schreiner, *Are You Alone Wise? The Search for Certainty in the Early Modern Era* (Oxford: Oxford University Press, 2011), 209–59. Schreiner usefully emphasizes the interconfessional nature of this post-Reformation emphasis on affective faith, and she traces it back to the *devotio moderna* movement and to Spanish mysticism. In fact, affective devotion is present in the beginnings of Western monasticism, as Amy Hollywood demonstrates in "Song, Experience, and Book in Benedictine Monasticism," in *The Cambridge Companion to Christian Mysticism,* ed. Amy Hollywood and Patricia Z. Beckman (Cambridge: Cambridge University Press, 2012), 66–69.

6. In the context of devotion, the Elizabethan theologian William Perkins writes of "an especiall persuasion imprinted in the hart by the holye Ghost, wheby every faithfull man doth particularlye apply unto himselfe, those promises which are made in the Gospel." Perkins, *A Golden Chaine* (London, 1591), sig. P7ᵛ. Following Barbara Lewalski's *Protestant Poetics and the Seventeenth-Century Religious Lyrics* (Princeton, NJ: Princeton University Press, 1979), seeing devotional poetry as influenced by this notion of affective application to the self has been a major trend in the scholarship.

7. When Strier reads the poems from the perspective of the Protestant affective devotion that he explained in *Love Known,* he finds that the poems present difficulties or failures in devotional terms, which for Strier ultimately imply aesthetic failures as well, insofar as the poems do not acknowledge their devotional problems. See "John Donne Awry and Squint: The 'Holy Sonnets,' 1608–1610," *Modern Philology* 86 (1989): esp. 380–81 and 384.

8. For the range of meanings associated with *affectus,* see Hollywood, "Song, Experience, and Book in Benedictine Monasticism," 67.

9. Readers familiar with T. S. Eliot's long and varied engagement with Donne's poetry will recognize that my argument confirms certain aspects of Eliot's account while challenging others. Eliot famously claimed that "a thought to Donne was an experience; it modified his sensibility" ("The Metaphysical Poets," in William Keast, ed., *Seventeenth-Century English Poetry: Modern Essays in Criticism* [Oxford: Oxford University Press, 1962], 27). Elsewhere, Eliot compared Donne's poetry with Herbert's in terms of cognition versus emotion: "In Donne thought seems in control of feeling, and in Herbert feeling seems in control of thought" (T. S. Eliot, *George Herbert* [London: Longman's, 1962], 19).

10. "Dem philologischen Wissen ist ein dynamisches Moment eigen . . . weil es nur in der fortwährenden Konfrontation mit dem Text bestehen kann, nur in der ununterbrochenen Zurückführung des Wissens auf Erkenntnis, auf das Verstehen des dichterischen Wortes." German original in Peter Szondi, *Hölderlin-Studien. Mit einem Traktat über philologische Erkenntnis.* (Frankfurt am Main: Suhrkamp Verlag, 1979), 11. English text in Peter Szondi, *On Textual Understanding and Other Essays,* trans. Harvey Mendelsohn (Minneapolis: University of Minnesota Press, 1986), 5.

11. This is hardly a coincidence: Szondi's claim is likely influenced by biblical hermeneu-
tics. For Szondi's engagement and debate with the hermeneutic tradition, see Peter
Szondi, "Schleiermacher's Hermeneutics Today," in *On Textual Understanding and Other
Essays*, 95–114.

12. The editors of the *Variorum* edition point out that "a signal feature of the manuscript
transmission of the Holy Sonnets is that none of the poems has a history of individual
circulation. However ordered, these sonnets invariably traveled in groups, a fact suggesting that the concept of sequence was integral to Donne's understanding of the
genre from the very beginning. . . . The details of Donne's handling of individual texts
as they move forward in the stream of transmission confirm that the ordering of the
sonnets was a matter of continuing authorial attention" (Stringer, *Holy Sonnets*, lx–lxi).

13. The fact that Donne circulated the poems in groups also raises the *different* question
of whether or not he meant them to be read in a specific order. The order of the *Holy
Sonnets* has been a matter of both research and speculation since at least Helen Gardner's edition of the divine poems, in which she presents both textual and interpretative evidence to support her argument that the poems cohere in individual groups:
two groups of six sonnets from the twelve that appeared in the 1633 *Poems*, four sonnets that appear in the 1635 edition, and three more ["Show me deare Christ," "Oh,
to vex me," and "Since She whome I lovd,"] that according to Gardner were written
after Donne's ordination (Helen Gardner, ed., *John Donne: The Divine Poems* [Oxford:
Clarendon Press, 1978], xxxvii–lv). The *Variorum* presents strong evidence in favor of
Donne's investment in arranging the poems in particular sequences. It prints both an
original and a revised sequence, which according to the editors represent two stages
in Donne's ordering of the poems. The two authorial sequences raise the question of
whether we can interpret these two sequences differently. While I have not been able
to discover either a narrative or a thematic order in either sequence, scholars have
proposed various interpretations. For instance, R. V. Young's essay "The Religious
Sonnet," in *The Oxford Handbook of John Donne*, 218–32, and Theresa M. DiPasquale's
and Kirsten Stirling's unpublished essays (I am grateful to them for sharing their work
with me).

14. For an overview of the reception of the *Holy Sonnets* and the unique role of "Death be
not proud" in it, see Raoul Granquist, *The Reputation of John Donne 1779–1873* (Stock-
holm: Almquist & Wiksell, 1975), 128. Praisers of "Death be not proud" include De Quin-
cey, Wordsworth, and Leigh Hunt (for a selection of their comments, see Stringer, *Holy
Sonnets*, 293–97).

15. Leigh Hunt, "An Essay on the Sonnet," in *The Book of Sonnet*, first published in Boston
in 1867. Quoted in A. J. Smith, ed., *John Donne: The Critical Heritage* (London: Routledge & Kegan Paul, 1975), 316.

16. The first ironic readings of the poem, readings that suggest that Donne's intent is to
reveal the speaker's bragging and lack of confidence rather than his defeat of death,
emerge in the second half of the twentieth century, in Thomas E. Sanders's *The Discovery of Poetry* (Glenview: Scott, Foresman 1967), 353, and most notably in John Carey's
John Donne: Life, Mind, and Art (New York: Oxford University Press, 1981), 199. Theresa M. DiPasquale argues, in the presidential address of the John Donne Society's

Annual Conference in 2007, that the revised sequence supports the modern, ironic readings of the poem (I thank Theresa DiPasquale for sharing this essay with me).

17. Quotations of *La Corona* are from Robin Robbins, ed., *The Complete Poems of John Donne* (Harlow: Longman, 2010), 476–87. In the 1633 edition, the title *La Corona* is placed under the all-capital heading "HOLY SONNETS," creating the impression that *La Corona* and the following twelve *Holy Sonnets* belong in a single group of poems, though the title "Holy Sonnets" is repeated again after *La Corona* and before the twelve sonnets. For the poem's textual history, see the discussions in Gardner, *The Divine Poems*, lvii–xcvi; Stringer, *Holy Sonnets*, lx–ci (although the editors' focus here is the *Holy Sonnets*, *La Corona* is also discussed as a poem that was often circulated together with the *Holy Sonnets*); and Robbins, *Complete Poems of John Donne*, 475–76.

18. "This first last end" is in the MS whereas the 1633 *Poems* edition has "The first last end," which leaves the reference of "first last end" more open, though still suggesting that the primary theological sense is redemption (see Robbins, *Complete Poems of John Donne*, 478). For more on additional meanings of the line with a "the," see my discussion of the poem in chap. 5.

19. See Robbins, *Complete Poems of John Donne*, 478, fn.11. For a particularly elegant interpretation of how Donne's use of the sonnet-crown represents the difficulty temporality poses to devotion, see Margaret Mauer, "The Circular Argument of Donne's 'La Corona,'" *Studies in English Literature, 1500–1900* 22:1: 51–68.

20. Annabel Patterson has suggested that in *La Corona* Donne sought to salvage a Catholic form by re-forming it and by making it compatible with Protestant doctrine and devotion, which would explain the proem's concern with devotional labor ("Donne's Reformed La Corona," *John Donne Journal* 23 [2004]: 80–81 and 86).

21. For reasons I explain below, here I follow the 1633 *Poems'* punctuation rather than Robbins's.

22. See, for instance, John T. Shawcross's edition, *The Complete Poetry of John Donne* (Garden City: Doubleday Anchor Books, 1967), 334, fn.12. Gardner quotes the Roman Breviary's "Ego autem ad Dominum aspiciam, et exspectabo Deum Salvatorem meum" (Gardner, *The Divine Poems*, 58); Robbins cites Psalm 61:1 ("Truly my soul waiteth upon God" in the KJV; Robbins, *Complete Poems of John Donne*, 478).

23. Gardner argues that "'[po]ssest' qualifies the soul, which is 'wholly occupied' by its thirst" (Gardner, *The Divine Poems*, 58). Robbins even prints the lines with a different punctuation: "This first last end now, zealously possessed, / With a strong, sober thirst, my soul attends" (Robbins follows the Westmoreland MS, but his punctutation of the line is based on his interpretation—the Westmoreland MS does not have any commas in these two lines).

24. For more about attention in liturgical contexts, see my discussion in chap. 3.

25. There are interesting differences between Catholic and Protestant treatments of this difficulty, with Catholics often focusing on finding remedies, while Protestants lament the difficulty and its significance for the human condition. Catholic discussions offer attention-techniques (which overlap significantly with the *ars memoria*), or develop scholastic vocabularies that seem to be designed to allow a great deal of leniency (for instance, there's a distinction between "actual" attention and "virtual" attention where

actual attention is the attention that is being paid to an object right now, whereas virtual attention is the prolonged effect of an earlier act of attention. The category of virtual attention thus allows one to find attentiveness in and therefore attribute efficacy to seemingly slack acts of devotion. Protestant discussions similarly emphasize the difficulty of concentrating in prayer, but with a different meaning: for them, it often comes up as a sign of the fallenness and imperfection of human devotion. What's generally true of all these discussions, though, is that they don't offer an answer to my question about attention and redemption; indeed they don't address the issue of why attention would be important at all. For more about these discussions, see chaps. 3 and 4.

26. By "mental prayer" authors of the *devotio moderna* movement and Catholic reformers in general meant not just silent prayer but a wide range of practices including meditation and contemplation. On this, see H. Outram Evennett, "Counter-Reformation Spirituality," in David M. Luebke, ed., *The Counter-Reformation* (Malden, MA: Blackwell, 1999), 58.

27. John Ashbery, "The Painter," in *Poetry* 87:3 (1955): 154.

28. The rest of the neighbors' advice is also pertinent: "Select, for a portrait, / Something less angry and large, and more subject / To a painter's moods, or, perhaps, to prayer."

29. "Temptation" may be described as a false promise of attentiveness: though it may lead to an experience of absorption, what distinguishes this experience from devotional attentiveness is its indissoluble attachment to an object.

30. Although far less explicitly articulated in traditional discussions of Christian devotion, what I call here the art of attention has significant overlaps with the *ars memoria* that has been articulated in the work of Frances Yates, Mary Carruthers, and Lina Bolzoni. For an essay that highlights some common traits between the arts of memory and attention, see Rachel Fulton Brown, "My Psalter, My Self; or, How to Get a Grip on the Office according to Jan Mombaer: An Exercise in Training the Attention for Prayer," *Spiritus* 12:1 (2012): 75–195.

31. When in the later 1920s Eliot began expressing doubts about Donne's qualities, he often brought up Donne's supposed distractions. For instance, in a notorious essay on Lancelot Andrewes, Eliot quotes two of Donne's sermons that address the issue of distraction, and he uses these passages to compare Donne unfavorably to Andrewes on the grounds that "[Donne] is constantly finding an object which shall be adequate to his feelings; [whereas] Andrewes is wholly absorbed in the object and therefore responds with the adequate emotion" (T. S. Eliot, "Lancelot Andrewes," in *Essays, Ancient and Modern* [London: Faber & Faber, 1936], 27).

32. John Donne, "Sermon Preached at the funerals of Sir William Cokayne Knight, Alderman of London, December 12. 1626," in George Potter and Evelyn M. Simpson, eds., *The Sermons of John Donne*, 10 vols. (Berkeley: University of California Press, 1953–62), 7:265.

33. For more about Augustine and Donne, see chap. 5.

34. "Sermon preached at Lincoln's Inn on Job 19:27: And though, after my skin, wormes destroy this body, yet in my flesh shall I see God," in Potter and Simpson, *Sermons*, 109–10.

35. Donne's "Extasie" is one of the many poems in the *Songs and Sonets* in which lovers pay exclusive and undistracted attention to each other. Among the many examples, the last line in "The Good-Morrow" stands out by drawing a parallel between attention and immortality: "Love so alike, none do slacken, none can die" imagines the lovers as paying equal and equally intense attention to each other and thereby perpetuating their love. I quote "The Good-Morrow" from the 1633 *Poems;* Robbins replaces the line with "Love just alike in all, none of these loves can die" (Robbins, *Complete Poems of John Donne,* 199). But see L. M. Crowley, "Establishing a 'Fitter' Text for Donne's 'The Good Morrowe,'" *John Donne Journal* 22 (2003): 5–21.

36. Stringer, *Holy Sonnets,* 13. The *Variorum* prints three versions of the sequence: the *Devine Meditations* (the original sequence containing twelve poems), the Westmoreland sequence (the only sequence containing all nineteen poems today known as the *Holy Sonnets*), and the Revised sequence (which contains twelve poems). Unless indicated otherwise, I quote from the Westmoreland sequence, though occasionally I refer to differences between it and the two twelve-poem sequences.

37. Louis Martz, *The Poetry of Meditation: A Study in English Religious Poetry* (New Haven, CT: Yale University Press, 1954), esp. 25ff.

38. Anthony Low notes the *Holy Sonnets'* tendency to break down after their initial attempt to perform their exercises, though he locates the change later, in the sestet ("Absence in Donne's Holy Sonnets: Between Catholic and Calvinist," *John Donne Journal* 23 [2004]: 98).

39. The revised sequence abandons the theological hesitation in line 7 and states instead, "But my ever wakeing part shall see that face / Whose feare already shakes my every ioynt" (Stringer, *Holy Sonnets,* 22). For a discussion of this change, see chap. 4, n. 64.

40. Richard Strier argues that in the final lines the "Reformation vocabulary does not correspond to the vision presented; the matter will not take this print," and he adds that in general in the *Holy Sonnets* we see "Donne's deep inability to accept the paradoxical conception of a regenerate Christian." See Strier, "John Donne Awry and Squint," 373–74.

41. The fact that Friedrich Heiler's *Das Gebet: Eine religionsgeschichtliche und religionspsychologische Untersuchung* (München: Verlag von Ernst Reinhardt, 1921) remains the most comprehensive theoretical account of Christian prayer is telling, not only because Heiler's work is nearly a century old, but because of Heiler's consistent Protestant bias that prioritizes spontanous and expressive prayer over set prayers and prayers as exercises. Recently, however, a great deal of work has been done to articulate devotion's practical and rhetorical aspects both within and beyond Christianity. See esp. Mary Carruthers, *The Craft of Thought: Meditation, Rhetoric, and the Making of Images* (New York: Cambridge University Press, 1998); Brian Stock, *After Augustine: The Meditative Reader and the Text* (Philadelphia: University of Pennsylvania Press, 2001); Rachel Fulton, *From Judgment to Passion: Devotion to Christ and the Virgin Mary, 800–1200* (New York: Columbia University Press, 2002); Saba Mahmood, *Politics of Piety* (Princeton, NJ: Princeton University Press, 2005); and Jennifer Herdt, *Putting on Virtue: The Legacy of the Splendid Vices* (Chicago: University of Chicago Press, 2008). One thing that connects these works is their shared interest in the role of practice, rhetoric, and habit

in devotion; an interest that bears out both neo-Aristotelian trends and the influence of Michel Foucault's work on power and subjectivity, which in turn is itself influenced by Pierre Hadot's work on devotional practices from antiquity to modern philosophy.

42. On this broad meaning of the phrase, see James O'Donnell's commentary in his edition of Augustine's *Confessions,* 3 vols. (Oxford: Clarendon Press, 1992), 3:4.

43. Alexander Pope, *An Essay on Criticism* (London, 1711), 11.

44. Though the association between grace and movement goes much further back in history, it is certainly present in Renaissance discussions (the *linea serpentinata* fascinated theorists of painting as a "moving" line). See William Guild Howard, "Reiz ist Schönheit in Bewegung," *PMLA* 24 (1909): 286–93.

45. "He was eminently illiterate; wrote bad English, and spelt it worse. . . . His figure was beautiful but his manner was irresistible. It was by this engaging, graceful manner, that he was enabled, during all his wars, to connect the various and jarring powers of the grand alliance, and to carry them on to the main object of the war, notwithstanding their private and separate views, jealousies, and wrongheadedness" (William Hazlitt, "On Manner," in *The Round Table* [New York: Scribner, 1869], 49). I thank Denise Gigante for this reference.

46. The *locus classicus* is Pliny the Elder's *Historia naturalis,* which describes the Greek painter Apelles' work as surpassing all other painters' by its *charis.* See Pliny the Elder, *Historia naturalis,* xxxv. 36, 79. *Charis* is translated here as *venustas;* but when Quintilian repeats the same anecdote, he uses *gratia.* See Quintilian, *Institutio Oratoria,* xii. 10, 6. The anecdote is immensely influential both in classical and early modern rhetoric, and *charis* and its translations become synonymous with the kind of expression that ensures the most delight and efficiency with and because of a certain facility and ease of movement, but cannot be defined, taught, or learned (in addition to Quintilian, see also Dionysius of Halicarnassus, *On Lysias;* and Cicero, *Oratoria,* xxv 84, xxvi 87, and *De Oratore,* i 31, 32). This is the point where grace becomes an anomaly within rhetoric: it holds the key of efficient *elocutio,* but the level of efficiency associated with it is declared an enigma, a *nescio-quid. Nescio quid* is Augustine's expression, which will become influential through the Renaissance Neoplatonists. I use the Latin here, instead of the more familiar French, in order to distinguish the doctrine of grace as enigma from the later career of the *je-ne-sais-quoi.* The latter has been the subject of a number of excellent studies including Vladimir Jankélévitch's *Le je-ne-sais-quoi et le presque-rien* (Paris: Seuil, 1980), and particularly its first volume, *La manière et l'occasion;* as well as Richard Scholar's *The Je-ne-sais-quoi in Early Modern Europe: Encounters with a Certain Something* (Oxford: Oxford University Press, 2005).

47. Giorgio Vasari, *Le Vite,* ed. Luciano Bellosi (Torino: Einaudi, 1986), 883.

48. Heinrich von Kleist, "Über das Marionettentheater," in *Sämtliche Werke und Briefe,* ed. Helmut Sembdner (München: Deutsche Taschenbuch Verlag, 2001), 2:338–45.

49. Making any universal statement about the concept of grace is difficult because even within Western Christian cultures the words denoting the various notions of grace are often widely different. While most Romance languages and English have inherited their vernacular words for grace from the Latin *gratia,* the German word for aesthetic grace is *Anmut* while the standard theological term for divine grace is *Gnade.* While

in Italian or in English the words for "grace" invite comparisons between the religious and the aesthetic, in German any similar association must be actively created by the speaker against the evidence of language. It is striking that in the *Marionettentheater* the word *Gnade* does not appear at all, not even in the final discussion, which focuses on the biblical notion of an original state of grace. Instead, Kleist's main terms are *Anmut* and the Latinate *Grazie,* as well as various adjectives. Had Kleist used the term *Gnade,* he would have inevitably evoked associations of asking for grace (by using religious prayer)—and perhaps this is precisely what he wanted to avoid. For an etymological history of *gratia* from the early Latin to the Christian period, see Claude Moussy, *Gratia et sa famille* (Paris: Presses Universitaires de France, 1966).

50. The author of one of the most acknowledged studies of the *Courtier,* Eduardo Saccone, criticizes those accounts that highlight Castiglione's debt to the classical rhetorical tradition. See Eduardo Saccone, "*Grazia, Sprezzatura, Affettazione* in the *Courtier,*" in Robert W. Hanning and David Rosand, eds., *Castiglione: The Ideal and the Real in Renaissance Culture* (New Haven, CT: Yale University Press, 1983), 45–67. Saccone emphasizes the significance of the Aristotelian theory of *aretē* as the ethical doctrine of the mean in the *Courtier:* "Neither [Wittkower's or Blunt's] formulation sees the word as an element of Castiglione's larger plan (one that is essential to the pedagogical scheme of the *Courtier*): to delimit an area of human activity that can serve as an Aristotelian middle ground between two exceptional conditions, the 'mean' between absolute perfection and imperfection, between 'eccelente grazia' and 'insensata sciochezza'" (50). Here, however, Saccone is unnecessarily reductive: the Aristotelian virtue may well be an important component of Castiglione's treatment of grace, but Saccone makes no mention of the fact the theory of the middle is just as important for classical theories of *elocutionis genera,* as in the case of Demetrius's locating the graceful style between the low and the grand styles. Overlooking this leads Saccone to misleading arguments. Thus, speaking about *sprezzatura,* Saccone asks "Whenever did grace come to consist in the avoiding of affectation?" (55). The fact of the matter is that Demetrius in his treatment of *charientismos* explicitly argues that the ultimate characteristic of the proper graceful style is that it is perilously near to affectation, yet manages to avoid it. Although Saccone does not cite any of the relevant passages from Demetrius, he does recognize the continuity between *sprezzatura* and classical rhetorical formulations of grace in Cicero and Quintilian. But he suggests that the difference of Castiglione's version is that it expands the notion of grace to "all human affairs whether in word or deed" (56)—which, he claims again, shows that Castiglione follows Aristotle. But to say this requires overlooking the whole Stoic tradition of grace as an ethical and social concept, the tradition that survives in the Middle Ages in the mythographers' treatments of *Gratia* as *liberalem mentis affectionem* and the Graces as the movement of gift giving. Moreover, this social and ethical aspect of grace is revived in the Renaissance by the Neoplatonists, who reconnect it with Christian doctrine. I do not question Saccone's claim that Aristotle's *aretē* is important for the *Courtier,* but it seems to me that this influence does not invalidate statements about the continuities between Castiglione's work and the different classical traditions of *charis, gratia,* and *venustas.* I find more useful Saccone's remarks on the relevance of Aristotle's *eirōneia* for *sprezzatura.*

For three competing accounts of the *Courtier*, see Daniel Javitch, "*Il Cortegiano* and the Constraints of Despotism," in Hanning and Rosand, *Castiglione: The Ideal and the Real*, 17–28; Amedeo Quondam, "Questo povero Cortegiano," in *Castiglione, il libro, la storia* (Roma: Bulzoni, 2000); and Jon R. Snyder's discussion of *sprezzatura* in *Dissimulation and the Culture of Secrecy in Early Modern Europe* (Berkeley: University of California Press, 2009), 71–77.

51. Baldassar Castiglione, *Il libro del Cortegiano* (Milan: Garzanti, 1981), 128.

52. What I'm trying to articulate here bears some resemblance to what Debora Shuger calls the Renaissance "pneumatic self," a self that is at least partly defined by its lack of autonomy. As Shuger explains, this self is "both permeable and passive . . . not a bounded ego but a space—a void, if you like—where God comes (or doesn't come)" (*Habits of Thought in the English Renaissance* [Berkeley: University of California Press, 1990], 100). But unlike Shuger, who articulates this sense of the self in contradistinction to the social, performative, and fully autonomous self, I am interested in the way grace is a simultaneously religious and secular ideal.

53. Consider the first stanza of Samuel Daniel's oft-quoted sonnet: "Care-charmer sleepe, sonne of the Sable night, / Brother to death, in silent darknesse borne: / Relieve my languish, and restore the light, / With darke forgetting of my cares returne" (Samuel Daniel, *Delia* [London, 1592], 49). This is a poem that begins, as poems in this subgenre often do, with insomnia, and ends with death; in between, there is an invitation for sleep to come and take hold of the speaker. Sidney, whose *Astrophil and Stella* was first published with a selection of Daniel's poems, dedicated sonnet 39 to the same theme. "Come Sleep, O Sleep" attempts to invite sleep by promising various gifts to it, and ends with this final invocation: "And if these things, as being thine by right, / Move not thy heavy grace, thou shalt in me, / Livelier than elsewhere, Stella's image see" (Katherine Duncan-Jones, ed., *Sir Philip Sidney: The Major Works* [Oxford: Oxford University Press, 2002], 168). An eminent precedent is Chaucer's *The Book of the Duchess*, which begins with the sleepless poet promising gifts to Morpheus; but it is important to note that one of the first Christian poems, Ambrose's hymn "Deus creator omniuminsert," is itself a prayerful meditation on the *soporis gratia*.

54. Cf. Maurice Merleau-Ponty's account: "I lie down in bed, on my left side, with my knees drawn up: I close my eyes and breathe slowly, putting my plans out of my mind. But the power of my will or consciousness stops there. As the faithful, in the Dionysian mysteries, invoke the god by mining scenes from his life, I call up the visitation of sleep by imitating the breathing and posture of the sleeper. The god is actually there when the faithful can no longer distinguish themselves from the part they are playing, when their body and consciousness cease to bring in, as an obstacle, their particular opacity, and when they are totally fused in the myth. There is a moment when sleep 'comes,' settling on this imitation itself which I have been offering to it, and I succeed in becoming what I was trying to be" (Maurice Merleau-Ponty, *Phenomenology of Perception* [London: Routledge, 2002], 189–90). The context of Merleau-Ponty's analysis of falling asleep is aphonia.

55. What Burke calls "secular prayer," prayer in an extended sense that goes beyond liturgy and devotion, is "the coaching of an attitude by the use of mimetic and verbal

language." Cf. Kenneth Burke, *Attitudes toward History* (Berkeley: University of California Press, 1984), 321–27.

56. Apart from Izaak Walton's *The Life of John Donne* (London, 1658), the best sources for studying Donne's life are Donne's *Letters to Severall Persons* (London, 1651), a full scholarly edition of which is being prepared by Dennis Flynn; R. C. Bald's *John Donne: A Life* (New York: Oxford University Press, 1970); John Carey's *John Donne: Life, Mind, and Art* (London: Faber & Faber, 1981); and most recently, John Stubbs's *John Donne: The Reformed Soul* (New York: Norton, 2007). David Colclough, ed., *John Donne's Professional Lives* (Cambridge: D. S. Brewer, 2003), includes a series of essays that seek to mediate between what earlier authors (particularly Carey) saw as tensions and contradictions in Donne's life.

57. Whether and to what extent Donne may have remained faithful to the confessional identity of his ancestors is a contested subject. Dennis Flynn's *John Donne and the Ancient Catholic Nobility* (Bloomington: Indiana University Press, 1995) is the classical statement of Donne's continuing loyalty to the "corrupted religion," and a response to Carey's *John Donne,* which argues that Donne's guilt over his apostasy motivates much of his poetry, particularly the emphasis on female unfaithfulness. On apostasy and conversion, see Molly Murray, *The Poetics of Conversion in Early Modern English Literature* (Cambridge: Cambridge University Press, 2011), 69–104. On the difficulties of determining Donne's confessional identity in the sermons, see Debora Shuger, *Habits of Thought in the English Renaissance: Religion, Politics, and the Dominant Culture* (Berkeley: University of California Press, 1990), 176–77, and Achsah Guibbory, "Donne's Religion," *English Literary Renaissance* 31 (2001): 412–39, reprinted in Guibbory, *Returning to Donne* (Burlington, VT: Ashgate, 2015), 175–200, which, in addition to arguing for Donne's association with Montagu and Armenianism, offers a helpful overview of the matter. See also the essays by Jeanne Shami, Achsah Guibbory, Dennis Flynn, and Hugh Adlington in *The Oxford Handbook of John Donne,* ed. Jeanne Shami, Dennis Flynn, and M. Thomas Hester (Oxford: Oxford University Press, 2011). One problem with talking about Donne's conversion is that oftentimes the poems themselves are used as its "proof." For a brilliant account of the inconsistencies and self-contradictions of this view, see Dayton Haskin's critique of Edmund Gosse's reading of the *Holy Sonnets* as expressions of Donne's converted state of mind in *John Donne in the Nineteenth Century* (Oxford: Oxford University Press, 2007), 174–77. As Brian Cummings has shown, Donne's sermon on Paul's conversion expresses both longing for a Pauline revelation and skepticism about its possibility. See Brian Cummings, *The Literary Culture of the Reformation: Grammar and Grace* (Oxford: Oxford University Press, 2002), 395. The most sustained and influential accounts of Donne's ambition and its relationship to the poetry are Carey, *John Donne;* and Arthur Marotti, *Donne, Coterie Poet* (Madison: University of Wisconsin Press, 1986).

58. Jorge Louis Borges's dictum comes to mind: "Blind to all sins, destiny can be ruthless at the slightest distraction" ("The South," in *Ficciones* [Buenos Aires: Grove Press, 1962], 167). Donne's marriage letters give the sense that Donne's mistake was one of inattention in prayer: the letters he wrote to Anne More's father and to Egerton are simultaneously abject petitions for forgiveness and arrogant requests to ask for more. As

prayers for mercy, they failed miserably; and at least one reason they failed is that Donne had not yet paid enough attention to the question of how to ask. In one sense, Donne's entire life after this fiasco could be seen as an attempt to learn from this original mistake by becoming better at prayer. The marriage letters are available in Thomas Hester at al., eds., *John Donne's Marriage Letters in the Folger Shakespeare Library* (Washington, DC: Folger Shakespeare Library, 2005).

59. Peter McCullough, "Donne and Court Chaplaincy," in Shami et al., *Oxford Handbook of John Donne*, 558.

60. See Bald, *John Donne: A Life*, 227.

61. While traditionally Donne's devotional poems were seen as the product of Donne's life as a divine, Helen Gardner and Louis Martz were among the first to suggest that many of the *Holy Sonnets* must have been written at the time Donne hesitated about his vocation (though for Martz this leaves open the rather large window between 1601 and 1615). A critique of Gardner's dating of the sonnet that suggests instead that they were written in the 1590s is in Dennis Flynn, "'Awry and Squint': The Dating of Donne's Holy Sonnets." *John Donne Journal* 7:1: 35–46. For a more recent discussion of the *Holy Sonnets'* textual history and the problems of dating them, see the editor's comments in Stringer, *Holy Sonnets*, lxxxvii–ci, and 133–46. Ironically, as late as the nineteenth century critics still saw Donne's hesitation, which I propose was really a gathering of his attention, as "distraction": "His life is as distracted and dependent as his thought. He cannot fairly decide to be the divine, and apologizes for his want of learning while he is displaying learning enough for a whole bench of bishops" (Sir Leslie Stephen quoted in Jeanne Shami, "Donne's Decision to Take Orders," in *Oxford Handbook of John Donne*, 527.

62. Donne's methodical processing of the theological debates of the period began well before the king's offer. According to his testimony in *Pseudo-Martyr*, his long "irresolution" concerning religious matters was a period of deliberate study, during which he "surveyed and digested the whole body of Divinity, controverted between ours and the Romane Church" (*Pseudo-Martyr* [London, 1610], 9–10). While it makes little sense to draw a rigid distinction between Donne's theological and devotional engagement with Christianity, it seems fair to say that in the prose Donne often focuses on theology, while in the poems and letters his concern is primarily with devotional action.

63. For an elaboration of Martz's argument, see Helen B. Brooks, "Donne's 'Vexations' and the Ignatian Meditative Model," *John Donne Journal* 19 (2000): 101–37. Ignatius's journals record the way the founder of the Jesuit order himself practiced meditations in order to arrive at a decision. For a selection, see *Saint Ignatius of Loyola: Personal Writings*, trans. Joseph A. Munitz and Philip Endean (London: Penguin, 1996).

64. Lewalski's *Protestant Poetics* counters Martz's reading and insists that the *Holy Sonnets* are Protestant poems. Less influential but similarly emphatic on Donne's Protestantism is William Halewood's *The Poetry of Grace: Reformation Themes and Structures in Seventeenth-Century English Poetry* (New Haven, CT: Yale University Press, 1970).

65. Or, to use Anthony Low's terms, in the *Holy Sonnets* there is a "joint presence of Catholic method and Calvinist anxiety" ("Absence in Donne's Holy Sonnets: Between Catholic and Calvinist," *John Donne Journal* 23 [2004]: 101).

66. Robert Nye compares the "intricate rhymes" of the *Holy Sonnets* to a hair shirt in "'The Body Is His Book: The Poetry of John Donne,'" *Critical Quarterly* 14:345–60, 357.

67. See Gardner's commentary in *The Divine Poems*, 67. The penultimate line's temporality poses further questions; for a more detailed discussion of these questions, see chap. 4.

68. For a provocative study of Luther's scatological imagery, see Norman O. Brown's *Life against Death: The Psychoanalytical Meaning of History* (New York: Random House, 1959), esp. 234–307.

69. Emphasis mine.

70. Though some of Donne's readers speak of a similar disappointment in the context of the *Songs and Sonets*; see, for instance, Christopher Ricks, "John Donne: 'Farewell to Love,'" in *Essays of Appreciation* (Oxford: Oxford University Press, 1996), 19–51, which argues that "the success of the ending is the failing of the poem, because it demeans" (20), and associates this dislike of ending with Donne's supposed "dislike of having come" (19).

71. For a classic statement of this view, see Roman Jakobson, "Linguistics and Poetics," in *Selected Writings*, ed. Stephen Rudy (The Hague: Mouton Publishers, 1981), 18–51.

72. Stringer, *Holy Sonnets*, 13.

73. My use of the term "given" is influenced by Jean-Luc Marion's phenomenological account of the concept, which itself goes back to Husserlian and Heideggerian precedents. In his 1919–20 lectures titled *Grundprobleme der Phänomenologie*, Heidegger compares givenness to Paul's stumbling block: "Was heißt 'Gegeben,' 'Gegebenheit'— dieses Zauberwort der Phänomenologie und der 'Stein des Anstoßes' bei den anderen" (Martin Heidegger, *Gesamtausgabe*, ed. Hans-Helmuth Gander [Frankfurt am Main: Klostermann, 1993], 58:5). By referring to 1 Corinthians 1:22, Heidegger draws a parallel between phenomenology and the Pauline Gospel, and the parallel is based on *charis*, that is, on the underivable givenness of divine grace/the phenomenon. This is the agenda that Marion picks up in his two books, in which he calls attention to the "unfinished" project of phenomenology in the concepts of *Gegeben* (the given) and *Gegebenheit* (givenness). Since Husserl's work, phenomenology's project was to go back to the "phenomena"; the phenomenological reduction is supposed to reach back to the object as it is given to intentionality. Marion argues that both Husserl and Heidegger missed an opportunity when, although they both emphasized the importance of the given (*Gegeben* or *es gibt*), they tried to explain it away—Husserl by identifying it with the "object," and Heidegger by deriving it from *Ereignis*. Marion argues that in doing so they both stepped beyond the limits of phenomenology toward metaphysics. The properly phenomenological procedure, Marion suggests, is to focus on the givenness of the given: how the given appears as *being* given. See Jean-Luc Marion, *Étant donné: essai d'une phénoménologie de la donation* (Paris: Presses universitaires de France, 1997); English translation in *Being Given: Toward a Phenomenology of Givenness*, trans. Jeffrey L. Kosky (Stanford, CA: Stanford University Press, 2002).

74. Calvin, *The Psalmes of David and Others*, 231.

75. Two foundational works for the relationship between devotion and philosophy influencing the following paragraphs are Paul Rabbow, *Seelenführung* (München: Kösel Verlag, 1954); and Pierre Hadot, *Philosophy as a Way of Life* (Oxford: Blackwell, 1995).

76. "A prayer is, for instance, a sentence but neither has truth nor has falsity. Let us pass over all such, as their study more properly belongs to the province of rhetoric or poetry" (Aristotle, *On Interpretation*, trans. Harold P. Cooke [Cambridge, MA: Harvard University Press, 1983], 121).

77. See chaps. 3 and 5 for detailed discussions of the overlap between prayer and theology.

78. Three accounts of address have been particularly influential for my discussion here and elsewhere in the book. The first is Jonathan Culler's "Apostrophe," in *The Pursuit of Signs* (Ithaca, NY: Cornell University Press, 1981), 135–54, an influential exposition of lyric address and apostrophe in poetry, which Culler has further developed for the recent *Theory of the Lyric* (Cambridge, MA: Harvard University Press, 2015), 186–243. The second is Jean-Louis Chrétien's "The Wounded Word," in *The Ark of Speech*, trans. Andrew Brown (New York: Routledge, 2004), esp. 17–39, which offers a phenomenology of prayer as address. The third is Jahan Ramazani's *Poetry and Its Others* (Chicago: University of Chicago Press, 2014), chap. 4.

79. Herbert J. C. Grierson's *Metaphysical Lyrics and Poems of the Seventeenth Century* (Oxford: Clarendon Press, 1921) began with a selection of Donne's poetry ("The goodmorrow" opened the collection), and the response from T. S. Eliot and the English and American literary critics of the era established Donne as the paradigmatic poet not only of the seventeenth century, but in many ways of the English language—before Eliot.

80. John Crowe Ransom, *The World's Body* (Baton Rouge: Louisiana State University Press, 1968), 286.

81. Cleanth Brooks quoting Coleridge in *The Well Wrought Urn: Studies in the Structure of Poetry* (New York: Reynal & Hitchcock, 1947), 26.

82. I. A. Richards, *Practical Criticism* (London: Kegan Paul, Trench, Trubner & Co., 1929), 272–73 (emphasis mine).

83. Ibid., 291–92 (emphasis mine).

84. That Protestant devotional ideals might be influencing the discussion, though, becomes quite clear in the passage that describes "something like a technique or ritual for heightening sincerity." Here is Richards's advice: "Sit by the fire (with eyes shut and fingers pressed firmly upon the eyeballs), and consider with as full 'realisation' as possible:—i, Man's loneliness (the isolation of human situation). ii. The facts of birth, and of death, in their inexplicable oddity. iii. The inconceivable immensity of the Universe. iv. Man's place in the perspective of time. v. The enormity of his ignorance" (Ibid., 290–91). The irony is that Richards proposes spiritual exercises as preparation for reading poetry that was itself a kind of spiritual exercise.

85. Martz, *Poetry of Meditation*, 67.

86. Lewalski's *Protestant Poetics* counters Martz's reading and insists that the *Holy Sonnets* are Protestant poems, as does Halewood's *The Poetry of Grace*. R. V. Young's *Doctrine and Devotion in Seventeenth-Century Poetry* (Cambridge: D. S. Brewer, 2000), 1–32, depicts Donne hesitating between Catholicism and Protestantism, embracing a type of Christian ecumenism, and thereby contributing to the rise of the *via media* in the Church of England. While many note hesitations in the *Holy Sonnets*, the most insistent analyses of religious doubt in the poems are Strier's "John Donne Awry and

Squint," Carey's *John Donne,* 57–58, and Stanley Fish's "Masculine Persuasive Force: Donne and Verbal Power," in *Soliciting Interpretation: Literary Theory and Seventeenth-Century English Poetry,* ed. Elizabeth D. Harvey and Katharine Eisaman Maus (Chicago: University of Chicago Press, 1990), 223–52. For a powerful critique of reading early modern poetry for hints of confessional identity, see Kimberly Johnson, *Made Flesh: Sacrament and Poetics in Post-Reformation England* (Philadelphia; University of Pennsylvania Press, 2015), 1–6.

87. See, for instance, Strier's *Love Known;* Shuger's *Habits of Thought;* Michael Schoenfeldt's *Prayer and Power* (Chicago: University of Chicago Press, 1991); Achsah Guibbory's *Ceremony and Community from Herbert to Milton: Literature, Religion, and Cultural Conflict in Seventeenth-Century England* (Cambridge: Cambridge University Press, 1998); and Ramie Targoff's *Common Prayer: The Language of Public Devotion in Early Modern England* (Chicago: University of Chicago Press, 2001).

88. For a convincing historical critique, see Kimberly Coles's account in *Religion, Reform, and Women's Writing,* which argues against Lewalski's thesis on the grounds that it prevents us from seeing how difficult it was for Protestant poets to begin writing *authorial* religious poetry; that is, poetry that reclaims poetic invention and acknowledges poetic authority. In Coles's view, it was female poets from Anne Lock to Mary Sidney who bridged the gap between the antipoetic sentiment of sixteenth-century English Calvinism and seventeenth-century devotional poetry. See Coles, *Religion, Reform, and Women's Writing,* 113–14.

89. Lewalski, *Protestant Poetics,* 282.

90. Marotti, *John Donne, Coterie Poet,* 245–68.

91. The catch-all adjective that Marotti deploys to refer to the poems' *formal* complexity is a word familiar from Lewalski's argument: "The poems no doubt express Donne's private psychological, religious, and moral struggles, but they were also, to a great extent, *witty* performances designed for an appreciative readership" (245, emphasis mine).

92. Targoff argues that the Romantic notion of poetry as private, original, and spontaneous reflects Puritan critiques of seventeenth-century modes of devotional poetry, which were in contrast predominantly public. For her, the poetry of Herbert is representative of this "common" poetry. But when it comes to Donne, she states that in Donne's case "the project of writing devotional verse that reflects a simultaneously individual and collective voice never seems to have materialized. Neither the impersonal and detached speaker of the 'La Corona' sonnets, nor the personal and often anguished voice of the nineteen *Holy Sonnets* offers a devotional paradigm for common expression" (*Common Prayer,* 92).

93. Ramie Targoff, *John Donne: Body and Soul* (Chicago: University of Chicago Press, 2008), 106–29.

94. In addition to Targoff, two particularly forceful readings that insist on Donne's inability or unwillingness to let go of hesitation and ambiguity are Strier, "John Donne Awry and Squint," and Brian Cummings, *The Literary Culture of the Reformation: Grammar and Grace* (Oxford: Oxford University Press, 2002), 406. While I agree with the obser-

vation that in the *Holy Sonnets* Donne's speakers make a habit out of hesitation, I suggest that we should indeed read this as a habit or even a method that serves a purpose in the poems' devotional exercises. For more about this, see the Coda.

95. Franco Moretti, *Distant Reading* (London: Verso, 2013), 48.

96. Although my method is in this sense formal, it isn't *formalist* either in an old or a new sense because unlike most formalist approaches, mine does not seek either to demarcate literature from other forms of discourse (obviously), or to reclaim form's precedence over context—though my argument shows some affinities with the latter tendency in new formalist works. For an overview of new formalism, see Marjorie Levinson, "What Is New Formalism?" *PMLA* 122 (2007): 558–69. For a related discussion of "surface reading," see Stephen Best and Sharon Marcus, "Surface Reading: An Introduction," *Representations* 108 (2009): 1–21.

97. Alex Woloch, *The One vs. the Many: Minor Characters and the Space of the Protagonist in the Novel* (Princeton, NJ: Princeton University Press, 2003). For a discussion of the contemporary relevance of attention as a limited resource, see Richard A. Lanham's *The Economics of Attention* (Chicago: University of Chicago Press, 2006).

98. Specifically, it is the Cartesian, temporary but consistent suspension of knowledge, both historical and conceptual, in order to be able to focus on the given subject. This method, which Husserl called "Cartesian meditation," does not require a repression of one's knowledge, of one's judgments. The "phenomenological epoché" implies a suspension of knowing and judging in order to be able to pay attention to how knowing and judging themselves operate. Such a suspension can never be complete; it is, rather, a shift of attention, and indeed the subject of such philosophical meditations is, both in Descartes and in Husserl, the attentive self. Recently Christopher Mole has pointed out that in the *Meditations* Descartes defines the core term of his method, the "clear and distinct" ideas, by introducing a notion of attention: "The crucial first move in Descartes's epistemology—the move from radical doubt to certainty about the truth of particular clear and distinct ideas—is, therefore, a transition that is mediated by attention" (Christopher Mole, "Attention," in the *Stanford Encyclopedia of Philosophy*, http://plato.stanford.edu/entries/attention [accessed 11/24/2012]). In Husserl, a comparable emphasis on attention appears much earlier in the argument. In the "First Meditation," Husserl explains phenomenological *epoché* and transcendental subjectivity in the following way: "The concrete subjective processes . . . are indeed the things to which this attentive regard [*aufmerkende Blick*] is directed: but the attentive Ego, qua philosophizing Ego [*aufmerkende Ich*], practices abstention with respect to what he intuits" (*Cartesianische Meditationen* [Hamburg: Meiner, 1977], 21; *Cartesian Meditations*, trans. Dorion Cairns [The Hague: M. Nijhoff, 1973], 20). The attentive Ego is a stepping back from knowing into the position of asking and observing, and it is in this basic yet essential sense of philosophy that my investigation may be called phenomenological, searching not into the historical facticity and conditions of poetry, but into the conflicts that poetry had to overcome to come to existence. I should add that insofar as Donne's poems and the Cartesian origins of phenomenology are both influenced by early modern spiritual exercises, one might draw a direct line from Donne's method in

the *Holy Sonnets* to phenomenology. Indeed, Merleau-Ponty's account of the method makes the resemblance between holy attention and phenomenology even more striking: "Reduction does not withdraw from the world towards the unity of consciousness as the world's basis: it steps back to watch the forms of transcendence fly up like sparks from a fire; it slackens the intentional threads which attach us to the world, and thus brings them to our notice. It, alone, is consciousness of the world, because it reveals the world as strange and paradoxical" (*Phenomenology of Perception*, xii). For more about the connection between the *Holy Sonnets* and Cartesianism, see my Coda.

99. A crucial exception being Augustine, whose accounts of attention I discuss later in the Introduction as well as in chaps. 4 and 5. In Rabbow's *Seelenführung*, especially 223–60, the ancient philosophical ideal of *prosochē* (vigilance, attentiveness) provides one of the continuities between antique philosophy and early modern spiritual exercises. Building on Rabbow's work, Hadot has argued for an even longer continuity connecting antique philosophy, medieval and early modern Christian devotion, and early modern and modern philosophy as "ways of life," and he has similarly argued that an ideal of attention played a significant role in this continuous tradition. See Hadot, *Philosophy as a Way of Life*, 47–145, esp. 84–85.

100. See particularly Simone Weil's essays collected in *Waiting for God* (New York: G. P. Putnam's Sons, 1951); and Iris Murdoch, "On 'God' and 'Good'" in *The Sovereignty of Good* (London: Routledge, 1970).

101. See esp. Benjamin's classic "The Work of Art in the Age of Mechanical Reproduction," included in *Illuminations*, ed. Hannah Arendt, trans. Harry Zohn (New York: Harcourt, Brace & World, 1968). Benjamin's concept of distraction has been immensely influential in the humanities and social sciences, as demonstrated by Jonathan Crary's *Suspensions of Perception: Attention, Spectacle, and Modern Culture* (Cambridge, MA: MIT Press, 1999), or more recently, by Paul North's *The Problem of Distraction* (Stanford, CA: Stanford University Press, 2012).

102. Indeed, before finding in distraction a positive model, Benjamin, like many of his contemporaries including Siegfried Kracauer and Theodor Adorno, was keenly interested in ascetic and monastic ideals of attention. See Carolin Duttlinger, "Between Contemplation and Distraction: Configurations of Attention in Walter Benjamin," *German Studies Review* 30 (Feb., 2007): 33–54. On *extentus*, see chap. 6.

CHAPTER ONE

─────────

1. Within the English canon, a classical formulation of why poetry and religion are incompatible is given by Samuel Johnson, who in *Lives of the Poets* criticizes Edmund Waller's devotional poetry because "the essence of poetry is invention; such invention as, by producing something unexpected, surprises and delights. The topicks of devotion are few, and, being few, are universally known; but, few as they are, they can be made no more; they can receive no grace from novelty of sentiment, and very little

from novelty of expression." Samuel Johnson, *The Lives of the Poets,* 2 vols. (London: Oxford University Press, 1952), 1:134. For an analysis of the assumptions and consequences of Johnson's statement, see Michael Schoenfeldt, "The Poetry of Supplication: Toward a Cultural Poetics of Religious Lyrics," in John R. Roberts, ed., *New Perspectives on the Seventeenth-Century Religious Lyric* (Columbia: University of Missouri Press, 1994), 75–76.

2. Stringer, *Holy Sonnets,* 16.

3. On the Renaissance rediscovery and influence of Aristotle's *Poetics,* see Bernard Weinberg, *A History of Literary Criticism,* vol. 1 (Chicago: University of Chicago Press, 1961), 349–423; and Daniel Javitch, "The Assimilation of Aristotle's *Poetics* in Sixteenth-Century Italy," in *The Cambridge History of Literary Criticism,* ed. Glyn P. Norton, vol. 3: *The Renaissance* (Cambridge: Cambridge University Press, 2001), 53–66.

4. "A Defence of Poesy," in *Miscellaneous Prose Works of Sir Philip Sidney,* ed. Katherine Duncan-Jones and Jan van Dorsten (Oxford: Clarendon Press, 1973), 136.

5. Though Donne's text in the Easter sermon of 1623 is Acts 2:36, he follows closely Paul's argument from 1 Corinthians 15 about faith and the resurrection. It is in this context that he paraphrases Acts 1:22 to state, "All the Gospell, all our preaching, is contracted to that one text, *To beare witnesse of the Resurrection.*" Potter and Simpson, *Sermons,* 4:355.

6. Cf. Helen Vendler's discussion of Herbert's originality: "Herbert often begins poems with, or bases poems upon, a traditional image or scene or prayer or liturgical act of Biblical quotation; but the question crying out for answer is what he makes of the traditional base. . . . My answer, in general, appears in the title of this chapter ["The Reinvented Poem"], and in the examples I have so far offered: Herbert 'reinvents' the poem afresh as he goes along" (*The Poetry of George Herbert* [Cambridge, MA: Harvard University Press, 1975], 29). For Vendler, this tendency to reinvent the given signals Herbert's willingness to critique received ideas. As I will show, in Donne's poems this privileging of the aesthetic and the critical over the devotional makes little sense; the point of these poems is to make the seemingly incompatible, the given and the invented, work together. This is one of the reasons I stress the "invention" (rather than "reinvention") of the given.

7. Grierson, *Metaphysical Lyrics and Poems,* xlix.

8. Lewalski, *Protestant Poetics,* 5.

9. Sidney, "Defence," 106–7.

10. Sidney explicitly frames his discussion as a search for available proofs: "In these my not old years and idlest times having slipped into the title of the poet, [I] am provoked to say something unto you in defense of that my unelected vocation, which if I handle with more good will than good reason, bear with me, since the scholar is to be pardoned that followeth the steps of his master. And yet I must say that, as I have more cause to make a pitiful defence of poor poetry, which from almost the highest estimation of learning is fallen to be the laughingstock of children, so have I need to bring some more available proofs, since the former is by no man barred of his deserved credit, the silly later hath even the names of philosophers used to defacing of it, with great danger of civil war among the Muses" ("Defence," 103).

11. "Defence," 108–11.

12. Ibid., 110.

13. Ibid., 110.

14. Ibid., 110–11.

15. Ibid., 111.

16. See the discussion of Sidney's argument in John Guillory, *Poetic Authority: Spenser, Milton, and Literary History* (New York: Columbia University Press, 1983), 9–11.

17. This, of course, is where the Horatian argument about poetry's goal to "teach and delight" becomes relevant.

18. Sidney's text is often described as idiosyncratic even within the early modern era. But on the subject of Christian poetry, the argument of the *Defence of Poesy* is symptomatic of the ambivalent position of poetry within a much longer history of Christian culture. For its first few centuries, Christianity expressed hostility toward poetry. Culturally, poetry was associated with the heathen world of the late Roman Empire. More importantly, poetry as fiction was seen as incompatible with the truth of the Christian revelation, and poetry as rhetorical eloquence was contrasted with the plain, democratic style of the Gospels. Thus, when the first instances of Christian poetry emerged, and when for the first time commentators began to argue that some of the sacred texts of Christianity contained poetry, the notion of "Christian poetry" became the foothold of poetry *in general* within Christian culture. See Anton Hilhorst and Jan den Boeft, *Early Christian Poetry* (Brill, 1993); Willemien Otten and Karla Pollmann, *Poetry and Exegesis in Premodern Latin Christianity* (Brill, 2007). Cf. Northrop Frye's introduction to *The Great Code* (New York: Harcourt, 1982); and Erich Auerbach, "Sermo humilis," in *Literary Language and its Public in Late Latin Antiquity and in the Middle Ages*, trans. Ralph Manheim (Princeton, NJ: Princeton University Press, 1993), 25–83.

19. Kimberly Coles, *Religion, Reform, and Women's Writing* (Cambridge: Cambridge University Press, 2008), 113–14.

20. There are, of course, exceptions, such as Barnabe Barnes, but the exceptions emerge only toward the end of the sixteenth century.

21. Although this would take us too far from the goals of this chapter, I also find a too rigid insistence on historicism epistemologically problematic. Throughout *Protestant Poetics*, Lewalski seeks to demonstrate that the individual poems she analyzes conform to the scheme of Protestant poetics that she finds in the broader historical and religious environment of early seventeenth-century England. The implicit but clear goal of her work is to demonstrate that seventeenth-century devotional poems had been latent as possibilities in the historical precedents and circumstances of their own genealogy. The problem is that during this process of demonstration, individual poems become symptoms of their own possibility. This means that they are doubly removed from the actual focus of the investigation: the primary concern of Lewalski's investigation is not the historical possibility of the poems themselves, but rather the possibility of their generic facticity, what Lewalski calls "Protestant poetics." Henri Bergson's critique of this type of historicism shows how an ontological approach may open up different avenues of historical investigation. The target of Bergson's criticism in "Le possible et le réel" is the historian's concept of the possible (Bergson delivered "Le possible et le

réel" first as a lecture at Oxford in 1920. The text was later published in *Le pensée et le mouvant* [1934]. I use the recent critical edition of Frédéric Cossutta, ed., *Lire Bergson: Le possible et le réel* [Paris: Presses universitaires de France, 1998]). For Bergson, when historians assume that the possibility of a phenomenon precedes the actuality (or full reality) of the same phenomenon, what they really do is create a specter of the phenomenon, or what Bergson calls "the mirage of the present in the past." This mirage, the historical possibility of the actual phenomenon, is for Bergson only an abstract, empty figure of the phenomenon stripped of its actuality and then projected back onto its historical context, thus creating a figure of its own existence. Finding the historical possibility of a poem within the poem's social or political environment is for Bergson a self-inflicted treasure hunt, an exercise in self-deception: we are looking for the possible in places where we ourselves hid it, thereby distracting ourselves from its real location: the phenomenon itself. Whether Bergson's caricature of "history" is a fair depiction of what historians do, and whether the ontological foundations of Bergson's argument are philosophically justifiable are beyond my present concerns. But one does not have to accept Bergson's metaphysics to be intrigued by the epistemological and heuristic implications that his insight holds for literary history. The metaphysical question of whether phenomena might be entirely new is independent of the methodological problem of how, *insofar* as a phenomenon is new and singular, we might be able to approach it *as* new and singular. If the poem as a singular entity comes to existence by overcoming those factors that would favor its non-existence, if singularity creates its own possibility, then insofar as we want to grasp it in its singularity, we cannot rely on the poem's external and precedent conditions of possibility. The conflicts that any phenomenon has to overcome in order to come to being do not disappear with the birth of the phenomenon; on the contrary, they are preserved as the tectonic vestiges of the original conflict, as the internal tensions and paradoxes of the existing phenomenon. The promise of attending to the fault lines within the poem and reigniting its original tensions is that it might lead to a minor resurrection.

22. See φανερὸν δὲ ἐκ τῶν εἰρημένων καὶ ὅτι οὐ τὸ τὰ γενόμενα λέγειν, τοῦτο ποιητοῦ ἔργον ἐστίν, ἀλλ᾽ οἷα ἂν γένοιτο καὶ τὰ δυνατὰ κατὰ τὸ εἰκὸς ἢ τὸ ἀναγκαῖον (Aristotle, *Poetics*, trans. W. H. Fyfe, revised by Donald Russell [Cambridge, MA: Harvard University Press, 2005], 1451b, 58–59).

23. Whether Aristotle's notion of poetry as fictional discourse in this particular sense is restricted to dramatic poetry or also applies to lyric poetry can be debated with regard to Aristotle's argument. The text's arrangement seems to imply that it applies to all kinds of poetry; but it is also plausible that even though the appearance of the argument suggests such a general application, Aristotle's intention is to talk only about dramatic poetry here; and indeed, the ensuing discussion of poetry versus history and myth seems to support this latter interpretation. For my argument, however, this is a question of little importance, for my interest is not in clarifying Aristotle's original intention, but to point out an Aristotelian tradition in poetics, a tradition that thinks about poetry as fiction in Aristotelian terms.

24. "In tragedy," Aristotle says, "they adhere to the actual names [a name that exists, *genomenon onomaton*]" (*Poetics*, 60). These are not necessarily names of historically real

people, but also (in fact, mainly) names of mythical figures, which further confirms that by *ta genomena* Aristotle does not mean real, existing things, people, or events, but rather words signifying concrete particular entities, independent of whether or not these entities have ever existed in reality.

25. "The reason is that the possible [*dunaton*] seems plausible [or credible, *pithanon*]: about the possibility of things [*dunata*], which have not occurred [*ta men oun me genomena*] we are not yet sure [*oupo pisteuomen*], but it is evident that actual events [*ta genomena*] are possible [*dunata*]—they could not have otherwise occurred" (*Poetics*, 60).

26. I have modified the translation by changing "plausible" to "credible." This is a crucial passage in the *Poetics* because it is here that the argument comes closest to the argument of the *Rhetoric*. By introducing terms so crucial to the goals of the *Rhetoric*, *pistis* and *pithanon*, trust and credibility, Aristotle redefines poetry's tasks in epistemological, rather than ontological, terms. The distinction between *Poetics* and *Rhetoric* remains there, however, and it consists in the fact that the poet uses the plot's internal possibility, probability, or necessity to move his audience, while the orator uses proofs.

27. "So even should his poetry concern actual events [*genomena*], he is no less a poet for that, as there is nothing to prevent some actual events being probable [*eikos*] as well as possible [*dunata*], and it is through probability that the poet makes his material from them [or: it is by virtue of this that he is a poet]" (*Poetics*, 61–63).

28. "One cannot remember the future, but of this one has opinion and expectation [*doxaston kai elpiston*] . . . what we remember is the past [*he de mneme tou genomenou*]" (*Aristotle on Memory and Recollection*, trans. David Bloch [Leiden: Brill, 2007], 24–25).

29. 1 Cor. 15:54. Unless indicated otherwise, all quotations from the KJV are from *The Bible: Authorized King James Version*, ed. Robert Caroll and Stephen Prickett (Oxford: Oxford University Press, 1998). I depart here from the KJV translation, which replaces the second occurrence of the Greek word for death with "grave" (ποῦ σου, θάνατε, τὸ νῖκος; ποῦ σου, θάνατε, τὸ κέντρον). (All quotations from the *Novum Testamentum Graece* are from the English 28th Nestle-Aland edition, *The Greek-English New Testament* [Wheaton, IL: Crossway, 2012.])

30. Cf. Aristotle, *Poetics*, chap. 14, and *Rhetoric*, bks. 1–2.

31. Cf. the anonymous but enormously influential *Rhetorica ad Herennium*, 1.2.3; Cicero, *De Inventione*, 1.7.9; and Quintilian, *Institutio Oratoria*, 3.3.1.

32. See, for instance, Lorna Hutson, *The Invention of Suspicion: Law and Mimesis in Shakespeare and Renaissance Drama* (Oxford: Oxford University Press, 2007), 1–2 and 64–102; and Roland Greene, *Five Words: Critical Semantics in the Age of Shakespeare and Cervantes* (Chicago: University of Chicago Press, 2013), 15–40. For an account of how the meaning of *inventio* shifts earlier with the rise of Christian rhetoric, see Rita Copeland, *Rhetoric, Hermeneutics, and Translation in the Middle Ages* (Cambridge: Cambridge University Press, 1991), 127–79.

33. Thus the Pauline proclamation and mockery of death is itself a reiteration of the prophecy, providing Donne's poem with the paradigm of using the given to say what is coming. For a detailed account of what role the passages from Isaiah and Hosea play

in Paul's saying, see John Paul Hay, *The Rhetorical Role of Scripture in 1 Corinthians* (Atlanta: Society of Biblical Literature, 2005), 247–61.

34. A comment on recent rhetorical approaches to Paul's letter is necessary here. In the early and mid-twentieth century, rhetoric was not a focal issue in discussions of the Pauline letters. Though there were exceptions (e.g., the German classical-philologist Eduard Norden's work), the general though often only implicit agreement in the scholarship was that the Pauline message took a form that was *sui generis* in the Hellenistic context, and which therefore couldn't be fruitfully compared with rhetorical precedents (the most emblematic and influential version of this position is of course Rudolf Bultmann's theory of the unique New Testamental form of the "kerygma" or proclamation). It was only almost forty years after Bultmann's 1941 *Neues Testament und Mythologie* that scholars returned to the question of rhetoric. With some simplification, one can identify two main trends within this rhetorical turn in scholarship about Paul. The first argues that Paul's letters should be analyzed with the tools of Greco-Roman rhetoric. While this position offers diverse arguments to justify the rhetorical reading of Paul, there is a growing agreement about the crucial role of rhetoric in the educational systems of the first century Hellenistic territories. One of the most influential early proponents of this position is George Kennedy, who in his 1984 *New Testament Interpretation through Rhetorical Criticism* defined his goal in determining how an early Christian with an average rhetorical education would have read the New Testament. The second approach is characterized by the question of how identifying rhetoric as an important aspect of Paul's letters affects our understanding of Paul's theology. One of the influential studies of this trend is Duane Litfin's *St. Paul's Theology of Proclamation* (1994), in which Litfin provides a new version of Bultmann's original position about the *sui generis* nature of the kerygma for contemporary Paul scholarship and argues that the first four chapters of 1 Corinthians are Paul's critical engagement with the rhetorical practices and ideology of his period. The question that emerges in between these two positions is the question that probably made Bultmann and his disciples refrain from asking the question of rhetoric in the first place: if Paul has an explicit and apparently all-encompassing critique of the rhetorical practices and ideology of the period, what are we to make of the fact that he seems to use some of the very methods that he criticizes, and indeed, he seems to use them in a manner that is quite excessive by Hellenistic standards? The standard answer to this question, that Paul wanted to emphasize the importance of "content" over "form," of substance over words, seems to me to misunderstand both the question itself and the notion of rhetoric in ancient Greece and Rome. Other scholars simply oppose the rhetorical analysis of Paul. Carl J. Classen in "St. Paul's Epistles and Ancient Greek and Roman Rhetoric," in Mark Nanos, ed., *The Galatians Debate: Contemporary Issues in Rhetorical and Historical Interpretation* (Peabody, MA: Hendrickson, 2002), 106, argues that the problems encountered by the rhetorical approach are due to the epistolary nature of Paul's letters. Jeffrey Reed agrees in "Using Ancient Rhetorical Categories to Interpret Paul's Letters: a Question of Genre," in Stanley E. Porter and Thomas H. Olbricht, eds., *Rhetoric and the New Testament* (Sheffield: Continuum, 1993), 304, 308. So does Stanley E. Porter in "The Theoretical Justification for Application of Rhetorical

Categories to Pauline Epistolary Literature," in Porter and Olbricht, *Rhetoric and the New Testament*, 115–16. For an overview of the rhetorical approaches to Paul's letters, see Troy W. Martin, "Investigating the Pauline Letter Body: Issues, Methods, and Approaches," in Stanley E. Porter and Sean A. Adams, eds., *Paul and the Ancient Letter Form* (Leiden: Brill, 2010).

35. This has not been recognized by the scholarship. Most rhetorical studies of Paul in general and the first letter to the Corinthians in particular avoid the issue entirely. The few studies that do concern themselves with the question of proof offer divergent answers to the question of what, if any, kind of proof the crucifixion may be, but none of them identifies the crucifixion as an inartificial proof (Kinneavy proposes to see grace itself as inartificial proof, which is a somewhat bizarre suggestion given that perhaps the most important aspect of the inartificial proofs is that they can simply be pointed out). Kennedy's review of Kinneavy's book raises the possibility: "Kinneavy speaks of 'The classical appeal to the authority of the speaker, which Aristotle called the [ethical]' (106–7). Well, yes and no. Aristotle never considers the 'authority' of a speaker, and makes it very clear that artistic ēthos inheres only in the actual language of the speaker, not in any external claim to authority such as that made by Jesus. Logically, Aristotle should have considered external authority, that of Pericles, for example, as a non-artistic mode of persuasion, but he doesn't do that either. The reason presumably is that he was thinking of judicial oratory in which a Greek speaker had no particular authority, and the speech-writer employed for the occasion had even less." See Robert A. Kennedy's review of Kinneavy's book in *Philosophy & Rhetoric* 22 (1989): 76.

36. *Atechnos* may be translated as atechnological, nontechnological, non-artificial or inartificial. For simplicity's sake, here and throughout this book I generally use the term "inartificial" to refer to the Aristotelian notion of *atechnoi*. Similarly, while *entechnos* may be translated as technological, artificial, or "entechnical" (the last being Kennedy's translation), my general practice is to use the simplest "artificial," unless the specific context requires a different translation. By translating these terms as "artificial" and "inartificial," I also want to indicate that I am applying them in the realm of poetry, where they become terms referring to that which is created inherently by the poetic artifice (the "artificial"), and that which precedes the poetic artifice, which is prior to and outside the poetic artifice (the "inartificial"). When I depart from this general practice, I indicate the specific reasons to do so.

37. As is well known, for Aristotle rhetoric is not simply the art of persuasion but "the faculty of discovering the possible means of persuasion in reference to any subject whatsoever." From this definition it follows that the *pisteis*, the proofs or proofs, insofar as they belong among the means of persuasion, constitute the very subject of rhetoric as invention. This is why immediately after defining the subject of rhetoric, Aristotle turns to the question of proofs and introduces the distinction between artificial and inartificial: "As for proofs (*pisteon*), some are inartificial (*atechnoi*), others artificial (*entechnoi*). By the former I understand all those which have not been furnished by ourselves but were already in existence, such as witnesses, tortures, contracts, and the like; by the latter, all that can be constructed by system and by our own efforts. Thus

we have only to make use of the former, whereas we must invent the latter." Aristotle, *Rhetoric*, 15.

38. For an account of the role of the *pisteis atechnoi* in forensic rhetoric and in the Greek juridical system, see Christopher Carey, "'Artless' Proofs in Aristotle and the Orators," *Bulletin of the Institute of Classical Studies* 39 (1994): 95–107.

39. Scholars have long been puzzled by the resistance of the Pauline letters to rhetorical generization. Since Betz published his study of the Galatians and categorized the letter as forensic oratory, and since Kennedy responded by suggesting that the Galatians is deliberative in its intent, critics have read virtually every letter in terms of virtually every one of the potential three rhetorical genres. On this, see Troy W. Martin, "Investigating the Pauline Letter Body," in Porter and Adams, *Paul and the Ancient Letter Form*, 197.

40. Though of course the Greeks had a concept of such foreknowledge, which they called divination. Elsewhere Aristotle even allows the possibility of a "science" (*epistēmē*) of predicting the future, which he contrasts with the regular modes of knowing future events (which fall in the lower epistemic category of *doxa* and *elpiston*, opinion and expectation). The point I am making here is simply that such foretelling of the future is entirely outside the scope of *Rhetoric* as Aristotle understood it, because rhetoric in Aristotle's view deals with human action and its consequences. See *Aristotle on Memory and Recollection*, trans. David Bloch (Leiden: Brill, 2007), 24–25.

41. In classical rhetorical terms, Paul's argument might be described as an *apagoresis*, an argument designed to dissuade the audience from doing something by reminding them of the action's consequences.

42. Paul uses several different terms to express this "vanity" of faith: *kenos, mataios,* and *eike*, which express emptiness, purposelessness, belief without proof or authority.

43. See Calvin's recapitulation of Paul's argument in the *Commentaries*: "Nowe he beginneth to prove the resurrection of us all by the resurrection of Christ. For thys is a mutuall and reciprocall consequence, which serveth as well affirmatively as negatively, from Christ to us in this manner, if Christ be risen agayne, then shall we rise agayne. If Christ be not risen agayne, then shall not we rise agayne. From us to Christ, after a contrary manner, if we shal rise agayne, then Christ is risen: if we rise not agayne, then Christ is not risen. The reason of bringing the Argument from Christ to us, is this, in the former consequence, Christ died not neyther rose againe to hymselfe, but to us and for us, therefore hys resurrection is the substance of our resurrection: and that which was done in hym, must also be fulfilled in us. And in the negative consequence, this, otherwyse he rose in vayne and unprofitably: bycause the fruite is not to be thought in his person, but in his members. An lyke manner the reason of bringing the former consequence from us unto hym, is, for the resurrection is neyther of nature, nor of any other thing than of Christ alone. For in Adam we al die, and recover life in no other than in Christ. Whereuppon it followeth, that hys resurrection is the foundation of ours: the which being taken awaye, the other cannot stand. The reason of the negative consequence is already set downe. For bycause he should not have risen agayne, but for our sake: his resurrection should be nothing, if it had not profited us. John Calvin, *A Commentarie Upon S. Paules Epistles to the Corinthians*, trans. Thomas Timme (London, 1577), sig. Aa1.

44. Overwhelmingly, the term "pistis" refers to faith in the Pauline corpus. The only occurrence of *pistis* in the sense of proof or assurance is in Acts 17:31: "Because he hath appointed a day, in the which he will judge the world in righteousness by *that* man whom he hath ordained; *whereof* he hath given assurance [*pistis*] unto all men, in that he hath raised him from the dead." The context of this passage is Paul's explanation of the *euangelion* to the Greek Epicureans and Stoics in Athens—in other words he appeals to their understanding of *pistis*.

45. The question whether or not the Pauline use of the noun *pistis* (faith) and the verb *pisteuein* (to believe) can in some way be related to the Aristotelian use of the same terms has received surprisingly little attention within biblical scholarship, even within the past four decades, which have seen much new work on the rhetorical aspects of Paul's letters. Besides works that focus on analyzing Paul's arguments in Aristotelian or generally in Greek rhetorical terms, the work that most explicitly addresses the question of rhetorical in Paul is by someone who is neither a Paul scholar nor a classicist but a scholar of English and rhetoric. James Kinneavy's *Greek Rhetorical Origins of Christian Faith: An Inquiry* (Oxford: Oxford University Press, 1987) argues that "a substantial part of the concept of faith found in the New Testament can be found in the rhetorical concept of persuasion, which was a major meaning of the noun *pistis* (faith *or* persuasion) and the verb *pisteuein* (to believe) in the Greek language at the period the New Testament was written" (143). David E. Hay goes one step further when he argues that *pistis* does in fact mean proof or ground in the Pauline corpus, though some of the evidence that he provides seem to me circumstantial and not conclusive. Yet Hay's argument is convincing enough to suggest a more modest thesis, namely that Paul might have been aware of the meaning of *pistis* as proof, and that he could have both intentionally avoided to use the term in this sense and played on this well-known Hellenistic meaning of *pistis* without explicitly referring to it. See David E. Hay, "Pistis as 'Ground for Faith' in Hellenized Judaism and Paul," *Journal of Biblical Literature* 108 (1989): 461–76.

46. On the meanings of *pistis* in Aristotle, see William M. Grimaldi, "A Note on the Pisteis in Aristotle's *Rhetoric*, 1354–1356," *American Journal of Philology* 78 (1957): 188–92; as well as "Appendix: The Role of the πίστεις in Aristotle's Methodology," in *Aristotle, Rhetoric I: A Commentary*, 349–57. In both of these papers, Grimaldi introduces a threefold distinction to explain the different meanings of *pistis*. He distinguishes (1) *pisteis* as "source areas for the material of convincing argumentation"; (2) *pistis* as the actual argument that uses these materials; and (3) *pistis* as the state of mind induced in an audience or judge. Apart from the fact that this distinction is not there, at least explicitly, in Aristotle (a fact that Grimaldi concedes), it is also unclear why Aristotle would distinguish between *entechnoi* and *atechnoi* proofs, if both can mean source areas. For a discussion of Grimaldi's position, see Joseph T. Lienhard, "A Note on the Meaning of Pistis in Aristotle's *Rhetoric*," *American Journal of Philology* 87 (1966): 446–54.

47. In a sense this is what Hebrews 1:11 argues: Now faith is the substance [*hupostasis*, confidence] of things hoped for, the evidence [*elenchos*] of things not seen.

48. Carey makes this point even concerning Aristotle, although admitting that Aristotle himself did not relativize the *pisteis atechnoi*. See Carey, "'Artless' Proofs in Aristotle and the Orators," 95–96.

49. The awareness of Paul with regard to this potential of his work to become the foundation for others is striking in the famous passage in 1 Cor. 3:10: "According to the grace of God which is given unto me [*kata tēn charin tou theou tēn dotheisan moi*] as a wise masterbuilder [*sophos architekōn*], I have laid the foundation [*themelion*], and another buildeth thereon. But let every man take heed how he buildeth thereupon."

50. Stringer, *Holy Sonnets*, 16.

51. Jonathan Culler, "Apostrophe," in *The Pursuit of Signs* (Ithaca, NY: Cornell University Press, 1981), 135–54.

52. Stringer, *Holy Sonnets*, 16.

53. Ibid.

CHAPTER TWO

—————————

1. George R. Potter and Evelyn M. Simpson, *The Sermons of John Donne*, 10 vols. (Berkeley: University of California Press, 1953–62), 6:39. All references to Donne's sermons are to this edition.

2. For a discussion of thanksgiving sermons, see Ronald E. McFarland, "The Response to Grace: Seventeenth-Century Sermons and the Idea of Thanksgiving," *Church History* 44 (1975): 199–203.

3. The popular thanksgiving psalms were Psalms 66 and 100, or those that are included in the Book of Common Prayer as thanksgiving psalms (92, 95, 98).

4. Donne was particularly interested in Psalm 6; he preached a total of six times on the ten verses of this psalm. The six sermons appeared consecutively in the *LXXX Sermons* in 1640. Others have noted the peculiarity of Donne's decision to choose a penitential psalm and focus on thanksgiving; for a discussion of Donne's sermons on the penitential psalms, and particularly on Psalm 6, see Philip Michael George, *The Sacramental Art of John Donne's Sermons on the Penitential Psalms* (PhD diss., University of British Columbia, 1996), 96ff.

5. A typical thanksgiving psalm or prayer that might be integrated in the order of the liturgy is preceded by a series of liturgical acts, so that the thanksgiving is prepared by repentance, penitence, and depending on the place of the thanksgiving prayer, even the sacramental offering.

6. On the one hand, early modern commentators tend to accept a division of prayer into prayers of petition and prayers of thanksgiving (the latter being synonymous with prayers of praise). Such divisions follow Paul's fourfold distinction in 1 Tim. 2 ("I exhort therefore before all things, that requests, supplications, intercesssions, and giving of thanks, be made for all men"). On the other hand, the line between petition and thanksgiving is constantly called into question; thus Calvin in the *Institutes* argues that "though prayer is properly restricted to wishes and petitions, yet there is so great an affinity between petition and thanksgiving, that they may be justly comprehended under the same name" (John Calvin, *Institutes of the Christian Religion*, trans. John

Allen [Philadephia: Presbyterian Board, n.a.], 134). For a discussion of further subdivisions within the categories of petition and thanksgiving, see Lancelot Andrewes's "The Pattern of Cathechistical Doctrine," in *Selected Sermons and Lectures*, ed. Peter McCullough (Oxford: Oxford University Press, 2005), 11–21 (see also McCullough's helpful notes to these pages).

7. One particularly interesting place where the distinction between gift and giving appears is James 1:17, "where the author declares that "every good giving [*dosis*] and every perfect gift [*dōrēma*] is from above," a distinction that the Vulgate maintains by translating the words as *datum* and *donum*, but that both Luther and the KJV erase by translating both words as *Gabe*/gift. I thank Steve Justice for calling my attention to the passage.

8. In addition to Marcel Mauss's classical *Essai sur le don* (1924), this discussion relies on Claude Levi-Strauss, *Introduction to the Work of Marcel Mauss* (London: Routledge, 1987); Maurice Godelier, *The Enigma of the Gift* (Chicago: University of Chicago Press, 1999); and Jacques Derrida, *Given Time I: Counterfeit Money* (Chicago: University of Chicago Press, 1992). None of these works seems to be particularly interested in the concept of thanksgiving.

9. For instance Giovanni Boccaccio's account of the three graces in *Genealogia deorum gentilium*.

10. Pliny the Younger, *Letters, and Panegyricus* (Cambridge, MA: Harvard University Press, 1969). See also *In Praise of the Later Roman Emperors: The Panegyrici Latini*, trans. C. E. V. Nixon and Barbara Saylor Rogers, with the Latin text of R. A. B. Mynors (Berkeley: University of California Press, 1994).

11. Here I refer to Burrow's *The Poetry of Praise* (Cambridge: Cambridge University Press, 2008), and especially Burrow's discussion of the concept of *auxesis* or *auxetic* (12–13); that is, the magnifying element that is central to the poetry of praise. Three further works on praise have informed my account: O. B. Hardison's classic *The Enduring Monument: A Study of the Idea of Praise in Renaissance Literary Theory and Practice* (Chapel Hill: University of North Carolina Press, 1962); Lewalski's *Donne's Anniversaries and the Poetry of Praise*; and Leslie Kurke's *The Traffic of Praise: Pindar and the Poetics of Social Economy* (Ithaca, NY: Cornell University Press, 1991).

12. As in Tertullian, "super panem Dei gratiarum actionibus fungi" (*Adv. Marcion*, i. 9).

13. "I exhort therefore, that, first of all, supplications, prayers, intercessions, and giving of thanks, be made for all men" (2 Tim. 1).

14. See particularly the essays collected in S. E. Porter and S. A. Adams, eds., *Paul and the Ancient Letter Form* (Leiden: Brill, 2010).

15. Clement of Alexandria in the seventh book of the *Stromata*, in chap. 7, launches his discussion of prayer with this sentence: "Further, we are bidden to worship and honour the Son and Word, being persuaded that He is both Saviour and Ruler, and honour the Father through Him, doing this not on special days, as some others do, but continuously all our life through, and in all possible ways." When still in the same paragraph Clement further explains what he means by honoring God [*tima ton theōn*], he says this: "Wherefore it is neither in a definite place or special shrine, nor yet on certain feasts and days set apart, that the gnostic honours God returning thanks to Him for the

knowledge bestowed and the gift of the heavenly citizenship; but he will do this all his life in every place, whether he be alone by himself or have with him some who share his belief" (Clement of Alexandria, *Miscellanies: Book VII*, ed. and trans. by Fenton John, Anthony Hort, and Joseph A. Mayor [London: Macmillan, 1902], 61–63).

16. 1 Thess. 5:17–18: "Pray without ceasing [*adialeptōs proseucheste*; in the Vulgate: *sine intermissione orate*]; In every thing give thanks [*eucharisteite* and *gratias agite*] for this is the will of God in Christ Jesus concerning you."

17. 2 Cor. 9:15: "Thanks be unto God for his unspeakable gift" [χάρις τῷ θεῷ ἐπὶ τῇ ἀνεκδιηγήτῳ αὐτοῦ δωρεᾷ].

18. "Naturall and morall men are better acquainted with the duty of gratitude, of thankesgiving, before they come to the Scriptures, then they are with the other duty of repentance, which belongs to Prayer; for in all *Solomons* bookes, you shall not finde halfe so much of the duty of thankfulnesse, as you shall in *Seneca* and in *Plutarch*. No book of Ethicks, of morall doctrine, is come to us, wherein there is not, almost in every leafe, some detestation, some Anathema against ingratitude; but of repentance, not a word amongst them all" (Potter and Simpson, *Sermons*, 6:41–42).

19. One of Donne's earliest sermons is on this issue. He considers "Esay" 52:3. "Ye have sold your selves for nought, and ye shall be redeemed without money." Potter and Simpson, *Sermons*, 1:151.

20. This is already clear in Seneca's *De beneficiis*, though its scholarly formulation is most famous from Marcel Mauss's *Essai sur le don*.

21. Donne's emphasis on God's glory stands out throughout the sermons, which return time and again to the point that unless an action's sole purpose is to serve divine glory, it cannot be seen as genuinely pious. See Potter and Simpson, *Sermons*, 2:309, and 9:248. For a discussion of these two passages as representing Donne's "spiritual rigorism," see Debora Shuger, *Habits of Thought*, 178–79.

22. For a study on how thanksgiving (*eucharistia*) could increase the glory of God (*doxa theōu*) according to Paul's letters, see George Henry Boobyer, *"Thanksgiving" and the "Glory of God" in Paul* (Borna-Leipzig: Universitätsverlag von Robert Noske, 1929).

23. 1 Thess. 5:18–19. Cf. the notion of petition and intercession according to the will of God, *kata theōn*, in Rom. 8:27. See the discussion of *kata theōn* in Boobyer, *"Thanksgiving" and the "Glory of God" in Paul*, 21.

24. Although this prioritization of thanksgiving was particularly prevalent in the early modern period, scholarship has paid scant attention to it. E. Catherine Dunn's *The Concept of Ingratitude in Renaissance English Moral Philosophy* (Washington, DC: Catholic University of America Press, 1946) focuses on ingratitude in mostly secular contexts, except for the last chapter on devotion.

25. Henry Peacham, *The Garden of Eloquence* (London, 1577), 85.

26. For two superb discussions of the role of the Psalms in the English early modern context, see Rivkah Zim, *English Metrical Psalms: Poetry as Praise and Prayer* (Cambridge: Cambridge University Press, 1987); and Hannibal Hamlin, *Psalms Culture and Early Modern English Literature* (Cambridge: Cambridge University Press, 2007).

27. On this subject, see Klaus Westermann's *Praise and Lament in the Psalms* (Westminster: John Knox Press, 1987), which points out that in Hebrew there is no word that could

be accurately translated as "thanking," and argues that ultimately thanking is a modality of praise, which in turn is the generic category for all psalms, even if laments are numerically dominant among them.

28. See Brooke Conti, "The Mechanical Saint: Early Modern Devotion and the Language of the Automaton," in Wendy Beth Hyman, ed., *The Automaton in English Renaissance Literature* (Farnham: Ashgate, 2011), 95–109. For a study of early modern "literary" automata, see Jessica Wolfe, *Humanism, Machinery, and Renaissance Literature* (Cambridge: Cambridge University Press, 2004).

29. The phrase is curiously ambiguous: does Donne mean that one function of thanking is that it invites more gifts (a theme that appears elsewhere in the sermons and the letters), or that it helps winning other people over to Christianity?

30. There is, however, a long tradition of seeing the entirety of creation as a praying creation; see the last, soaring passages of Tertullian's *On Prayer*: "Every creature prays; cattle and wild beasts pray and bend their knees; and when they issue from their layers and lairs, they look up heavenward with no idle mouth, making their breath vibrate after their own manner. Nay, the birds too, rising out of the nest, upraise themselves heavenward, and, instead of hands, expand the cross of their wings, and say somewhat to seem like prayer." Alexander Roberts, James Donaldson, and A. Cleveland Coxe, eds., *Ante-Nicene Fathers*, vol. 3, trans. S. Thelwall (Buffalo, NY: Christian Literature Publishing Co., 1885). (I thank Joanna Picciotto for this reference.) The concept returns in the early modern period, when Godfrey Goodman suggests that nature is in fact more proficient at the act of praising the creator than humans, and that humans need to learn the art of thanksgiving from other creatures. See *The Creatures Praysing God: Or, The Religion of Dumbe Creatures* (London, 1622). See also the existentialist version of this argument in Kierkegaard's "The Lily in the Field and the Bird of the Air," where the lily and the birds are portrayed as devotional authorities by virtue of their silent obedience to their own nature. Søren Kierkegaard, *Without Authority*, trans. Howard V. Hong and Edna H. Hong (Princeton, NJ: Princeton University Press, 1997), 1–47.

31. In spite of the fact that it is frequently cited in scholarship, no one has to my knowledge given serious consideration to the fact that Donne here makes thanksgiving the end of poetry. Many scholars who quote the passage omit not only the context but even the references to devotion within the passage. For examples, see John Carey, "Donne and Coins," in *English Renaissance Studies* (Oxford: Clarendon Press, 1980), 158–59; Helen Gardner, *The Metaphysical Poets* (London: Penguin, 1985), 22; Christopher Ricks, *Essays in Appreciation* (Oxford: Clarendon Press, 1996), 31–32; Marotti, *John Donne, Coterie Poet*, 69; and perhaps most strikingly Barbara Herrstein Smith in *Poetic Closure: A Study of How Poems End* (Chicago: University of Chicago Press, 1968), 37, where the passage appears without any explanation or commentary, purely in the service of the author's quite different argument. The only scholar who to my knowledge acknowledges the devotional significance of Donne's passage, though without considering the specific relevance of thanksgiving, is Siobhán Collins in "Riddling Wonders: Gold Coins and the Phoenix in Donne's Genre-Defying

Verse," *Appositions: Studies in Renaissance / Early Modern Literature & Culture* 1 (2008).

32. Praying to the "father of Heaven," in sonnet 62 of the *Canzoniere* Petrarch says, "miserere del mio non degno affanno, / reduci I pensier vaghi a miglior luogo, / rammenta lor come oggi frusti in croce" ["have mercy on my unworthy pain, lead my wondering thoughts back to a better place, remind them that today you were on the Cross"]. *Petrarch's Lyric Poems*, trans. Robert M. Durling (Cambridge, MA: Harvard University Press, 1976), 140–41.

33. The ambiguities of the Greek text leave this passage open to different interpretations, but the most likely reading is that Esau, who sold his birthright to Jacob for a bowl of pottage, later sought to change the mind of their father, Isaac, but couldn't. Though "metanoia" is usually translated as repentance, the passage is interesting precisely because by meaning "change of mind," this *metanoia* is simultaneously Isaac's mercy and Esau's repentance. The passage and Esau's story in general are used in the early modern period in discussions of predestination and double predestination (for Esau's rejection, the Vulgate has "reprobatus est"), though the doctrine isn't necessarily implied in the passage. See Helen Thomas, "Jacob and Esau: 'Rigidly Calvinistic'?" *Studies in English Literature, 1500–1900* 9:2 (Spring 1969): 199–213.

34. For the verb "find," the Greek text uses *heuriskō*, while the Vulgate has "non enim invenit poenitentiae locum."

35. See Carruthers, *The Craft of Thought*, 77ff. Discussing mainly Fortunatianus, Carruthers focuses on *ductus* as the movement of the mind, as well as on *skopos* as goal. Here I heed Carruthers's suggestion: "I would . . . urge the value . . . of the concept of *ductus*, and of its attendant colors and modes (moods)" (263).

36. Several times during the sermon Donne's discussion is reminiscent of Platonic views of recollection and of *ars memoria*. This aspect of thanksgiving is not immediately relevant to my discussion, but it is worth noting that insofar as thanksgiving acknowledges "that God hath given," it is necessarily grounded in remembering the gift. Indeed thanksgiving may be called a way of remembering, one that not only recalls but holds onto the given. Insofar as this remembering, which is the ground of thanksgiving, and which in turn itself ought to be remembered, is the task of the poem's end, the poem is heir to the medieval and Renaissance tradition of the *machina memorialis*. Thanks largely to the work of generations of medievalists and early modern scholars, and most recently to Mary Carruthers's studies, particularly *The Craft of Thought*, we have abundant evidence for the centrality of both the *machina memorialis* and of the art of memory in general to medieval and early modern Christian devotional life. It is now clear that the Roman *ars memoria* became the foundation of the monastic *memoria spiritualis* or *sancta memoria*, and that the ancient rhetorical and cognitive technologies of invention were employed from the Middle Ages in the service of lifting one's mind toward God—as Donne himself notes in another sermon, "The art of salvation, is but the art of memory" (Potter and Simpson, *Sermons*, 2:73). In light of this tradition of *memoria spiritualis*, the psalm that Donne interprets and, consequently, devotional poetry as well become technologies, "machines" of remembering the given and offering

thanks for it. For a recent work emphasizing the technological character of early modern poetry, see Rayna Kalas, *Frame, Glass, Verse: The Technology of Poetic Invention in
the English Renaissance* (Ithaca, NY: Cornell University Press, 2007), a study informed
by Heidegger's critique of modern technology versus what he saw as the ancient view
of a correspondence between *technē* and *poiesis*. The classical essay is "The Question
concerning Technology," in *The Question concerning Technology and Other Essays*, trans.
William Lovitt (New York: Harper & Row, 1977).

37. This is what Montrose calls "prestation" gifts ("I use prestation to connote an implic-
    itly obligatory or coercive act of giving"), following Mauss's terminology (Louis A.
    Montrose, "Gifts and Reasons: The Contexts of Peele's Araygnment of Paris," *English
    Literary History* 47 [1980]: 433).

38. Thanksgiving is thus a speech-act that strives to undo itself as language; it is an utter-
    ance of words that strives to negate the meaning of the very words that it utters. Of
    relevance here is the long tradition of associating thanksgiving with nonverbal, ritual
    action. Apart from the obvious connotations in Christianity, the same nonlinguistic
    character is also present in Greek and Roman antiquity. Frances Hickson Hahn points
    out that while Livy often describes and quotes prayers, he rarely quotes thanksgiv-
    ing. Pondering this discrepancy, Hahn suggests that the lack of quotations is due to
    Livy's almost exclusive emphasis on the physical, nonverbal expression of gratitude.
    See Hickson Hahn, "Ut diis immortalibus honos habeatur: Livy's Representation of
    Gratitude to the Gods," in Alessandro Barchiesi, ed., *Rituals in Ink* (Stuttgart: Franz
    Steiner Verlag, 2004), 57–77.

39. Contemporaries writing about prayer sometimes make a distinction between "natu-
    ral" and "right" prayer. "Naturall prayers," to use John Preston's terminology from his
    popular *The Saints Daily Exercise* (London, 1629), are "the expressions of our own spir-
    its"; that is, spontaneous prayers. A "right" prayer, however, is "*an expression of holy
    and good dispositions.*" Preston adds that he uses the term "disposition" instead of "de-
    sire" because "there is some part of *prayer* that stands in thanksgiving, when you desire
    nothing at Gods hands, but give thanks for that you have received" (3–4).

40. For a catalog of such "supplications" of *gratiarum actio* and an analysis of their tradi-
    tion, see Léon Halkin, *La supplication d'action de graces chez les Romains* (Paris: Les
    Belles Lettres, 1953).

CHAPTER THREE

----

1. John Norden, *A Poor Mans Rest* (London, 1620), sig. B2ᵛ.

2. Potter and Simpson, *Sermons*, 6:39.

3. Potter and Simpson, *Sermons*, 6:39.

4. As Bradley suggested, Shakespeare is generally fond of using ellipses in building his
    characters: "acts and omissions [are] thoroughly expressive of the doer" (A. C. Bradley,
    Shakespearean Tragedy [New York: Palgrave Macmillan, 2007], 6).

5. *Hamlet* in Stephen Greenblatt, ed., *The Norton Shakespeare* (New York: Norton, 1997), 1747 (All subsequent quotations of *Hamlet* are from this edition).

6. For a recent critical overview, see Margreta De Grazia, "Hamlet's Delay," *Hamlet without Hamlet* (Cambridge: Cambridge University Press, 2007), 158–205.

7. Oftentimes Claudius's failure is seen in terms of religious hypocrisy, as in Alex Nevell's *The Soliloquies in Hamlet* (London: Associated University Press, 1991), 114–19, which characterizes Claudius's attempt to pray as "shuffling" and "self-deception." Eleanor Prosser's discussion of the scene is more careful and recognizes that Claudius's soliloquy is not only the single most explicitly Christian passage in the play, but also a theologically sound and psychologically sincere attempt to repent. Yet she also finds its failure evident, though she sees the reason in the fact that even in the course of performing his prayer, "Claudius was rejecting the call of grace" (*Hamlet and Revenge* [Stanford, CA: Stanford University Press, 1971], 185–87).

8. Targoff, *Common Prayer..* See also Targoff's earlier "The Performance of Prayer: Sincerity and Theatricality in Early Modern England," *Representations* 60 (1997): 49–69.

9. Targoff, *Common Prayer*, 3.

10. The Aristotelian behaviorism that Targoff mentions as the philosophical background of this view reveals an inherent tension at the heart of Protestantism in England and beyond. Aristotle's concept of "habit" (*hexis*), translated as *habitus* in Latin, is central to his concept of virtue in the *Nicomachean Ethics*, but it is also one of the main reasons Luther vehemently criticized Aristotle. For an account of habit from Aristotle to the early modern period and beyond, see Jennifer Herdt, *Putting on Virtue* (Chicago: University of Chicago Press, 2008). Both Targoff and Herdt could be seen as scholars working within a recent trend of neo-Aristotelianism, a rediscovery of an ethics in which rituals, practices, and habits play a central role. For a seminal articulation of this turn to Aristotle (through Foucault), see Saba Mahmood, *Politics of Piety; The Islamic Revival and the Feminist Subject* (Princeton, NJ: Princeton University Press, 2005), chaps. 1 and 4.

11. "However ambivalent Hamlet may ultimately may have been, the Church of England was firmly aligned behind it. There were no absolute divisions between sincerity and theatricality, inwardness and outwardness within the early modern English church." Targoff stops here; for her, "the play does not pursue any further the state of Claudius mind, nor does it burden Hamlet with discovering the folly of his misreading" (Targoff, *Common Prayer*, 4). See also Targoff, "The Performance of Prayer," 64.

12. In other words, what Targoff's account doesn't explain is how and why it is possible that while the scene is a "detailed exploration of the devotional process," ultimately this process "fails to produce a sincere state of contrition" (*Common Prayer*, 1). On a side note, "contrition" is surely not the right term in this context. Claudius does in fact reach a state of sincere contrition already at the outset; what his soliloquy does not produce is a sincere state of repentance and prayer—and what "sincerity" means in this context is the question.

13. Targoff generally avoids an explicit characterization of Claudius's attempt to pray as insincere. Instead, she uses neutral characterizations (Claudius is "devoid of the internal sentiment whose presence the established churchmen fought so hard to maintain" or

"his efforts fail to produce any correspondence between his outward and inward self" (Targoff, "The Performance of Prayer," 62). Yet at other times she uses formulations that allow an association between Claudius's generally hypocritical role in the play and his character in this scene, for instance: "Hamlet's failure to consider the possible discrepancy between Claudius's inward and outward state of devotion threatens to undermine the critical consensus about his ability to penetrate the insincere" (Targoff, *Common Prayer*, 3). It is this latter association that I disagree with: Claudius may be dissembling throughout the play, but in this scene he seems to me entirely sincere.

14. Targoff recognizes the tension: "Indeed, notwithstanding Claudius's apparent belief in the performative logic that shaped conformist accounts of devotional efficacy—he does imagine that if only his knee bow, his heart itself will soften—his efforts fail to produce any correspondence between his outward and inward self" (Targoff, "The Performance of Prayer," 62).

15. A particularly widespread version of this notion of a hierarchical order in devotion was the so-called "ladder of repentance," comprising contrition, confession, faith, and satisfaction or amendment of life. For versions of this notion, see William Tyndale's "Prologue upon The Gospel of St. Matthew," in *Doctrinal Treatises and Introductions to the Different Portions of the Holy Scriptures*, ed. Rev. Henry Walter (Cambridge: Cambridge University Press, 1848), 477–78; and the "Homilie or Sermon concerning prayer" in the *Second Tome of Homilies* (London, 1582).

16. What I call "preparatio" is to be distinguished from the use of the term that Latin translators of Eusebius made famous by translating Εὐαγγελικὴ Προπαρασκευή as *Praeparatio Evangelica*, where the term refers to the ways in which non-Christian cultures may be prepared to receive the Christian gospels. The term "preparation" is used and discussed extensively by Aquinas; for a few particularly relevant examples, see *Summa Theologiae* Ia. 23 (where *preparatio* is discussed in relation to predestination) and 1a2æ. 109–13 (a crucial section where *preparatio* appears in the context of a discussion of grace). For relevant discussions of devotion and particularly prayer as actions of religion, see 2a2æ. 82.1 and 2a2æ. 83.3. The term "preparation" is central in early modern English Protestant contexts. Thomas Becon dedicates a chapter to the eightfold preparation for prayer ("How a Christen man shoulde prepare himself to praye") in *The Right Pathwaye unto Prayer* (London, 1542). Preparation remained equally important for dissenters in the seventeenth century: "The Puritan project sometimes seemed nothing less than a wholesale revision of the values by which English men and women lived. At the heart of the program was a prescription for rigorous introspection—readying the soul for the reception of grace. Puritans called this process 'preparation.'" Alen Heimert and Andrew Delbanco, eds., *The Puritans in America: A Narrative Anthology* (Cambridge, MA: Harvard University Press, 1985), 20. For a "preparationist" text, see Thomas Hooker, *The Soul's Preparation for Christ, or, a Treatise on Contrition* (London, 1632).

17. Samuel Hieron proposes prayer as preparation for prayer: "Marvaile not that I make Praying a preparative to Prayer. A little eating prepareth a weake stomacke, and setteth an edge uppon the appetite to eat more" (*Helpe unto Devotion* [London, 1611], sig. B²). Becon discusses faith as one of the crucial conditions of prayer. But he adds that if one

does not have strong enough faith, one should pray: "But if it be so that we are yette weake, & have no sure trust of the clemencye & great goodnes of God toward us, nor can not persuade our selves that our prayer is heard, but doubte & waver peradventure of the divine promises, than after the example of the Apostles let us pray, 'Lorde encrease our fayth' " (*The Right Pathwaye unto Prayer*, sig. H1ʳ).

18. This account is indebted to what remains one of the most original discussions of action in Maurice Blondel's *L'action* (Paris: Presses Universitaires de France, 1973; orig. 1893), a groundbreaking work that attempted both a philosophy of action and a philosophy of religion.

19. In the broader context of the scene, it is a meditation on Claudius's past and his immediate future; and like meditations in the context of Loyola's *Spiritual Exercises*, it is supposed to help the king arrive at a *decision* (for, one should recall, Claudius's hesitation is not merely between the "affects" of the murder and true repentance; at this point he is also aware that if he wants to hold onto power, he might have to have Hamlet murdered). Heminge's play suggests that contemporaries were aware of this dimension of the soliloquy as meditation. Eleazer in his "To be or not to be" soliloquy explicitly contemplates the two options: contrition and virtuous life, or seizing power by crime.

20. Aquinas discusses this problem of infinite regress in preparation, and he introduces "gratuitous assistance of God" to solve the problem (Aquinas, *Summa Theologiæ* Ia2æ, 109, 6). *Summa Theologiæ*, vol. 30, trans. and ed. by Cornelius Ernst O.P. (Oxford: Blackfriars, 1972), 87–91.

21. Which might be seen as identical with his original intention to murder old Hamlet and thereby gain possession of the queen and the crown. "Guilt" then would mean not simply the remembrance of a past crime, but the conscience that the crime is not past, that its seed, its intention is still present. This presence of the guilt is further confirmed by the king's potential thinking about murdering Hamlet as well.

22. "An Homilie or Sermon concerning prayer" in *The Seconde Tome of Homilies* emphasizes that the recognition of sin ought to propel one to pray even more fervently: "What if wee bee sinners, shall wee not therefore pray vnto GOD? or shall wee despaire to obtaine any thing at his handes? Why did Christ then us to aske forgivenesse of our sinnes, saying, And forgive us our trespasses, as wee forgive them that trespasse against us?" (sig. Kk5ʳ).

23. "An Homilie of repentance and of true reconciliation unto God" characterizes contrition and confession in comparable but distinct terms. Contrition consists in being "earnestly sorry for our sinnes," and willing to "unfeignedly lament and bewayle that wee have by them so grievously offended our most bounteous and mercifull GOD." The second step is "an unfained confession and acknowledging of our sinnes unto GOD, whom by them we have so grievously offended, that if he should deale with us according to his iustice, wee doe deserve a thousand helles, if there could bee so many." (*Second Tome of Homilies*, sig. Yy1ʳ.)

24. Targoff suggests that there is a contradiction here in *The Subject of Prayer: Models of Public Devotion in Early Modern England* (PhD diss., University of California, Berkeley, 1996), 107.

25. This is not a view that theologians of most affiliations would explicitly embrace—and yet it is something that follows from the conception of grace and often appears in theology in sufficiently recognizable form. A good place to start is Aquinas's pivotal, if complex, discussion of preparation for grace in the *Summa*. Aquinas addresses the question "can man prepare himself for grace by himself without the external assistance of grace?" [*utrum homo posit seipsum ad gratiam præparare per seipsum absque exteriori auxilio gratiæ*]. This article is particularly relevant because it discusses the question of *preparatio* and grace in terms of "turning toward God" [*Nihil audem est aliud se ad gratiam præparare quam Deum converti*], a phrase that may characterize not only virtuous action, but also prayer in particular. Aquinas's answer is that one cannot prepare for this turn without habitual grace, which is the gift of God (*sine habituali gratiæ dono*); at the same time, one cannot prepare for receiving habitual grace without "some gratuitous assistance of God moving the soul within." Indeed, he comes to this conclusion because, he points out, "in order that someone should prepare himself to receive the gift [of habitual grace], there is no need to presuppose some further habitual gift in the soul, *because otherwise we should go on to infinity* [*quia sic procederetur in infinitum*]" (my emphasis). In other words, preparation for the action of turning to God, understood as the work of human will habituated by grace, is itself prepared not by further human preparation, but by external, transcendent, "gratuitous" divine assistance. See *Summa Theologiæ* Ia2æ, 109, 6; quoted from Ernst, *Summa Theologiæ*, 87–91.

26. Helen Wilcox suggests that the *Holy Sonnets* are prayers precisely insofar as they recognize this problem: "These lines reflect the dilemma of much of Donne's devotional writing and the agonizing complexity of his particular doctrinal circumstances, caught as he was between the active vocation of his Catholicism and the predestination of Calvinism. Could the speakers of the *Holy Sonnets* do anything to influence God's final judgment—and if so, what? The implied answer given by the sonnets—their response to the profound personal and doctrinal difficulties—is prayer. The sonnets are themselves a form of dialogue, and their meditation often leads, as in 'If faithful soules,' to a resolution to pray." Helen Wilcox, "Devotional Writing," in *The Cambridge Companion to John Donne*, ed. Achsah Guibbory (Cambridge: Cambridge University Press, 2006), 154.

27. Stringer, *Holy Sonnets*, 13.

28. Aquinas's position confirms that only an external, entirely transcendent divine grace can prepare the human will for the "turning toward God," and thus for the reception of grace. At the same time Aquinas's notion of "habitual grace" enables human will to cooperate with grace. What the majority of Protestant Reformers (certainly the early Luther) objected to was precisely this idea of habitual grace; the idea that grace could become inherent in the individual, and thus the individual could in some fashion contribute to his own salvation. For a discussion of the *sola gratia* formula in connection with the other *sola* doctrines in the Reformation, see Heiko Augustinus Oberman's *The Reformation: Roots and Ramifications* (Grand Rapids, MI: W. B. Eerdmans, 1994), 218ff. For accounts of the widespread acceptance of the *sola gratia* doctrine in the early seventeenth century in England, as well as its waning influence in the second half of the

century, see Derek D. Wallace, Jr., *Puritans and Predestination: Grace in English Prot-estant Theology, 1525–1695* (Chapel Hill: University of North Carolina Press, 1982); and J. Wayne Baker, "Sola Fide, Sola Gratia: The Battle for Luther in Seventeenth-Century England," *Sixteenth Century Journal* 16 (1985): 115–33.

29. "Naturall prayers," says John Preston in his popular *The Saints Daily Exercise* (London, 1629), are "the expressions of our own spirits." These are "naturall" not only in the sense that they are spontaneous but also in the more specific sense that "any naturall man may make [them] to the Lord" (compare this with Sir Thomas Harriot's empha-sis on the "natural religion" of Native Americans in *A briefe and true report of the new found land of Virginia* [London, 1588]). "Right" prayers, however "arise from the regenerate part which is within us, which is quickened and inlarged to pray from the immediate helpe of the *Holy Ghost*" (Preston, *The Saints Daily Exercise*, 2–3).

30. Lancelot Andrewes, *Institutiones Piae or Directions to Pray* (London, 1630), 4. This definition of prayer as conversation goes back to early Christianity; among others, Clement of Alexandria suggests that "prayer [*euchē*], then, to speak somewhat boldly, is converse [*homilia*] with God." See Boulluec's edition of the *Stromata*, where Boul-luec suggests that the definition appears in Maximus of Tyre, the second century AD Greek rhetorician and Platonist philosopher, often considered as a precursor of Neo-platonism. He adds that the definition might go back to Plato, and to Aristotle's mythic work on prayer. Cf. the Greek text here: *homilia pros ton theōn hē euchē*, in Clément D'Alexandrie, *Les stromates: stromate 7*, ed. Alain Le Boulluec (Paris: Éditions du Cerf, 1997), 46. For the English, see Clement of Alexandria, *Miscellanies*, 69.

31. Cynthia Garrett, "The Rhetoric of Supplication: Prayer Theory in Seventeenth-Century England," *Renaissance Quarterly* 46 (1993): 331.

32. Raymond Williams, *Writing in Society* (London: Verso, 1991), 31–67; and Debora Shuger, "Life-Writing in Seventeenth-Century England," in Patrick Coleman et al., eds., *Representations of the Self from the Renaissance to Romanticism* (Cambridge: Cambridge University Press, 2000), 73–76.

33. See Robert Sturges's introduction to his translation of a Middle English version of the text in Anne Clarke Bartlett and Thomas H. Bestul, eds., *Cultures of Piety: Medi-eval English Devotional Literature in Translation* (Ithaca, NY: Cornell University Press, 1999), 41–42. For a discussion of the text's English reception, see Julia D. Staykova, "The Augustinian Soliloquies of an Early Modern Reader: A Stylistic Relation of Shake-speare's Hamlet?" *Literature & Theology* 23 (2009): 121–41.

34. In *Liber soliloquiorum*, Augustine talks to Reason in what seems to be a Christian version of the Platonic dialogues. I discuss Augustine's *Soliloquies* in detail in chap. 5. For discussions of the concept of soliloquy in Augustine, see Brian Stock, *Augustine's Inner Dialogue: The Philosophical Soliloquy in Late Antiquity* (Cambridge: Cambridge University Press, 2010), and "Self, Soliloquy, and Spiritual Exercises in Augustine and Some Later Authors," *Journal of Religion* 91 (2011): 5–23.

35. Claudius's prayer to angels is of course significant in that Protestant audiences may have found his devotion therefore flawed. Then again, this is certainly not the only crypto-Catholic reference in *Hamlet*, and one wonders just how much attention audi-ences would have paid to the theological flaw if otherwise Claudius's attempt to repent

seemed genuine. Claudius, like Hamlet's father, might also be seen as that other generation in whom Protestants at the turn of the century might have recognized their own parents, as Stephen Greenblatt argues in *Hamlet in Purgatory* (Princeton, NJ: Princeton University Press, 2001).

36. Q1 reduces the soliloquy to a mere thirteen lines; and these two lines on petition for grace conclude Claudius's speech. I quote Q1 from Bernice W. Kliman and Paul Bertram, eds., *The Three-Text Hamlet* (New York: AMS Press, 2003), 150 (I lightly modernized the spelling).

37. A classic example for a reprobate in the period is the Italian Catholic Francesco Spira; John Preston, for instance, describes Spira as someone who "cryed so earnestly for grace, that hee might have but a drop of it, because he could not be saved without it, he gives the reason himselfe; hee said withall, he saw no excellencie in it, he desired it not for it selfe; and therefore hee thought his prayers should not be heard" (Preston, *The Saints Daily Exercise*, 6). On double predestination, see Nicholas Watson, "Despair," in Brian Cummings and James Simpson, eds., *Cultural Reformations* (Oxford: Oxford University Press, 2010), 342–61.

38. Sermons and handbooks on prayer often include sections on how the repentant may know "whether you have this repentance or not." Indeed, I am quoting the question itself from Robert Hill's popular *Pathway to Prayer* (London, 1609), which goes on to identify the "markes" or signs of repentance, which include "godly sorrow," being "displeased with myself," and a "changing of the mind" (133–34). Importantly, Hill discusses these signs of repentance in the context of preparing for the Eucharist.

39. One of the reasons "attention" and "intention" are complex notions with somewhat unclear shared histories is that starting with Franz Brentano's 1874 *Psychologie vom empirischen Standpunkt*, intentionality has become an essential concept for phenomenology and philosophy in general. Brentano's theory of intentionality implies yet another sense of intention: in the philosophical context, "intentionality" usually refers to the notion that mental phenomena are always directed toward an object. Because of the enormous influence of Brentano's discussion, "intentionality" and to a lesser but nevertheless significant degree "intention" have become technical philosophical terms, usually discussed without any reference to the concept of attention. And since Brentano took the concept of intentionality from Scholastic philosophy, studies dedicated to the premodern history of intention often focus on the precedents of Brentano's (and Husserl's) notions of intention in classical and medieval philosophies, rarely considering the flexibility of the term and its connection to attention in the original contexts. Thus the entries dedicated to intention ("Intentio") and attention ("Aufmerksamkeit") in the *Historisches Wörterbuch der Philosophie*, while among the best in tracing the histories of the two notions, also exemplify this bias by all but neglecting each other. See Joachim Ritter, ed., *Historisches Wörterbuch der Philosophie*, vols. 1, 4 (Basel: Schwabe & Co. 1971), 1:635–45; 4:466–74.

40. Becon, *The Right Pathwaye unto Prayer*.

41. Norden, *A Poor Mans Rest*, sig. B6^r.

42. Ibid.

43. Interpreting Claudius's devotional failure as a matter of distraction also helps us see its role in the play. Hamlet and Claudius are never closer to each other than in 3.3, not only physically but also in finding themselves in a similar predicament: they both want to perform an action but fail to do so. Despite the morbidity of comparing prayer and murder, it is clear that Shakespeare wants us to see them as parallel: the Ghost puns on praying and preying (1.5.42ff.), and Hamlet himself compares his "swift" revenge to meditation (1.4.29ff. and 1.5.130ff.). The latter comparison proves to be ironic, of course, because Hamlet's revenge turns out to be meditation-like not because it's swift but because it takes so long. One of the reasons of its delay is Hamlet's "distraction." The early modern sense of distraction as "madness" is relevant here (see Carol Thomas Neely, *Distracted Subjects: Madness and Gender in Shakespeare and Early Modern Culture* [Ithaca, NY: Cornell University Press, 2004]), but it is also the case that Hamlet is actually distracted from his task, primarily by his thoughts about Gertrude (his father's Ghost warns him early on against thinking about Gertrude's potential complicity, and the only time the Ghost returns in the play is in the bedchamber scene, to remind Hamlet that he has forgotten about his task). It is then important to note that the single most important reference to distraction in the New Testament is Paul's characterization of the unmarried as less distracted by worldly concerns and therefore more attentive to God. In Andrewes's paraphrase, "the unmarried may *the better attend upon the Lord without distraction. They* may be more constant in adhering to Christ, and suffering for his cause, more willing to die and to follow Christ, *Minus mali metuit, qui minus delicias gustavit,* he feares the evil of affliction the lesse, who hath had a least tast of the delights and pleasures of the world" (*The Pattern of Catechistical Doctrine at Large* [London, 1650], 453). Hamlet's misogyny throughout the play, his excessively cruel treatment of Ophelia, and his attempts to make his mother repent are evidence that he and the king share the same distractions. In this sense, Claudius's failure to pray is an allegory of the entire play, Shakespeare's way of using the example of devotion to shed light on Hamlet's "long prayer." See Peter Iver Kaufman, *Prayer, Despair, and Drama: Elizabethan Introspection* (Urbana: University of Illinois Press, 1996), esp. chap. 3, "Hamlet's 'Kind of Fighting.'"

44. Jeremy Taylor, *Holy Living* (London, 1650), 295.

45. The concern with distraction was partly due to the growth of the breviary itself; clergy often complained about the difficulty of paying sustained attention to text. See Pierre Batiffol, *History of the Roman Breviary*, trans. Atwell M. Y. Baylay (London: Longmans, 1912), 173–74 and 195.

46. See, for instance, Francisco Suarez's *De horatione, devotione, et horis canonicis*, chaps. 4 and 5, in *Opera Omnia*, vol. 15, ed. Carolo Berton (Paris, 1859), 224–32.

47. Domingo de Soto, O.P., *De iustitia et iure*, q. 5, a. 5 (Salamanca, 1549), 883. Thanks to Steven Justice for this quotation.

48. "Nam in mentali, cum ipsa eadem attentio sit ipsissima oratio, vanum est quaerere utrum illie requiratur attentio." Ibid., 884.

49. "Utrum de necessitate orationis sit quod sit attenta" (2a2æ. 83, 13), in *Summa Theologiæ*, 82–83.

50. Ibid., 82–85.

51. Ibid., 86–87.
52. Ibid., 80–83. The Augustine quotation is from *Ad Probam*, cxxx, 9. PL 33, 501.
53. Ibid., 82–83.
54. Ibid., 84–85.
55. Ibid., 84–85.
56. The clearest practical example of this notion of devotional decision is Ignatius of Loyola's *Spiritual Exercises*, in which the exercises are meant to help the meditator to find the decision that is right for her. This explains the seemingly paradoxical beginning of the *Exercises*, where Ignatius explains that in order to make the right decision, one needs to learn how to be "indifferent." What "indifference" means, however, is a kind of attentive receptivity that enables the meditator to find the right answer to her question. Reading the *Exercises* along with Ignatius's *Spiritual Diaries* is particularly instructive. In the *Diaries*, the reader follows Ignatius in the process of making decisions (most importantly, a decision about whether or not the newly founded Jesuit order should engage in financial activities). The preparation for making this decision consists in frequent prayers and meditations; and the decisions, or rather the "readiness" to make the decisions, arrive in the form of tears, which Ignatius identifies with God's grace. For more about this, see chap. 4.
57. Donne owned works by both Aquinas and de Soto; see Geoffrey Keynes, A *Bibliography of Dr John Donne* (Cambridge: Cambridge University Press, 1958), 209 and 221. At the same time, Donne's references to Aquinas aren't always appreciative; as Katrin Ettenhuber puts it, "he had no special affection for the Angelic Doctor" (*Donne's Augustine: Renaissance Cultures of Interpretation* [Oxford: Oxford University Press, 2011], 101–4).
58. Although Margaret Mauer notes the role of prayer in Donne's letter and even points out the parallel with *La Corona* in the sense that both works are concerned with both prayer and praise, she underplays prayer as as Donne's "nominal" concern and a part of his strategy of "indirection." As I try to show below, Donne's comments deserve consideration on their own right, and not only as an excuse for Donne to discuss friendship. See Margaret Mauer, "The Poetical Familiarity of John Donne's Letters," in Stephen Greenblatt, ed., *The Power of Forms in the English Renaissance* (Norman, OK: Pilgrim Books, 1982), 185–86.
59. The letter that I focus on in this chapter is incidentally the first letter included in the 1633 *Poems of J.D.* For discussions of how to interpret the fact that twelve of Donne's prose letters are included in the 1633 volume, see R. E. Bennett, "Donne's *Letters to Severall Persons of Honour*," PMLA 46 (1941): 126–27, and David Novarr, *The Making of Walton's Lives* (Ithaca, NY: Cornell University Press, 1958), 35–38. Donne's letters have received some critical attention recently, yet a reliable and full edition of them is still missing (one is being prepared by Dennis Flynn). A recent but partial edition is P. M. Oliver, ed., *John Donne: Selected Letters* (Manchester: Carcanet Press, 2002). This edition does not print the letter that I am concerned with in this chapter, and which I am therefore quoting from *Letters to Severall Persons of Honour* (London, 1651), 109–12. Literature on the letters is still somewhat limited; see Roger E. Bennett, 'Donne's

Letters to Severall Persons of Honour," *PMLA* 56 (1941): 120–40; John Carey, "John Donne's Newsless Letters," *Essays and Studies* 34 (1981): 45–65; Margaret Mauer, "The Poetical Familiarity of John Donne's Letters," and, recently, Ramie Targoff, *John Donne: Body and Soul* (Chicago: University of Chicago Press, 2008), 25–49.

60. "Prestation" is Marcell Mauss's term for that aspect of the gift which he calls *fait social total*, that once in circulation, the gift belongs to everyone who participates in the process, that it must be kept in circulation, and that this circulating gift pervades all aspects of social life. "Prestation-gift" is Louis Montrose's term, based on Mauss's theory, to denote gifts that are given in order to evoke a return; or in other words gifts that clearly indicate that they are part of a symbolic exchange system. On this, see chap. 2 on thanksgiving.

61. Donne, *Letters*, 109.

62. Ibid.

63. Ibid., 110.

64. Lancelot Andrewes, *The Pattern of Catechistical Doctrine*, 145.

65. Donne continues: "For in all *Solomons* bookes, you shall not finde half so much of the duty of thanksfulnesse, as you shall in *Seneca* and in *Plutarch*. No book of Ethicks, of morall doctrine, is come to us, wherein there is not, almost in every leafe, some detestation, some Anathema against ingratitude; but of repentance, not a word amongst them all. And therefore in that dutie of prayer which presumes repentance, (for he must stand *Rectus in curia* that will pray) *David* has insisted longest; and because he would enter, and establish a man, upon confidence in God, he begins with a deprecation of his anger; but for upon that ground, no man can stand; and because he would dismisse him with that which concerns him most, he chooseth to end in a Thanksgivinge" (Potter and Simpson, *Sermons*, 6:42).

66. Donne, *Letters*, 110.

67. One recalls that Erasmus's exercise in *De Copia* focuses on a sentence that expresses the gratitude of the receiver of a letter.

68. Donne, *Letters*, 111.

69. Ibid., 110–11.

70. In the Gospels, the idea is phrased in terms of divine knowledge: "But thou, when thou prayest, enter into thy closet, and when thou hast shut thy door, pray to thy Father which is in secret; and thy Father which seeth in secret shall reward thee openly. But when ye pray, use not vain repetitions, as the heathen do: for they think that they shall be heard for their much speaking. Be not ye therefore like unto them: for your Father knoweth what things ye have need of, before ye ask him" (Matt. 6:6–8).

71. Marotti cites this passage to suggest that here Donne prioritizes thanksgiving over petition and that "insofar as they request or demand divine help or become self-aggrendizing performances, the religious poems veer away from this devotional ideal" (Marotti, *John Donne, Coterie Poet*, 252). But this overlooks the extent to which in order to be able to give thanks, the speaker has to have received gifts/grace; and what Donne is thinking about here is precisely the question of how petition and thanksgiving depend on each other.

72. Donne, *Letters*, 111.

73. See, for instance, the Church of England clergyman Thomas Gataker's *Jacobs Thankfulnesse to God for Gods Goodnesse to Jacob* (London, 1624), where Gataker notes that "Thanksgiving is the best, and the most effectual forme of Prayer" (4).

74. Donne, *Letters*, 111.

75. Ibid., 110–111. This sentence stands out in the whole letter, not the least by virtue of its puzzling grammatical structure. Or rather, by its rhetoricization of grammar, a method that Donne employs in the *Holy Sonnets* as well. At first sight, the grammar suggests a highly logical arrangement of the parts by virtue of the conjunctions. But at closer look, the hypotactic relations seem to dissolve in an implicit but more general parataxis; the parts that are supposed to be controlled by the conjunctions seem to resist the control and remain oddly indeterminate within the sentence. Does "being composed of thought and breath" explain the subtle and delicate nature of words or, on the contrary, their muddy and thick character? Does the only "because" of the sentence explain something about words or thoughts? And in either case, if, despite being the most subtle and delicate that human beings are capable of creating, words are still as muddy and thick as our thoughts, then what does this "because they are ever leavened with passions and affections" really explain? The muddiness and thickness of thoughts and/or words? Or rather, their subtle and delicate character, at least by human measures?

76. What is the subject of this "first rising"? The grammar seems to suggest that it refers back to words (Words are as muddy and thick as our thoughts, because—except at the first rising—they are ever leavened with passions and affections). At the same time, the syntax does not exclude that it refers to thoughts instead, if simply by virtue of the word's vicinity. Semantically, "rising" may have an implicit relationship to both breath and leaven (which derives of the Latin *levare*, to raise). Meanwhile, especially in the light of the immediately following reference to Christ's incarnation, we cannot forget about the possible theological meanings of the words either: "rising" as incarnation may be a reference to any and all of the essential theological doctrines of the Logos, of the incarnation, or of the resurrection. While in terms of its precise subject this first rising is even vaguer than the rest of the sentence, in all its vagueness it clearly states an exception within the rule that claims the general impossibility of addressing God. Later in the letter, he confirms the insight that in the beginning there is an exception. In the context of condemning long prayers because they have "more of the Devil by often distractions," Donne says "for, after in the beginning we have well intreated God to hearken, we speak no more to him." One recalls Donne's generally astonishing first lines; one may also remember that Donne's poems ever so often speak their words in a tone of the waking body, when the senses are fresh and perceptive and at the same time tender from the dreams that they just saw; "The Good-Morrow" is the poem that thematizes this sense of the beginning through the alba/aubade tradition.

77. Emphases mine. The printed letter ends here without period or signature. Donne, *Letters*, 112.

CHAPTER FOUR

1. "Es sah aber der achtsame Mann / Das Angesicht des Gottes." Quoted from the fragments of the later version of the poem in Friedrich Hölderlin, *Poems and Fragments*, trans. Michael Hamburger (London: Anvil, 2004), 572–73.

2. Michel De Certeau, *The Mystic Fable*, trans. Michael B. Smith (Chicago: University of Chicago Press, 1992), 5.

3. "The metrical form destroys the hearer's trust and diverts his attention, making him watch for metrical recurrences." Aristotle, *Rhetoric*, trans. W. R. Roberts (New York: Modern Library, 1954), bk. 3., chap. 14.

4. Of course pure prayer itself has a long and varied tradition, with ideals of pure prayer rather different from the ascetic, Evagrian version of the concept in which I am interested in this chapter (see, for instance, Rachel Fulton Brown's discussion of Hugh of St. Victor's *De modo orandi* in her essay "Oratio/Prayer," in *The Cambridge Companion to Christian Mysticism*, ed. Amy Hollywood and Patricia Z. Beckman (Cambridge: Cambridge University Press, 2012), 170–71). My interest in this chapter isn't in tracing the history of pure prayer, but in understanding how the ascetic ideal has influenced more ubiquitous modes of devotion.

5. John Donne, "Sermon Preached at the Funerals of Sir William Cokayne Knight, Alderman of London, December 12. 1626," in George Potter and Evelyn M. Simpson, eds., *The Sermons of John Donne*, 10 vols. (Berkeley: University of California Press, 1953–62), 7:264–65. For a brilliant interpretation of this sermon, see Peter McCullough, "Preaching and Context: John Donne's Sermon at the Funerals of Sir William Cokayne," in *The Oxford Handbook of the Early Modern Sermon*, ed. Peter McCullough et al. (Oxford: Oxford University Press, 2011), 213–67.

6. See Clement of Alexandria: "To [the Gnostic] the flesh is dead; but he himself lives alone, having consecrated the sepulchre into a holy temple to the Lord, having turned towards God the old sinful soul. . . . Such a one is no longer continent, but has reached a state of passionlessness, waiting to put on the divine image." *Strōmateis*, IV.22 and VI.9 in *Fathers of the Second Century*, ed. Alexander Roberts, James Donaldson, and A. Cleveland Coxe, *The Ante-Nicene Fathers*, vol. 2 (Buffalo, NY, 1885), 434–35, 496. For the Greek, see Nicolai Le Nourry, *Clementis Alexandria Opera Omnia*, vol. 1., in J-P. Migne, *Patrologia Graeca*, 8 vols. (Paris, 1857), 292.

7. What Clement calls "Gnosis" is different from Gnosticisim, of which Clement held critical views.

8. "Wherefore it is neither in a definite place or special shrine, nor yet on certain feasts and days set apart, that the gnostic honours God, returning thanks to Him for knowledge bestowed and the gift of the heavenly citizenship; but he will do this all his life in every place, whether he be alone by himself or have with him some who share his belief." This continuous devotion aims at a contemplative union with God: "The gnostic at all events prays all his life through, striving to be united with God in prayer." Clement of Alexandria, *Miscellanies, Book VII*, 61, 71.

9. See Clement of Alexandria, *Miscellanies*, 74-75. Clement's definition in turn evokes Paul's discussion of marriage in 1 Corinthians 7:37: "And this I speak for your own profit; not that I may cast a snare upon you, but for that which is comely, and that ye may attend upon the Lord without distraction." What the KJV renders "without distraction" is the Greek *aperispaston*, the same term that Clement uses to characterize prayer as undistracted. The other crucial term in Clement's definition is *epistrophē* or "turning," one of the synonyms of *metanoia* or "conversion"; see Acts 15:3. But in certain contexts it may also imply attention; see Henry George Liddel and Robert Scott, *A Greek-English Lexicon*, rev. Henry Stuart Jones and Roderick McKenzie (Oxford: Clarendon Press, 1940), s.v. *epistrophē*, A.II.3.

10. Apart from being implied in the notion of the "undistracted turn" itself, Pythagorean and Stoic notions of *tonos* may be the influence behind some of Clement's discussions of the "physics" of prayer, including the emphasis on corporeal "stretching toward" the sky (*Miscellanies*, 69–70), as well as the speculations about how angels and God may perceive prayer (*Miscellanies*, 66–67).

11. For a historical essay of the idea of harmony as a musical and metaphysical notion, see Leo Spitzer's *Classical and Christian Ideas of World Harmony: Prolegomena to an Interpretation of the Word 'Stimmung'* (Baltimore: Johns Hopkins University Press, 1963). Incidentally, Spitzer's book (which he left unfinished) concludes with a passage from Donne's *Sermons*, where Donne uses the figure of a musical instrument to describe salvational history, and with a brief discussion of distraction and *divertissiment* in Pascal. For a discussion of Cicero's translation of *tonos* as *intentio*, see Mary Carruthers's *The Craft of Thought*, 15. See the entry on "Intentio" in Joachim Ritter, ed., *Historisches Wörterbuch der Philosophie*, vol. 4 (Basel: Schwabe & Co. 1971), 469.

12. 5.1.69, in Greenblatt, *The Norton Shakespeare*, 1170.

13. On Stoic and Epicurean notions of *prosochē*, see Paul Rabbow, *Seelenführung* (München: Kösel-Verlag, 1954), 223–60, and Pierre Hadot, *Philosophy as a Way of Life*, trans. Michael Chase (Oxford: Blackwell, 1995), esp. 130–33. On the afterlife of *prosochē* in early Christian monasticism, see Douglas Burton-Christie, "Early Monasticism," in Hollywood and Beckman, *The Cambridge Companion to Christian Mysticism* (Cambridge: Cambridge University Press, 2012), 47–56.

14. In this sense, it seems to me that this antique conception of attention is closer to the philosophical-phenomenological intention of Brentano and Husserl than to the common meanings of intention as "purpose" or "plan." It also shows similarities with the view that has been recently advocated by philosophers of mind who argue that attention is not a faculty or a particular activity but rather the ways in which all cognitive activities are organized into a unit. Where I see a crucial difference is the ordering of attention vis-à-vis the particular cognitive activities; the classical and Christian notion of attention seems to imply that attention as the unity of all other "cognitive" (or intentional) activities *precedes* these particular activities. For recent philosophical accounts of attention, see Christopher Mole, Declan Smithies, and Wayne Wu, eds., *Attention: Philosophical and Psychological Essays* (Oxford: Oxford University Press, 2011); for a critique of traditional psychological approaches to the question of attention, see

Christopher Mole, *Attention Is Cognitive Unison: An Essay in Philosophical Psychology* (Oxford: Oxford University Press, 2011).

15. The Greek word that appears in Clement's description of prayer, *aperispaston*, or "without distraction," is itself an important category for both Skeptic and Stoic philosophy; it appears, for instance, in Epictetus, *Discourses* 3.22.69.

16. To be sure, Stoic philosophy would also discuss attention to God; yet the two notions of transcendence are fundamentally different. This is a point somewhat neglected in Pierre Hadot's *Exercises spirituels et Philosophie Antique*, which seeks to shed light on the continuity between Greek and Latin (mainly Stoic) philosophy and Christian spiritual exercises, and in so doing often ignores the difference between the antique philosophical exercises and the Christian religious meditations.

17. Martha Nussbaum, in *The Therapy of Desire* (Princeton, NJ: Princeton University Press, 1994), makes virtually no mention of *apatheia*, except for a passage in which she admits that she would rather see a Stoic philosophy free of *apatheia*: "As in the case of Epicurus, I have preferred those Stoic works that acknowledge the pressure of the Aristotelian position, recognizing, especially, the depth of ties to others in a truly reasonable and complete life. It seems to me a major contribution of Hellenistic ethics to have urged us to think humanly, like the finite beings we are. I believe this insight should have moved the argument, in some cases, away from *apatheia* and toward both *erōs* and compassion" (199).

18. On Evagrius, perfect prayer, *apatheia*, and images, see Elizabeth A. Clark's seminal discussion in *The Origenist Controversy* (Princeton, NJ: Princeton University Press, 1992), 67: "For Evagrius, 'pure prayer,' which in essence he identifies with contemplation, requires that worshippers rid themselves of both emotions and images from the sense world. Prayer demands a kind of 'purgation' that entails a moral, spiritual, and (we would say) psychological discipline. The time of prayer serves as a kind of 'mirror' through which we can judge the condition of our own souls: it is, he posits, a 'state' (*katastasis*)."

19. Evagrius of Pontus, *The Greek Ascetic Corpus*, trans. Robert E. Sinkewicz (Oxford: Oxford University Press, 2003), 196.

20. Both Luther and Calvin were critical of the ideal of *apatheia*. For instance, when in the context of commenting on 1 Thessalonians 4:13 ("But I would not have you to be ignorant, brethren, concerning them which are asleep, that ye sorrow not, even as others which have no hope"), Calvin approves of Paul's call for moderation in grief, he also adds: "Those that abuse this testimony, so as to establish among Christians Stoical indifference, that is, an iron hardness, will find nothing of this nature in Paul's words." John Calvin, *Commentaries on the Epistles of Paul the Apostle to the Philippians, Colossians, and Thessalonians*, trans. John Pringle (Edinburgh: Calvin Translation Society, 1851), 280. For more on Calvin's critique of *apatheia*, see William S. Bouwsma, *John Calvin: A Sixteenth-Century Portrait* (Oxford: Oxford University press, 1988), 133–34.

21. "All who had believed in Evagrian or Origenist-derived monastic teachings now faced being discredited on two grounds. They not only ran the risk of being classed, in the eyes of influential figures such as Jerome and Augustine, as followers of the 'heretical' Origen, but also being identified with the Pelagians, anathematized at the council of

Carthage in 418" (Marilyn Dunn, The *Emergence of Monasticism: From the Desert Fathers through the Early Middle Ages* [Oxford: Blackwell, 2000], 73).

22. See Jerome's Letter 133 "To Ctesiphon": "Evagrius of Ibera in Pontus who sends letters to virgins and monks and among others to her whose name bears witness to the blackness of her perfidy, has published a book of maxims on apathy, or, as we should say, impassivity or imperturbability; a state in which the mind ceases to be agitated and—to speak simply—becomes either a stone or a God. His work is widely read, in the East in Greek and in the West in a Latin translation made by his disciple Rufinus." Philip Schaff and Henry Wace, eds., *Nicene and Post-Nicene Fathers, Second Series,* vol. 6, trans. W. H. Fremantle, G. Lewis and W. G. Martley (Buffalo, NY: Christian Literature Publishing Co., 1893), 274.

23. Augustine, *Confessions II: Books IX–XIII,* ed. and trans. William Watts (Cambridge, MA: Harvard University Press, 1997), 278–81.

24. Martin Luther, *Works,* vol. 43: *Devotional Writings* II, ed., J. J. Pelikan, H. C. Oswald and H. T. Lehmann (Philadelphia: Fortress Press, 1999), 203.

25. Similar instructions to be attentive in prayer are ubiquitous in Protestant devotional manuals. Robert Hill even produces a catechism in *Pathway to Prayer* (London, 1609; c. 1606) on what he considers as the center of Christian practice: "As I am bound to pray continually, so am I bound to watch continually . . . that I bestow no more care and thought upon the world, then I needs must, for the moderate maintaining of my selfe, and those that belong to me, lest my thoughts be distracted from too much from heavenly things" (153–56).

26. "In all actions which are of long continuance, deliberation and abode, let your holy and pious intention be actual, that is, that it be by a special prayer, or action, by a peculiar act of resignation or oblation given to God: but in smaller actions, and little things, and indifferent, fail not to secure a pious habitual intention." Jeremy Taylor, *Holy Living* (London, 1650), 21–22.

27. John Christopherson, Queen Mary's chaplain, explains in 1554 that "it is much better for them not to understand the common service of the church, because when they hear others praying in a loud voice, in the language that they understand, they are letted from prayer themselves, and so come to such a slackness and negligence in praying, that at length as we have seen in these late days, in manner pray not at all." In Thomas Frederick Simmons, *The Lay Folks' Mass Book* (Oxford: Oxford University Press, 1879), 365.

28. Targoff, *Common Prayer,* 15.

29. For Donne's familiarity with Granada, see José Ramón Fernández Suárez, "Repercusiones de la Obra de Fray Luis de Granada en los sermones de John Donne," *Revista de filología inglesa* 4 (1974): 109–31.

30. Luis Granada, *Meditations* (London, 1633), 2–3.

31. One recalls that in the early modern era the term "distraction" often refers to political tumult (the "distracted multitude" that Claudius references in *Hamlet* 4.3.4), and at times specifically to a scattering of a former political unity.

32. Loyola's *Spiritual Exercises,* which until the very last section might seem like a work that would enable the individual to practice Christianity on their own, in the end declares

that the goal of the meditations is to prepare one to render their services to the "militant church."

33. The classic treatment of Evagrius and Cassian is Salvatore D. Marsili, *Giovanni Cassiano ed Evagrio Pontico: Dottrina sulla carità e contemplazione* (Roma: Herder, 1936). For an account of the transition, see Dunn, *Emergence of Monasticism*, 59–111.

34. John Cassian, *The Conferences*, trans. Boniface Ramsey, O.P. (New York: Newman Press, 1997), 43.

35. "Cassian had another problem to overcome: the fact that much of his spiritual doctrine depended on that of Evagrius, an Origenist whose concept of apatheia has, in 415, been specifically singled out by Jerome for criticism. . . . In his hands, the tricky notion of *apatheia* becomes the less controversial (and less technical) 'purity of the heart' [*puritas cordis*] nevertheless preserving the Evagrian idea that it was the gateway to something more significant." Dunn, *Emergence of Monasticism*, 77ff.; and Columba Stewart, *Cassian the Monk*, 42ff.

36. Cassian, *Conferences*, 50.

37. See Amy Hollywood's account of Cassian's "fiery prayer": "Although the fullness of fruition in God will never occur in this life, the monk trains himself daily, through obedience, chastity, poverty, and, most importantly, prayer, to attain it." In Hollywood, "Song, Experience, and Book in Benedictine Monasticism," 69.

38. "It is, indeed, impossible for the mind not to be troubled by thoughts, but accepting them or rejecting them is possible for everyone who makes an effort. . . . Therefore we practice the frequent reading of and constant meditation on the Scripture, so that we may be open to a spiritual point of view. For this reason we frequently chant the psalms, so that we may continually grow in compunction. For this reason we are diligent in vigils, fasting, and praying, so that the mind which has been stretched to its limits may not taste earthly things but contemplate heavenly ones." Cassian, *Conferences*, 56–57.

39. "The preoccupation with technique is already the effect of what it opposes. Unbeknownst even to some of its promoters, the creation of mental constructs (imaginary compositions, mental voids, etc.) takes the place of attention to the advent of the Unpredictable." Michel De Certeau, *The Mystic Fable*, 5.

40. Giles Constable's *The Reformation of the Twelfth Century* (Cambridge: Cambridge University Press, 1996) traces medieval movements to extend monastic practices beyond the walls of the monasteries. Eamon Duffy's *The Stripping of the Altars* (New Haven, CT: Yale University Press, 1992) stresses the reformation movement within the framework of Roman Catholicism. See also Katherine Zieman, *Singing the New Song* (Philadelphia: University of Pennsylvania Press, 2008), xiii, and Charles Lloyd Cohen, *God's Caress: The Psychology of Puritan Religious Experience* (Oxford: Oxford University Press, 1986), 6.

41. Ignatius was familiar with medieval attention exercises at least indirectly through Cardinal García Jiménez de Cisneros's *Ejercitatorio de la vida espiritual*. See Fulton Brown, "My Psalter, My Self; or, How to Get a Grip on the Office According to Jan Mombaer: An Exercise in Training the Attention for Prayer," *Spiritus* 12:1 (2012): 77, 99, 100.

42. The first annotation defines the goal of the exercises in "preparing and disposing the soul to rid itself of all inordinate attachments [*affecciones desordenadas*], and, after their removal, of seeking and finding the will of God in the disposition of our life for the salvation of our soul." Louis J. Puhl, S.J., *The Spiritual Exercises of Ignatius of Loyola* (Chicago: Loyola Press, 1952), 1; for the Spanish, see P. José Calveras, S.I., *Ejercicios espirituales y Directorio de Ignacio de Loyola* (Barcelona: Editorial Balmes, 1958), 41.

43. Pedroche's *Censura* is printed in Juan Alfonso de Polanco's *Chronicon* (Madrid, 1895), 3:503–524. On Pedroche's criticism, see Ignacio Iparraguirre, S.J., *Práctica de los Ejercicios de San Ignacio de Loyola en vida de su autor, 1522–1556* (Roma: IHSI, 1946), 98–102, and John W. O'Malley, *The First Jesuits* (Cambridge, MA: Harvard University Press, 1993), 43.

44. Some of the *alumbrados* held heterodox views, some departed more radically from the doctrines of the church, but early in the sixteenth century the entire group was condemned as heretical by the Spanish Inquisition. They became easily identifiable after a 1525 edict that condemned them and listed the main reasons of their conviction. See Nora E. Jaffary, *False Mystics* (Lincoln: University of Nebraska Press, 2004), 29–30.

45. Cf. Schreiner, *Are You Alone Wise?* 271–72.

46. Pedroche, *Censura*, 509–10. Similar charges were articulated against Ignatius by others, including the Dominican Melchor Cano. On Cano, see Schreiner, *Are You Alone Wise?* 272–74.

47. The bulk of Nadal's text is printed after Pedroche's *Censura* in Polanco's *Chronicon*, 3:526–73. Though the controversy continued into the early years of Trent, where papal legates interviewed two prominent Jesuits about it, the Holy Seat, which first approved of the *Spiritual Exercises* in the *Pastoralis Officii Cura* in 1548, continued to favor the Society and the exercises, and the controversy eventually abated. It is telling that in responding to the charges, Nadal's consistent strategy is to distinguish the practice of the exercises from theology. But this is the point: what Nadal wants to show is that the *Spiritual Exercises* can be entirely in line with the orthodox teachings of the church. The practice of indifference is strictly within the context of the exercises themselves. This is a strategy that is reflected in the *Exercises* as well. In Annotation 15, even as he advises the director against influencing the exercitant in any way, Loyola emphasizes that this is a temporary, pragmatic indifference. When in the First Principle and Foundation, Ignatius restates the principle of indifference, he suggests that "we must make ourselves indifferent to all created things, as far as we are allowed free choice and are not under any prohibition" (12). In other words, indifference in the *Spiritual Exercises* is a practical principle, a temporary and strategic suspension of one's preexisting assumptions, judgments, and inclinations. It is restricted both in the sense that it is only valid within the space of the exercises, and in the sense that even within that space it is not absolute but includes the acceptance of the basic regulations of both church and state.

48. "El que da los ejercicios, no debe mover al que los recibe más a pobreza ni a promessa, que a sus contrarios, ni a un estado o modo de vivir, que a otro." Ignatius, *Spiritual Exercises*, 6; Spanish from *Ejercicios espirituales y Directorio*, ed. P. José Calveras (Bar-

celona: Editorial Balmes, 1958), 48. Further citations to the English are given parenthetically in the text.

49. Francesca Bugliani Knox suggests that Donne's Litany contains direct echoes of this
Ignatian idea of indifference in *The Eye of the Eagle: John Donne and the Legacy of
Ignatius of Loyola* (Oxford: Peter Lang, 2011), 94–98.

50. Writing in the first person, Ignatius suggests that the exercitant "should be like a balance at equilibrium, without leaning to either side, that I might be ready to follow
whatever I perceive is more for the glory and praise of God our Lord and for the salvation of my soul" (75).

51. Schreiner, *Are You Alone Wise?* 272–73.

52. The literature on the influence of Ignatius is already immense and rapidly growing;
three examples should suffice here: Mordechai Feingold, *Jesuit Science and the Republic
of Letters* (Cambridge, MA.: MIT Press, 2002); J. Michelle Molina, *To Overcome Oneself: The Jesuit Ethic and Spirit of Global Expansion, 1520–1767* (Berkeley: University of
California Press, 2013); and the essays in Thomas O'Malley et al., eds., *Jesuits II: Cultures, Sciences, and the Arts, 1540–1773* (Toronto: University of Toronto Press, 2006).

53. Often presented as if they had been between Protestants and Catholics only, in reality
the debates were a far more complicated affair with Arminians opposing Calvinists,
Dominicans accusing Jesuits, and Jesuits criticizing Jansenists. The Dominican accusations against the Jesuits in the *de auxiliis* debates are particularly pertinent here as the
Jesuit Juan de Molina's 1588 *Concordia* was accused of containing semi-Pelagian views;
the matter was later settled at the Congregation de auxiliis between 1598 and 1607. For
a brief overview of the affair, see Alastair E. McGrath, *Iustitia Dei* (Cambridge: Cambridge University Press, 1989), 280–82.

54. Francis of Sales, *A Treatise of the Love of God*, trans. Miles Car (Doway [Douai], 1630),
168–69. For the French, see *Traicté de l'amour de Dieu* (Lyon, 1616), par. 540–41.

55. Sales's "simple attente" is a precedent of Malebranche's attention as "natural prayer."
What for Sales is a model of *devotional* agency, for Malebranche becomes the model
of *philosophical* agency. In both cases, attention is key because it negotiates the gap between human action and divine grace: the labor of devotion aims at creating a disposition of holy attention that is no longer an action but a receptivity open to the event of
grace. There is concrete historical continuity at work here: Malebranche was a member
of the Congregatio Oratorii Iesu et Mariæ that Pierre de Bérulle founded in 1611 on the
model of St. Philip Neri's Oratory. Sales, who was friend with Bérulle, himself founded
an oratory of St. Philip Neri. On Bérulle's influence on Malebranche, see Blanchard,
L'Attention à Dieu, 201–19.

56. Martz, *Poetry of Meditation*, 31. Although Martz's account has often been criticized because of its focus on Catholicism, more recently Francesca Bugliani Knox has offered a
full-scale defense of the notion that Jesuit views and practices were a decisive influence
in Donne's life and work in *The Eye of the Eagle*. To some degree, Knox's discussion
confirms the notion that much of Donne's religious verse follows the model of vocal
prayers and meditations in preparation for mental prayer; see particularly *The Eye of
the Eagle*, 69–111, and especially the reading of "A Litany" on 89–98.

57. Lewalski, *Protestant Poetics*, 25.

58. Stringer, *Holy Sonnets*, 13.

59. Richard Strier, "John Donne Awry and Squint," 373–74. See R. V. Young's ecumenical and *via media* interpretation of the poem in *Doctrine and Devotion*, 18–32.

60. Holy Sonnet 6 in Stringer, *Holy Sonnets*, 13.

61. Quoted in Alexandre Brou, S.J., *Ignatian Methods of Prayer*, trans. William S. Young, S.J. (Milwaukee: Bruce Publishing Company, 1949), 97.

62. Ibid., 96.

63. "An attentive person is like a diver. All he sees of the things underwater is only as much as is allowed by the volume of air retained in his lungs, by the way he carefully husbands it, by his art of breathing, his resilience against death and suffocation. . . . In the end, we would always come back to . . . *ourselves*?" (Paul Valéry, *Cahiers/Notebooks*, trans. Norma Rinsler, Paul Ryan, Brian Stimpson [Frankfurt a. M.: Peter Lang, 2007], 291).

64. Although in the Westmoreland sequence line 7 expresses theological hesitation about whether or not the speaker would face God's face immediately after death or only later (presumably at the Last Judgment), the revised sequence eliminates this hesitation and states instead, "But my ever wakeing part shall see that face / Whose feare already shakes my every ioynt" (Stringer, *Holy Sonnets*, 22). Helen Gardner was the first to use this revision as a hint for dating the *Holy Sonnets* based on the idea that the revision in the poem reflects a change in Donne's theological views (John Donne, *The Divine Poems*, ed. Helen Gardner [Oxford: Oxford University Press, 1978], xliii–1 and 114–17). In my reading of the poem, however, lines 5–12 may be most fruitfully considered as a parodistic imagination of what might happen after death, and the poem's concluding couplet is precisely a recognition that the attempts to imagine what might happen after death were fundamentally misguided. I concur with the Variorum editors who object to Gardner's suggestion on the grounds that "the revision of line 7 rather reflects Donne's concern for the internal coherence of the poem than for the up-to-dateness of its theology" (Stringer, *Holy Sonnets*, xcix). If anything, the revision makes the error of the speaker more evident by imagining a direct encounter with God.

65. For a more extensive comparison of Donne's *Holy Sonnets* and Anne Lock's poetry, see my essay "The Divine Poems," in Michael Schoenfeldt, ed., *Donne in Context* (Cambridge: Cambridge University Press, forthcoming). In addition, I would like to thank Kirsten Stirling for sharing her unpublished essay "Anne Lock and John Donne: The Sonnet Sequence and Salvation; *or* One Damned Thing after Another."

66. Roland Greene, "Anne Lock's Meditation: Invention versus Dilation and the Founding of Puritan Poetics," in Amy Boesky and Mary Thomas Crane, eds., *Form and Reform in Renaissance England: Essays in Honor of Barbara Kiefer Lewalski* (Newark: University of Delaware Press, 2000), 153–70.

67. Susan M. Felch, *The Collected Works of Anne Vaughan Lock* (Tempe: Arizona Center for Medieval and Renaissance Studies, 1999).

68. "Se lo stile segna, per l'artista, il tratto più proprio, la maniera registra un inverso processo di disappropriazione e di inappartenenza. . . . Essi sono i due poli, nella cui tensione vive il libero gesto dello scrittore: lo stile è un'appropriazione disappropriante (una negligenza sublime, un dimenticarsi nel proprio), la maniera una disappropriazi-

one appropriante, un presentirsi o un ricordar sé nell'improprio" (Giorgio Agamben, "Disappropriata maniera," in *Categorie Italiane* [Venice: Marsilio, 1996], 99–100; English translation: "Expropriated Manner," in *The End of the Poem*, trans. Daniel Heller-Roazen [Stanford: Stanford University Press, 1999], 97–98).

69. Greene offers a different reading of Lock's use of the *volta*: "In 1560, following the aesthetically modern, but religiously unreformed poetics of Surrey and his contemporaries, the sonnet is practically a sort of technology for representing *voltas* or turns of all psychic sorts. Ironically, there are few actual turns in Lock's twenty-six sonnets. . . . What if Lock's sonnets were seen as being 'about' the turn it embodies rather than the speaker, persons, or consciousness undergoing the turn?" (Greene, "Anne Lock's Meditation," 166).

70. There is, to be sure, a tendency for the words that rhyme with "grace" to evoke, eventually, the word "grace" itself in virtually all English poetry of the early modern period. But the ubiquity of this grace-automaton in Lock's sequence is striking; see sonnets 2, 3, 4, 7, 9, 10, 12, 13, and 17.

71. *Meditations of a Penitent Sinner* was published unsigned, and Lock introduced it by saying it "was delivered me by my friend with whom I knew I might be so bolde to use & publishe it as pleased me" (Felch, *Lock*, 62).

72. Marot and de Bèze's French psalm translations appeared between 1533 and 1543. Thomas Sternhold published his first collection of psalm translations between 1547 and 1549. See Hannibal Hamlin, *Psalm Culture and Early Modern English Literature* (Cambridge, 2004), 25. Also relevant are paraphrase translations of other Bible books, for instance William Baldwin's *The Canticles, or Balades of Salomon* (1549).

73. Felch, *Lock*, 62.

74. In this sense, I agree with P. M. Oliver's claim that "Lok's sonnets are written from a securely Calvinist position," which Oliver contrasts with the *Holy Sonnets'* "lack of a fixed theological viewpoint" (P. M. Oliver, *Donne's Religious Writings: A Discourse of Feigned Devotion* [London: Longman, 1997], 134).

75. Stringer, *Holy Sonnets*, 13.

76. "Then when we see that God is juste in punisshynge us for oure synnes, let us come wyth head bowed downe, that we maye be releved by hys merye: and let us have no other confidence, nor truste of salvation, but in thys that it pleaseth him in the name of oure savioure Jesus Christ, to receave us to mercye, for as muche as in us there is nothyng but cursednes" (Felch, *Lock*, 21).

CHAPTER FIVE

1. *"Ne te flatte pas d'y réussir sans une attention poussée à l'extrême, dont le chef-d'œuvre sera de surprendre ce qui n'existe qu'à ses dépens."* Introduction to Jean de La Fontaine's *Adonis* (Paris, 1921), iv. English translation by Denise Folliot in *The Art of Poetry* (New York: Vintage Books, 1958), 11.

2. Augustine's relevance for Donne's poetry and theology has been an important theme of Donne scholarship for a long time. Some of these studies have focused on the theology of the *Holy Sonnets*. See Patrick Grant, "Augustinian Spirituality and the *Holy Sonnets* of John Donne," *English Literary History* 38 (1971): 542–61. R. V. Young's reading of the *Holy Sonnets* relates the sequence to post-Tridentine soteriology and finds it more Augustinian than Protestant. See "Donne's *Holy Sonnets* and Donne's Theology of Grace," in *Bright Shootes of Everlastingnesse: The Seventeenth-Century Religious Lyric*, ed. Claude Summers and Ted-Larry Pebworth (Columbia: University of Missouri Press, 1987). Mary Ann Koory in "'England's Second Austin': John Donne's Resistance to Conversion," *John Donne Journal* 17 (1998), argues that Donne relies on Petrarch's version of Augustinianism to both ask for and shelter himself from God's love. For a similar argument, see Gary Kuchar, "Petrarchism and Repentance in Donne's *Holy Sonnets*" in *Modern Philology*, 105:3 (2008): 535–70. I have found helpful Helen Brooks's argument in "Donne's 'Goodfriday, 1613. Riding Westward' and Augustine's Psychology of Time," in *John Donne's Religious Imagination: Essays in Honor of John T. Shawcross* (Conway: University of Central Arkansas Press, 1995), 284–306, which uses Augustine's discussion in Book XI of the *Confessions* to establish the way Donne's poems move between the structural parts of meditation that Louis Martz's *Poetry of Meditation* has identified. For a general account of Augustine's influence on Donne, see Mary Arshagouni Papazian, "The Augustinian Donne: How a "Second Augustine?" in *John Donne and the Protestant Reformation: New Perspectives,* ed. Mary Arshagouni Papazian (Detroit: Wayne University Press, 2003), 66–90. For a study of Donne's use of Augustine in the sermons, see Katrin Ettenhuber, *Donne's Augustine: Renaissance Cultures of Interpretation* (Oxford: Oxford University Press, 2011).

3. An important exception is James T. Chiampi, "Petrarch's Augustinian Excess," *Italica* 72 (1995): 1–20.

4. To be sure, whether "distraction" is the best word to translate "distentio" is a question to which I will return later, along with the problem of how "distentio" relates to "attentio" in the *Confessions*.

5. "A prayer is, for instance, a sentence but neither has truth nor has falsity. Let us pass over all such, as their study more properly belongs to the province of rhetoric or poetry." Aristotle, *On Interpretation*, trans. Harold P. Cooke (Cambridge, MA.: Harvard University Press, 1983), 121.

6. For discussions of the concept of soliloquy in Augustine, see Brian Stock, *Augustine's Inner Dialogue: The Philosophical Soliloquy in Late Antiquity* (Cambridge: Cambridge University Press, 2010), and "Self, Soliloquy, and Spiritual Exercises in Augustine and Some Later Authors," *Journal of Religion* 91 (2011): 5–23.

7. The quotation is from the second book of *De Ordine*. Cf. the English translation in *Divine Providence and the Problem of Evil* (New York: Cosmopolitan Science and Art Service Co., 1942), 159. Quoted in Thomas Gilligan, *The Soliloquies of Saint Augustine* (New York: Cosmopolitan Science and Art Service Co., 1943), 159. All quotations from the *Soliloquies* refer to Gilligan's Latin text and translation, though I occasionally refer to the Latin in Gerard Watson's edition (Saint Augustine, *Soliloquies and Immortality*

of the Soul [Warminster: Aris & Phillips, 1990]), which prints Wolfgang Hörmann's edition of the Latin text (*Soliloquiorum libri duo* [Vienna, 1986]).

8. Gilligan, *The Soliloquies of Saint Augustine*, 159.

9. Targoff, *Common Prayer*, 4.

10. What Burke calls "secular prayer," prayer in an extended sense that goes beyond liturgy and devotion, is "the coaching of an attitude by the use of mimetic and verbal language." Burke identifies the Socratic dialogues among the most exemplary secular prayers in the sense of its mimetic character building and dialectical transcendence. See Burke, *Attitudes toward History*, 321–27.

11. Gilligan, *The Soliloquies of Saint Augustine*, 102–5. In Watson's translation, "it strives towards being absolutely and yet does not exist." Augustine, *Soliloquies and Immortality of the Soul*, 93.

12. Gilligan, *The Soliloquies of Saint Augustine*, 99.

13. Ibid., 50–51.

14. Reason requires "tota intentione animi" (the mind's total attention" 50–51); it admonishes that "attende in ista diligentius." ("pay close attention to these things" 87), that "hic esto quantum potes, et vigilantissime attende" ("stay with me now as much as you are able and be most carefully attentive" 90–91), or simply "Nunc attende" (pay attention now; 96–97).

15. Gilligan, *The Soliloquies of Saint Augustine*, 122–23.

16. Ibid., 142–43. In Watson: "nullus est interitus tuus nisi oblitum esse, quod interire non possis." *Soliloquies and Immortality of the Soul*, 120.

17. Augustine's influence on Descartes has been explored many times, including in Stephen Menn's *Augustine and Descartes* (Cambridge: Cambridge University Press, 1998), which offers a helpful overview and critique of the history of comparing the two authors. Yet to my knowledge the significance of this passage in the *Soliloquies* for Descartes's system has not been noted, even though it foreshadows Descartes's account of what it means to perceive a truth clearly and distinctly. Here is Descartes: "as long as we attend to some truth which we perceive very clearly, we cannot indeed doubt it" (*The Philosophical Works of Descartes*, 2:266). For more about attention in Descartes, see the Coda.

18. Augustine, *The Retractions*, trans. M. Inez Bogan, R.S.M. (Washington, DC: Catholic University of America Press, 1968), 16–20.

19. Perhaps the most famous of the philosophical readings is Paul Ricoeur's *Time and Narrative*, vol. 1 (Chicago: University of Chicago Press, 1984), 5–30. For an overview of the philosophical interpretations of Book XI from Bergson to Russell in terms of its account of time, see Kurt Flasch, *Was ist Zeit? Augustinus von Hippo. Das XI Buch der Confessiones. Historisch-philologische Studie: Text, Übersetzung, Kommentar* (Frankfurt: Vittorio Klostermann Verlag, 2004), 27–74. Flasch briefly addresses the formal aspects of Augustine's discussion (see *Was ist Zeit?* 196–200); Jean-Luc Marion's recent work articulates the significance of the *Confessions'* formal features as prayer and praise for philosophy. See Jean-Luc Marion, *In the Self's Place: The Approach of Saint Augustine*, trans. Jeffrey L. Kosky (Stanford, CA: Stanford University Press, 2012), esp. 1–55 and 191–229.

20. Augustine, *Confessions*, trans. William Watts (Cambridge, MA.: Harvard University Press), 2:271 (hereafter all references to the *Confessions* are given to this edition parenthetically in the text).

21. Literally, a song, and at times it is unclear whether Augustine means reciting or singing it. See Andrea Nightingale, *Once out of Nature* (Chicago: University of Chicago Press, 2011), 88–89.

22. "Dicturus sum canticum, quod novi: antequam incipiam, in totum expectatio mea tenditur, cum autem coepero, quantum ex illa in praeteritum decerpsero, tenditur et memoria mea, atque distenditur vita huius actionis meae, in memoriam propter quod dixi, et in expectationem propter quod dicturus sum: praesens tamen adest attentio mea, per quam traicitur quod erat futurum, ut fiat praeteritum. quod quanto magis agitur et agitur, tanto breviata expectatione prolongatur memoria, donec tota expectatio consumatur, quum tota illa actio finita transierit in memoriam" (Augustine, *Confessions*, 2:276–79).

23. "Upon which ground it seems unto me, that time is nothing else but a stretching out in length; but of what, I know not, and I marvel, if it be not of the very mind" (*Confessions*, 2:269).

24. This is of course just one of the many instances that Augustine uses the words of the Psalms. On the role of the Psalms in the *Confessions*, see the seminal study of Georg Nicolaus Knauer, *Psalmenzitate in Augustins Konfessionen* (Göttingen: Vandenhoeck & Ruprecht, 1955), especially 150–62. For further literature on the *confessio laudis*, see James O'Donnell's commentary in his edition of Augustine's *Confessions* (Oxford: Clarendon Press, 1992), 1:9.

25. Augustine, *Confessions*, 1:3. Augustine's praise is composed of several passages from the Psalms, including 95:4, 144:3, and 47:2 in the Vulgate, and in the second half of the sentence he quotes 146:5.

26. "*Confiteri* is a verb of speaking, and *confessio* is speech that is made possible, and hence authorized, by God" (O'Donnell, "Introduction," in Augustine, *Confessions*, 2:5 and 9). See also Peter Brown, *Augustine of Hippo* (Berkeley: University of California Press, 2000), 169.

27. Augustine, *Confessions* 1:3.

28. Ibid.

29. "Numquid, domine, cum tua sit aeternitas, ignoras, quae tibi dico, aut ad tempus vides quod fit in tempore? cur ergo tibi tot rerum narrationes digero? non utique per me noveris ea, sed affectum meum excito in te et eorum, qui haec legunt, ut dicamus omnes: Magnus dominus et laudabilis valde" (*Confessions*, 2:208–9).

30. Particularly in the philosophical tradition; for instance, Origen's *On Prayer*.

31. Augustine, *Confessions*, 2:282–85.

32. Augustine, *De civitate Dei*, 11:21, trans. D. S. Wiesen (Cambridge, MA: Harvard University Press, 1972), 413.

33. Augustine, *Confessions*, 2:213. There are a number of places in the *Confessions* where Augustine makes it clear that the purpose of the *confessio* is to praise God not only using words that belong to God but by hearing those words. Another such passage is in chap. 29 of Book XI: "sequor ad palmam supernae vocationis, ubi audiam vocem

laudis." ["I follow hard on, for the garland of my heavenly calling, where I may hear the voice of thy praise."]

34. Augustine, *Confessions*, 2:275.

35. Ibid., 2:279.

36. *Confessions*, 2:208–209.

37. See, as in the case of Donne's discussion: "But thou, when thou prayest, enter into thy closet, and when thou hast shut thy door, pray to thy Father which is in secret; and thy Father which seeth in secret shall reward thee openly" (Matt. 6:6–7).

38. Aquinas, 2æ2a. 83, 12 in *Summa Theologiæ*, 80–83. Donne's "thanksgiving machine" in chap. 2 was founded on the very same duality between God's foreknowledge of prayer and prayer's impact on the devotion of others.

39. "Sed quondam melior est misericordia tua super vitas, ecce distentio est vita mea, et me suscepit dextera tua in domino meo, mediatore filio hominis inter te unum et nos multos, in multis per multa, ut per eum adprehendam, in quo et adprehensus sum, et a veteribus diebus colligar sequens unum, praeterita oblitus, non in ea quae futura et transitura sunt, sed in ea quae ante sunt *non distentus, sed extentus, non secundum distentionem, sed secundum intentionem* sequor ad palmam supernae vocationis, ubi audiam vocem laudis et contempler delectationem tuam nec venientem nec praetereuntem" (*Confessions*, 278–81; emphases mine).

40. See Andrea Nightingale's discussion in *Once out of Nature*, 96–104.

41. Augustine only uses the adjective *extentus*, of which *extensus* is a more common nominal form.

42. Cf. Augustine, *Confessions,* IX.10.23 and XII.16.23.

43. Phil. 3:13–14: "Fratres, ego me non arbitror comprehendisse; unum autem: quae quidem retro sunt, obliviscens, ad ea vero, quae ante sunt, extendens me" [in KJV: "Brethren, I count not myself to have apprehended: but this one thing I do, forgetting those things which are behind, and reaching forth unto those things which are before"].

44. Cassian, *Conferences*, 44.

45. "Et quis negat praesens tempus carere spatio, quia in puncto praeterit? Sed tamen perdurat attentio, per quam pergat abesse quod aderit [And who can deny that the present moment has no space, because it passeth away in a moment? But yet our attentive marking of it continues so that that which shall be present proceedeth to become absent]" (XI.28). I should note that in the attention research of contemporary cognitive science this is a much debated, and usually rejected position about attention; indeed one of the most popular research fields is precisely divided attention, attention that may be able to focus on more than one things at a time. But while Augustine's account may seem vulnerable to this criticism, in its defense one may note that Augustine insists on the temporal singularity of attention; he insists on the notion that in any given instant attention can only mark one thing. This is of course a metaphysical rather than physical or cognitive position, for the "instant" is hardly an empirical concept, but it does show that Augustine's notion of attention is not quite the same as the attention of today's cognitive scientists.

46. In *Once out of Nature*, Andrea Nightingale argues for a reading of Augustine's treatment of attention in the *Confessions* in terms of the body; see particularly chap. 2.

47. For Augustine's conception of desire, see Bernard McGinn, *Foundations of Mysticism* (New York: Crossroads, 1991), 144ff.

48. Is not the divine *attentio* in fact *misericordia*, the way the divine listens to someone even before the person would speak? Cf. "sed quoniam melior est misericordia tua super vitas, ecce distentio vita mea [but because thy loving kindness is better than life itself, behold my life is a distraction]." *Confessions*, XI. 29.

49. "non in ea quae futura et transitura sunt, sed in ea quae ante sunt [not to what shall be and shall pass away, but to those that are *ante*]" (XI.29) (and this is why *extentio* must be first distinguished sharply from *expectatio*, to understand how it is still *expectatio*, but of a different kind—not an *expectatio* of the future but that which is after the future). And "extendatur etiam in ea, quae ante sunt, et intellegant te ante omnia tempora aeternum creatorem omnium temporum [let them stretch forth rather towards those things which are before; and understand thee the eternal Creator of all times, to have been before all times]" (XI.30).

50. Robbins, *Complete Poems of John Donne,* 478. For reasons explained in the Introduction (see note 23), in line 11 I follow the 1633 *Poems*' punctuation rather than Robbins's.

51. Whether this "success" would be a work of the poem itself or the Holy Spirit is of course left deliberately open in the penultimate line of *La Corona*. I discuss the relevance of this ambiguity for holy attention in the Coda.

52. John Freccero, "The Fig-Tree and the Laurel: Petrarch's Poetics," *Diacritics* 5:1 (1975): 40.

53. Petrarch may have found inspiration for Rime 190 in Augustine's *City of God*, and particularly in the following passage: "For bodily beauty is indeed created by God; but it is a temporal and carnal, and therefore a lower, good; and if it is loved more than God is, Who is eternal, inward, and everlasting Good, that love is as wrong as the miser's when he forsakes justice out of his love for gold." The figure of the miser also turns up in the conversation between Augustine and Petrarch in the *Secretum*, where Augustine calls "love and glory" the golden chains that the miser is reluctant to lose. See *My Secret Book*, trans. J. G. Nichols (London: Hesperus, 2002), 55–56.

54. This is in fact conjectural. The so-called Giovanni form corresponds to one of the two MSS of the *Canzoniere*. Vat. Lat. 3195 is written partly by Petrarch, partly by a scribe. The scribe's transcription has two parts, and the first of them seems to end with 190. There is however little evidence to suggest that this was at any time an intended division. On the Giovanni form, see Ernest Hatch Wilkins, *The Making of the "Canzoniere"* (Roma: Edizioni di Storia e Letteratura, 1951), esp. 165–70.

55. With this alteration, the poem comes close to being an actual parable of the beginnings of grace's Christian history. When in the first-century Hellenistic context Paul appropriates the term and makes it the key term of his theology, the main connotation of *charis* is at the core of the very texture that holds together the Roman Empire. In the beneficiary system, it means gift. Rather than being restricted to the particular gift, however, it also means everything that one can associate with gifts: giving, receiving, returning gifts, the joy that accompanies each and every part of the process, the social status that is indicated by the gift—and, in the end, the entire process itself. The cohesive force of society, *charis* in the first century is simultaneously the idea of reciprocity

and all its manifestations, especially the pleasure of being part of the process. This *charis*, the coin with two sides that connects everyone with everyone else by making relationships proportionate, commensurate, and potentially mutual is the *charis* that Paul appropriates in the first century and makes it mean the exact opposite—the Christian *charis* being the unilateral, excessive and even infinite mercy of God—a gift that no human being should ever dare or hope to return. But to state the difference between Saint Paul's usage of the word and the general understanding of *charis* in the first century in such clear-cut terms is, at the same time, not entirely fair. By the time of the late Augustus, though the common use of *charis* was the above-mentioned one that emphasized reciprocity and commensurability, a new connotation also appeared: the caesar's gift to his subjects. This singular type of gift constituted an exception among gifts: it was considered, just as Paul's *charis*, abundant to the extent of being infinitive and arbitrary, thus representing the divine sovereignty of the caesar. And yet there is something that sets the Pauline *charis* wide apart from the imperial concept. Imperial grace is a constitutive element of the eschatological ideology of Hellenistic Rome; it is infinite and arbitrary but it is wholly present: it is part of an earthly yet divine kingdom. For Paul, in contrast, grace is present only through the body of Jesus the Christ; the Messiah *is* grace. And since the Christ is dead, grace is not so much a present gift of God but rather the promise that God will, eventually, bestow on his people an even more significant gift—one that redeems them not only of the original sin but also of their temporal life. The Eu*charist*, the ritual blending of anthropophagy and theophagy, is to keep this promise alive and present: it is the ritual through which God's grace is present on earth even after the Messiah's death. The sacrament is precisely that which makes the invisible visible. By describing grace as present and yet absent, as the promise of a future event (the *parousia*), Saint Paul opens up a temporal dimension within the semantics of grace that is entirely new to the pre-Pauline tradition of *charis*. *Charis*, all of a sudden, becomes the concept that connects the two ends of history: the prelapsarian and the post-apocalyptic. As the fulfillment of the promise is delayed, over and over again, this in-between, empty, purely chronological time (in contrast to the kairotic, "due" time of the *parousia*) becomes more and more indefinite: it becomes the secular, that is, temporal history of humanity. And yet, despite its growing significance, it always remains chronological, empty time, expanding between the repelling force of the Fall and the attractive force of the apocalypse. The temporal grace of Pauline theology is, in fact, apocalyptic grace. This grace, the grace that first replaces mutuality by the caesar's exclusive pleasure, and then pushes this pleasure further ahead in time, in an infinitely remote future is at the core of Petrarch's poem, and indeed at the core of Petrarch's *Canzoniere*, along with all the questions that surround it: How does it appear to the senses? How is one to negotiate between the senses and language? Is language capable at all of holding onto the mutability of grace's experience? See James R. Harrison's study in the *Wissenschaftliche Unterschungen zum Neuen Testament* series under the title *Paul's Language of Grace in Its Graeco-Roman Context* (Tübingen: Mohr Siebeck, 2003).

56. William A. Ringler, Jr., ed., *The Poems of Philip Sidney* (Oxford: Clarendon Press, 1962), 270–71.

57. Hannibal Hamlin et al., eds., *The Sidney Psalter* (Oxford: Oxford University Press, 2009), 11.

58. On "consist," see Roland Greene, "Sidney's Psalms, the Sixteenth-Century Psalter and the Nature of the Lyric," *Studies in English Literature, 1500–1900* 30:1 (1990): 28.

59. Donne's complex relationship to Petrarchism in the *Songs and Sonets* has been treated extensively in the scholarship; the Petrarchist elements in the *Holy Sonnets* have also received some, though not as much, attention. For a classical study of Donne's Petrarchism, see Donald L. Guss, *John Donne, Petrarchist: Italianate Conceits and Love Theory in the Songs and Sonets* (Detroit: Wayne State University Press, 1966). For an insightful account of Petrarchism in the *Holy Sonnets*, see Gary Kuchar, *The Poetry of Religious Sorrow in Early Modern England* (Cambridge: Cambridge University Press, 2008), 151–83.

60. The 1633 *Poems by J. D.* includes a psalm translation that is now attributed to Francis Davison. See Francis Davison, *The Poetical Rhapsody*, ed. Harris Nicholas (London, 1826), 2:321–23. On the Davison psalm, see Hamlin, *The Sidney Psalter*, 132.

61. Jean-Claude Milner, "Réflexions sur le fonctionnement du vers français," *in Ordres et Raisons de Langue* (Paris: Seuil, 1982), 301.

62. Stringer, *Holy Sonnets*, 14.

63. Ibid., 12.

64. Ibid., 11.

65. The most important departures are not the definite ones but rather those that leave it unclear how exactly they depart from the regular meter. Thus in a line like "All whom the Flood did and fyre shall overthrow" (Sonnet 8), the monosyllables in the middle ("the Flood did and fyre shall") leave it entirely open how one should accentuate them; but in every attempt there will be at least one element in the line that is either off-beat or departs from the speech rhythm (for instance, either "fyre" or "Flood" would have to be unaccented in a regular iambic pentameter. Though "fyre" may be a bisyllable, it still leaves the problem unresolved).

66. In a mostly forgotten but fascinating book, *The Rhetoric of Verse in Donne* (Baltimore: J. H. Furst, 1906), Wightman Fletcher Melton quotes a scholar named Belden to say that "Donne's verse is never lyric. . . . Instead, he leaves you, line after line and phrase after phrase in doubt of the pattern, or of how the line is to be fitted to the pattern, producing thereby a searching pause on almost every syllable—a sort of perpetual 'hovering accent'" (56). The idea of "hovering accent" (*schwebende Betonung*) seems to come from Rudolph Richter, "Der Vers bei Dr. John Donne," *Beitrage zur Neueren Philologie* (1902): 391–415. It is also evoked by Roman Jakobson in his essay "Linguistics and Poetics," in Stephen Rudy, ed., *Selected Writings* (The Hague: Mouton, 1981), 37. Donne's metrical practices are often considered more liberal than those of his contemporaries, but see Kristin Hanson, "Nonlexical Word Stress in the English Iambic Pentameter: A Study of John Donne," in Kristin Hanson and Sharon Inkelas, eds., *The Nature of the Word: Studies in Honor of Paul Kiparsky* (Cambridge, MA.: MIT Press, 2009), 21–63.

67. Stringer, *Holy Sonnets*, 14.

68. Giorgio Agamben, *The End of the Poem*, trans. Daniel Hellen-Roazen (Stanford, CA: Stanford University Press, 1999), 114.

69. Agamben cites Valéry's famous definition of poetry as hesitation between sound and sense in *The End of the Poem*, 109.

70. The Calvinist doctrine of double predestination is the most radical theological explication of this problem, which is also the doctrinal figure for religious dispair. For a helpful discussion of the double election, see Nicholas Watson, "Despair," in Brian Cummings and James Simpson, eds., *Cultural Reformations* (Oxford: Oxford University Press, 2010), 342–60.

71. George Puttenham, *The Arte of English Poesie*, ed., Frank Whigham and Wayne A. Rebhorn (Ithaca, NY: Cornell University Press, 2007), 184.

CHAPTER SIX

1. Augustine, *De civitate dei* xiii.18.

2. "Donne has a general tendency to carry a given idea, metaphor, or assertion out to its logical extreme . . . this extension of the logical argument has as its primary purpose the pushing of a given argument to a point when its inadequacy for reflecting reality becomes fully recognizable" (Michael McCanles, "Paradox in Donne," in John Roberts, ed., *Essential Articles for the Study of John Donne's Poetry* [Hemden: Archon Books, 1975], 226). What I call distension in this chapter is essentially what McCanles calls extension. McCanles's argument concerns mostly poems in the *Songs and Sonets*, the classical locus for the New Critical search for the paradoxes and tensions of poetry. McCanles's discussion of the apparent inadequacy of the extension is less intriguing; he identifies the inadequacy as "palpable nonsense," and makes it clear in other ways as well that he finds the poems "inadequate" when they do not match common sense or some other mode of belief. But this external inadequacy is not relevant for the *Holy Sonnets*; what moves these poems is always internal inadequacy.

3. Medieval and early modern commentators used various spellings for the Greek σαρκασμός. In addition to the original Greek, the Late Latin *sarcasmus*, and further variants like *sarchasmos* and *sarchosmos*, there were also vernacular versions like the Italian *sarcasmo* or the German *sarkasmus*. Here and throughout the chapter I use the transliteration of the Greek in order to emphasize the distinction between historical conceptions and uses of *sarcasmos* and the modern notion of sarcasm. Later in the chapter I shall discuss how this historical distinction has conceptual grounds as well. My account of the trope is indebted to Dilwyn Knox's *Ironia: Medieval and Renaissance Ideas on Irony* (E. J. Brill: Leiden, 1989), esp. 170–77.

4. *Stimmung* or mood has recently been regaining critical traction, not the least because it is sometimes presented as an alternative to interpretation, critique, or what Ricoeur famously called the "hermeneutics of suspicion." The theory of poetic mood that I present below is based on a more traditional Aristotelian-Christian account in which moods are seen not as alternatives to but rather prompts toward thinking, and they are in this sense an initial stage in a process of understanding. This seems to me to be in

accord with Heidegger's own account of mood in *Sein und Zeit* (see esp. §§ 28–32), as well as his reading of Aristotle's *Rhetoric* (see below). For recent discussions of *Stimmung* and mood in literary criticism and aesthetics, see Gernot Böhme, "Atmosphere as the Fundamental Concept of a New Aesthetics," *Thesis Eleven* 36 (1993): 113–26; David E. Wellbery, "Stimmung," in: *Historisches Wörterbuch Ästhetischer Grundbegriffe*, hg. Karlheinz Barck et al., Bd. 5 (Stuttgart/Weimar: Metzler, 2003), 703–33; Hans Ulrich Gumbrecht, *Atmosphere, Mood, Stimmung: On a Hidden Potential of Literature* (Stanford, CA: Stanford University Press, 2012); and Rita Felski, *The Limits of Critique* (Chicago: University of Chicago Press, 2015).

5. Stringer, *Holy Sonnets*, 19.

6. See the discussions of this poem in Heather Dubrow, *Echoes of Desire* (Ithaca, NY: Cornell University Press, 1995), 227, and Kuchar, *The Poetry of Religious Sorrow*, 173–78. Kuchar in particular marks the poem's bitterness and its ambivalence toward both Petrarchism and Neoplatonism.

7. Whether the allusion should be seen as yet another instance of Donne's Catholic influences is unclear; despite the Reformation propaganda against holy water, it remined a widely popular concept. See Terje Oestigaard, "The Topography of Holy Water in England after the Reformation," in K. V. Lykke Syse and T. Oestigaard, eds., *Perceptions of Water in Britain from Early Modern Times to the Present: An Introduction* (Bergen: BRIC Press, 2010), 21–24.

8. In noting the speaker's bitterness, Gary Kuchar argues that "the poem laments not only the death of a woman, but the death of a world view that made the Petrarchan elegy possible" (*The Poetry of Religious Sorrow*, 177).

9. Indeed, scholarship has been puzzled by the moods and attitudes of the poem and responded in various terms. No doubt encouraged by the apparent relationship between the sonnet and Anne More's death, those critics who have taken note of how the poem's mood seems to be in discord with its devotional movement interpreted the discord in biographical terms as a sign of Donne's mourning of Anne and perhaps even his inability to completely turn away from her memory to God. Thus the poem emerges in the scholarship as "the most personal" of the *Holy Sonnets* (Peter Porter, *The Illustrated Poets: John Donne* [London: Aurum Press, 1991]); as "movingly restrained and dignified" (A. J. Smith, "John Donne," in *Seventeenth-Century British Nondramatic Poets*, ed. Thomas Hester [London: Gale, 1992]), expressing "deep sorrow" (Peter Milward, *A Commentary on the Holy Sonnets of John Donne* [Tokyo: Renaissance Institute, 1988]), perhaps with a "tone of resignation" (Gardner, *The Divine Poems*), or passionately (David Novarr, *The Disinterested Muse: Donne's Texts and Contexts* [Ithaca, NY: Cornell University Press, 1980]); and one critic even argues that Donne's "feelings are subject to a pervasive and controlling, if agonised, irony," and he wonders if Donne's turn to the "jealous God" of the Exodus is "quite as unadulterated as he pretends" (T. R. Langley, "Having Donne," *Cambridge Quarterly* 22 [1993]: 188–210).

10. Eduardo Saccone emphasizes the ironic aspect of *sprezzatura* to support his argument that Castiglione works toward an Aristotelian ethics. See Eduardo Saccone, "Grazia, Sprezzatura, Affettazione in the Courtier," in Robert W. Hanning and David Rosand, eds., *Castiglione: The Ideal and the Real in Renaissance Culture* (New Haven, CT: Yale

University Press, 1983). For a succinct discussion of political and rhetorical irony, see Heinrich Lausberg, *Handbook of Literary Rhetoric: A Foundation for Literary Study* (Leiden: Brill, 1998), 403–7. Lausberg addresses the ethical relevance of irony in relation to Aristotle's theory of the middle; he also usefully differentiates between *ironia* as *simulatio* and as *dissimulatio*.

11. Hilary Gatti, *The Renaissance Drama of Knowledge: Giordano Bruno in England* (London: Routledge, 1989), 138; Marvin Rosenberg, *The Masks of Hamlet* (Newark: University of Delaware Press, 1992), 881.

12. Laertes has asked for a "foil" (a blunt type of sword used in fencing, OED "foil" sb.4), but Hamlet uses the word primarily in the sense of advantage (sb.1 5b and 6: The setting (of a jewel).

13. "Hamlet's 'No, by this hand' may repeat the offer of a handshake; but given the provocative mood in Hamlet, it may convey a ruder or more aggressive gesture. . . . Potter heard it said in a puzzled tone that could be even more infuriating" (Rosenberg, *The Masks of Hamlet*, 881).

14. Rosenberg, *The Masks of Hamlet*, 881.

15. For a psychoanalytical interpretation of Hamlet's sarcasm (which is also one of the very few studies dedicated solely to Hamlet's sarcasm in the play), see M. D. Faber, "Hamlet, Sarcasm and Psychoanalysis," *Psychoanalytic Review* 55 (1968): 79–90.

16. Gardner, *The Metaphysical Poets*, 19.

17. Crucial to this layer of the remark is Hamlet's use of "stick off." For this phrase, OED has only Hamlet's remark and a phrase in Chapman, both interpreted as "[showing] to advantage." Both the second Quarto and the Folio has "stick off"; the first Quarto has the unhelpful "I'le be your foyle Laertes, these foyles, / Have all a laught, come on sir." One potential thread in interpreting "stick off" would be to compare it with all those senses of "off" in which the adverb implies some sort of cessation, completion, exhaustion. If "stick off" is thus comparable to phrases like "clear off," "finish off," "bring off" or "cool off," it may suggest that Hamlet's words predict not only Hamlet's own death by Laertes' sword, but also that Laertes' star might be in fact a shooting star that "shows off" against the darkness of Hamlet's night but then falls into it and fades away.

18. Although the ironic interpretation makes Hamlet's remark uncharacteristically facile. This is why scholars who want to interpret the remark ironically then struggle with its meaning. Rosenberg comments: "Hamlet seems to be suppressing his heart's unease, confident that heaven's ordinance protects him. Nothing can hurt him now. (Does he touch his cross for luck?) He is playful, even cheeky. Hyper about what lies ahead with Claudius?" (Rosenberg, *The Masks of Hamlet*, 881).

19. While there is no shortage of modern studies of sarcasm, I know only one book discussing early modern conceptions of *sarcasmos*. In addition to being a useful historical account of these conceptions, the section on *sarcasmos* in Knox's *Ironia: Medieval and Renaissance Ideas on Irony*, esp. 170–77, also offers valuable suggestions about the complex relationship between *ironia* and *sarcasmos*. See also the entry on "Sarkasmus" by B. Meyer-Sickendiek in *Historisches Wörterbuch der Rhetoric*, ed. Gert Ueding (Tübingen: Max Niemeyer Verlag, 2007). Although both Knox and Meyer-Sickendiek note the replacing of epic examples with biblical ones in medieval and early modern

commentaries, they do not address the issue of conceptual differences between classical and Christian conceptions of *sarcasmos*.

20. The first to find *sarcasmos* in the Scriptures is apparently Bede, who associates it with the crucifixion: "Sarcasmos est plena odio atque hostilis inrisio, ut: 'Alios salvos fecit, se ipsum non potest salvum facere; si rex Israel est, discendat nunc de cruce, et credimus ei'" [Sarcasm is a mockery, which is filled with hatred and hostility, as in [Matt. 27:42]: 'He saved others; himself he cannot save. If he is the King of Israel, let him now come down from the cross, and we will believe him"] (Calvin B. Kendall, ed., *De schematibus et tropis* [Saarbrücken: AQ-Verlag, 1991], 196 and 201).

21. 1 Cor. 15:55: "*Ubi est, mors, victoria tua? Ubi est, mors, stimulus tuus?*" Knox, on p. 30 of *Ironia*, cites Blebel (1584) and Dieterich (1616) for an ironic interpretation of the phrase, and Lonicer (1538), Treutler (1602), Keckermannus (1614) and others to see it as *sarcasmos*.

22. That is, both the world as "flesh" and the *kata sarka* attitude (or *ēthos*) toward the world. For recent accounts of what "kata sarka" means in Paul, see James G. D. Dunn, *The Theology of Paul the Apostle* (Grand Rapids: W. B. Eerdmans, 1998); and Daniel Boyarin, *A Radical Jew: Paul and the Politics of Identity* (Berkeley: University of California Press, 1994). Some of the most useful accounts of how Renaissance authors understood the Pauline conceptions of *sarx* and *kata sarka* focus on *The Merchant of Venice*; see for instance James Shapiro's *Shakespeare and the Jews* (New York: Columbia University Press, 1996).

23. The issue of a "Christian style" emerged as a scholarly topic in the early twentieth century, addressed mainly by German scholars. Traditionally, the discussion has focused on Augustine's view of Christian rhetoric as it appears *in De doctrina Christiana*, especially in the final book where Augustine discusses the issue of the Christian orator and importantly severs the *genera dicendi* from any particular *res*, thereby introducing the concept of a Christian mixed style based on the conviction that for the Christian orator every matter has the same weight. In *Die antike Kunstprosa* (1918), one of the first surveys of the Christian ideal of a low style, Eduard Norden already calls attention to the contradiction between theory and practice in Christian rhetoric: while early Christians recommended low style, they actually used rhetorical ornaments and the grand style. Hans Robert Curtius continued to analyze the Christian literary style in *European Literature and the Latin Middle Ages* (1948). Curtius focused on the continuity between antique and Christian rhetoric and literature; yet he pointed out the "affected modesty" of Christian writers. Erich Auerbach, first in *Mimesis: The Representation of Reality in Western Literature* (1946) and then in "Sermo Humilis" (published in *Literary Language and Its Public in Late Latin Antiquity*), focused on the mixed Christian style. For Auerbach, Christian concepts of style differed from the classical rhetorical notions of *elocutio* in that they did not assume the same sense of appropriateness of style with regard to the represented reality; on the contrary, the Christian concept assumes that there is an essential discrepancy between appearance and meaning, and therefore between reality and style. For a recent account on the debates about and evolution of the Christian style, see Peter Auksi, *Christian Plain Style: The Evolution of a Spiritual*

Ideal (McGill-Queen's University Press, 1995). For a particularly influential account of the Christian style in the English Renaissance, see Debora Shuger, *Sacred Rhetoric: The Christian Grand Style in the English Renaissance* (Princeton, NJ: Princeton University Press, 1988).

24. Although Quintilian is one of the most influential sources of this categorization of *sarcasmos*, his own treatment of the trope in 8.6 of *Institutio Oratoria* is already ambiguous in ways that foreshadow the later debates about the relationship between irony and *sarcasmos*, and the place of *sarcasmos* in rhetoric. After identifying allegory as that which "presents one thing by its word and either a different or sometimes even a contrary thing by its sense [allegoria . . . aut aliud verbis, aliud senses ostendit, aut etiam interim contrarium]," Quintilian specifies that irony is "the type in which meaning and the words are contrary [in eo vero genere quo contraria ostenduntur ironia est.]" The ensuing cursory characterization of *sarcasmos* does not clarify whether *sarcasmos* is a type of *ironia*, a type of *allegoria*, or a trope in its own right. Quintilian says, "On occasion, the opposite to what is intended is said in a mocking way [aliquando cum inrisu quodam contraria dicuntur iis quae intellegi volunt,]," and he later seems to identify this with the trope of *sarcasmos*. But right after doing so, he notes about *sarcasmos*, *asteismos*, *antiphrasis*, and *paroimia*, that "some even regard these not as species of Allegory but as Tropes in their own right [ipsa tropos]; this is a shrewd view because Allegory is more obscure, whereas in all these our intentions are obvious [illa obscurior sit, in his omnibus aperte appareat quid velimus]." I modified the Loeb translation at certain places (trans. Donald A. Russel [Cambridge, MA: Harvard University Press, 2001]).

25. While definitions of *sarcasmos* do not explicitly say that *sarcasmos* is necessarily either allegorical or ironic, the reason may be that they traditionally regard *sarcasmos* as being both ironic and allegorical. The fact that most of the examples that commentators use to illustrate *sarcasmos* are indeed ironic (and therefore also allegorical) would seem to support this assumption. That said, some early modern rhetoricians explicitly debated the classification of *sarcasmos* as irony and argued that *sarcasmos* is simply an exceptionally aggressive way of speaking, potentially not even figurative at all.

26. I refer to an Italian-Latin bilingual edition, Angelo Valastro Canale, ed., *Etimologie o origini / di Isidoro di Siviglia* (Torino: UTET, 2004), 87. In English: Stephen A. Barney, *The Etymologies of Isidore of Seville* (Cambridge: Cambridge University Press, 2006), 63.

27. Lucio Giovanni Scoppa, *Grammatices Institutiones* (Venezia: P. de Paganinis, 1508), 378. Quoted in Knox, *Ironia*, 171.

28. "Or when we deride with a certain severity, we may call it the Bitter Taunt, *sarcasmus*" (George Puttenham, *The Arte of English Poesie* [1589]). It is interesting to note that Puttenham's examples all refer to rulers mocking their courtiers. I refer to Puttenham's work in the edition of Frank Whigham and Wayne A. Rebhorn (Ithaca, NY: Cornell University Press, 2007), 274.

29. Michael Rudick, *The Poems of Sir Walter Ralegh: A Historical Edition* (Tempe: Arizona Center for Medieval and Renaissance Studies, 1999), prints different versions of the

poem. I quote 20B (the Bod. Rawlinson Poetry copy). Ralegh's authorship remains contested.

30. "First of all, *ressentiment* is the repeated experiencing and relieving of a particular emotional response/reaction against someone else. The continual reliving of the emotion sinks it more deeply into the center of the personality, but concomitantly removes it from the person's zone of action and expression. It is not a mere intellectual recollection of the emotion and of the events to which it "responded"—it is a re-experiencing of the emotion itself, a renewal of the original feeling. Secondly, the word implies that the quality of this emotion is negative, i.e. that it contains a movement of hostility. Perhaps the German word "Groll" (rancor) comes closest to the essential meaning of the term. "Rancor" is just such a suppressed wrath, independent of the ego's activity, which moves obscurely through the mind. It finally takes shape through the repeated reliving of intentionalities of hatred or other hostile emotions. In itself it does not contain a specific hostile intention, but it nourishes any number of such intentions." Max Scheler, *Ressentiment*, trans. William Holdheim (New York: Free Press of Glencoe, 1961), 39–40.

31. From the Bodleian Rawlinson Poetry 212, fols. 88–91v. Quoted in Rudick, *The Poems of Sir Walter Ralegh*, 35.

32. This reply appears along with the poem in a unique manuscript source, the Bodleian Tanner 306, fol. 188–8v. Quoted in Rudick, *The Poems of Sir Walter* Ralegh, 42.

33. John Haiman suggests a potential connection between sarcasm and the liar's paradox: "Unlike the liar, the sarcast has no wish to deceive; sarcasm differs from falsehood in the presence of the honest metamessage. . . . Among lies, however, sarcasm is especially close to self-referential paradoxical utterances like the Cretan's 'this statement is false.' . . . One may legitimately inquire how a sarcastic "thanks a lot!" differs from such well-known examples and why sarcastic expressions in general pose no paradoxical conundrums (for they do not). The difference between the two is perfectly clear on examination: the liar's single statement is both message and metamessage, while the sarcast is actually making not one statement but two clearly separated statements simultaneously: first, a message 'X,' and second, a commentary along the general lines that 'X is bunk.' . . . The peculiarly self-referential (and self conscious) nature of sarcasm is one of its most striking features" (John Haiman, *Talk Is Cheap: Sarcasm, Alienation, and the Evolution of Language* [Oxford: Oxford University Press, 1998], 21).

34. "Ironiae formae, cum victor victum irridet." Melanchthon uses both classical and Christian examples; thus he quotes Virgil ["En agros et quam bello Troiane petisti, Hesperiam métier iaces"], the standard passage from Matt. 24 ["Si filius Dei es descende de cruce"], and, unusually, the Psalms ["Speravit in domino eripiat salvum faciet eum, quoniam vult eum"] (Philipp Melanchthon, *Institutiones Rhetoricae* [Wittenberg, 1521]; I am using the 1523 edition of the Bibliotheca Palatina). Cf. Melanchthon's later discussion in the so-called Wittenberg Rhetoric (*Elementa rhetorices*, 1531): "Vocant *sarcasmos* cum hostis calamitatem exprobrat hosti, ut, En agros, et quam bello Troiane petisti, Hesperiam metire iacens. Talia sunt: Ave rex Iudaeorum. Si filius Dei es, descende de cruce. Verbum *sarkazein* significant rictum irritati canis, hinc

translatum est ad exprobriationem, ut significet irridere cum quadam irae significa-
tione, quails est rictus irritati canis." I am using Joachim Knape's *Philipp Melanchthon's
"Rhetorik"* (Tübingen: Max Niemeyer Verlag 1993), 474. Note that Melanchthon lists
eironeia and *sarcasmos* as two different kinds of *allegoria*; it is also worth mentioning
that his discussion of allegory and within it *sarcasmos* follows right after his discussion
of the fourfold interpretation of the Scriptures. See also Knox, *Ironia*, 171.

35. "Est enim sarcasmos hostilis irrisio super mortuo." Later he elaborates on this definition: "Nos in Originibus ita commenti sum carnis vocabulum vix et raro in vivente nisi
apud philosophos. At vulgus cadaveris carnem dicebat, quae iam careret vita. Itaque
carnifex is a Latinis dictus est, qui carnem facit ex vivente. Igitur cum sarcasmos non-
nisi in hostem victum legatur eumque vel iam mortuum vel mox certo moriturum, ab
ea causa nomen accepisse crederim" (Julius Caesar Scaliger, *Poetices libri septem*, ed.
Luc Deitz [Stuttgart: Frommann-Holzboog, 1994], 3:550–51).

36. Knox quotes this from *Barbarismus*, a "prose treatise dealing with the same matter as
the section of Donatus' *Ars Maior* which medieval authors commonly called *Barbarismus*." See Knox, *Ironia*, 172 and 185.

37. "In eo vero genere quo contraria ostenduntur ironia est (illusionem vocant)" (Quintilian, *Institutio Orato*ria, 8.6.54).

38. Scaliger himself held that *sarcasmos* can be, but does not have to be, ironic: "Inter elo-
gia quidem enumeranda, si spectes accomodationem; sin autem vim ipsam consideres
orationis, frequentus ad ironiam accedit, sine qua etiam saepe fit." Later he declares,
"Non est igitur verum, quod aiunt grammatici, sarcasmum esse ironiam; non enim
semper" (Scaliger, *Poetices libri septem*, 550–51).

39. On the problematic place of *sarcasmos* in rhetoric, see Knox, *Ironia*, 176–78.

40. Thus in 1638, John Clarke translates *sarcasmos* and *charientismos* as opposites: "Logis-
mus iste meus Charientismus fuit non Sarcasmus. I meant you no harm" (John Clarke,
Phraseologia puerilis Anglo-Latina [London: Imprinted by Felix Kyngston for Robert
Mylbourne, 1638], n.p). *Charientismos* is defined in a number of ways; to say that it is
the trope that makes the unpleasing pleasing is to select that one aspect that the different definitions share. When *charientismos* is discussed more strictly under irony
as mockery, it is described as pretended good will toward the enemy. For a concise
summery of *charientismos*, see Heinrich Lausberg, *Handbook of Literary Rhetoric: A
Foundation for Literary Study* (Leiden: Brill, 1998), 267 and 690. *Charientismos* as a
kind of irony should not be confused with *charientismos* as a *genus*, even though there
are parallels between the two.

41. Much of the confusion concerning the Christian doctrine of resurrection derives from
the fact that Paul proclaimed the resurrection of the body (*soma*) but the irreversible
destruction of the flesh (*sarx*). On St. Paul's notions of body and flesh, see James D. G.
Dunn, *The Theology of Paul the Apostle* (Grand Rapids, MI: Wm. B. Eerdmans Publishing, 2006), 72ff. Dunn differentiates between the two notions by suggesting that the
body (*soma*) refers to the specifically human *being* in the world, the given of existence,
whereas flesh (*sarx*) implies a way of *belonging* to the world. I will return to the issue of
sarx later in this chapter to focus on one of its crucial meanings in the Pauline context.
Kata sarka, a derivative of *sarx* that is arguably more important for Paul than *sarx* itself,

means according to the flesh. *Kata sarka* is a relationality, an attitude, a mood; it is a way of relating to the world and to others. On this level, *kata sarka* means primarily any relationship based on family, race, ethnicity, nationality. Cf. Daniel Boyarin's reading of the Galatians, *A Radical Jew: Paul and the Politics of Identity* (Berkeley: University of California Press, 1994).

42. Pierre Lefranc, *Sir Walter Ralegh, écrivain, l'œuvre et les idées* (Paris: Les Presses de l'Université Laval, 1968), 86–94. Lefranc places the poem in the Ralegh-Essex antagonism and debates Ralegh's authorship on both stylistic and historical grounds.

43. Stephen Greenblatt has contested Lefranc's assumptions; he points out, for instance, that even though Ralegh despised the Puritan movement, "he shared the Puritan disillusionment with the practices of the world. . . . In Ralegh this mood was derived not so much from the doctrines of Calvin as from an almost medieval *contemptus mundi*. But in the late sixteenth century, the resemblance between Puritanism and medieval pessimism is often striking." While Lefranc found the repetitive and now angry, now pretentious phrases of the poem indications of the poet's ineptitude, Greenblatt finds in the same phrases "instances of [Ralegh's] use of irony. The poet repeatedly and deftly turns praise into condemnation. . . . The language, like the poem itself, is lean, mocking, and effective" (Stephen Greenblatt, *The Renaissance Man and His Roles* [New Haven, CT: Yale University Press, 1973], 174–76).

44. See the debate between Louis Martz and Barbara Lewalski.

45. Charles Darwin, *The Expression of Emotion in Man and Animals* (London: John Murray, 1872), 254–77.

46. On this, see Haiman, *Talk Is Cheap*, 30.

47. Gary Stringer, ed., *The Variorum Edition of the Poetry of John Donne, Volume 6: The Anniversaries, Epicedes, and Obsequies* (Bloomington: Indiana University Press, 1995), 16–17.

48. In the following, I take into account Aristotle's discussion of *ēthos* and *pathos* in other works (certainly in the *Metaphysics* but even in the *Poetics*) only tangentially, insofar as they clarify his concern with *ēthos* and *pathos* within the *Rhetoric*. All the references from Aristotle's *Rhetoric* are to the Loeb edition (trans. John Henry Freese [Cambridge, MA: Harvard University Press, 1975]).

49. Aristotle, *Rhetoric*, I.ii.2–3.

50. Aristotle, *Rhetoric*, II.i.8.

51. Although Aristotle himself does not make direct connection between *pathos* and tragedy on the one hand, and *ēthos* and comedy on the other, later rhetoricians did not hesitate to make this move. See esp. Quintilian's discussion: "Diversum est huic quod πάθος dicitur quodque nos adfectum proprie vocamus, et, ut proxime utrisque differentiam signem, illud comoediae, hoc tragoediae magis simile" (*Institutio Oratoria*, 6.2.20–21).

52. John Stuart Mill, "Thoughts on Poetry and Its Varieties," *The Crayon* 7 (1860): 95.

53. In other words, my argument does not imply that devotional poetry, including the *Holy Sonnets*, did not have an audience, was not written for an audience, etc. On this level, my argument is entirely structural: I speak about how the poem constructs its own terms of relating to the world.

54. This is indeed a coincidence: for the roles of the speaker and the listener are distinguished; they just happen to coincide in the person who meditates. In this regard, it is important to remember that meditation in the early contexts means primarily reading aloud; and that this meaning remains operative until the late seventeenth century, so that treatises of meditation often have a separate category (sometimes called "literal meditation") for meditation as reading aloud or recital of Scriptural passages. Of course, in prayer there is an audience other than the speaker—the divinity that is addressed in the speech act. But it is crucial to differentiate between prayer and meditation. In prayer, divinity is indeed the addressee of the speech act, and this raises further questions that I discuss in my chapter on attention. But meditation is different from prayer in that it is not, in its entirety, an address to the divine; meditation is primarily the speaker's preparation, attempt to turn to the divine, to enable herself to address the divine. In this sense, the *Holy Sonnets* may become prayers, may reach the point when they actually turn into a *gratiarum actio*; but primarily they are rhetorical and poetic (rather than psychological) preparations to address the divine in the proper mood, with the proper attitude.

55. Haiman suggests that sarcasm may be compared to the subjunctive in that they both express the speaker's attitude toward the propositional content of her message (Haiman, *Talk Is Cheap*, 28). I accept Haiman's suggestion of thinking about a "sarcastive mood"; that is, a mood that is like the subjunctive in every respect except for its nongrammatical indices.

56. What I have been calling, in the preceding pages, the "attitude" and "mood" of the poem are sometimes called "tone" in English. In literary criticism, the term "tone" was given a technical definition by I. A. Richards in *Practical Criticism*: "The speaker has ordinarily *an attitude to his listener*. He chooses or arranges his words differently as his audience varies, in automatic or deliberate *recognition of his relation to them*. The tone of his utterance reflects his awareness of his relation, his sense of how he stands towards those he is addressing. Again the exceptional case of dissimulation, or instances in which the speaker unwittingly reveals an attitude he is not consciously desirious of expressing, will come to mind." I should also quote Richards's definition of "feeling," which is not too far from the classical rhetorical concept of "pathos": "We also, as a rule, have some feelings *about these items* [i.e., the "items of consideration" to which "we use words to direct our hearer's attention"], about the state of affairs we are referring to. We have an attitude towards it, some personal flavor or colouring of feeling; and we use language to *express* these feelings, this nuance of interest. Equally, when we listen we pick it up, rightly or wrongly; it seems inexplicably part of what we receive; and this whether the speaker be conscious himself of his feelings towards what he is talking about or not" (I. A. Richards, *Practical Criticism: A Study of Literary Judgment* [London: Kegan Paul, 1929], 175–76). That this definition creates a whole set of new problems is evidenced by how handbooks of literary terms attempt to rephrase it. Thrall and Hibbard, for instance, in the *Handbook to Literature* write of tone that it "has been used, following I. A. Richards' example, for the attitudes toward the subject and toward the audience implied in a literary work." Previously, however, they defined mood as "the emotional-intellectual attitude of the author toward the subject. . . . If a

distinction exists between mood and tone, it will be a fairly subtle one between mood as the attitude of the author toward the subject and tone as the attitude of the author toward the audience" (Flint Thrall and Addison Hibbard, *Handbook to Literature* [Indianapolis: Odyssey Press, 1972]).

57. My account of Aristotle's theory of *ēthos* and *pathos* in the *Rhetoric* is indebted to Martin Heidegger's discussion of the Aristotelian concepts in his 1924 lecture course at the University of Marburg, *Grundbegriffe der Aristotelischen Philosophie*, vol. 18 of Heidegger's *Gesamtausgabe*, in 2002. A note of explanation is due here: why apply antique Greek philosophical terms as they are interpreted by a twentieth-century German phenomenologist to seventeenth-century devotional poetry? What seems a double anachronism begins to make more sense when we notice that Heidegger's Aristotle is not unlike the Philosopher of the Scholastics. During his Marburg years, Heidegger was developing a number of concepts that were to serve as key terms in *Sein und Zeit*. Among them, *pathos* and its derivatives are especially noteworthy: already in the *Grundbegriffe*, Heidegger translates and interprets *pathos* by introducing a number of German terms that include *Stimmung* (mood or attunement) and *Befindlichkeit* (disposition). It is in the course of this philosophical appropriation of *pathos* that one may begin to feel that Heidegger's interpretation may be driven by a Christian agenda in the broadest sense. In particular, Heidegger's emphasis on *pathos* being the movement away from an *ēthos* in a conversion that involves the entirety of the *Dasein* appears to be an attempt to ground a Christian conception of conversion as an existential event in Aristotelian philosophy. Regardless of whether Heidegger's interpretation can be substantiated on historical or philosophical grounds, in itself, it seems to me that this Christian element is what makes the Heideggerian-Aristotelian theory of *pathos* particularly suitable for the interpretation of Christian poetry in the early modern period, particularly when this poetry, as Donne's *Holy Sonnets* and the devotional poetry of the period in general, is profoundly concerned with devotional movement and particularly with conversion. See Martin Heidegger, *Grundbegriffe der Aristotelischen Philosophie* (Frankfurt am Main: Vittorio Klostermann, 2002); English translation by Robert D. Metcals and Mark B. Tanzer, *Basic Concepts of Aristotelian Philosophy* (Bloomington: Indiana University Press, 2009).

58. Potter and Simpson, *Sermons*, 5:42.

59. The notion is of course common in the period; cf. Hamlet's "My mother. Father and mother is man and wife, man and wife is one flesh, and so, my mother."

60. Aquinas, *Summa Theologiæ*, esp. 1a. 54–58.

61. Such a reading of *Hamlet* also implies that the prince's drama reflects the Pauline conflict between *gnosis* and *praxis*, between knowledge or desire and action. Paul in Romans 7:16–24, and Augustine in *De civitate dei* emphasize that the Fall brought about a breach between desire and will, or between knowledge and action; the kind of indecision that Hamlet struggles with is an accurate reflection of this breach. Read this way, Hamlet's drama becomes the drama of a Christian character who prays and meditates to enable himself to act according to the revelation he has received from the Ghost. For a similar reading, see Peter Iver Kaufman, *Prayer, Despair, and Drama: Elizabethan Introspection* (Urbana: University of Illinois Press, 1996), esp. chap. 3.

62. Anthony Bale, *The Jew in the Medieval Book: English Antisemitism, 1350–1500* (Cambridge: Cambridge University Press, 2006), 145. In the chapter "Passion: The Arma Christi in Medieval Culture," Bale offers an account of Middle English manuscripts representative of the late medieval *Arma Christi* tradition. For *the Arma Christi* tradition in general, see R. Berliner, "Arma Christi," *Münchner Jahrbuch der bildenden Kunst* 6 (1955): 35–152.

63. *A Gloryous Medytacyon of Ihesus Crystes Passyon* (London, 1523, printed by Rychard Fakes), sig. B1ʳ (I have slightly modernized the spelling). The image depicts two grotesque Jewish characters standing on both sides of Christ, spitting at him; the four lines follow under the image. The poem's implications for early modern anti-Semitism are discussed by Bale, *The Jew in the Medieval Book,* 145–68 and 177–81.

64. The Gospels have precedents for both of these, cf. Matt. 27:40 and Mark 15:29. For examples cited by rhetoricians, see Bede: "Sarcasmos est plena odio atque hostilis inrisio, ut: 'Alios salvos fecit, se ipsum non potest salvum facere; si rex Israel est, discendat nunc de cruce, et credimus ei.'" [Sarcasm is a mockery which is filled with hatred and hostility, as in [Matt. 27:42]: 'He saved others; himself he cannot save. If he is the King of Israel, let him now come down from the cross, and we will believe him"] (Calvin B. Kendall, ed., *De schematibus et tropis* [Saarbrücken: AQ-Verlag, 1991], 196 and 201). Melanchthon uses both classical and Christian examples; thus he quotes Virgil ("En agros et quam bello Troiane petisti, Hesperiam métier iaces."), the standard passage from Matt. 24 ("Si filius Dei es descende de cruce"), and, somewhat unusually, the Psalms ("Speravit in domino eripiat salvum faciet eum, quoniam vult eum") (Melanchthon, *Institutiones Rhetoricae*). In the English context, both Sherry and Peacham use the example. Sherry: "Sarcasmus. Amara irrisio is a bitter sporting a mocke of our enemye, or a maner of iesting or scoldinge bytynglye, a nyppyng taunte, as: The Jewes saide to Christ, he saved other, but he could not save hym selfe" (Richard Sherry, *A Treatise of Schemes and Tropes* [London, 1550]; Peacham: "An example of the Holy Scripture. . . . Thou which does destroy the Temple, and build it again in three dayes, have thy self and come down from y crosse. Another: He saved others, him selfe he cannot save. Let that Christ the king of Israel come down now from the crosse, the wee may see and believe him. These examples of the Jewes against Christ are here set down to teach the forme of this figure, and not to confirme the abuse" (Peacham, *The Garden of Eloquence*).

65. See Calvin B. Kendall, ed., *De schematibus et tropis* (Saarbrücken: AQ-Verlag, 1991), 196 and 201.

66. Melanchthon, *Institutiones Rhetoricae.*

67. Sherry, *A Treatise of Schemes and Tropes.*

68. Peacham, *The Garden of Eloquence.*

69. Melanchthon, *Institutiones Rhetoricae.*

70. The system of signification that *sarcasmos* constitutes may be seen as an alternative to typology. Daniel Boyarin has argued that in typology the *figura* is essentially allegorical, even if its apocalyptic dimensions remain crucial. I suggest that in contrast to allegory, in the case of *sarcasmos* the sign and its meaning are essentially identical even despite the intention behind the utterance. *Sarcasmos,* in other words, may be a

type of hyperbolical irony that says what it says *despite* the intention of the speaker. Cf. Daniel Boyarin, *A Radical Jew: Paul and the Politics of Identity* (Berkeley: University of California Press, 1994), 13–38. Typology is an important comparison because it calls attention to how *sarcasmos* may be the basis for a consistent view of history as well. It is quite common to dichotomize the possible views of history in the West as continuous decline or as continuous progress. Both of these views can claim Christian eschatology as their model: for Christian eschatology may be seen as pessimistic (until the Second Coming things will just get worse, as in Foxe's narrative of the increasing number of martyrs indicating the coming apocalypse), or as optimistic (the apocalyptic process is somehow pre-programmed inside history so that no matter what actually happens on the surface the process is teleological). The sarcastic view of history challenges both of these views; instead, it envisions history as a process in which everything that is new (even when it appears to be positive, as a discovery or an invention) indicates only the vanity of the past (thus a new discovery does not approach the truth but only unveils the errors of the past). The *Anniversaries* are permeated by this sense of history: when "new Philosophy cals all in doubt," this apparent progress in knowledge becomes, in Donne's poem, nothing but a proof for the inevitable fallacy of human knowledge. This sense of a sarcastic history is ubiquitous in the early seventeenth century. Thomas Scot's *Philomythie* (London, 1622), for instance, begins with a verse introduction that bears the title *Sarcasmus mundo* and uses history as a proof of the vanity of human knowledge and judgment (2–4).

71. "Dicuntur autem ista ex persona crucifixi. nam de capite Psalmi huius sunt uerba quae ipse clamauit cum in cruce penderet, personam etiam seruans ueteris hominis, cuius mortalitatem portauit. nam uetus homo noster confixus est cruci cum illo" (Augustine, *Enarrationes Psalmos* 21.1.1. Quoted from Augustine, *Opera Omnia* [Charlottesville, VA: InteLex Corporation, 2000]; English translation by Maria Boulding in *Expositions on the Psalms*, 1–32. Volume III/15 [New York: New City Press, 2000], 222).

72. "'Omnes qui conspiciebant me subsannabant me'. Omnes qui conspiciebant me, irridebant me. 'Et locuti sunt in labiis, et mouerunt caput'. Et locuti sunt non in corde, sed in labiis. nam irridenter mouerunt caput, dicentes: 'Sperauit in dominum, eruat eum; saluum faciat eum, quoniam uult eum'. Haec uerba erant, sed in labiis dicebantur" (Augustine, *Enarrationes Psalmos* 21.1.8–9. *Expositions*, 223).

73. Augustine, *Enarrationes Psalmos* 21.2.1. *Expositions*, 228.

74. The "English Donatists": Robert Browne's followers criticized them in works like *A short treatise against the Donatists of England* (London: Printed by J. Windet for Toby Cooke, 1590). See also the religious separatist Henry Barrow's answer, *A plaine refutation of M. G. Giffardes reprochful booke* (Dordrecht, 1591).

75. John Andrewes, *Christ His Crosse or The Most Comfortable Doctrine of Christ Crucified* (Oxford, 1614), 51–52.

76. Indeed, one might suggest that the reason texts like the *Enarrationes Psalmos*, the Arma Christi poem quoted above, or Donne's *Holy Sonnet* all associate mockery with Jewishness is because of the typological appropriation of Psalm 21. In all these texts, the "Jew" is the emblem of mockery, or the literal or *kata sarka* understanding of the Passion; but precisely as such a *kata sarka* interpretation of the Passion, the "Jew" also stands

for the Christian's self-understanding as a sinner. This is why a few passages later Andrewes bursts into a virulent diatribe against the Jews who "despoiled all their senses of common humanitie" when "spitting, smitting, and mocking the sonne of God." Andrewes, *Christ His Crosse*, 54–55.

77. *The English Poems of George Herbert*, ed. Helen Wilcox (Cambridge: Cambridge University Press, 2007), 92.

78. Ibid., 102.

79. Ibid., 103

80. Ibid., 112–13.

81. *The holy Gospel of Iesus Christ, according to Iohn, with the Commentary of M. Iohn Calvine*, trans. Christopher Fetherstone [printed with *A Harmonie vpon the three Euangelists, Matthew, Mark, and Luke, with a Commentarie of M. Iohn Caluine* (London, 1584)], 19.

82. "Sermon preached at S. Pauls, in the Evening, upon Easter-day. 1623." In Potter and Simpson, *Sermons*, 4:352.

CHAPTER SEVEN

1. "The Dry Salvages," in *Collected Poems, 1909–1962* (London: Harcourt Brace, 1990), 199.

2. When Alain Badiou begins what has since become one of the most influential postmodern secular defenses of Paul, he feels necessary to dissociate his argument from Paul's belief in the resurrection: "Let us be perfectly clear: so far as we are concerned, what we are dealing here is precisely a fable. And singularly so in the case of Paul, who for crucial reasons reduced Christianity to a single statement: Jesus is resurrected. Yet this is precisely the fabulous element [*point fabuleux*], since all the rest, birth, teachings, death, *might* after all be upheld. A "fable" that is part of a narrative that, so far as we are concerned, fails to touch on any Real, unless it be by virtue of that invisible and indirectly accessible residue sticking to every obvious imaginary. In this regard, it is to its element of fabulation [*point de fable*] alone that Paul reduces the Christian narrative, with the strength of one who knows that holding fast to this point as real, one is unburdened of all the imaginary that surrounds it. If it is possible for us to speak of belief from the outset (but Paul's entire problem concerns the question of belief or faith, or of that which is presupposed beneath the word *pistis*), let us say that so far as we are concerned in it vigorously impossible to believe in the resurrection of the crucified." Alain Badiou, *The Foundation of Universalism*, trans. Ray Brassier (Stanford, CA: Stanford University Press, 2003), 4–5.

3. Caroline Walker Bynum, *The Resurrection of the Body in Western Christianity, 200–1336* (New York: Columbia University Press, 1995).

4. Potter and Simpson, *Sermons*, 4:355.

5. "Nay, the Immortality of the soule, will not so well lie in the proofe, without a resuming of the body." Ibid., 4:357–58. At the same time, Donne is also willing to expand

to meaning of resurrection; influenced by Augustine, in the same sermon he distinguishes three kinds of resurrection, "a Resurrection from worldly calamities, a resurrection from sin, and a resurrection from the grave." Ibid., 4:359.

6. Shawcross, *The Complete Poetry of John Donne*, 142.

7. For a review of resurrection imagery in the *Songs and Sonets* and in some of the devotional poems, see Kathryn R. Kremen, *The Imagination of the Resurrection: The Poetic Continuity of a Religious Motif in Donne, Blake, and Yeats* (Lewisburg: Bucknell University Press, 1972), 96–128.

8. Stringer, *Holy Sonnets*, 18.

9. *Poems by J. D. With Elegies on the Authors Death* (London, 1633), 161–62.

10. Robbins, *Complete Poems of John Donne*, 519.

11. Or at least the church, the body of the faithful. While the fact that line 21 leaves somewhat open the question of *whose* body resembles a soul, I don't see any potential reading in which the observer could see his own body as the soul of "the whole." It is also worth mentioning that the 1633 *Poems* has "this body a soul" rather than "his body a soul" (Robbins here follows Dolau Cothi MS 6748 [National Library of Wales], "the only MS without obvious error" [Robbins, *Complete Poems of John Donne*, 517]).

12. Juan de Valdés is an intriguing character, influential among Italian mannerist artists such as Pontormo; *Ciento i Diez Consideraciones* was first entirely suppressed by the Spanish inquisitions, so that Valdés fled to Italy, where the considerations were published in 1550.

13. Juan Valdés, *Hundred and Ten Considerations* (Oxford, 1638), 95–97.

14. Stringer, *Volume 6: The Anniversaries, Epicedes, and Obsequies*, 29.

15. Bynum, *The Resurrection of the Body*, 200.

16. "Preached at Lincoln's Inn on Job 19:27: And though, after my skin, wormes destroy this body, yet in my flash shall I see God," in Potter and Simpson, *Sermons*, 109–10. After the passage about distraction, Donne goes on to say, "We shall see the Humanity of Christ with our bodily eyes, then glorifyed; but, that flesh, though gloryfed, cannot make us see God better, nor clearer, then the soul alone hath done, all the time, from our death, to our resurrection" (112).

17. See Eliot's curious commentary on this and another sermon passage: "These are thoughts which would never have come to Andrewes. When Andrewes begins his sermon, from beginning to end you are sure that he is wholly in his subject, unaware of anything else, that his emotion grows as he penetrates more deeply into his subject, that he is finally 'alone with the Alone,' with the mystery which he is seeking to grasp more and more firmly. . . . But with Donne there is always the something else, the 'baffling' of which Mr. Pearsall Smith speaks in his introduction! Donne is a 'personality' in a sense in which Andrewes is not: his sermons, one feels, are a 'means of self-expresion.' He is constantly finding an object which shall be adequate to his feelings; Andrewes is wholly absorbed in the object and therefore responds with the same adequate emotion." T. S. Eliot, *Essays, Ancient and Modern* (London: Faber & Faber, 1936), 26–27. Even if we ignore the ideological and religious motives here, it is odd that Eliot would not consider the possibility that Donne's passages on distraction, rather

than being expressions of Donne's modern, distracted personality, may in fact act as rhetorical strategies allowing his audiences to feel "wholly absorbed in the object" precisely by tending to their own distractions.

18. Ramie Targoff quotes the sermon as evidence of Donne's interest and confidence in the resurrection of the body in *John Donne, Body and Soul* (Chicago: University of Chicago Press, 2008), 118; Kimberly Johnson instead emphasizes Donne anxiety about the fate of the body in *Made Flesh: Sacrament and Poetics in Post-Reformation England* (Philadelphia: University of Pennsylvania Press), 91–94.

19. All the more interesting because Augustine's letter was written to a woman, Proba, "the devoted handmaid of God."

20. "Dicuntur fratres in Aegypto crebras quidem habere orationes, sed eas tamen brevissimas, et raptim quodammodo iaculatas, ne illa vigilanter erecta, quae oranti plurimum necessaria est, per productiores moras evanescat atque hebetetur intentio. Ac per hoc etiam ipsi satis ostendunt, hanc intentionem, sicut non est obtundenda, si perdurare non potest, ita si perduraverit, non cito esse rumpendam. Absit enim ab oratione multa locutio, sed non desit multa precatio, si fervens perseverat intentio" (Letter 130 "Ad Probam," in Augustine, *Letters,* vol. 3 [83–130], trans. Sister Wilfrid Parsons, S.N.D. [Washington, DC: Catholic University of America Press, 1953], 391).

21. Robbins, *Complete Poems of John Donne,* 197.

22. In Milton's text, this is a moment of postcoital depression, when Adam and Eve understand the first time the result of their Fall, which they didn't immediately see, due to the "force of that fallacious Fruit, / That with exhilerating vapour bland / About thir spirits had plaid." The comparison with "The Good-Morrow" is all the more appropriate: as an alba poem, "The Good-Morrow" depicts not so much the moment of falling in love, but the reflection on it, the next morning.

23. In the seventeenth century, this effort to remedy distraction as a consequence of the Fall by attention was characteristic not only of the ascetic and devotional literature of the period but of the rising experimentalist and scientific thinking, in texts such as Robert Boyle's "Occasional Reflections upon Several Subjects," in *The Works of Robert Boyle,* ed. Michael Hunter and Edward B. Davis, 14 vols. (London: Pickering & Chatto, 1999–2000), 5:3–188. On *curiositas* and its relationship to attention and receptivity, see Lorraine Daston, "Curiosity in Early Modern Science," *Word and Image* 11 (1995): 391–404, and Joanna Picciotto, *Labors of Innocence in Early Modern England* (Cambridge, MA.: Harvard University Press, 2010), esp. chap. 4. On Boyle, see also my essay "Easy Attention: Ignatius of Loyola and Robert Boyle," *Journal of Medieval and Early Modern Studies* 44 (2014): 135–71.

24. I quote "The Good-Morrow" here from the 1633 *Poems*; Robbins replaces the line with "Love just alike in all, / none of these loves can die" (Robbins, *Complete Poems of John Donne,* 199). But see L. M. Crowley, "Establishing a 'Fitter' Text for Donne's 'The Good Morrowe,'" *John Donne Journal* 22 (2003): 5–21.

25. And, as I pointed out in chap. 2, the letter ends with a thanksgiving: "But thanks *be* unto God, who hath given us the victory through our Lord Jesus Christ."

26. Helen Gardner observes that all the MSS. "agree in giving the second 'death' a capital." Gardner, *The Divine Poems,* 70.

27. Derrida defines the gift of death as "the marriage of responsibility and faith" and suggests that "the gift of death puts me into relation with the transcendence of the other, with God as selfless goodness, and that gives me what it gives through a new experience of death" (Jacques Derrida, *The Gift of Death* [Chicago: University of Chicago Press, 1996], 5–6).

28. The poem's end foreshadows Heidegger's analysis in *Being and Time*. In Agamben's account, "Even in proper Being-toward-death and proper decision, Dasein seizes hold of its impropriety alone, mastering an alienation and becoming attentive to a distraction" (Giorgio Agamben, "The Passion of Facticity," in *Potentialities: Collected Essays in Philosophy*, trans. Daniel Hellen-Roazen [Stanford, CA: Stanford University Press, 2000], 197).

CODA

1. *Recherche de la Vérité* in *Œuvres de Malebranche*, ed. Jules Simon (Paris: Charpentier, 1842), 458; English translation from the *Treatise concerning the Search after Truth*, Vols. 1–2, trans. T. Taylor (London, 1700), 2:37.

2. For some classical contributions, see Pierre Mesnard, "L'arbre de la sagesse," *Descartes, Cahiers de Royaumont, Philosophie*, II (Paris, 1957), 350–59; L. J. Beck, *The Metaphysics of Descartes: A Study of the Meditations* (Oxford: Oxford University Press, 1965), 28–38; Arthur Thomson, "Ignace de Loyola et Descartes: L'influence des exercises spirituels sur les oeuvres philosophiques de Descartes," *Archive de philosophie* 35 (1972), 61–85; Walter John Stohrer, "Descartes and Ignatius Loyola: La Flèche and Manresa Revisited," *Journal of the History of Philosophy* 17 (1979): 11–27; Amélie Oksenberg Rorty, "Experiments in Philosophical Genre: Descartes' Meditations," *Critical Inquiry* (1983): 545–64; Gary Hatfield, "The Senses and the Fleshless Eye: The *Meditations* as Cognitive Exercises," in *Essays on Descartes' "Meditations"* (Berkeley: University of California Press, 1986), 45–79; Zeno Vendler, "Descartes' Exercises," *Canadian Journal of Philosophy* 19 (1989): 193–224; Matthew L. Jones, "Descartes' Geometry as Spiritual Exercise," *Critical Inquiry* 28 (2001): 40–71, and *The Good Life in the Scientific Revolution: Descartes, Pascal, Leibniz, and the Cultivation of Virtue* (Chicago: University of Chicago Press, 2006), 1–86. Many of these works (Jones's study in particular) are either directly influenced by or echo the classical statement about Descartes's philosophy as a practice of virtue in Pierre Hadot's *Philosophy as a Way of Life*.

3. Two things are important to note here. The first is that insofar as in Christian discussions attention in prayer is an act of the will, the proem's last line is in accord with the idea that the work of prayer is the work of attention. The second, though, is that although the proem ends with what may seem as a jab at Calvinist notions of predestination, the very next poem throws this conclusion into question by revising the meaning of "all": "*Salvation to all that will is nigh*: / That All, which always is everywhere." In other words, the poem hedges its bets about devotional agency in a way

that anticipates (as we shall see) the sonnet crown's end: if the proem seems to suggest that human will and actions may participate in the work of salvation, the second poem takes this back by suggesting that the "all" whose will can lead to salvation is in fact God. See Robbins, *Complete Poems of John Donne.* 478, f. 14.

4. Ibid., 487, f. 13.

5. Margaret Mauer, "The Circular Argument of Donne's 'La Corona,'" *Studies in English Literature* 22:1 (1982): 68.

6. Stringer, *Holy Sonnets*, 20.

7. Stringer, *Holy Sonnets*, 20.

8. Lewalski, *Protestant Poetics*, 274–75.

9. Insofar as this fearful, silent knowing of God implies a holy attentiveness, my argument concurs with Gary Kuchar's analysis of the opening of the soul toward God in the *Holy Sonnets* in Kuchar, *Divine Subjection: The Rhetoric of Sacramental Devotion in Early Modern England* (Pittsburgh: Duquesne University Press, 2005), 219–25, and *The Poetry of Religious Sorrow*, 173.

10. "Objections IV" in *The Philosophical Works of Descartes* II, trans. Elizabeth S. Haldane and G. R. T. Ross (Cambridge: Cambridge University Press, 1977), 92. The italicized text belongs to Arnauld.

11. The answer to Arnauld proceeds along the same lines: "Finally, to prove that I have not argued in a circle in saying, that the only secure reason we have for believing that what we clearly and distinctly perceive is true, is the fact that God exists; but that clearly we can be sure that God exists only because we perceive that, I may cite my explanation that I have already given at sufficient length in my reply to the second set of Objections, numbers 3 and 4. There I distinguished those matters that in actual truth we clearly perceive from those we remember to have formerly perceived. For first, we are sure that God exists because we have attended to the proofs that established this fact; but afterwards it is enough for us to remember that we have perceived something clearly, in order to be sure that it is true; but this would not suffice, unless we knew that God existed and that he did not deceive us" (Descartes, *The Philosophical Works,* II, 114–15). Descartes's argument here bears a resemblance to scholastic discussions of actual and virtual attention, actual attention being the attention that is being paid to prayer's words in the present moment, while virtual attention is the "force" of the initial attention that carried over in the rest of the prayer without actual attention being sustained.

12. "Objections VII" in Descartes, *The Philosophical Works,* II, 266.

13. In René Descartes, *Principles of Philosophy*, trans. Valentine Rodger Miller and Reese P. Miller (Dordrecht: Kluwer, 1991), 20.

14. Though Augustine's influence on Descartes has been the subject of much critical debate, the potentially Augustinian origins of Descartes's notion of attention have not been pointed out. See Stephen Menn, *Descartes and Augustine* (Cambridge: Cambridge University Press, 1998), 3–70 and 130–94.

15. "Toute ma methode se réduit à une attention sérieuse à ce qui m'éclaire et à ce qui me conduit." Nicolas Malebranche, *Entretiens sur la Métaphysique,* 2 vols. (Paris: Vrin, 1948), 2:175. For an overview of the role of attention in Malebranche's philosophy,

see Pierre Blanchard, *L'attention à Dieu selon Malebranche: Méthode et doctrine* (Lyon: Desclée de Brouwer, 1955).

16. References are to Malebranche, *Recherche de la Vérité*; English trans., *Treatise*.

17. *Recherche de la Vérité*, 457, *Treatise*, 2:36.

18. *Recherche de la Vérité*, 460, *Treatise*, 2:38.

19. L. J. Beck expresses this surprise about Descartes's reliance on the concept of attention in the *Principia* and the *Regulae* in *The Method of Descartes* (Oxford: Clarendon Press, 1952), 56.

20. Although attention is not among the more significant philosophical concepts, philosophers have been interested in it since at least the early modern period. In the twentieth century, attention was discussed predominantly in the context of psychology, but some philosophers, particularly in phenomenology, showed interest in it; see, for instance, Edmund Husserl's late work published as *Wahrnehmung und Aufmerksamkeit: Texte aus dem Nachlass* in volume 38 of the *Husserliana* (Dordrecht: Springer, 2004). More recently attention has become a concept of interest in philosophy of mind; see particularly Christopher Mole, *Attention Is Cognitive Unison* (Oxford: Oxford University Press, 2011), and Christopher Mole, Declan Smithies, and Wayne Wu, eds., *Attention: Philosophical and Psychological Essays* (New York: Oxford University Press, 2011).

INDEX